DISCOVERING THE WESTERN PAST

A LOOK AT THE EVIDENCE

VOLUME I: TO 1789

SIXTH EDITION

Merry E. Wiesner
University of Wisconsin—Milwaukee

Julius R. Ruff
Marquette University

William Bruce Wheeler
University of Tennessee

HOUGHTON MIFFLIN COMPANY   Boston   New York

Publisher: Patricia Coryell
Sponsoring Editor: Nancy Blaine
Senior Marketing Manager: Katherine Bates
Senior Development Editor: Jeffrey Greene
Project Editor: Aimee E. Chevrette
Art and Design Manager: Jill Haber Atkins
Cover Design Manager: Anne S. Katzeff
Photo Editor: Jennifer Meyer Dare
Composition Buyer: Chuck Dutton
New Title Project Manager: Susan Brooks-Peltier
Editorial Assistant: Adrienne Zicht
Marketing Assistant: Lauren Bussard
Editorial Assistant: Andrew Laskey

Cover Image: *View of Kensington High Street*, 1898, Lithograph by Emery Walker. © Eileen Tweedy/The Art Archive

Printed in the U.S.A.

Library of Congress Control Number: 2007926148

Instructor's exam copy:
ISBN-13: 978-0-618-83418-1
ISBN-10: 0-618-83418-4

For orders, use student text ISBNs:
ISBN-13: 978-0-618-76610-9
ISBN-10: 0-618-76610-3
6789-EB-00 09 08 07

CONTENTS

CHAPTER SEVEN
Life at a Medieval University   147

CHAPTER EIGHT
Infidels and Heretics: Crusades of the High Middle Ages   172

PREFACE

The title of this book begins with a verb, a choice that reflects our basic philosophy about history. History is not simply something one learns about; it is something one does. One discovers the past, and what makes this pursuit exciting is not only the past that is discovered but also the process of discovery itself. This process can be simultaneously exhilarating and frustrating, enlightening and confusing, but it is always challenging enough to convince those of us who are professional historians to spend our lives at it. And our own students, as well as many other students, have caught this infectious excitement.

The recognition that history involves discovery as much as physics or astronomy does is often not shared by students, whose classroom experience of history frequently does not extend beyond listening to lectures and reading textbooks. The primary goal of *Discovering the Western Past: A Look at the Evidence* is to allow students enrolled in Western Civilization courses to *do* history in the same way we as historians do—to examine a group of original sources in order to answer questions about the past.

The unique structure of this book clusters primary sources around a set of historical questions that students are asked to "solve." Unlike a source reader, this book prompts students to actually *analyze* a wide variety of authentic primary source material, to make inferences, and to draw conclusions in much the same way that historians do.

The evidence in this book is more varied than that in most source collections. We have included such visual evidence as coins, paintings, statues, literary illustrations, historical photographs, maps, cartoons, advertisements, and political posters. In choosing written evidence we again have tried to offer a broad sample—eulogies, wills, court records, oral testimonies, and statistical data all supplement letters, newspaper articles, speeches, memoirs, and other more traditional sources.

In order for students to learn history the way we as historians do, they must not only be confronted with the evidence but must also learn how to use that evidence to arrive at a conclusion. In other words, they must learn historical methodology. Too often methodology (or even the notion that historians *have* a methodology) is reserved for upper-level majors or graduate students; beginning students are simply presented with historical facts and interpretations without being shown how these were unearthed or formulated.

Students may learn that historians hold different interpretations of the significance of an event or individual or different ideas about causation, but they are not informed of how historians come to such conclusions.

Thus, along with evidence, we have provided explicit suggestions about how one might analyze that evidence, guiding students as they reach their own conclusions. As they work through the various chapters, students will discover both that the sources of historical information are wide-ranging and that the methodologies appropriate to understanding and using them are equally diverse. By doing history themselves, students will learn how intellectual historians handle philosophical treatises, economic historians quantitative data, social historians court records, and political and diplomatic historians theoretical treatises and memoirs. They will also be asked to consider the limitations of their evidence, to explore what historical questions it cannot answer as well as those it can. Instead of remaining passive observers, students become active participants.

Following an approach that we have found successful in many different classroom situations, we have divided each chapter into five parts: The Problem, Sources and Method, The Evidence, Questions to Consider, and Epilogue. The section called "The Problem" presents the general historical background and context for the evidence offered and concludes with the central question or questions explored in the chapter. Your students should refer to the central questions frequently as they analyze the evidence in the chapter. These serve as guideposts for their analysis, and can always be found right at the end of "The Problem" section.

The section titled "Sources and Method" provides specific information about the sources and suggests ways in which students might best study and analyze this primary evidence. It also discusses how previous historians have evaluated such sources and mentions any major disputes about methodology or interpretation. In keeping with the active learning that this book encourages, "Sources and Methods" often guides students by posing specific questions about the evidence. These are meant to encourage careful reading, and certainly do not all need to be answered.

"The Evidence" forms the core of each chapter, presenting a variety of original sources for students to use in completing the central task. In "Questions to Consider," suggestions are offered about connections among the sources, and students are guided to draw deductions from the evidence. Again, possible connections among pieces of evidence are often proposed in the form of questions rather than statements, for we believe this technique helps reinforce the process of discovering. "Questions to Consider" is just that—additional issues for students to think about as they develop answers to the chapter's central questions.

The final section, "Epilogue," traces both the immediate effects of the issue under discussion and its impact on later developments.

Within this framework, we have tried to present a series of historical issues and events of significance to the instructor as well as of interest to the student. We have also aimed to provide a balance among political, social, diplomatic, intellectual, and cultural history. In other words, we have attempted to create a kind of historical sampler that we believe will help students learn the methods and skills used by historians. These skills—analyzing arguments, developing hypotheses, comparing evidence, testing conclusions, and reevaluating material—will not only enable students to master historical content; they will also provide the necessary foundation for critical thinking in other college courses and after college as well.

Discovering the Western Past is designed to accommodate any format of the Western Civilization course, from the small lecture/discussion class of a liberal arts or community college to the large lecture with discussions led by teaching assistants at a sizable university. The chapters may be used for individual assignments, team projects, class discussions, papers, and exams. Each is self-contained, so that any combination may be assigned. The book is not intended to replace a standard textbook, and it was written to accompany any Western Civilization text the instructor chooses. The *Instructor's Resource Manual,* written by the authors of the text, offers suggestions for class discussions, suggestions for ways in which students' learning may be evaluated, and annotated lists of suggestions for further reading.

New to the Sixth Edition

The first five editions of *Discovering the Western Past: A Look at the Evidence* elicited a very positive response from instructors and students alike, and that response encouraged us to proceed with this Sixth Edition. As authors, we were particularly gratified by the widespread acceptance of the central goal of *Discovering the Western Past,* that of making students active analysts of the past and not merely passive recipients of its factual record.

The Sixth Edition of *Discovering the Western Past* incorporates the responses to the book that we have received from our own students, as well as from student and faculty users of the book around the country. Many of the chapters in the two volumes have received some reworking, and new chapters are included in each volume.

Volume I includes new chapters on barbarian invaders and medieval village life, and the return of a chapter on the Reformation brought back by request from users of the book. Volume II offers a new chapter on European material life (1600–1800), a chapter on women in Russian revolutionary movements, and a new final chapter on the European nation-state and regional ethnic nationalism.

Acknowledgments

In the completion of this book, the authors received assistance from a number of people. Our colleagues and students at the University of Wisconsin—Milwaukee, Marquette University, and the University of Tennessee, Knoxville, have been generous with their ideas and time. Merry E. Wiesner (-Hanks) wishes especially to thank Judith Bennett, Judith Beall, Martha Carlin, Abbas Hamdani, and Marci Sortor for their critiques and suggestions, and Neil Wiesner-Hanks and Kai and Tyr Wiesner-Hanks for their help in maintaining the author's perspective. Julius Ruff acknowledges the assistance of two valued colleagues who aided in preparing all six editions of this work: the Reverend John Patrick Donnelly, S.J., of Marquette University and Michael D. Sibalis of Wilfrid Laurier University. He also wishes to thank Laura, Julia, and Charles Ruff for their continued support. William Bruce Wheeler wishes to thank Owen Bradley and John Bohstedt for their valuable assistance.

We wish to acknowledge particularly the following historians who read and commented on the manuscript of this Sixth Edition as it developed:

Steve Alvin, *Illinois Valley Community College*

William S. Arnett, *West Virginia University*

Anne M. Breedlove, *Las Positas College*

Christopher Carlsmith, *University of Massachusetts-Lowell*

Marie Seong-Hak Kim, *St. Cloud State University*

Lynn Lubamersky, *Boise State University*

Matthew R. Lungerhausen, *Winona State University*

Sherri Olson, *University of Connecticut*

Jeremy D. Popkin, *University of Kentucky*

Paul Townend, *University of North Carolina-Wilmington*

Finally, the authors extend their thanks to the staff of Houghton Mifflin Company for their enthusiastic support.

M.E.W.

J.R.R.

W.B.W.

CHAPTER ONE

THE NEED FOR WATER

IN ANCIENT SOCIETIES

The title of the course for which you are using this book is probably a variant of "Western Civilization." Why do we use the term "civilization"? What distinguishes human cultures that are labeled civilizations from those that are not? Though great differences separate them, all civilizations share some basic characteristics. The most important of these similarities is the presence of cities; indeed, the word "civilization" comes from the Latin word *civilis* (meaning "civic"), which is also the root of "citizen" and "civil." Historians and archaeologists generally define a city as a place inhabited by more than 5,000 people, and they have discovered the remains of the earliest communities of this size in ancient Mesopotamia, which is present-day Iraq.

Why should the presence of cities be the distinguishing mark of cultural development? It is not the cities themselves but what they imply about a culture that makes them so important. Any society in which thousands of people live in close proximity to one another must have some sort of laws or rules governing human behavior. These may be either part of an oral tradition or, as in ancient Mesopotamia, written down. A city must provide its residents with a constant supply of food, which means developing ways to transport food into the city from the surrounding farmland, to store food throughout the year, and to save it for years marked by poor harvests. Not only does the presence of cities indicate that people could transport and store food effectively, but it also reveals that they were producing enough surplus food to allow for specialization of labor. If all work time had been devoted to farming, it would not have been possible to build roads, produce storage bins, or enforce laws on which the city depended. This specialization of labor, then, gave some members of society the opportunity and time to create and produce goods and artifacts that were not directly essential to daily survival. Urban residents in Mesopotamia began to construct large buildings and decorate them with sculptures, paintings, and mosaics; to write poetry and history; and to develop religious and philosophical ideas, all of which are pursuits we consider essential to a civilization. As the cities themselves grew, they required greater and greater amounts of food to feed their inhabitants, which led to further technological development.

Mesopotamia was in many ways an odd location for the beginning of a civilization. True, the soil is so rich that the region is called the Fertile Crescent, but it does not receive enough natural rainfall to grow crops steadily year after year. In fact, this region is not where agriculture began in the West; that happened closer to the Mediterranean, where the rainfall was more regular. Apparently, as techniques of planting and harvesting crops spread into Mesopotamia, the inhabitants realized that they would be able to use these techniques effectively only through irrigation. They needed to tap the waters flowing in the Tigris and Euphrates Rivers, a project requiring the cooperation of a great many people. Thus, rather than proving a block to further development, the need for irrigation in ancient Mesopotamia may have been one of the reasons that cities first arose there. We may never be able to know this with certainty, because irrigation systems were already in place when written records began and because cities and irrigation expanded at the same time. We do know, however, that in Mesopotamia, neither

could have existed without the other; cities could survive only where irrigation had created a food surplus, and irrigation could survive only where enough people were available to create and maintain ditches and other parts of the system.

Building irrigation systems presented both technical and organizational problems. The Tigris and Euphrates were fast-flowing rivers that carried soil as well as water down from the highlands. This rich soil created new farmland where the rivers emptied into the Persian Gulf. (The ancient Persian Gulf ended more than 100 miles north of its present boundary; all that land was created as the rivers filled in the delta.) The soil also rapidly clogged up the irrigation ditches, which consequently required constant cleaning. Every year these deposits were excavated and piled on the banks until the sides of the ditches grew so tall that cleaning could no longer be easily accomplished. At this point the old ditch was abandoned and a new ditch was cut, tasks that required a great deal of work and the cooperation of everyone whose land was watered by that ditch.

Mesopotamian farmers used several types of irrigation. One technique, known as *basin irrigation,* was to level large plots of land fronting the rivers and main canals and build up dikes around them. In the spring and other times during the year when the water was high, farmers knocked holes in the dikes to admit water and fresh soil. Once the sediment had settled, they let the water flow back into the channel. They also built small waterways between their fields to provide water throughout the year, thereby developing a system of *perennial irrigation*. In the hillier country of northern Mesopotamia, farmers built terraces with water channels running alongside them. The hillside terraces provided narrow strips of flat land to farm, and the waterways were dug to connect with brooks and streams.

Farmers could depend on gravity to bring water to their fields during spring and flood seasons, but at other times they needed water-raising machines. They devised numerous types of machines, some of which are still in use today in many parts of the world. These solved some problems but created others, as farmers with machines could drain an irrigation ditch during times of low water, leaving their neighbors with nothing. How were rights to water to be decided? Solving this problem was crucial to human social organization, and the first recorded laws regarding property rights in fact concern not rights to land but rights to water. In Mesopotamia, land was useless unless it was irrigated.

Many of the irrigation techniques developed in Mesopotamia either spread to Egypt or were developed independently there. Because it received even less rainfall than Mesopotamia, Egypt was totally dependent on the Nile for watering crops. Fortunately, the Nile was a much better source of water than the Tigris and Euphrates because it flooded regularly, allowing easy basin irrigation. The rise and fall of the Nile was so regular, in fact, that the Egyptians based their 365-day calendar on its annual flooding. The Egyptians also constructed waterways and

water-lifting machines to allow for perennial irrigation. As in Mesopotamia, irrigation in Egypt both caused and resulted from the growth of cities. It contributed as well to the power of the kings, whom the Egyptian people regarded as responsible for the flood of the Nile.

Irrigation was more difficult in places that did not have flood-prone rivers, including many parts of North Africa and the Near East. Here people adapted techniques to conserve water from sporadic heavy rainfalls. They dammed the temporary lakes (termed *wadis*) created by these rainfalls and built ditches to convey the water to fields, rather than allowing it simply to flow off onto the desert. Sometimes this wadi irrigation involved a whole series of small dams down the course of rivers that ran only after storms. Besides providing water, wadi irrigation also built up terraces because the rivers carried soil with them.

The earliest water systems were for crop irrigation, but people also began to demand good drinking water. In many parts of the ancient world, the demand for drinking water led to the establishment of a second system because river water that is suitable for irrigation may be brackish, unpleasant, or even unhealthful to drink. In southern Europe, where lakes were often not far from growing cities, people solved the problem by building channels made of timber, stone, or clay earthenware to carry water from the lakes to the city. These channels might be open or closed, depending on the terrain and the level of technical development of the culture that built them. Generally they relied on gravity flow and fed into underground tanks or reservoirs in the city; the oldest known water channels are in Jerusalem and date from about 1000 B.C. The construction of such systems, which demanded even more technical expertise than the building of irrigation ditches, provoked additional legal problems about ownership of the right to this clean, cool water.

When lakes were not located close enough to make aboveground channels feasible, people had to rely on water from *aquifers,* underground water-bearing layers of gravel or porous rock. The water could be obtained from wells drilled in the ground, but wells could supply only a small amount of water at a time. Once an aquifer had been discovered, however, a horizontal channel could be dug to lead the water to an outside channel or reservoir. A horizontal channel worked only in hilly areas where the aquifer stood higher than a nearby valley, but such channels, called *qanats,* have been found in Iran, Syria, Egypt, and Turkey that are over 2,000 years old. If the amount of water it yielded was large enough, the qanat could be used for irrigation as well as drinking water.

When the Romans conquered the Middle East and North Africa in the second century B.C., they inherited irrigation systems that in some cases had already been in existence for more than 2,000 years. The Romans carried many ideas to other parts of their empire and made innovations as the terrain or distance required. Most of the European territory in the Roman Empire received adequate rainfall for farming without irrigation, but many Roman cities, especially Rome itself, experienced a chronic shortage of drinking water. The Romans solved this problem by building *aqueducts,* covered or uncovered channels that brought water into the cities from lakes and springs. The first of these in Rome was built in 312 B.C., and the system expanded continuously up to about A.D. 150. Over 300 miles of aqueducts served the city of Rome alone, with extensive systems in the outlying provinces as well. Although Roman engineers went to great lengths to avoid valleys, they were occasionally forced to construct enormous bridges to carry the aqueducts over valleys. Some of these bridges were over 150 feet high, and a few, such as the bridge-aqueduct in Segovia, Spain, still bring water to city residents. The Romans' sophisticated architectural and construction techniques—the arch and water-resistant cement, for example—enabled them to build water systems undreamed of in Mesopotamia and Egypt. Legal problems were not as easily solved, however, and disputes about water rights recur frequently throughout the long history of Rome.

Supplying cities with water was not simply a technological problem; it had economic, legal, and political implications. Through their solutions to these complex problems, ancient societies created what we call civilization. Your task in this chapter will be to use both visual and written evidence of ancient water systems to answer the question, How did the need for a steady supply of water shape civilization?

SOURCES AND METHOD

Historians use a wide variety of sources when examining ancient irrigation and water supply systems. Since many of these systems were created before the development of writing, archaeological evidence is extremely important, especially in examining technological development. This evidence may be the actual remains of ancient ditches, machines, or aqueducts, but in many areas these have completely disappeared. This does not mean that they have left no trace, however, for the ancient uses of modern landscapes are often revealed through patterns of depressions and discoloration.

The best way to see these patterns is through aerial photography. Analyzing aerial photographs can be a difficult task, and learning how to read ancient land-use patterns through the overlay of modern development takes a great deal of training. Occasionally the older patterns can be quite clear, however, and only a small amount of additional information is necessary for you to begin to decode them. The first piece of evidence, Source 1, is an aerial photograph of the site of a pre-Roman city in Italy. Examine the picture carefully. Can you see the old grid pattern of irrigation ditches, which shows up as light and dark marsh grass? The dark lines are the outlines of ancient irrigation ditches, the lighter squares are ancient fields, and the white parallel lines superimposed on the top are part of a modern drainage system. To examine the ancient system, you will need to strip away the modern system mentally. What do you think the broader black strip at the top left is? Does this system look like basin or perennial irrigation? Look at the flatness of the landscape. Would silting be a problem?

A more sophisticated type of aerial photography involves the use of satellites rather than airplanes. Satellites can take extremely detailed pictures of the earth's surface that reveal natural and artificially constructed features, both ancient and contemporary. The sharpest images are produced by high-resolution military satellites whose pictures are not available to the public. Low-power images produced by LANDSAT, the only U.S. commercial imaging satellite system, are adequate for most archaeological and historical purposes, however. Source 2 is a map of the major ancient irrigation ditches between the Tigris and Euphrates Rivers that were identifiable in a recent LANDSAT image. What does the size of the system reveal about Mesopotamian technology? What does it imply about the political systems in this area—would you expect, for example, the cities in Mesopotamia to be hostile to one another? New technologies such as LANDSAT imagery not only provide answers to questions, but also guide future research. How could you use this map to plan further investigations of irrigation systems?

Aerial photography provides visual evidence of entire irrigation systems but not of the specific tools and machines used to lift water to the fields. For these we must look to the remains of the tools themselves or to

[5]

depictions of them in tomb paintings, mosaics, and pottery. Source 3 is the earliest depiction of irrigation ditches that has survived from ancient Egypt, carved on the head of a ceremonial mace dating from around 3100 B.C. The large figure in the middle is one of the early kings of Egypt, who is holding a hoe and who is flanked by two palm-fan bearers and a man holding a basket for the dirt dug up by the hoe. At the bottom are two other workmen, also with hoes, excavating or deepening the ditches. Based on what you already know about Eygptian society, would you expect the king himself to be digging ditches? Why might this mace, which signified royal authority, show the king involved in building irrigation ditches?

Some of the machines depicted in ancient paintings are still in use today, showing that many techniques for lifting water have not changed at all for thousands of years. Sources 4 through 7 show four different machines for raising water that we know were in use in ancient times and are still in use in many parts of the world today: the shaduf, saqiya, Archimedes' screw,[1] and noria. To assess their role and importance, you must consider a number of different factors while carefully examining the four diagrams. Some of these factors are technical: How complicated is the machine to build? Does it have many moving parts that must all be in good repair? How much water can it lift?

How high can it lift the water? Can it work with both flowing and stationary water? Some factors are economic: Does the machine require a person to operate it, thus taking that person away from other types of labor? Does it require a strong adult, or can it be operated by a child? Does it require an animal, which must be fed and cared for? Some factors are both economic and political: Does the machine require a variety of raw materials to build, more than one family might possess? Does it require any raw materials, like metal, that would have to be imported? (Such questions are political because someone has to decide which families get the raw materials necessary for their fields.) Some factors are legal: Does the machine raise so much water that laws about distribution would become necessary? At this point, you may want to make a chart summarizing your assessment of the advantages and disadvantages of each machine, which will help you in making your final conclusions.

We will now turn from visual to written sources. Because water is such a vital commodity, mention of water systems appears very early in recorded human history. The next five sources are written accounts of the construction or operation of water systems. Source 8 contains sections from the Code of Hammurabi, a Babylonian legal code dating from 1750 B.C., that refer to irrigation. Source 9 is a description of the Roman aqueduct system written by Vitruvius during the first century B.C., and Source 10 is a description of the water-system projects undertaken by

1. Archimedes (287–212 B.C.) was a Greek mathematician and inventor who is credited with inventing this machine.

Emperor Claudius during his reign (A.D. 41–54), written by the Roman historian Suetonius. The next selection is a discussion of some of the problems associated with Rome's water system written about A.D. 100 by Frontinus, who was commissioner of the water supply. The last is a proclamation issued by Emperor Theodosius in 438 as part of his code of laws, an edict that had probably been in effect for many earlier decades as well.

As you read these sources, notice first of all the technical issues that the authors are addressing. What problems in tapping, transportation, and storage of water do they discuss? What solutions do they suggest? Then look at legal problems, which you can find most clearly stated in the selection by Frontinus and the law codes of Hammurabi and Theodosius. Keep in mind when you are reading the law codes that laws are generally written to address those problems that already exist, not those

the lawmakers are simply anticipating. The presence of a law, especially one that is frequently repeated, is often a good indication that the prohibited activity was probably happening, and happening often. How did people misuse or harm the water systems? What penalties were provided for those who did? Who controlled the legal use of water, and who decided how water was to be distributed?

The written sources also include information about political and economic factors in ancient water supply systems that is nearly impossible to gain from archaeological evidence. Careful reading can reveal who paid for the construction of such systems and who stood to gain financially from them once they were built. What reasons, other than the simple need for water, might rulers have had for building water systems? What political and economic factors entered into decisions about the ways in which water was to be distributed?

THE EVIDENCE

Source 1 from Leo Deuel, Flights into Yesterday: The Story of Aerial Archeology *(New York: St. Martin's Press, 1969), p. 236. Photo by Fotoaerea Valvassori, Ravenna.*

1. Aerial Photograph of Pre-Roman City in Italy

Source 2 from Robert MaC. Adams, Heartland of Cities: Surveys of Ancient Settlements and Land Use on the Central Floodplains of the Euphrates *(Chicago: University of Chicago Press, 1981), p. 34.*

2. Major Ancient Levees Identifiable in LANDSAT Imagery

Source 3 from Walter B. Emery, Archaic Egypt *(Baltimore: Penguin, 1961), p. 43.*

3. Early Egyptian King Cutting an Irrigation Ditch, Drawn from Mace-head Carving, 3100 B.C.

Sources 4 through 7 adapted from sketches by Merry E. Wiesner.

4. Shaduf

5. Saqiya

6. Archimedes' Screw   7. Noria

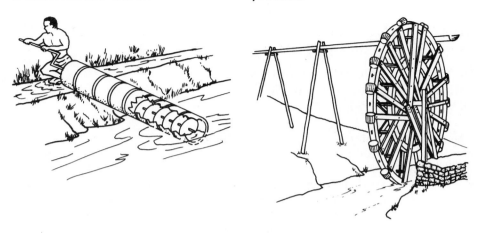

Source 8 from Robert F. Harper, The Code of Hammurabi *(Chicago: University of Chicago Press, 1904).*

8. Sections from the Code of Hammurabi Referring to Irrigation, 1750 B.C.

53. If a man neglects to maintain his dike and does not strengthen it, and a break is made in his dike and the water carries away the farmland, the man in whose dike the break has been made shall replace the grain which has been damaged.

54. If he is not able to replace the grain, they shall sell him and his goods and the farmers whose grain the water has carried away shall divide [the results of the sale].

55. If a man opens his canal for irrigation and neglects it and the water carries away an adjacent field, he shall pay out grain on the basis of the adjacent field.

56. If a man opens up the water and the water carries away the improvements of an adjacent field, he shall pay out ten gur of grain per bur [of damaged land]. . . .

66. If a man has stolen a watering-machine from the meadow, he shall pay five shekels of silver to the owner of the watering-machine.

Sources 9 and 10 from Naphtali Lewis and Meyer Reinhold, editors and translators, Roman Civilization *(New York: Columbia University Press, 1955), pp. 304–306; pp. 151–152. Reprinted with permission of Columbia University Press, 562 W. 113th St., New York, NY 10025, via Copyright Clearance Center, Inc.*

9. Vitruvius's Description of the Roman Aqueduct System, first century B.C.

The supply of water is made by three methods: by channels through walled conduits, or by lead pipes, or by earthenware pipes. And they are arranged as follows. In the case of conduits, the structure must be very solid; the bed of the channel must be leveled with a fall of not less than half a foot in 100 feet. The walled conduits are to be arched over so that the minimum amount of sun may strike the water. When it comes to the city walls, a reservoir is to be made. To this reservoir a triple distribution tank is to be joined to receive the water; and three pipes of equal size are to be placed in the reservoir, leading to the adjoining tanks, so that when there is an overflow from the two outer tanks, it may deliver into the middle tank. From the middle tank pipes will be laid to all basins and fountains; from the second tank to the baths, in order to furnish an annual revenue to the treasury; to avoid a deficiency in the public supply, private houses are to be supplied from the third, for private persons will not be able to divert the water, since they have their own limited supply from the distribution sources. Another reason why I have made these divisions is that those who take private supplies into their houses may by their taxes paid through tax farmers contribute to the maintenance of the water supply.

If, however, there are hills between the city and the source, we must proceed as follows: underground channels are to be dug and leveled to the fall mentioned above. If the bed is of tufa or stone, the channel may be cut in it; but if it is of soil or sand, the bed of the channel and the walls with the vaulting must be constructed, and the water should be thus conducted. Air shafts are to be so constructed that they are 120 feet apart. . . .

Water supply by earthenware pipes has these advantages. First, in the construction: if a break occurs, anybody can repair it. Again, water is much more wholesome from earthenware pipes than from lead pipes. For it seems to be made injurious by lead, because white lead is produced by it; and this is said to be harmful to the human body. So if what is produced by anything is injurious, there is no doubt that the thing itself is not wholesome. We can take an example from the workers in lead who have complexions affected by pallor. For when lead is smelted in casting, the fumes from it settle on the members of the body and, burning them, rob the limbs of the virtues of the blood. Therefore it seems that water should by no means be brought in lead pipes if we desire to have it wholesome. Everyday life can be used to show that the flavor from earthenware pipes is better, because everybody (even those who load their table with silver vessels) uses earthenware to preserve the purity of water.

But if we are to create springs from which the water supplies come, we must dig wells.

But if the soil is hard, or if the veins of water lie too deep, then supplies of water are to be collected from the roofs or higher ground in concrete cisterns. . . . If the cisterns are made double or triple, so that they can be changed by percolation, they will make the supply of water much more wholesome. For when the sediment has a place to settle in, the water will be more limpid and will keep its taste without any smell. If not, salt must be added to purify it.

10. Suetonius's Description of the Water Projects Undertaken by Emperor Claudius (r. A.D. 41–54)

The public works which Claudius completed were great and essential rather than numerous; they were in particular the following: an aqueduct begun by Caligula; also the drainage channel of Lake Fucine and the harbor at Ostia, although in the case of the last two he knew that Augustus had refused the former to the Marsians in spite of their frequent requests, and that the latter had often been considered by the deified Julius but given up because of its difficulty. He brought to the city on stone arches the cool and abundant springs of the Claudian aqueduct . . . and at the same time the channel of the New Anio, distributing them into many beautifully ornamented fountains. He made the attempt on the Fucine Lake as much in the hope of gain as of glory, inasmuch as there were some who offered to drain it at their own cost provided the land that was drained be given them. He finished the drainage canal, which was three miles in length, partly by leveling and partly by tunneling a mountain, a work of great difficulty requiring eleven years, although he had 30,000 men at work all the time without interruption.

Source 11 from B. K. Workman, editor and translator, They Saw It Happen in Classical Times *(New York: Barnes & Noble, 1964), pp. 179–181. Reprinted by permission of Littlefield, Adams & Company and Basil Blackwell Publishers.*

11. Frontinus's Discussion of Rome's Water System, ca A.D. 100

The New Anio[2] is drawn from the river in the district of Sinbrinum, at about the forty-second milestone along the Via Sublacensis. On either side of the

2. An aqueduct completed under the emperor Claudius in A.D. 52.

river at this point are fields of rich soil which make the banks less firm, so that the water in the aqueduct is discoloured and muddy even without the damage done by storms. So a little way along from the inlet a cleansing basin was built where the water could settle and be purified between the river and the conduit. Even so, in the event of rain, the water reaches the city in a muddy state. The length of the New Anio is about 47 miles, of which over 39 are underground and more than 7 carried on structures above the ground. In the upper reaches a distance of about two miles in various sections is carried on low structures or arches. Nearer the city, from the seventh Roman milestone, is half a mile on substructures and five miles on arches. These arches are very high, rising in certain places to a height of 109 feet.

. . . All the aqueducts reach the city at different levels. So some serve the higher districts and some cannot reach loftier ground. For the hills of Rome have gradually increased in height because of the rubble from frequent fires. There are five aqueducts high enough at entrance to reach all the city, but they supply water at different pressures. . . .

Anyone who wants to tap water for private consumption must send in an application and take it, duly signed by the Emperor, to the Commissioner. The latter must take immediate action on Caesar's grant, and enroll one of the Imperial freedmen to help him in the business. . . . The right to water once granted cannot be inherited or bought, and does not go with the property, though long ago a privilege was extended to the public baths that their right should last in perpetuity. . . .

Now that I have explained the situation with regard to private supply, it will be pertinent to give some examples of the ways in which men have broken these very sound arrangements and have been caught red-handed. In some reservoirs I have found larger valves in position than had been granted, and some have not even had the official stamp on them. . . .

Another of the watermen's intolerable practices is to make a new outlet from the cistern when a water-grant is transferred to a new owner, leaving the old one for themselves. I would say that it was one of the Commissioner's chief duties to put a stop to this. For it affects not only the proper protection of the supply, but also the upkeep of the reservoir which would be ruined if needlessly filled with outlets.

Another financial scheme of the watermen, which they call "puncturing," must also be abolished. There are long separate stretches all over the city through which the pipes pass hidden under the pavement. I found out that these pipes were being tapped everywhere by the "puncturers," from which water was supplied by private pipe to all the business premises in the area, with the result that only a meagre amount reached the public utilities. I can estimate the volume of water stolen in this way from the amount of lead piping which was removed when these branch pipes were dug up.

Source 12 from Naphtali Lewis and Meyer Reinhold, editors and translators, Roman Civilization *(New York: Columbia University Press, 1955), pp. 479–480. Reprinted with permission of Columbia University Press, 562 W. 113th St., New York, NY 10025, via Copyright Clearance Center, Inc.*

12. Proclamation of Emperor Theodosius, A.D. 438

It is our will that the landholders over whose lands the courses of aqueducts pass shall be exempt from extraordinary burdens, so that by their work the aqueducts may be cleansed when they are choked with dirt. The said landholders shall not be subject to any other burden of a superindiction,[3] lest they be occupied in other matters and not be present to clean the aqueducts. If they neglect this duty, they shall be punished by the forfeiture of their landholdings; for the fisc[4] will take possession of the landed estate of any man whose negligence contributes to the damage of the aqueducts. Furthermore, persons through whose landed estates the aqueducts pass should know that they may have trees to the right and left at a distance of fifteen feet from the aqueducts, and your[5] office shall see to it that these trees are cut out if they grow too luxuriantly at any time, so that their roots may not injure the structure of the aqueduct.

QUESTIONS TO CONSIDER

Now that you have looked at both visual and written evidence, you will need to put together the information you have gathered from each type of source to achieve a more complete picture. Because sources for the earliest period of human development are so scanty, we need to use every shred of information available and use it somewhat creatively, making speculations where no specific evidence exists.

Take all the evidence about technical problems first. Keeping in mind that the ancient world had no power equipment and no tools more elaborate than axes, hammers, saws, and drills (the Romans also had planes and chisels), what would you judge to be the most difficult purely technical problem involved in constructing water systems? In keeping them operating? The four diagrams of the water-raising machines are arranged in chronological order of their development: The shaduf may be as old as 2500 B.C., and the other three did not appear until 1,000 years later. Looking at your chart on the advantages and disadvantages of each machine,

3. That is, any special taxes.

4. **fisc**: the imperial treasury.

5. This proclamation was addressed to the administrator of the water supply, the same office that Frontinus held earlier.

in what ways did the later machines improve on the shaduf? What additional problems might these improvements have produced? What types of technological experimentation did the need for water encourage?

Technological advance is not always an unmitigated blessing. For example, water standing in irrigation ditches can become brackish, providing a good breeding ground for mosquitoes and other carriers of disease. Cities that depend on irrigation suffer food shortages and famine when ditches cannot be kept clear or when river levels are low. The diversion of large quantities of water for irrigation makes rivers much smaller when they finally reach their deltas, which means that the deltas become increasingly salty from seawater and unable to support the types of plant and animal life they originally fostered. Judging by the aerial photograph and the LANDSAT map, would you expect any of these problems in ancient Italy or Mesopotamia? Do you find evidence in the written sources for problems in the later Roman water systems that were caused by technical advances? Do the written sources offer suggestions for solving these problems?

Now consider what you have learned about the economic issues associated with water systems. You have doubtless noticed that tremendous numbers of people were needed to construct irrigation ditches and aqueducts. Some of the written sources, such as the extract from Suetonius, provide exact figures. The size and complexity of the systems in the other sources also imply a substantial work force, given the lack of elaborate equipment. The rulers of Egypt, Mesopotamia, and Rome saw the need for a large labor force as no problem; it was, rather, a solution to the greater problem of unemployment. According to a story told about the Roman emperor Vespasian, when he was offered a labor-saving machine, he refused to allow its use because that would put people out of work and lead to social problems in Rome. We might regard this concern for full employment as a positive social attitude, but it should also tell you something about the value of labor in ancient societies. What would you expect wages to be for construction workers? What class of people would you expect to find working on these water systems?

Large numbers of workers were needed not only to build but also to maintain irrigation systems and to operate water-lifting machines. What does this fact tell you about the value of labor? What would happen with a sudden drop in the population, such as that caused by a famine or epidemic? How would a loss of workers affect the available food supply?

The sources also reveal information about political factors associated with water systems. What does the construction of these systems indicate about the power of rulers to coerce or hire labor? How do rulers control the building and maintenance of machines and ditches? How might their control affect the power and independence of local communities or of individual families? What does this tell you about the role of water in expanding centralized political power?

Finally, the sources provide evidence of alterations in the law made necessary by the search for water. Previously unrestricted and unregulated actions now came under the control of public authorities, which meant that the number of enforcement agents and courts had to increase. What would this do to taxation levels? In what ways would political concerns shape the regulations?

Political issues affect not only the types of laws to be passed, but also the stringency or selectivity with which those laws are enforced. We have very little information about how rigidly law codes were implemented in ancient societies, for few legal documents have survived; law codes were frequently recopied and reissued, but the outcome of individual cases was not.

It is therefore dangerous to assume that the prescribed penalties were actually levied or that the law was regularly obeyed. (Think for a minute the mistake a person 2,000 years from now would make in describing traffic patterns in twentieth-century America if he or she assumed that the posted speed limit described the actual speed at which traffic moved!) Looking again at the law codes of Hammurabi and Theodosius, would you expect the penalties to be carried out, or do they appear to serve more as a strong warning? How would the penalties differ in their effects on poor and rich people?

You are now ready to answer the question posed at the beginning of the chapter. How did the need for a steady supply of water affect the development of civilization in the West?

EPILOGUE

The irrigation and water supply systems of the ancient world not only required huge amounts of labor, but also made necessary a strong central authority to coerce or hire that labor and to enforce laws to keep the channels flowing. At first, each Mesopotamian city managed its own irrigation system, but the wealthy and advanced cities were attractive targets for foreign conquerors. The political history of ancient Mesopotamia was one of wave after wave of conquerors coming down from the north—the Akkadians, Babylonians, Assyrians, Persians, Greeks, and finally the Romans. Most of these conquerors realized the importance of irrigation and ordered the conquered residents to maintain or expand their systems. When the Muslims invaded the region in the seventh century, they also learned Mesopotamian techniques and spread these westward into North Africa and Spain, where Roman irrigation systems had in many places fallen apart.

Irrigation could also be overdone, however, and during periods of political centralization many areas were overirrigated, which led to salinization, making the land useless for farming. This, combined with the rivers of Mesopotamia changing their courses, meant that many cities could not survive. Centuries of irrigation combined with too little fertilization made even land that was not salinized less and less productive.

[17]

The benefits and problems produced by irrigation are not limited to the ancient world, however; they can be seen in many modern societies. One of the best modern examples comes from the same part of the world we have been studying in this chapter. Throughout the twentieth century, Egypt expanded its irrigation system watered by the Nile with a series of dams, culminating in the Aswan High Dam; this dam, begun in 1960, was designed to provide hydroelectric power and limit the free flow of water at the height of the flood season. The enormous reservoir formed by the dam can also be tapped at low-water times to allow for perennial irrigation. The Aswan Dam serves all its intended purposes very well, but it has also created some unexpected problems. The river's regular flooding had brought new fertile soil to the Nile Valley and carried away the salts that resulted from evaporation. Once the dam stopped the flooding, Egyptian fields needed artificial fertilizer to remain productive, a commodity many farmers could not afford. The soil of the Nile Valley has a high clay content, rendering drainage difficult, and a steady supply of water makes many fields waterlogged and unusable. The large reservoir created by the dam sits in the middle of the Sahara, allowing a tremendous amount of evaporation and significantly decreasing the total flow of water in the Nile; it has also put many acres of farmland under water and forced the relocation of tens of thousands of people. Ending the flooding allowed snails carrying bilharzia or schistosomiasis—an intestinal parasite that makes people very weak—to proliferate in the fields and irrigation ditches. The high water table resulting from the dam is destroying many ancient monuments, such as the temples of Luxor and Karnak, that have survived for millennia. Thus, like the lead pipes that brought water to the Romans, the Aswan High Dam has proved a mixed blessing in modern Egypt.

As you reflect on what you have discovered in this chapter, you may want to think about problems associated with the distribution of water in your own region. How does the need for water affect the political and economic structures of your city or state? What technological solutions has your region devised, and how have these worked? Thinking more globally, why might analysts be predicting that by the end of the twenty-first century the distribution of water will be a far greater political and economic issue than the distribution of oil?

CHAPTER TWO

POLYTHEISM AND MONOTHEISM

IN THE FERTILE CRESCENT,

CA 3000–500 B.C.

Ancient men and women, like all peoples, struggled with answering basic questions about their existence. What were the origins of human beings and their world? What was the purpose of human existence? How could they explain the events that occurred in their lives? How could they establish order in their societies? Ancient men and women answered such questions chiefly in religious terms, and indeed spiritual thought and institutions largely defined their cultures. Thus an understanding of religious thought and practice is essential to the study of ancient civilization.

Especially significant in the study of ancient civilization is the region of the Fertile Crescent, the relatively well watered band of arable soil in southwestern Asia extending through modern Israel, Lebanon, and Syria along the shore of the Mediterranean Sea to the Tigris and Euphrates River valleys in Iraq. In this zone ancient men and women first began the transition from hunting and gathering to domesticating animals and farming. Here, too, they established the urban centers in which the first civilizations of the West were founded. And in this region they also developed writing systems, now accessible to modern scholars, in which they propounded some of the first formal religious answers to the existential questions with which all ancient peoples struggled. Indeed, these ancient men and women developed two very different religious traditions. One tradition typified ancient religious thought in many ways; the other, as we will see, established the theological foundation for the three great religions of the modern West: Judaism, Christianity, and Islam.

The first of these religious traditions chronologically was polytheism, the worship of many gods and goddesses. It was virtually the universal fashion in which ancient men and

[19]

Chapter 2

Polytheism and

Monotheism in

the Fertile

Crescent, ca

3000–500 B.C.

women in the Fertile Crescent answered questions about their existence and the world around them. They associated deities with every conceivable physical phenomenon, human emotion, event, or even their cities, clans, or trades. Thus ancients might have prayed to the sea god for a safe voyage, or to the fertility god for a good harvest or a fecund herd. Individuals worshipped personal gods, too. All such worship was anthropomorphic; that is, its practitioners envisioned their gods and goddesses as living beings and portrayed them in human or animal form, and they believed that their deities, although immortal, ate, drank, married, reproduced, and experienced a full range of emotions just like humans. Although the followers of such beliefs frequently venerated one deity above others as a sort of supreme god in their pantheon of gods and goddesses, they almost never worshipped one god, a practice called monotheism.

The oldest formal religious practices of which scholars have any significant knowledge are the polytheistic rites of the peoples of ancient Mesopotamia, the area that forms the eastern portion of the Fertile Crescent between the Tigris and Euphrates Rivers in Iraq. As we have seen in Chapter 1, the search for reliable water supplies was central to the existence of ancient communities, and scholars long have assumed that the waters of these two rivers drew the earliest inhabitants to Mesopotamia. Indeed, the region's water, and its lack of great natural barriers to human movement, drew a number of different peoples to the region.

Thse first significant inhabitants of early Mesopotamia were the Sumerians, a people of uncertain origins whose language was unrelated to any known today, including those of the Semitic language groups native to Mesopotamia. Settling in southern Mesopotamia sometime in the fourth millennium B.C. the Sumerians created flourishing cities like Uruk, Ur, and Nippur and traded widely throughout the Fertile Crescent. The cultural life that they created in their cities constituted the first civilization of the West and shaped the culture of Mesopotamia for three millennia. Central to this cultural life was the Sumerians' invention of a writing system, *cuneiform*, with which they kept their business records and created their literature. Cuneiform was a complicated system of wedge-shaped characters (*cuneus* is Latin for "wedge") that were typically inscribed on clay tablets with reed styli by scribes specially schooled in its intricacies. It constituted the universal writing system of scholars, theologians, and diplomats of the Fertile Crescent for several millennia; indeed, Alexander the Great and his soldiers found scribes of the region still using cuneiform in the fourth century B.C. The polytheistic religious beliefs of the Sumerians also became universal in Mesopotamia and much of the Fertile Crescent. Thus, even though the Sumerians eventually disappeared from the region as a distinct people, subsumed by successive conquerors and the Semitic-language natives of the region, their achievements formed the basis for a common ancient Mesopotamian culture. Among the peoples sharing this culture were the Akkadians from northern Mesopotamia, who conquered the Sumerian cities and merged them into an empire ruled by Sargon I about 2350 B.C.; the Babylonians, who, under Hammurabi (r. ca 1792–1750), created a major state centered on their capital of Babylon; the Elamites, who built a large Mesopotamian realm in the late second and early first millennia with its capital at Susa in modern Iran; and the Assyrians, who created a large, warlike state that conquered much of the region in the first millennium B.C.

The first Sumerian settlers of the region and their successors found that they had to cope with a difficult environment. They had to drain marshland for cultivation along the rivers' banks, and they could expand their area of arable land only by building irrigation systems. They found, too, that the Tigris and Euphrates flooded unpredictably and that their waters might quickly kill large numbers of inhabitants along with their livestock and destroy the irrigation works so vital to those who survived inundations. Weather was difficult, too, for early men and women. Today the sun parches the region, producing temperatures as high as 125 degrees Fahrenheit in the warmer months, while heavy winter rains can turn much of the area into mud. Human action also rendered the region dangerous for early men and women. Ancient Mesopotamians fought each other for water supplies at the same time that they had to struggle with invaders of this region, which had few natural barriers to attack.

The grim realities of life in ancient Mesopotamia shaped the religious outlook of its inhabitants. Ancient Mesopotamians could not assume that order, stability, and personal safety would be their lot, and in their quest to explain the difficulties that surrounded them and to ward off imminent dangers they devised a polytheistic belief system. They saw individual human beings as having little consequence in the cosmic order, and one Mesopotamian author wrote: "Mere man—his days are numbered; whatever he may do, he is but the wind."[1] Indeed, Mesopotamians saw themselves as pawns in the hands of capricious gods whose needs they were created to serve and whose ways they were incapable of knowing. One Babylonian text conveys the dilemma of these ancient peoples in their relations with such gods:

> What seems good to oneself, is a
>   crime before a god.
> What to one's heart seems bad, is
>   good before one's god.
> Who may comprehend the minds
>   of gods in heaven's depth?
> The thoughts of (those) divine deep
>   waters, who could fathom them?
> How could mankind, beclouded,
>   comprehend the ways of the
>   gods?[2]

1. Gilgamesh Epic, Old Babylonian version, Yale Tablet IV, 7–8, quoted in Thorkild Jacobsen and William A. Irwin, *The Intellectual Adventure of Ancient Man: An Essay on Speculative Thought in the Ancient Near East* (Chicago: University of Chicago Press, 1946), p. 125.

2. W. G. Lambert, ed., *Babylonian Wisdom Literature* (Oxford: Clarendon Press, 1960), p. 40, lines 34–38.

Chapter 2

Polytheism and

Monotheism in

the Fertile

Crescent, ca

3000–500 B.C.

Ancient Mesopotamians believed in the existence of a pantheon of literally thousands of deities whom they arranged in a hierarchy. There were, however, four especially significant deities in this Mesopotamian pantheon, although their names changed somewhat over the centuries. (We will provide the Sumerian name of each with the Babylonian equivalent in parentheses.) An (Anu or Anum), whose name is the Sumerian word for "sky," was the god of the heavens, and may have been venerated as the chief god in the period prior to the invention of writing. By the time written religious records came into use, however, this deity, though important, was not the chief god. The second important deity for the Sumerians, Enlil, whose name means "Lord Storm," was a god of great power, a kind of chief executive who executed the will of the gods. The Babylonians ascribed many of Enlil's powers to a god they called Marduk. The third significant god was Enki (Ea), god of wisdom and organizer of the earth under Enlil's direction, and the fourth key deity was Ninhursaga (Ninmah, Nintur, and other names), the mother of all living things. In addition to these four central gods and goddesses, Mesopotamians also particularly worshipped three astral deities: Nanna (Sîn), the moon god; Nanna's son, the sun god Utu (Shamash), whose dispelling of darkness made him the deity associated with equity and justice; and Nanna's daughter, Inanna (Ishtar), the goddess of love and fertility, but also war. Mesopotamians believed that these gods and numerous other deities controlled the fate of the world and

mankind in an assembly in which An and Enlil proposed action which the other deities deliberated. When the deities reached a decision, Enlil, or a god or demon designated by him, carried it out. Mesopotamians sought to influence the outcomes of these divine deliberations in several ways. Most individuals had personal gods, deities often long venerated by their families, who they hoped might intercede with the main deities in their behalf. Indeed, the Sumerian word for "good luck" means "to acquire a god," that is, a personal deity who would work for the earthly success of an individual.

The main fashion in which Mesopotamians attempted to influence their deities, however, was in the elaborate cultic activities of their temples, and each deity enjoyed particular veneration in certain locations. Mesopotamians believed that each city was the possession of an individual deity who was entitled to all of its wealth and the labor and devotion of its inhabitants. Thus Uruk was the possession of An, while Nippur was the city of Enlil, and Babylon that of Marduk. To adequately fund the worship of these divinities, Mesopotamian temples owned considerable land, employed tenant farmers to work it, and ran business enterprises, but we now know that they did not own all property, as scholars once thought. Nevertheless, Mesopotamians, anxious to find favor in the eyes of their gods, turned over considerable wealth to the temples, which scribes carefully recorded on clay tablets. This wealth supported a virtual household for the deity in each temple. Priests dressed the god's

[22]

image in rich clothing, prepared ritual meals for him, and entertained him with music. Such wealth also supported elaborate public festivals honoring the gods with ceremonies and parades. Eventually, too, the priesthood devised an elaborate system to interpret natural omens that they alleged predicted the gods' intentions toward humans.

These practices represent a belief system, dominated by a professional priesthood, which established little direct relationship between the individual and the divine, beyond the prayers and offerings that the individual rendered to his or her personal god. Reward for service to the gods, and obedience to the kings whom Mesopotamians saw as deputies of their deities, came in the form of divine protection from the dangers of this life and was measured in good health, long life, and material success. But death, in the end, overtook all, and while Mesopotamian notions of the afterlife still remain vague to modern scholars, they seem to have offered the individual little prospect of a reward for a virtuous life on earth. The Mesopotamian view was that all of the dead seem to share a miserable afterlife, even the greatest of heroes.

The second religious tradition of the ancient Fertile Crescent, monotheism, is inextricably linked with the history of the Hebrews, who were originally nomadic herdsmen. Their recorded history began in the second millennium B.C. as they left Mesopotamia led by the patriarch Abraham and settled first in Canaan, a region along the eastern shore of the

Mediterranean Sea that partially included the territory of the modern state of Israel. Further migration, possibly because of a drought in Canaan, led the Hebrews to Egypt, where the government eventually reduced them to doing forced labor on its building projects in the Nile Delta.

In approximately 1250 B.C., a remarkable leader named Moses led the Hebrews' escape from Egypt, an event remembered as the Exodus. Received by the Hebrews as a messenger of God, Moses spiritually unified them in the midst of their Exodus by committing them to the worship of one deity, referred to as *YHWH* in ancient Hebrew texts (ancient Hebrew employed no vowels) and *Yahweh* in much of modern scholarship. The Hebrews' vision of their deity was unique in the second millennium B.C. For them, Yahweh was the all-powerful creator of the world, and, unlike Mesopotamian deities, he alone controlled every aspect of the universe. He was invisible and omnipresent, too, and because the Hebrews believed him to be eternal, they never envisioned him as being born or having physical needs like Mesopotamian gods and goddesses. Most importantly in the Hebrews' religious vision, Yahweh was kind, merciful, and slow to anger, and he chiefly demanded that his followers exhibit their devotion to him through their obedience to the ethical code revealed in laws associated with him.

Committed to following the laws and teachings of Yahweh, the Hebrews returned to Canaan, which they believed Yahweh had promised to them, and conquered the land with

[23]

Chapter 2

Polytheism and

Monotheism in

the Fertile

Crescent, ca

3000–500 B.C.

military force. Their first-millennium B.C. sojourn in this land was often difficult. Organized first as a tribal federation, the Hebrews had to defend their conquests. Indeed, their military needs required them to abandon tribal government for a monarchy under King Saul (r. ca 1024–1000 B.C.). Following Saul's death in battle, the throne passed first to King David (r. ca 1000–961 B.C.) and then to King Solomon (r. ca 961–922 B.C.). Under the latter monarch, the Hebrew state grew to its greatest extent, and a great spiritual center arose in the temple built in the royal capital, Jerusalem.

At Solomon's death, however, the Hebrew state divided. The northern part of the state, resentful of Solomon's high taxes and the favoritism he showed the south, established itself as the kingdom of Israel, with its capital at Samaria. The south, the kingdom of Judah, retained Jerusalem as its capital. This division of the Hebrew state occurred at a most unfortunate time, just as dangerous and powerful new states were emerging in the Fertile Crescent. Thus Israel fell to the Assyrians in 722 B.C., and these conquerors transported the Hebrews of the north to other parts of their growing empire. There, the Hebrew tribes of northern Canaan lost their religious identity as other Middle Eastern peoples culturally subsumed them.

The kingdom of Judah survived to 586 B.C., when the forces of a new Babylonian empire captured Jerusalem and carried the Hebrews of the south off into captivity in Babylon. There was a real risk that the captives would lose their religious identity in such an exile, just as had their northern kinsmen, but remarkably their religious culture survived. Priests and scholars undertook to preserve religious tradition by drawing together the laws and oral traditions of the Hebrews into texts that would become the Old Testament, and preachers rekindled religious belief with predictions that Yahweh would restore the Hebrews to their homeland. Indeed, such a prediction bore fruit when the Persians conquered Babylon and allowed the Hebrews to return to Judah, by that time a Persian province. There, the Hebrews, henceforth usually called Jews because of their residence in Judah, rebuilt the temple destroyed by the Babylonians.

Although Persian and Babylonian conquests—followed by those of Alexander the Great and the Romans—ended ancient Hebrew political independence, Judaism survived as a distinct faith. Indeed, it survived even as Roman conquerors in the first century A.D. scattered Jews around the West in a diaspora that left many of them living far from their traditional homeland. They often survived as a religious minority among peoples who shared little of their religious culture. In part, this survival was the result of the distinctiveness of that culture. The Jews' adherence to the traditional laws of Yahweh gave them an identity that made their assimilation into other religious traditions difficult and that bound the individual to the religious tradition.

Your goal in this chapter is to analyze the ways in which the polytheism of ancient Mesopotamia and the monotheism of the Hebrews proposed answers to the basic questions posed at the opening of this chapter. What were the origins of human beings and their world? How did they explain the events that occurred in their lives? How could they establish order in their societies? As you develop answers to these questions, you should better understand ancient religion and the societies that produced it.

SOURCES AND METHOD

As we found in Chapter 1, archaeology is an essential tool in reconstructing the life of the ancient world. Archaeological excavations, systematically carried on by modern scholars, are recovering increasing evidence of the art, architecture, and learning of the ancient world, and in recent years their discoveries have dramatically increased historians' knowledge of the Fertile Crescent and its religious life. Indeed, modern scholars have amassed virtually all of their knowledge of ancient Mesopotamia in the past two centuries. Their systematic recovery of the physical remains of the region's ancient civilization commenced only in the 1830s when the French scholar Paul Emile Botta (1805–1870) began to excavate the mysterious mounds, called *tells* in Arabic, that dotted the otherwise flat Mesopotamian landscape. Formed by centuries of drifting sand accumulating around the ruins of ancient cities and temples, these mounds yielded ancient artifacts and architecture to archaeologists. Scholars' efforts to interpret the significance of their findings advanced considerably when the German philologist Georg Friedrich Grotefend (1775–1853) successfully deciphered the cuneiform writing of ancient scribes.

Equipped with such linguistic skills, archaeologists have been able to exploit dramatic discoveries to increase their knowledge of Mesopotamian civilization. One such discovery was the excavation of the library of the Assyrian king Ashurbanipal (r. 668–627 B.C.) in Nineveh. That monarch had attempted to assemble all of the region's learning in his library, and the 22,000 tablets that archaeologists discovered there have proven to be a remarkable source for the study of Mesopotamian civilization.

Sources 1 and 2 offer pictorial evidence of archaeologists' work and provide us with an introduction to the physical remains of ancient Mesopotamian religious life. Both sources illustrate the ziggurat constructed by King Ur-Nammu at Ur about 2100 B.C., a time when that Sumerian city was the capital of a considerable empire. Ziggurats were stepped pyramids, as Source 1 shows, that were characteristic features of Mesopotamian temple sites. Source 1 is a sketch based on the work of Sir Leonard Wooley, a twentieth-century archaeologist who led some of the most important digs at Ur. The ziggurat illustrated in the sketch was part of the shrine of the moon god, Nanna, who was the patron god of Ur, and it was the center of a massive temple complex including shrines to Nanna

[25]

Chapter 2
Polytheism and
Monotheism in
the Fertile
Crescent, ca
3000–500 B.C.

and his wife Ningal, offices for the priests, and storehouses for the temple's wealth. Many scholars think that the Mesopotamians believed that the god dwelt atop the ziggurat in a shrine that was open only to priests, who reached it by mounting staircases like those illustrated in Source 1.

Source 2, a photograph of this ziggurat after archaeologists removed the tell that had concealed the structure for centuries, shows this religious site as it looks today. Its two top terraces have been lost to the ravages of time, but the scale of the structure may be gauged by comparing it to the automobile in the foreground. Constructed in the sun-baked mud brick of the region and faced with harder, fired bricks, the ziggurat measures about 200 feet by 150 feet at its base and today stands about 50 feet high. Four millennia ago, temple attendants planted the terraces with trees and green plants, which must have made the ziggurat look like a mountain. What impression do you think that the ziggurat made on ancient residents of Ur? If you combine this impression with the closure of the inner sanctum of the ziggurat to laypeople, and recall the riches that Mesopotamians offered to their temples, what sort of religious sentiments do you suppose worshippers at such a shrine might have experienced? Why might you agree with a modern scholar who has written that the divine in ancient Mesopotamia "was above all something grandiose, inaccessible, dominating, and to be feared"?[3] Why can you find little

3. Jean Bottéro, *Religion in Ancient Mesopotamia*, translated by Teresa Lavender Fagan (Chicago: University of Chicago Press, 2001), p. 37.

connection between the individual and the deity in this architectural expression of ancient polytheism?

Mesopotamian religious thinkers produced no systematic theological treatises yet discovered by archaeologists. Thus modern students of the region must reconstruct Mesopotamian religion from the texts of actual religious rites that archaeologists have uncovered. The precise ancient purpose of the text in Source 3 is unclear; its words come from an early second-millennium column found near Babylon on the Euphrates River that is in a poor state of preservation. Perhaps the words originally were a prayer or incantation, but scholars do know that they present us with a vision of human origins that was widespread in Mesopotamia. What does this text tell us about the position of mankind in the Mesopotamian cosmos? Why did the gods create humans? Why do you suppose the gods created the first man from a mixture of divine blood and clay? Given this vision of human origins, what do you suppose Mesopotamians believed that they owed their deities?

Source 4 reminds us that the various linguistic groups of Mesopotamia shared a common cultural heritage. It is a prayer found on a tablet at King Ashurbanipal's palace in Nineveh, with a text in both Sumerian and the Akkadian language of northern Mesopotamia. Impossible to precisely date, this was a prayer to the moon god known as Nannar (or Nanna) to the Sumerians and Sîn to the Babylonians. Why does the prayer exalt the moon god as "supreme" when, in the Sumerian pantheon, Enlil largely occupied that position, while among Babylonians the supreme deity was Marduk? Assessing the text, why might you conclude that this attribution of superior status was an attempt to win the favor of the god? What are the alleged powers of this moon god? Is this god loved by his worshippers or feared by them?

Source 5 presents four excerpts from the oldest work of Western literature yet identified by scholars, the *Epic of Gilgamesh*, a poem of over 3,000 lines. Archaeologists discovered the first, partial text of this great epic in the ruins of King Ashurbanipal's palace library in Nineveh. That first discovery, however, yielded only part of the epic, and only slowly have scholars pieced the rest of it together with discoveries of additional portions of the text at archaeological digs elsewhere in Mesopotamia. Indeed, their task still is under way. Nevertheless, the result of their labors is an ancient text that gives us further insight into Mesopotamian religion, even though the epic itself is not a religious work.

The hero of the epic, Gilgamesh, was king of Uruk about 2600 B.C., and according to tradition he built the city's walls. Poetry recounting his legendary exploits dates from at least 2000 B.C. and was written in cuneiform in the major languages of the region. The epic presents Gilgamesh as part god, a vigorous ruler who embellished his city and who had many adventures with his friend, Enkidu. Together, however, they ran afoul of the gods. They slew Huwawa, a monster assigned by Enlil to guard a forest, and they felled the cedar trees in it. Gilgamesh insulted the goddess

Ishtar when she sought his hand in marriage, and he and Enkidu slew the bull of heaven that the goddess sent to Uruk to punish him. Divine punishment, envisioned in a dream, caused Enkidu's death, as the first lines of Source 5 show. Gilgamesh deeply mourned the loss of his friend, but the king resolved to avoid the fate of Enkidu, and all mortals, and set off on a quest to find the secret of immortality. That quest set Gilgamesh searching for the sole survivor of the all-killing flood that was part of Mesopotamian mythology. The gods had granted immortality to that survivor, Utnapishtim, and Gilgamesh sought to learn from him the secret of eternal life.

In undertaking his search for Utnapishtim, Gilgamesh ignored the prescient warnings of a tavern-keeper, referred to as an alewife in the translation in Source 5, that he was disregarding mankind's proper relationship with the cosmos. When Gilgamesh finally managed to meet Utnapishtim by crossing the waters that separated the realm of death from that of the living, the latter gave Gilgamesh a test requiring that he remain awake for seven days and nights. The king promptly went to sleep, however, losing his chance to learn the secret of immortality, and Utnapishtim ordered Gilgamesh to return to the land of the living, where he, of course, would face eventual death. But thanks to the intervention of the wife of Utnapishtim, Gilgamesh got one more chance to avoid early death with a magical plant that offered rejuvenation. How did he lose this opportunity, too? What does the

[27]

Chapter 2

Polytheism and

Monotheism in

the Fertile

Crescent, ca

3000–500 B.C.

epic tell us about Mesopotamians' belief in their gods' control of their destinies? How did Mesopotamians view the afterlife? Did the powerful and wealthy fare any better there than commoners? Is there any sense here that the gods even cared about man's fate? What was Gilgamesh's fate? Why do you think that this part of the epic ends with Gilgamesh taking the boatman who had conveyed him back and forth across the waters on a tour of the walls and sights of Uruk?

Source 6 presents us with the Mesopotamians' quest to establish earthly order. Ancient Mesopotamians viewed their world as an extension of the divine world. The gods simply delegated their authority on earth to kings, and ancient authors often used the words "the Enlil functions" to designate the power of these kings, which, in their view, reflected the almighty power of the god Enlil. Thus, just as that chief god kept order in the divine world, the king kept order on earth. And, indeed, there was considerable need for an authority figure to keep order in the ancient Tigris and Euphrates River valleys. Mesopotamians lived in densely populated cities and engaged in competitive commercial and agricultural activities that created ample opportunity for human conflict. Moreover, there was little in the way of social control in Mesopotamian religion; the ancient polytheism of Mesopotamia seems not to have obligated its followers to adhere to an ethical code as part of their spiritual devotion. Thus, archaeologists have found evidence that Mesopotamian rulers began attempting to regulate human behavior

with detailed law codes by 2400 B.C., if not earlier.

Source 6 presents the most famous Mesopotamian law code, that of Hammurabi, the ruler of Babylon (r. ca 1792–1750 B.C.). First discovered by French archaeologists in 1901 carved in cuneiform characters on a stele, or upright stone slab, the laws of Hammurabi have now been found at a number of Mesopotamian sites. What does the prologue of the law code suggest that Mesopotamians saw as the source of law and order in their earthly realm? The code itself represents what legal scholars call case law; that is, it describes specific actions and circumstances and then posits their legal consequences. Why do you think Babylonian society required such a detailed law code? What aspects of life did the code regulate? Did its scope exceed the bounds of modern law? Did Hammurabi's code regulate a society in which all citizens were equal? Why might you characterize the sections dealing with criminal law as harsh by modern standards?

If the sources of ancient Mesopotamian polytheism have been known to Western scholars for only about two centuries, the sources of the religion of the ancient Hebrews have been the object of serious scholarly study for two millennia. Those sources are the texts that constitute the Hebrew Bible, what Jews call *Tanak* (an acronym based on the first letters of the three divisions of the Hebrew Bible: Torah ["Law"], Nebi'im ["Prophets"], and Kethubim ["Writings"]), and the first part of the Christian Bible, the Old Testament.

[28]

Traditionally scholars have studied these works through intense textual analyses in which they apply their theological, linguistic, and historical knowledge to better understand the origins and development of these biblical texts, which are the essential foundations for the religious beliefs of many in the West.

Such study has allowed modern scholars to identify differences in textual authorships and actually to date the books of the Old Testament. They know, for example, that they have yet to find a single biblical text dating to the traditional second-millennium B.C. origins of Hebrew monotheism. Instead, they have found that much of the Old Testament commentary on the origins of Hebrew monotheism was written considerably later. The first Old Testament books, including Genesis and Exodus, which recount the Creation story and the early history of the Hebrews through about 1200 B.C., were written later, perhaps between about 950 and 800 B.C. Thus these and other Old Testament texts were not the work of authors who actually witnessed the events that they recounted. Instead, these were the work of extremely talented, later authors who wove Hebrew oral traditions, songs, prayers, and laws into coherent texts of often beautiful literary quality.

Scholars' knowledge of this evolution of the Old Testament text caused some among them in the early and mid-twentieth century to question the traditional second-millennium B.C. origins of Hebrew monotheism in the time of Abraham and Moses. They reasoned that the authors of the Old Testament books who recounted the earliest Hebrew history probably projected their own monotheism onto their ancestors. These scholars placed the origin of true monotheism later, at the time of the prophetic writings of the eighth and ninth centuries B.C., in part because their textual analyses suggested that the authors of the prophetic texts indeed described events that they witnessed.

More recently, however, Old Testament scholarship has been powerfully affected by the results of archaeological excavations in the western Fertile Crescent. These excavations at non-Hebrew sites are now providing important verification of much found in the Old Testament accounts of the earliest Hebrew experiences. The most important of these sites is that of Ugarit (modern Ras Shamra) on the Mediterranean coast of Syria. There, archaeological digs under way since 1928 have uncovered the remains of a port city and cultural center that flourished at the time of the Hebrews' flight from Egypt. Texts discovered at Ugarit, written in the local language that was closely related to Hebrew, contain the poetry and myths of the Hebrews' close neighbors and confirm many of the stories and practices of the Old Testament books like Genesis and Exodus. As a result, recent scholars have been better able to place Hebrew monotheism into the cultural context of the ancient Middle East as well as to better understand its earliest origins.

It is clear that Hebrew monotheism and Mesopotamian polytheism shared certain geographic and cultural roots. The Old Testament places the origin

Chapter 2

Polytheism and

Monotheism in

the Fertile

Crescent, ca

3000–500 B.C.

of Abraham and his kin squarely in southern Mesopotamia at Ur, and they also dwelt at Haran in northern Mesopotamia before moving on to Canaan. Thus Mesopotamian and Hebrew cultures share certain elements; both have very similar Creation accounts, and both traditions recall an all-destroying flood. But despite these similarities, we can discern marked differences in the religious thought of the two groups in even the earliest Hebrew texts.

Source 7 presents the Creation account from Genesis 2:1–24. Biblical scholars know that this account is one of three originally distinct Creation stories that eventually became part of Genesis, and on the basis of close textual analysis they identify this as the oldest of the three. In Genesis it follows another, relatively more recent, Creation account that opens the book and that presents Yahweh creating the universe in seven days. The opening lines of the selection in Source 7 refer to that process. Compare this account with the Creation story in Source 3. What similarities do you note? How, for example, was the first man formed in each story? What location do you suspect for the Garden of Eden based on two of the rivers identified in the selection? Why do such similarities in the two accounts suggest that they, or their authors, had similar origins? Next examine the text of Source 7 for its differences from the Mesopotamian account. For what reason did Mesopotamian deities form human beings? What did Yahweh intend for his human creations? What do you conclude from the fact that Yahweh permitted humans to name

the animals that he had created? Why might you determine that the Hebrew account portrays a more benevolent deity than does the Mesopotamian story?

Source 8 describes the central event of the Hebrews' religious experience, their acceptance of the covenant with Yahweh that established them as his chosen people. The event described here occurred in the wilderness of Sinai, after the Hebrews' exodus from Egypt, when Yahweh descended to Mount Sinai and enunciated the covenant to Moses. In return for obeying Yahweh's law, the Hebrews would enjoy divine protection. The laws that form the covenant are known as the Ten Commandments, and Source 8A presents these from Exodus 20:1–17. Following the laws, in Source 8B, is the Hebrews' acceptance, described in Exodus 24:3, of Yahweh's terms for the covenant.

The laws contained in Source 8 are part of a broad general statement of law contained in the first five books of the Old Testament—Genesis, Exodus, Leviticus, Numbers, and Deuteronomy—that for Jews constitute the Torah or law. The Ten Commandments are quite different from the case law that we observed in Hammurabi's Code; they are what legal scholars call absolute, or apodictic, law. Such law states broad, absolute principles that cannot be violated, and it can be extremely important in ordering the lives of those subject to it, although it is essential that case law provide concrete applications of its principles. Although some biblical scholars have questioned whether this covenant truly established monotheism since it acknowledges the existence of "other gods," many others accept it as clearly establishing a special relationship between Yahweh and the Hebrews defined by a monotheistic faith. What did Yahweh expect of his people in the Ten Commandments? When you consider the commandments, why will you probably conclude that they established definite behavioral responsibilities for the individual within the covenanting group? What does Yahweh expect of his followers that Mesopotamian deities did not require of those who worshipped them? Why might you conclude that the phrase "ethical monotheism" is an apt description of the faith established by this covenant?

Source 9 presents sources from some of the books of the Torah that offer case law. Like Hammurabi's Code, they give us a fuller vision of the behavior that Yahweh expected of his followers. What is the source of the law in Source 9, and, ultimately, who is the guarantor of the peace that the law seeks to protect? Contrast your answers with those that you would give to the same questions posed about Hammurabi's Code. Who is the protector of the marginal members of Hebrew society: resident aliens, widows, orphans, and the poor? In Leviticus 19:17, what do you find demanded of Yahweh's followers that goes well beyond simple adherence to the "law" in our modern sense of that word? Why might you conclude that these selections also spell out a code of personal ethics? Why might you probably conclude that the Hebrew laws demanded far more of those subject to them than did the laws of Hammurabi?

In return for their adherence to the Ten Commandments, the Old Testament tells us that Yahweh promised to deliver the land of Canaan into the possession of the Hebrews. The Hebrews' subsequent conquest and settlement of this region were fraught with problems. Traditionally nomadic herdsmen, the Hebrews had to adjust to a sedentary, agricultural life in Canaan, and they had to deal with dangerous neighbors like the warlike Philistines. But the greatest danger that they faced, according to the Old Testament, was a spiritual one. They had settled among Canaanite neighbors who, archaeological evidence shows, were more materially advanced than their Hebrew conquerors, and Canaanite culture must have tempted many Hebrews. But embracing aspects of that culture risked the cultural distinctiveness of the Hebrews, particularly in the area of religion. The Canaanites were polytheists, much of whose religious life centered on fertility cults that included ritualized sexual acts. These acts were fiercely condemned by Hebrew religious leaders, known as prophets.

The prophets represented a Hebrew manifestation of a long-standing Middle Eastern tradition in which religious figures prophesized the future and tried to shape human behavior. The Hebrew prophets of the first millennium B.C.—men like Elijah, Elisha, Isaiah, Hosea, and Amos—proclaimed that they were messengers of Yahweh and that they spoke his words. Thus biblical passages often start the words of the prophets with phrases like "Thus says the Lord. . . ." The words that followed such phrases typically condemned the kings of Israel and

Chapter 2

Polytheism and

Monotheism in

the Fertile

Crescent, ca

3000–500 B.C.

Judah who did not provide proper leadership to their people, the moral failings of Hebrew society, and most particularly the tendency of the Hebrews to adopt Canaanite religious practices. Usually, too, the prophets threatened divine action against Hebrews who did not change their ways, and they portrayed the conquests of Israel and Judah as acts of divine retribution.

Source 10 offers the words of several prophets as examples of the Hebrews' relationship with Yahweh and the struggle of the prophets to uphold the religious beliefs and practices of the covenant. Source 10A is from the book of Isaiah, a prophet active in the eighth century B.C. His writings suggest that Isaiah was a man of considerable culture and learning, and he warned of the moral and ethical failings of the Hebrews as well as of the growing threat from the Assyrians. Scholars believe that the later part of the book of Isaiah, including the selection in 10A, was the work of one of the great prophet's disciples. What does the author of these verses remind his readers about Yahweh's power? What does he say that Yahweh values in his followers? How are such expectations consistent with Hebrew ethical monotheism?

Source 10B is a selection from the book of Hosea. His book includes an account of his marriage to Gomer, a woman who bore him three children and then was unfaithful to her marital vows. Hosea divorced her for this unfaithfulness and she became a prostitute, but he subsequently forgave Gomer and remarried her. Biblical scholars generally see Hosea's story as an allegory that represents the Hebrews' unfaithfulness to Yahweh and his ultimate mercy and forgiveness. What does Hosea condemn? Why might you conclude that he condemns religious syncretism, that is, the Hebrews' adoption of Canaanite rites? Source 10B also gives an eloquent account of Yahweh's relationship with the Hebrews. Why would you characterize that relationship as a parental one? Why do think that Yahweh, like many parents, punished with extreme reluctance? Why do you conclude that Hosea saw Yahweh as a merciful god?

Despite the personal relationship between Yahweh and the individual Hebrew, there remained a certain distance between him and mortals, and his ways often remained inscrutable to them. This is evident even in Old Testament books written relatively late in time. One such book is that of Job, which may have been written as late as the fourth century B.C. Stylistically, it is one of the Old Testament's most remarkable books, comprising, in part, poetry of exceptional beauty. Its story, however, is its most compelling aspect, that of a righteous man who, despite his virtues and religious devotion, is afflicted by evil. This theme appears in Mesopotamian and Egyptian literature, too, but in the book of Job, excerpted in Source 11, the main theme is not the incidence of evil but the individual's relationship with Yahweh.

In the book, Yahweh tests Job, depriving him of his children and his property and afflicting him with illness. What is Job's response to these afflictions? How does he despair in an age that assumed that virtue would be rewarded not in the next life but with material success and good health in this life? How does Job even despair of ever getting a fair hearing from Yahweh? How does Yahweh respond to Job? Why might you find Yahweh's questions of Job almost mocking the weakness of mortals? What vision of Yahweh's power do you detect in his response to Job? Why can Job not know Yahweh's ways? What sort of profession of faith from Job led to the restoration of what he had lost?

Using this background information on ancient polytheism and monotheism in the Fertile Crescent, now turn to the sources themselves. As you read them, reflect on how the ancient followers of each religious tradition answered the basic existential questions with which we opened this chapter. What were the origins of human beings and their world? How did they explain events that occurred in their lives? How could they establish order in their societies?

THE EVIDENCE

Source 1 from The Granger Collection. *New York.*

1. The Ziggurat of Ur-Nammu, King of Ur, ca 2100 B.C.

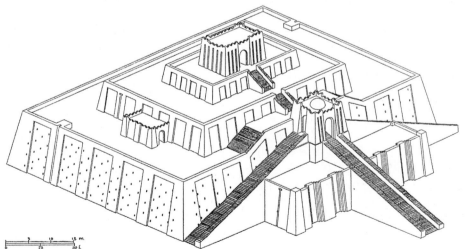

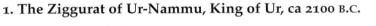

Chapter 2
Polytheism and
Monotheism in
the Fertile
Crescent, ca
3000–500 B.C.

Source 2 from The Granger Collection. *New York.*

2. The Ziggurat of Ur-Nammu, King of Ur, ca 2100 B.C., As It Looked After Twentieth-Century Archaeological Excavation Work

Source 3 from James B. Pritchard, Ancient Near Eastern Texts Relating to the Old Testament, *third edition with supplement. © 1950, 1955, 1969, renewed 1978 by Princeton University Press. Reprinted by permission of Princeton University Press.*

3. Creation of Man by the Mother Goddess

"That which is slight he shall raise to abundance;
The work of god man shall bear!"
The goddess they called to enquire,
The midwife of the gods, the wise Mami:[4]
"Thou art the mother-womb,
The one who creates mankind.
Create, then, Lullu[5] and let him bear the yoke!
The yoke he shall bear, . . . [. . .];
The work of god man shall bear!"
Nintu opened her mouth,
Saying to the great gods:

4. **Mami:** one of a series of names Mesopotamians applied to the mother goddess. They also included, among others, Nihursaga and Nintur, as well as the name Nintu that appears later in this text.
5. **Lullu:** literally, "the savage first man," really a figure akin to Adam of the Old Testament.

"With me is the doing of (this) not suitable;
With Enki is (this) work (proper)!
He purifies everything,
Let him give me the clay, then I will do (it)!"
Enki opened his mouth,
Saying to the great gods:
"On the first of the month, the seventh and fifteenth days,
I will prepare a purification, a bath.
Let one god be slain,
And let the gods be purified by immersion
In his flesh and his blood.
Let Nintu mix clay,
God and man,
Let them together be smeared with clay.
Unto eternity let us hear the drum."

Source 4 from R. F. Harper, editor, Assyrian and Babylonian Literature: Selected Translations *(New York: Appleton, 1900), pp. 430–431.*

4. Prayer to the Moon God, Nannar or Sîn

O Lord, chief of the gods, who in heaven and on earth alone is supreme!
Father Nannar, lord of increase, chief of the gods!
Father Nannar, lord of heaven, great one, chief of the gods!
Father Nannar, lord of the moon, chief of the gods!
Father Nannar, lord of Ur, chief of the gods!
Father Nannar, lord of E-gis-sir-gal,[6] chief of the gods!
Father Nannar, lord of the moon-disk, brilliant one, chief of the gods!
Father Nannar, who rules with pomp, chief of the gods!
Father Nannar, who goes about in princely garb, chief of the gods!
O strong bull, with terrible horns, well-developed muscles, with a flowing beard of the colour of lapis lazuli,[7] full of vigour and life!
O fruit, which grows of itself, developed in appearance, beautiful to look upon, but whose luxuriance does not produce fruit!
O merciful one, begetter of everything, who has taken up his illustrious abode among living creatures!

6. **E-gis-sir-gal:** the name of the moon god's temple at Ur.
7. **lapis lazuli:** a semiprecious stone of deep blue color used by the ancients for beads and other ornaments.

Chapter 2

Polytheism and

Monotheism in

the Fertile

Crescent, ca

3000–500 B.C.

O merciful and forgiving father, who holds in his hand the life of the whole
country!
O Lord, thy divinity is full of fear, like the far-off heavens and the broad sea!
. . . .
O Father, begetter of everything . . .
O Lord, who determines the decisions of heaven and earth, whose command
no one [can set aside]!
O thou who holdest fire and water, who rulest over all creatures! What god can
attain thy position?
In heaven who is exalted? Thou alone art exalted!
On earth who is exalted? Thou alone art exalted!

Source 5 from James B. Pritchard, Ancient Near Eastern Texts Relating to the Old Testament,
*third edition with supplement. © 1950, 1955, 1969, renewed 1978 by Princeton University Press.
Reprinted by permission of Princeton University Press.*

5. The *Epic of Gilgamesh*

[The death of Enkidu]

Gilgamesh in his palace holds a celebration.
Down lie the heroes on their beds of night
Also Enkidu lies down, a dream beholding.
Up rose Enkidu to relate his dream,
Saying to his friend:
"My friend, why are the great gods in council?"

[And] Enkidu answered Gilgamesh:
"[He]*ar* the dream which I had last night:
Anu, Enlil, Ea, and heavenly Shamash
      [Were in council].
And Anu said to Enlil:
'Because the Bull of Heaven they have slain, and Huwawa
They have slain, therefore'—said Anu—'the one of them
Who stripped the mountains of the cedar
      [Must die!]'
But Enlil said: 'Enkidu must die;
Gilgamesh, however, shall not die!'. . .

That night [he pours out] his feelings to his friend:
". . . My friend, I saw a dream last night:
The heavens shouted, the earth responded;
While I was standing between them
(There was) a young man whose face was dark, . . .
Looking at me, he leads me to the House of Darkness,

      The abode of Irkalla,[8]
To the house which none leave who have entered it,
On the road from which there is no way back,
To the house wherein the dwellers are bereft of light,
Where dust is their fare and clay their food.
They are clothed like birds, with wings for garments,
And see no light, residing in darkness.
In the House of Dust, which I entered,
I looked at [rulers], their crowns put away;
I [saw princes], those (born to) the crown,
    Who had ruled the land from the days of yore.
[These *doubl*]es of Anu and Enlil were serving meat roasts;
They were serving bake[meats] and pouring
    Cool water from the waterskins.
In the House of Dust, which I entered,
Reside High Priest and acolyte,
Reside incantatory and ecstatic,
Reside the laver-anointers of the great gods,
Resides Etana,[9] resides Sumuqan. . . .[10]

[Gilgamesh mourns Enkidu.]

For Enkidu, his friend, Gilgamesh
Weeps bitterly, as he ranges over the steppe:
When I die, shall I not be like Enkidu?
Woe has entered my belly.
Fearing death, I roam over the steppe.
To Utnapishtim, Ubar-Tutu's son,
I have taken the road to proceed in all haste. . . .

[Gilgamesh meets the tavern-keeper.]

"Gilgamesh, whither rovest thou?
The life thou pursuest thou shalt not find.
When the gods created mankind,
Death for mankind they set aside,
Life in their own hands retaining.
Thou, Gilgamesh, let full be thy belly,
Make thou merry by day and by night.
Of each day make thou a feast of rejoicing,

8. **Irkalla:** in Mesopotamian mythology, the queen of the underworld.
9. **Etana:** a legendary king carried to heaven by an eagle.
10. **Sumuqan:** the god of cattle.

Chapter 2

Polytheism and

Monotheism in

the Fertile

Crescent, ca

3000–500 B.C.

Day and night dance thou and play!
Let thy garments be sparkling fresh,
Thy head be washed; bathe thou in water.
Pay heed to the little one that holds on to thy hand,
Let thy spouse delight in thy bosom!
For this is the task of [mankind]!" . . .

[Gilgamesh leaves Utnapishtim and returns to Uruk.]

His spouse says to him, to Utnapishtim the Faraway:
"Gilgamesh has come hither, toiling and straining.
What wilt thou give (him) that he may return to his land?"
At that he, Gilgamesh, raised up (his) pole,
To bring the boat nigh to the shore.
Utnapishtim [says] to him, [to] Gilgamesh:
"Gilgamesh, thou hast come hither, toiling and straining.
What shall I give thee that thou mayest return to thy land?
I will disclose, O Gilgamesh, a hidden thing,
And [*a secret of the gods* I will] tell thee:
This plant, like the buckthorn is [its . . .].
Its thorns will pr[ick thy hands] just as does the *rose.*
If thy hands obtain the plant, [thou wilt find new life]."
No sooner had Gilgamesh heard this,
    Than he opened the *wa[ter-pipe]*,[11]
He tied heavy stones [to his feet],
They pulled him down into the deep [and he saw the plant].
He took the plant, though it pr[icked his hands].
He cut the heavy stones [from his feet].
The [s]ea cast him up upon its shore.

Gilgamesh says to him, to Urshanabi, the boatman:
"Urshanabi, this plant is a plant *apart,*
Whereby a man may regain his *life's breath.*
I will take it to ramparted Uruk,
    Will cause [. . .] to eat the plant. . . !
Its name shall be 'Man Becomes Young in Old Age.'
I myself shall eat (it)
    And thus return to the state of my youth."
After twenty leagues they broke off a morsel,
After thirty (further) leagues they prepared for the night.
Gilgamesh saw a well whose water was cool.
He went down into it to bathe in the water.

11. **water-pipe:** meaning unclear because of the incomplete state of the original text. The pipe in
    some way related to Gilgamesh's dive.

A serpent snuffed the fragrance of the plant;
It came up [from the water] and carried off the plant.
Going back it shed [its] slough.[12]

Thereupon Gilgamesh sits down and weeps,
His tears running down over his face.
[He took the hand] of Urshanabi, the boatman:
"[For] whom, Urshanabi, have my hands toiled?
For whom is being spent the blood of my heart?
I have not obtained a boon for myself.
For the earth-lion[13] have I effected a boon!
And now the tide will bear (it) twenty leagues away!
When I opened the *water-pipe* and [. . .] the gear,
I found that which has been placed as a sign for me:
　I shall withdraw,
And leave the boat on the shore!"
　After twenty leagues they broke off a morsel,
After thirty (further) leagues they prepared for the night.
When they arrived in ramparted Uruk,
Gilgamesh says to him, to Urshanabi, the boatman:
"Go up. Urshanabi, walk on the ramparts of Uruk. . . ."

Source 6 from James B. Pritchard, Ancient Near Eastern Texts Relating to the Old Testament, *third edition with supplement. © 1950, 1955, 1969, renewed 1978 by Princeton University Press. Reprinted by permission of Princeton University Press.*

6. The Code of Hammurabi

The Prologue

When lofty Anum, king of the Anunnaki,[14]
(and) Enlil, lord of heaven and earth,
the determiner of the destinies of the land,
determined for Marduk, the first-born of Enki,
the Enlil functions over all mankind,
made him great among the Igigi,[15]
called Babylon by its exalted name,
made it supreme in the world,
established for him in its midst an enduring kingship,

12. **slough:** the outer skin that a snake periodically sheds.
13. **earth-lion:** the serpent.
14. **Anunnaki:** the lesser gods attending Annum.
15. **Igigi:** the lesser gods attending Enlil.

Chapter 2

Polytheism and

Monotheism in

the Fertile

Crescent, ca

3000–500 B.C.

whose foundations are as firm as heaven and earth—
at that time Anum and Enlil named me
to promote the welfare of the people,
me, Hammurabi, the devout, god-fearing prince,
to cause justice to prevail in the land,
to destroy the wicked and the evil,
that the strong might not oppress the weak,
to rise like the sun over the black-headed (people),[16]
and to light up the land. . . .

When Marduk commissioned me to guide the people aright, to direct the land,
I established law and justice in the language of the land,
thereby promoting the welfare of the people.
At that time I decreed:

THE LAWS

1: If a seignior[17] accused a(nother) seignior and brought a charge of murder against him, but has not proved it, his accuser shall be put to death. . . .

3: If a seignior came forward with false testimony in a case, and has not proved the word which he spoke, if that case was a case involving life, that seignior shall be put to death.

4: If he came forward with (false) testimony concerning grain or money, he shall bear the penalty of that case.

5: If a judge gave a judgment, rendered a decision, deposited a sealed document, but later has altered his judgment, they shall prove that that judge altered the judgment which he gave and he shall pay twelvefold the claim which holds in that case; furthermore, they shall expel him in the assembly from his seat of judgment and he shall never again sit with the judges in a case.

6: If a seignior stole the property of church or state, that seignior shall be put to death; also the one who received the stolen goods from his hand shall be put to death.

7: If a seignior has purchased or he received for safekeeping either silver or gold or a male slave or a female slave or an ox or a sheep or an ass or any sort of thing from the hand of a seignior's son or a seignior's slave without witnesses and contracts, since that seignior is a thief, he shall be put to death.

8: If a seignior stole either an ox or a sheep or an ass or a pig or a boat, if it belonged to the church (or) if it belonged to the state, he shall make thirtyfold restitution; if it belonged to a private citizen, he shall make good tenfold. If the thief does not have sufficient to make restitution, he shall be put to death.

16. **black-headed people:** a late Sumerian expression for mankind in general.

17. **seignior:** a free man of some standing in the community.

9: When a seignior, (some of) whose property was lost, has found his lost property in the possession of a(nother) seignior, if the seignior in whose possession the lost (property) was found has declared, "A seller sold (it) to me; I made the purchase in the presence of witnesses," and the owner of the lost (property) in turn has declared, "I will produce witnesses attesting to my lost (property)"; the purchaser having then produced the seller who made the sale to him and the witnesses in whose presence he made the purchase, and the owner of the lost (property) having also produced the witnesses attesting to his lost (property), the judges shall consider their evidence, and the witnesses in whose presence the purchase was made, along with the witnesses attesting to the lost (property), shall declare what they know in the presence of god, and since the seller was the thief, he shall be put to death, while the owner of the lost (property) shall take his lost (property), with the purchaser obtaining from the estate of the seller the money that he paid out.

10: If the (professed) purchaser has not produced the seller who made the sale to him and the witnesses in whose presence he made the purchase, but the owner of the lost property has produced witnesses attesting to his lost property, since the (professed) purchaser was the thief, he shall be put to death, while the owner of the lost property shall take his lost property.

11: If the (professed) owner of the lost property has not produced witnesses attesting to his lost property, since he was a cheat and started a false report, he shall be put to death. . . .

22: If a seignior committed robbery and has been caught, that seignior shall be put to death.

23: If the robber has not been caught, the robbed seignior shall set forth the particulars regarding his lost property in the presence of god, and the city and governor, in whose territory and district the robbery was committed, shall make good to him his lost property.

24: If it was a life (that was lost), the city and governor shall pay one mina[18] of silver to his people.

25: If fire broke out in a seignior's house and a seignior, who went to extinguish (it), cast his eye on the goods of the owner of the house and has appropriated the goods of the owner of the house, that seignior shall be thrown into that fire. . . .

88: If a merchant [lent] grain at interest, he shall receive sixty *qu* of grain per *kur* as interest.[19] If he lent money at interest, he shall receive one-sixth (shekel) six *še* (i.e. one-fifth shekel) per shekel of silver as interest.[20]

18. **mina:** a weight of 500 grams.
19. *qu, kur:* there were 300 *qu* in a *kur*. Thus, the interest rate was 20 percent.
20. *še:* there were 180 *še* in a shekel. Thus, the interest rate, again, was 20 percent.

Chapter 2

Polytheism and

Monotheism in

the Fertile

Crescent, ca

3000–500 B.C.

89: If a seignior, who [incurred] a debt, does not have the money to pay (it) back, but has the grain, [the merchant] shall take grain for his money [with its interest] in accordance with the ratio fixed by the king.

90: If the merchant increased the interest beyond [sixty *qu*] per *kur* [of grain] (or) one-sixth (shekel) six *še* [per shekel of money] and has collected (it), he shall forfeit whatever he lent. . . .

104: If a merchant lent grain, wool, oil, or any goods at all to a trader to retail, the trader shall write down the value and pay (it) back to the merchant, with the trader obtaining a sealed receipt for the money which he pays to the merchant.

105: If the trader has been careless and so has not obtained a sealed receipt for the money which he paid to the merchant, the money with no sealed receipt may not be credited to the account. . . .

195: If a son has struck his father, they shall cut off his hand.

196: If a seignior has destroyed the eye of a member of the aristocracy, they shall destroy his eye.

197: If he has broken a(nother) seignior's bone, they shall break his bone.

198: If he has destroyed the eye of a commoner or broken the bone of a commoner, he shall pay one mina of silver.

199: If he has destroyed the eye of a seignior's slave or broken the bone of a seignior's slave, he shall pay one-half his value.

200: If a seignior has knocked out a tooth of a seignior of his own rank, they shall knock out his tooth.

201: If he has knocked out a commoner's tooth, he shall pay one-third mina of silver.

202: If a seignior has struck the cheek of a seignior who is superior to him, he shall be beaten sixty (times) with an oxtail whip in the assembly.

203: If a member of the aristocracy has struck the cheek of a(nother) member of the aristocracy who is of the same rank as himself, he shall pay one mina of silver.

204: If a commoner has struck the cheek of a(nother) commoner, he shall pay ten shekels of silver.

205: If a seignior's slave has struck the cheek of a member of the aristocracy, they shall cut off his ear.

206: If a seignior has struck a(nother) seignior in a brawl and has inflicted an injury on him, that seignior shall swear, "I did not strike him deliberately"; and he shall also pay for the physician.

207: If he has died because of his blow, he shall swear (as before), and if it was a member of the aristocracy, he shall pay one-half mina of silver. . . .

7. The Creation, from
Genesis 2:1–24

Thus the heavens and the earth were finished, and all their multitude. And on the seventh day God finished the work that he had done, and he rested on the seventh day from all the work that he had done. So God blessed the seventh day and hallowed it, because on it God rested from all the work that he had done in creation.

These are the generations of the heavens and the earth when they were created.

In the day that the Lord God made the earth and the heavens, when no plant of the field was yet in the earth and no herb of the field had yet sprung up—for the Lord God had not caused it to rain upon the earth, and there was no one to till the ground; but a stream would rise from the earth, and water the whole face of the ground—then the Lord God formed man from the dust of the ground, and breathed into his nostrils the breath of life; and the man became a living being. And the Lord God planted a garden in Eden, in the east; and there he put the man whom he had formed. Out of the ground the Lord God made to grow every tree that is pleasant to the sight and good for food, the tree of life also in the midst of the garden, and the tree of the knowledge of good and evil.

A river flows out of Eden to water the garden, and from there it divides and becomes four branches. The name of the first is Pishon;[21] it is the one that flows around the whole land of Havilah,[22] where there is gold; and the gold of that land is good; bdellium[23] and onyx stone are there. The name of the second river is Gihon;[24] it is the one that flows around the whole land of Cush.[25] The name of the third river is Tigris, which flows east of Assyria. And the fourth river is the Euphrates.

The Lord God took the man and put him in the garden of Eden to till it and keep it. And the Lord God commanded the man, "You may freely eat of every tree of the garden; but of the tree of the knowledge of good and evil you shall not eat, for in the day that you eat of it you shall die."

---

21. **Pishon:** biblical scholars have been unable to locate this river.
22. **Havilah:** a region of northern Arabia.
23. **bdellium:** an aromatic gum from trees of the incense tree family found in northeastern Africa. It was used for perfumes and medicines.
24. **Gihon:** a stream that flows from a spring on Mount Zion in Jerusalem.
25. **Cush:** a name that appears in ancient sources to identify two different states, one in eastern Mesopotamia, the other in northeast Africa in the region of the modern nation of Sudan.

[43]

Chapter 2

Polytheism and

Monotheism in

the Fertile

Crescent, ca

3000–500 B.C.

Then the Lord God said, "It is not good that the man should be alone; I will make him a helper as his partner." So out of the ground the Lord God formed every animal of the field and every bird of the air, and brought them to the man to see what he would call them; and whatever the man called every living creature, that was its name. The man gave names to all cattle, and to the birds of the air, and to every animal of the field; but for the man there was not found a helper as his partner. So the Lord God caused a deep sleep to fall upon the man, and he slept; then he took one of his ribs and closed up its place with flesh. And the rib that the Lord God had taken from the man he made into a woman and brought her to the man. Then the man said,

"This at last is bone of my bones and flesh of my flesh; this one shall be called Woman, for out of Man this one was taken."

Therefore a man leaves his father and his mother and clings to his wife, and they become one flesh.

8. The Ten Commandments

A. Exodus 20:1–17

Then God spoke all these words: I am the Lord your God, who brought you out of the land of Egypt, out of the house of slavery; you shall have no other gods before me.

You shall not make for yourself an idol, whether in the form of anything that is in heaven above, or that is on the earth beneath, or that is in the water under the earth. You shall not bow down to them or worship them; for I the Lord your God am a jealous God, punishing children for the iniquity of parents, to the third and the fourth generation of those who reject me, but showing steadfast love to the thousandth generation of those who love me and keep my commandments.

You shall not make wrongful use of the name of the Lord your God, for the Lord will not acquit anyone who misuses his name.

Remember the sabbath day, and keep it holy. Six days you shall labor and do all your work. But the seventh day is a sabbath to the Lord your God; you shall not do any work—you, your son or your daughter, your male or female slave, your livestock, or the alien resident in your towns. For in six days the Lord made heaven and earth, the sea, and all that is in them, but rested the seventh day; therefore the Lord blessed the sabbath day and consecrated it.

Honor your father and your mother, so that your days may be long in the land that the Lord your God is giving you.

You shall not murder.

You shall not commit adultery.

You shall not steal.

You shall not bear false witness against your neighbor.

You shall not covet your neighbor's house; you shall not covet your neighbor's wife, or male or female slave, or ox, or donkey, or anything that belongs to your neighbor.

B. Exodus 24:3

Moses came and told the people all the words of the Lord and all the ordinances; and all the people answered with one voice, and said, "All the words that the Lord has spoken we will do."

9. Selections from the Torah

A. Exodus 21:12–18, 26–34

Whoever strikes a person mortally shall be put to death. If it was not premeditated, but came about by an act of God, then I will appoint for you a place to which the killer may flee. But if someone willfully attacks and kills another by treachery, you shall take the killer from my altar for execution.

Whoever strikes father or mother shall be put to death.

Whoever kidnaps a person, whether that person has been sold or is still held in possession, shall be put to death.

Whoever curses father or mother shall be put to death.

When individuals quarrel and one strikes the other with a stone or fist so that the injured party, though not dead, is confined to bed, but recovers and walks around outside with the help of a staff, then the assailant shall be free of liability, except to pay for the loss of time, and to arrange for full recovery. . . .

When a slaveowner strikes the eye of a male or female slave, destroying it, the owner shall let the slave go, a free person, to compensate for the eye. If the owner knocks out a tooth of a male or female slave, the slave shall be let go, a free person, to compensate for the tooth.

When an ox gores a man or a woman to death, the ox shall be stoned, and its flesh shall not be eaten; but the owner of the ox shall not be liable. If the ox has been accustomed to gore in the past, and its owner has been warned but has not restrained it, and it kills a man or a woman, the ox shall be stoned, and its owner also shall be put to death. If a ransom is imposed on the owner, then the owner shall pay whatever is imposed for the redemption of the victim's life. If it gores a boy or a girl, the owner shall be dealt with according to this same rule. If the ox gores a male or female slave, the owner shall pay to the slaveowner thirty shekels of silver, and the ox shall be stoned.

If someone leaves a pit open, or digs a pit and does not cover it, and an ox or a donkey falls into it, the owner of the pit shall make restitution, giving money to its owner, but keeping the dead animal.

[45]

Chapter 2

Polytheism and

Monotheism in

the Fertile

Crescent, ca

3000–500 B.C.

B. Exodus 22:1–7, 21–25

When someone steals an ox or a sheep, and slaughters it or sells it, the thief shall pay five oxen for an ox, and four sheep for a sheep. The thief shall make restitution, but if unable to do so, shall be sold for the theft. When the animal, whether ox or donkey or sheep, is found alive in the thief's possession, the thief shall pay double.

If a thief is found breaking in, and is beaten to death, no bloodguilt is incurred; but if it happens after sunrise, bloodguilt is incurred.

When someone causes a field or vineyard to be grazed over, or lets livestock loose to graze in someone else's field, restitution shall be made from the best in the owner's field or vineyard.

When fire breaks out and catches in thorns so that the stacked grain or the standing grain or the field is consumed, the one who started the fire shall make full restitution.

When someone delivers to a neighbor money or goods for safekeeping, and they are stolen from the neighbor's house, then the thief, if caught, shall pay double. If the thief is not caught, the owner of the house shall be brought before God, to determine whether or not the owner had laid hands on the neighbor's goods. . . .

You shall not wrong or oppress a resident alien, for you were aliens in the land of Egypt. You shall not abuse any widow or orphan. If you do abuse them, when they cry out to me, I will surely heed their cry; my wrath will burn, and I will kill you with the sword, and your wives shall become widows and your children orphans.

If you lend money to my people, to the poor among you, you shall not deal with them as a creditor; you shall not exact interest from them.

C. Leviticus 19:9–17

When you reap the harvest of your land, you shall not reap to the very edges of your field, or gather the gleanings of your harvest. You shall not strip your vineyard bare, or gather the fallen grapes of your vineyard; you shall leave them for the poor and the alien: I am the Lord your God.

You shall not steal; you shall not deal falsely; and you shall not lie to one another. And you shall not swear falsely by my name, profaning the name of your God: I am the Lord.

You shall not defraud your neighbor; you shall not steal; and you shall not keep for yourself the wages of a laborer until morning. You shall not revile the deaf or put a stumbling block before the blind; you shall fear your God: I am the Lord.

You shall not render an unjust judgment; you shall not be partial to the poor or defer to the great: with justice you shall judge your neighbor. You shall not go around as a slanderer among your people, and you shall not profit by the blood of your neighbor: I am the Lord.

You shall not hate in your heart anyone of your kin; you shall reprove your neighbor, or you will incur guilt yourself. . . .

10. Selections from the Prophets

A. Isaiah 66:1–2

Thus says the Lord: Heaven is my throne and the earth is my footstool; what is the house that you would build for me, and what is my resting place?

All these things my hand has made, and so all these things are mine, says the Lord. But this is the one to whom I will look, to the humble and contrite in spirit, who trembles at my word.

B. Hosea 11:1–4, 8–9; 14:4

When Israel was a child, I loved him, and out of Egypt I called my son. The more I called them, the more they went from me; they kept sacrificing to the Baals[26] and offering incense to idols.

Yet it was I who taught Ephraim[27] to walk, I took them up in my arms; but they did not know that I healed them.

I led them with cords of human kindness, with bands of love. I was to them like those who lift infants to their cheeks. I bent down to them and fed them. . . .

How can I give you up, Ephraim? How can I hand you over, O Israel? How can I make you like Admah? How can I treat you like Zeboiim?[28] My heart recoils within me; my compassion grows warm and tender.

I will not execute my fierce anger; I will not again destroy Ephraim; for I am God and no mortal, the Holy One in your midst, and I will not come in wrath. . . .

I will heal their disloyalty; I will love them freely, for my anger has turned from them.

11. The Book of Job

Job 1–3:3

There was once a man in the land of Uz[29] whose name was Job. That man was blameless and upright, one who feared God and turned away from evil. There

26. **Baals:** the chief deity in the Canaanite pantheon was called Baal.
27. **Ephraim:** one of the twelve tribes of the Hebrews.
28. **Admah, Zeboiim:** cities destroyed by Yahweh because of their wickedness along with Sodom and Gomorrah.
29. **Uz:** a region that modern scholars believe to have been in northern Arabia.

Chapter 2

Polytheism and

Monotheism in

the Fertile

Crescent, ca

3000–500 B.C.

were born to him seven sons and three daughters. He had seven thousand sheep, three thousand camels, five hundred yoke of oxen, five hundred donkeys, and very many servants; so that this man was the greatest of all the people of the east. His sons used to go and hold feasts in one another's houses in turn; and they would send and invite their three sisters to eat and drink with them. And when the feast days had run their course, Job would send and sanctify them, and he would rise early in the morning and offer burnt offerings according to the number of them all; for Job said, "It may be that my children have sinned, and cursed God in their hearts." This is what Job always did.

One day the heavenly beings came to present themselves before the Lord, and Satan[30] also came among them. The Lord said to Satan, "Where have you come from?" Satan answered the Lord, "From going to and fro on the earth, and, from walking up and down on it." The Lord said to Satan, "Have you considered my servant Job? There is no one like him on the earth, a blameless and upright man who fears God and turns away from evil." Then Satan answered the Lord, "Does Job fear God for nothing? Have you not put a fence around him and his house and all that he has, on every side? You have blessed the work of his hands, and his possessions have increased in the land. But stretch out your hand now, and touch all that he has, and he will curse you to your face." The Lord said to Satan, "Very well, all that he has is in your power; only do not stretch out your hand against him!" So Satan went out from the presence of the Lord.

One day when his sons and daughters were eating and drinking wine in the eldest brother's house, a messenger came to Job and said, "The oxen were plowing and the donkeys were feeding beside them, and the Sabeans[31] fell on them and carried them off, and killed the servants with the edge of the sword; I alone have escaped to tell you." While he was still speaking, another came and said, "The fire of God fell from heaven and burned up the sheep and the servants, and consumed them; I alone have escaped to tell you." While he was still speaking, another came and said, "The Chaldeans[32] formed three columns, made a raid on the camels and carried them off, and killed the servants with the edge of the sword; I alone have escaped to tell you."

While he was still speaking, another came and said, "Your sons and daughters were eating and drinking wine in their eldest brother's house, and suddenly a great wind came across the desert, struck the four corners of the house, and it fell on the young people, and they are dead; I alone have escaped to tell you."

---

30. **Satan:** the name used in the original Hebrew text for this figure means "accuser." It does not refer to the devil figure that appeared later in both Jewish and Christian thought. Rather, the figure called "Satan" apparently was an angel charged with investigating conditions on earth.

31. **Sabeans:** a nomadic people of Arabia.

32. **Chaldeans:** a people of southern Mesopotamia in the region of Babylon.

Then Job arose, tore his robe, shaved his head, and fell on the ground and worshiped. He said, "Naked I came from my mother's womb, and naked shall I return there; the Lord gave, and the Lord has taken away; blessed be the name of the Lord."

In all this Job did not sin or charge God with wrongdoing.

One day the heavenly beings came to present themselves before the Lord, and Satan also came among them to present himself before the Lord. The Lord said to Satan, "Where have you come from?" Satan answered the Lord, "From going to and fro on the earth, and from walking up and down on it." The Lord said to Satan, "Have you considered my servant Job? There is no one like him on the earth, a blameless and upright man who fears God and turns away from evil. He still persists in his integrity, although you incited me against him, to destroy him for no reason." Then Satan answered the Lord, "Skin for skin! All that people have they will give to save their lives. But stretch out your hand now and touch his bone and his flesh, and he will curse you to your face." The Lord said to Satan, "Very well, he is in your power; only spare his life."

So Satan went out from the presence of the Lord, and inflicted loathsome sores on Job from the sole of his foot to the crown of his head. Job took a potsherd with which to scrape himself, and sat among the ashes.

Then his wife said to him, "Do you still persist in your integrity? Curse God, and die." But he said to her, "You speak as any foolish woman would speak. Shall we receive the good at the hand of God, and not receive the bad?" In all this Job did not sin with his lips.

Now when Job's three friends heard of all these troubles that had come upon him, each of them set out from his home—Eliphaz the Temanite, Bildad the Shuhite, and Zophar the Naamathite.[33] They met together to go and console and comfort him. When they saw him from a distance, they did not recognize him, and they raised their voices and wept aloud; they tore their robes and threw dust in the air upon their heads. They sat with him on the ground seven days and seven nights, and no one spoke a word to him, for they saw that his suffering was very great.

After this Job opened his mouth and cursed the day of his birth. Job said: 'Let the day perish in which I was born, and the night that said, 'A man-child is conceived.'. . .

Job 9:1–4, 14–18, 22–24

Then Job answered: "Indeed I know that this is so; but how can a mortal be just before God?

---

33. **Temanite, Shuhite, Naamathite:** ethnic labels that identify Job's friends as residents of Arabia.

Chapter 2

Polytheism and

Monotheism in

the Fertile

Crescent, ca

3000–500 B.C.

If one wished to contend with him, one could not answer him once in a thousand.

He is wise in heart, and mighty in strength—who has resisted him, and succeeded?. . .

How then can I answer him, choosing my words with him?

Though I am innocent, I cannot answer him; I must appeal for mercy to my accuser.

If I summoned him and he answered me, I do not believe that he would listen to my voice.

For he crushes me with a tempest, and multiplies my wounds without cause;

he will not let me get my breath, but fills me with bitterness. . . .

It is all one; therefore I say, he destroys both the blameless and the wicked.

When disaster brings sudden death, he mocks at the calamity of the innocent.

The earth is given into the hand of the wicked; he covers the eyes of its judges—if it is not he, who then is it?"

Job 38:1–7

Then the Lord answered Job out of the whirlwind: "Who is this that darkens counsel by words without knowledge?

Gird up your loins like a man, I will question you, and you shall declare to me.

Where were you when I laid the foundation of the earth? Tell me, if you have understanding.

Who determined its measurements—surely you know! Or who stretched the line upon it?

On what were its bases sunk, or who laid its cornerstone

when the morning stars sang together and all the heavenly beings shouted for joy?"

Job 42:1–2,10–17

Then Job answered the Lord: "I know that you can do all things, and that no purpose of yours can be thwarted.". . .

And the Lord restored the fortunes of Job . . . and the Lord gave Job twice as much as he had before. Then there came to him all his brothers and sisters and all who had known him before, and they ate bread with him in his house; they showed him sympathy and comforted him for all the evil that the Lord had brought upon him; and each of them gave him a piece of money and a gold ring. The Lord blessed the latter days of Job more than his beginning; and he had fourteen thousand sheep, six thousand camels, a thousand yoke of oxen, and a thousand donkeys. He also had seven sons and three daughters.

He named the first Jemimah, the second Keziah, and the third Keren-happuch. In all the land there were no women so beautiful as Job's daughters; and their father gave them an inheritance along with their brothers. After this Job lived one hundred and forty years, and saw his children, and his children's children, four generations. And Job died, old and full of days.

QUESTIONS TO CONSIDER

One of the most important skills of the historian is the ability to think comparatively. Only by constantly comparing his or her data with those amassed by other students of historic societies can the historian fully understand the significance of his or her findings. Our sources on the religious history of the ancient Fertile Crescent offer us an opportunity for such comparative thought because, as we suggested at the outset of this chapter, both Mesopotamian polytheism and Hebrew monotheism were concerned with answering the same questions.

The first of those questions involved human origins. Consider again the Creation accounts that you have read in both Mesopotamian and Hebrew texts. In what ways are the accounts similar? Why do you suspect that the accounts shared similar roots? How do they differ as to the purpose of human existence? How would you explain that difference in terms of the religious vision of the ancient Hebrews?

Both ancient peoples believed that divine action shaped their lives. Did the Mesopotamians and the Hebrews believe that they could understand fully why their respective deities behaved the way they did in shaping the lives of mortals? Why do the Mesopotamian gods and goddesses emerge from our sources as capricious and rather uncaring entities? How did the Hebrews envision Yahweh? If not always predictable, why did they find him just and merciful?

Religious thought played a key role, both in Mesopotamia and among the Hebrews, in ancients' efforts to give order to their societies by controlling human behavior. Did ancient Mesopotamian polytheism include anything resembling a code of personal behavior in its religious practices and teachings? Why, then, was the gods' delegation of the "Enlil functions" to kings so important in giving order to their society? How was the religious thought of the Hebrews grounded in a code of behavior right from the first? How did this allow them to order their society? Most scholars of world religions identify Hebrew monotheism as the first personal religion. Why do you find that the Hebrews' covenant with Yahweh had profound implications for the individual believer?

Finally, if we consider Mesopotamian polytheism as generally characteristic of the ancient religions of the West, what strikes you as unique about the religious life of the ancient Hebrews? Why might you think that the essential aspects of their belief system might attract others?

Chapter 2

Polytheism and

Monotheism in

the Fertile

Crescent, ca

3000–500 B.C.

EPILOGUE

The relevance of the religious practices that we have examined in this chapter is not confined solely to the study of the ancient world. The religious ideas and rites that we have examined also have considerable relevance to the modern world in which we live.

The ancient polytheism, of the Mesopotamians may not survive in the form it assumed for over two millennia in the eastern Fertile Crescent, but its salient features persist in parts of the globe today. Primitive peoples still conceive of their deities as the embodiment of great natural forces, envision them in anthropomorphic forms, and attempt to appease their capriciousness through elaborate rites.

The monotheism of the ancient Hebrews has had great long-term global influence. Indeed, the ethical monotheism that was at its core constitutes the foundation of the three great Western religions, Judaism, Christianity, and Islam, faiths that claim the spiritual allegiance of approximately 4 billion people worldwide, representing the majority of the human race. As their foundation, all three Western religions emphasize adherence to broad ethical principles enunciated first by the ancient Hebrews. The ancient Hebrew texts that we have examined form not only the Hebrew Bible, but also the Old Testament of the Christian Bible, and early Christian leaders from the first recognized their spiritual debt to the ancient Hebrews, even as they sought to distinguish early Christianity from Judaism. Thus, Saint Paul, the apostle to the Gentiles, lauded "the faith of our ancestor Abraham" in his first-century A.D. letter to the Romans (Romans 4:12).

In Islam, the words of the Prophet Muhammad also acknowledge a spiritual inheritance from the ancient Hebrews. Ethical monotheism is the fundamental core of Islam, too, and we find the following words in the Qur'an, the sacred book of Islam:

> Who will turn away from the creed of Abraham but one dull of soul? . . . We believe in God and what has been sent down to us, and what has been revealed to Abraham and Ishmael and Isaac and Jacob and their progeny, and that which was given to Moses and Jesus and all other prophets by the Lord. We make no distinction among them, and we submit to Him. (Qur'an, 2:130, 136)

In short, the religious ideas of the ancient world still play a great role in our modern world.

CHAPTER THREE

THE IDEAL AND THE REALITY

OF CLASSICAL ATHENS

Athens during the fifth century B.C. is often identified as one of the main sources of Western values and standards. Later Europeans and Americans regarded the Athenians as the originators of democracy, drama, representational or realistic art, history, philosophy, and science. At different times over the past 2,500 years they have attempted to imitate this "Golden Age" of classical Athens in everything from buildings to literature. Many U.S. state capitols and government buildings are modeled on the Parthenon or other temples, complete with statuary of former governers in the manner of Greek gods. We still divide drama into tragedies and comedies in the same way the Athenians did, though now we sometimes use a prerecorded laugh track instead of grinning masks to indicate that a given work is a comedy. During some historical periods, such as the Renaissance, thinkers and writers made conscious attempts to return to classical ideals in all areas of life, combing the works of Athenian authors for previously overlooked material in their quest to draw guidance and learn everything possible from this unique flowering of culture.

Even more than as a model for literature and art, classical Athens has continued to serve as a relevant source for answers to basic questions about human existence. Though all cultures have sought to identify the ultimate aim and meaning of human life, the ancient Greeks, especially the Athenians, were the first in the West to provide answers that were not expressed in religious or mythological terms. Their thoughts on these matters grew out of speculations on the nature of the universe made by earlier Greeks, particularly Thales and his followers Anaximander and Heraclitus. These thinkers, living in the seventh and sixth centuries B.C., theorized about how the universe had been formed and what it was made of by means of rational explanations drawn from observation rather than from myth or religious tradition. Because they believed the natural universe could be explained in other than supernatural terms, they are often termed the first true scientists or first philosophers.

During the fifth century B.C., several Athenian thinkers turned their attention from the world around them to the human beings living in that world. They used this new method of philosophical inquiry to question the workings of the human mind and the societies humans create. They asked such questions as, How do we learn things? What should we try to learn? How do we know what is right or wrong, good or bad? If we can know what is good, how can we create things that are good? What kind of government is best? This type of questioning is perhaps most often associated with Socrates (469–399 B.C.) and his pupil Plato (427?–347 B.C.), who are generally called the founders of Western philosophy. Thales and his followers are thus known as the pre-Socratics; and a twentieth-century philosopher, Alfred North Whitehead, noted—only half jokingly—that "the European philosophical tradition . . . consists of a series of footnotes to Plato."

Both Socrates and Plato believed that goodness is related to knowledge and that excellence could be learned. For Plato especially, true knowledge was gained not by observation of the world but by contemplation of what an ideal world would be like. In their view, to understand goodness, justice, or beauty, it is necessary to think about what pure and ultimate goodness, justice, or beauty means. Plato thus introduced into Western thought a strong strain of idealism and was the first to write works on what an ideal society or set of laws would look like. He also described the education required to train citizens for governing this ideal state and the social and economic structure necessary to keep them at their posts. Though he probably recognized that these standards could never be achieved, he believed that the creation of ideals was an important component of the discipline of philosophy, a sentiment shared by many Western thinkers after him.

Plato's most brilliant pupil, Aristotle (384–322 B.C.), originally agreed with his teacher but then began to depart somewhat from idealism. Like the pre-Socratics, Aristotle was fascinated by the world around him, and many of his writings on scientific subjects reveal keen powers of observation. Even his treatises on standards of human behavior, such as those concerning ethics and politics, are based on close observation of Athenian society and not simply on speculation. Aristotle further intended that these works should not only describe ideal human behavior or political systems, but also provide suggestions about how to alter current practice to conform more closely to the ideal. Thus, although Aristotle was still to some degree an idealist, both the source and the recipient of his ideals was the real world.

In classical Athens, human nature was a subject contemplated not only by scientists and philosophers, but also by historians, such as Herodotus and Thucydides. They, too, searched for explanations about the natural order that did not involve the gods. For Herodotus and Thucydides, the Persian and Peloponnesian wars were caused by human failings, not by actions of vengeful gods such as those that Homer, following tradition, depicted in the *Iliad* as causing the Trojan War. Like Aristotle, they were interested in describing real events and finding explanations for them; like Plato, they were also interested in the possible as well as the actual. History, in their opinion, was the best arena for observing the true worth of various ideals to human society.

To the Athenians, war was the ultimate test of human ideals, morals, and values, but these could also be tested and observed on a much smaller scale in the way people conducted their everyday lives. Although for Plato the basis of an ideal government was the perfectly trained ruler or group of rulers, for Aristotle and other writers it was the perfectly managed household, which they regarded as a microcosm of society. Observing that the household was the smallest economic and political unit in Athenian society, Aristotle

began his consideration of the ideal governmental system with thoughts on how households should be run. Other writers on politics and economics followed suit, giving advice after observing households they regarded as particularly well managed.

Whereas Plato clearly indicated that he was describing an ideal, in the case of Aristotle and other Athenians, it is sometimes difficult to determine whether they were attempting to describe reality, what they wished reality was, or a pure ideal. Your task in this chapter will be to examine the relationship between idealism and reality in the writings of several Athenian philosophers, historians, and commentators and in an architectural diagram of an Athenian house. What ideals do the writers set forth for the individual, the household, and the government? How are these ideals reflected in more realistic descriptions of life in Athens and in the way Athenians built their houses?

SOURCES AND METHOD

All the written sources we will use come from Athenians who lived during the classical period and are thus what we term original or primary sources. They differ greatly from modern primary sources, however, in that their textual accuracy cannot be checked. Before the development of the printing press, the only way to obtain a copy of a work was to write it out by hand yourself or hire someone to do so. Therefore, each manuscript copy might be slightly different. Because the

originals of the works of Aristotle or Thucydides have long since disappeared, what we have to work with are translations of composites based on as many of the oldest copies still in existence after 2,500 years that the translators could find.

The problem of accuracy is further complicated with some of the authors we will read because they did not actually write the works attributed to them. Many of Aristotle's works, for instance, are probably copies of his students' notes combined with (perhaps) some of his own. If you think of the way in which you record your own instructors' remarks, you can see why we must be cautious about assuming that these secondhand works contain everything Aristotle taught exactly as he intended it. Socrates, in fact, wrote nothing at all; all his ideas and words come to us through his pupil Plato. Scholars have long debated how much of the written record represents Socrates and how much represents Plato, especially when we consider that Socrates generally spoke at social gatherings or informally while walking around Athens, when Plato was not taking notes. These problems do not mean that we should discount these sources; they simply mean that these sources differ from the printed documents and tape-recorded speeches of later eras.

We will begin our investigation with what is probably the most famous description of classical Athens: a funeral speech delivered by Pericles. Pericles, one of the leaders of Athens when the Peloponnesian War opened, gave this speech in 430 B.C. in honor of those who had died during the first year of the war. It was recorded by Thucydides and, though there is some disagreement over who actually wrote it, reflects Pericles' opinions. Read the speech carefully. Is Pericles describing an ideal he hopes Athens will achieve or reality as he sees it? How does he depict Athenian democracy and the Athenian attitude toward wealth? How does he compare Athens with Sparta? How does Athens treat its neighbors? What role does Pericles see for Athenian women? Before going on to the next readings, jot down some words that you feel best describe Athens and the Athenians.

Would you want to live in the Athens Pericles describes?

Source 2 comes from a later section of Thucydides' *Peloponnesian War,* and it describes Athenian actions in the sixteenth year of the war. As you read it, think about the virtues that Pericles ascribed to the Athenians. Are these virtues reflected in the debate with the Melians or in the actions against them? How do the Athenians justify their actions? After reading this selection, jot down a few more words that you think describe the Athenians. Would you now erase some entries from your first list?

Source 3 is taken from the first book of Aristotle's *The Politics.* In this selection, he describes the proper functioning of a household and the role of each person in it. As you read it, you will notice that Aristotle is concerned equally with the economic role of household members and their moral status. What qualities does he see as important in the ideal head of household? The ideal wife or child? The ideal slave? How does he justify the differences between household members? How do these qualities compare with those described by Pericles or exhibited by the Athenians in their contact with the Melians? Add a few more words to your list describing the Athenians.

The fourth selection, by an unknown author, presents another view of Athenian democracy and the Athenian empire. This passage was written about five years after the speech made by Pericles and about ten years before the Melian debate. How does this author view democracy and Athens's relations with its neighbors?

What words might he add to your list to describe his fellow Athenians? How do you think he would have responded had he been in the audience listening to Pericles' funeral speech?

The fifth selection is a discussion of household management cast in the form of a dialogue, from a treatise by Xenophon called *The Economist*. What does the main speaker, whose name is Ischomachus, see as the main roles of husband and wife? Would he have agreed with Aristotle's conclusions about the qualities necessary in an ideal husband and wife? What suggestions does he make for encouraging ideal behavior in wives and slaves? Does he appear to be describing an actual or an ideal marital relationship? What words would you now add to or subtract from your list?

The sixth selection is a very small part of *The Republic,* in which Plato sets out his views on the ideal government. Plato did not favor democracy; he advocated training a group of leaders, whom he called *guardians,* to work for the best interests of all. What qualities does Plato feel are most important in the guardians?

What economic and family structures does he feel will help them maintain these qualities? How does his description of the ideal female guardian compare with Pericles' and Xenophon's descriptions of the ideal Athenian wife? Do the qualities he finds important in guardians match up with any of those on your list?

Once you have read all the selections carefully, go back to Pericles' speech and read it again. Do you still have the same opinion about whether he is describing the ideal or reality? Which of the words describing Athens that were on your original list are left?

Now look at Source 7, the floor plan of a house from fifth-century B.C. Olynthus. Since it is based on archaeological discoveries, it is a clear representation of physical reality in classical Greece, but it tells us something about ideals as well, for people construct the space they live in according to their ideas about how society should operate. Does the actual house correspond to the one described by Xenophon? How does the layout of the house reinforce the roles prescribed for the ideal husband and wife?

THE EVIDENCE

Sources 1 and 2 from Thucydides, History of the Peloponnesian War, *translated by Richard Crawley (New York: Modern Library, 1951), pp. 103–106; p. 109.*

1. Pericles' Funeral Speech,
430 B.C.

That part of our history which tells of the military achievements which gave us our several possessions, or of the ready valour with which either we or our fathers stemmed the tide of Hellenic or foreign aggression, is a theme too familiar to my hearers for me to dilate on, and I shall therefore pass it by. But what was the road by which we reached our position, what the form of government under which our greatness grew, what the national habits out of which it sprang; these are questions which I may try to solve before I proceed to my panegyric upon these men: since I think this to be a subject upon which on the present occasion a speaker may properly dwell, and to which the whole assemblage, whether citizens or foreigners, may listen with advantage.

Our constitution does not copy the laws of neighbouring states; we are rather a pattern to others than imitators ourselves. Its administration favours the many instead of the few; this is why it is called a democracy. If we look to the laws, they afford equal justice to all in their private differences; if to social standing, advancement in public life falls to reputation for capacity, class considerations not being allowed to interfere with merit; nor again does poverty bar the way, if a man is able to serve the state, he is not hindered by the obscurity of his condition. The freedom which we enjoy in our government extends also to our ordinary life. There, far from exercising a jealous surveillance over each other, we do not feel called upon to be angry with our neighbour for doing what he likes, or even to indulge in those injurious looks which cannot fail to be offensive, although they inflict no positive penalty. But all this ease in our private relations does not make us lawless as citizens. Against this fear is our chief safeguard, teaching us to obey the magistrates and the laws, particularly such as regard the protection of the injured, whether they are actually on the statute book, or belong to that code which, although unwritten, yet cannot be broken without acknowledged disgrace.

Further, we provide plenty of means for the mind to refresh itself from business. We celebrate games and sacrifices all the year round, and the elegance of our private establishments forms a daily source of pleasure and helps to banish the spleen; while the magnitude of our city draws the produce of the world into our harbour, so that to the Athenian the fruits of other countries are as familiar a luxury as those of his own.

If we turn to our military policy, there also we differ from our antagonists. We throw open our city to the world, and never by alien acts exclude foreigners from any opportunity of learning or observing, although the eyes of an enemy may occasionally profit by our liberality; trusting less in system and policy than to the native spirit of our citizens; while in education, where our rivals from their very cradles by a painful discipline seek after manliness, at Athens we live exactly as we please, and yet are just as ready to encounter every legitimate danger. In proof of this it may be noticed that the Lacedæmonians[1] do not invade our country alone, but bring with them all their confederates; while we Athenians advance unsupported into the territory of a neighbour, and fighting upon a foreign soil usually vanquish with ease men

---

1. **Lacedæmonians:** Spartans.

who are defending their homes. Our united force was never yet encountered by any enemy, because we have at once to attend to our marine and to despatch our citizens by land upon a hundred different services; so that, wherever they engage with some such fraction of our strength, a success against a detachment is magnified into a victory over the nation, and a defeat into a reverse suffered at the hands of our entire people. And yet if with habits not of labour but of ease, and courage not of art but of nature, we are still willing to encounter danger, we have the double advantage of escaping the experience of hardships in anticipation and of facing them in the hour of need as fearlessly as those who are never free from them.

Nor are these the only points in which our city is worthy of admiration. We cultivate refinement without extravagance and knowledge without effeminacy; wealth we employ more for use than for show, and place the real disgrace of poverty not in owning to the fact but in declining the struggle against it. Our public men have, besides politics, their private affairs to attend to, and our ordinary citizens, though occupied with the pursuits of industry, are still fair judges of public matters; for, unlike any other nation, regarding him who takes no part in these duties not as unambitious but as useless, we Athenians are able to judge at all events if we cannot originate, and instead of looking on discussion as a stumbling-block in the way of action, we think it an indispensable preliminary to any wise action at all. Again, in our enterprises we present the singular spectacle of daring and deliberation, each carried to its highest point, and both united in the same persons; although usually decision is the fruit of ignorance, hesitation of reflexion. But the palm of courage will surely be adjudged most justly to those, who best know the difference between hardship and pleasure and yet are never tempted to shrink from danger. In generosity we are equally singular, acquiring our friends by conferring not by receiving favours. Yet, of course, the doer of the favour is the firmer friend of the two, in order by continued kindness to keep the recipient in his debt; while the debtor feels less keenly from the very consciousness that the return he makes will be a payment, not a free gift. And it is only the Athenians who, fearless of consequences, confer their benefits not from calculations of expediency, but in the confidence of liberality.

In short, I say that as a city we are the school of Hellas; while I doubt if the world can produce a man, who where he has only himself to depend upon, is equal to so many emergencies, and graced by so happy a versatility as the Athenian. And that this is no mere boast thrown out for the occasion, but plain matter of fact, the power of the state acquired by these habits proves. For Athens alone of her contemporaries is found when tested to be greater than her reputation, and alone gives no occasion to her assailants to blush at the antagonist by whom they have been worsted, or to her subjects to question her title by merit to rule. Rather, the admiration of the present and succeeding ages will be ours, since we have not left our power without witness, but have shown it by mighty proofs; and far from needing a Homer for our panegyrist, or other of his craft whose verses might charm for the moment only for the impression which they gave to melt at the touch of fact, we have forced every sea and land to be the highway of our daring, and everywhere, whether for evil or for good, have left imperishable monuments behind us. Such is the Athens for which these men, in the assertion of their resolve not to lose her, nobly fought and died; and well may every one of their survivors be ready to suffer in her cause. . . .

[I]f I must say anything on the subject of female excellence to those of you who will now be in widowhood, it will be all comprised in this brief exhortation. Great will be your glory in not falling short of your natural character; and greatest will be hers who is least talked of among the men whether for good or for bad.

My task is now finished. I have performed it to the best of my ability, and in words, at least, the requirements of the law are now satisfied. If deeds be in question, those who are here interred have received part of their honours already, and for the rest, their children will be brought up till manhood at the public expense: the state thus offers a valuable prize, as the garland of victory in this race of valour, for the reward both of those who have fallen and their survivors. And where the rewards for merit are greatest, there are found the best citizens.

And now that you have brought to a close your lamentations for your relatives, you may depart.

2. The Melian Debate, 415 B.C.

The Athenians also made an expedition against the isle of Melos with thirty ships of their own, six Chian, and two Lesbian vessels, sixteen hundred heavy infantry, three hundred archers, and twenty mounted archers from Athens, and about fifteen hundred heavy infantry from the allies and the islanders. The Melians are a colony of Lacedæmon[2] that would not submit to the Athenians like the other islanders, and at first remained neutral and took no part in the struggle, but afterwards upon the Athenians using violence and plundering their territory, assumed an attitude of open hostility. Cleomedes, son of Lycomedes, and Tisias, son of Tisimachus, the generals, encamping in their territory with the above armament, before doing any harm to their land, sent envoys to negotiate. These the Melians did not bring before the people, but bade them state the object of their mission to the magistrates and the few; upon which the Athenian envoys spoke as follows: . . .

ATHENIANS: We will now proceed to show you that we are come here in the interest of our empire, and that we shall say what we are now going to say, for

---

2. **Lacedæmon:** Sparta.

the preservation of your country; as we would fain exercise that empire over you without trouble, and see you preserved for the good of us both.

MELIANS: And how, pray, could it turn out as good for us to serve as for you to rule?

ATHENIANS: Because you would have the advantage of submitting before suffering the worst, and we should gain by not destroying you.

MELIANS: So that you would not consent to our being neutral, friends instead of enemies, but allies of neither side.

ATHENIANS: No; for your hostility cannot so much hurt us as your friendship will be an argument to our subjects of our weakness, and your enmity of our power.

MELIANS: Is that your subjects' idea of equity, to put those who have nothing to do with you in the same category with peoples that are most of them your own colonists, and some conquered rebels?

ATHENIANS: As far as right goes they think one has as much of it as the other, and if any maintain their independence it is because they are strong, and that if we do not molest them it is because we are afraid; so that besides extending our empire we should gain in security by your subjection; the fact that you are islanders and weaker than others rendering it all the more important that you should not succeed in baffling the masters of the sea.

MELIANS: But do you consider that there is no security in the policy which we indicate? For here again if you debar us from talking about justice and invite us to obey your interest, we also must explain ours, and try to persuade you, if the two happen to coincide. How can you avoid making enemies of all existing neutrals who shall look at our case and conclude from it that one day or another you will attack them? And what is this but to make greater the enemies that you have already, and to force others to become so who would otherwise have never thought of it?

ATHENIANS: Why, the fact is that continentals generally give us but little alarm; the liberty which they enjoy will long prevent their taking precautions against us; it is rather islanders like yourselves, outside our empire, and subjects smarting under the yoke, who would be the most likely to take a rash step and lead themselves and us into obvious danger.

MELIANS: Well then, if you risk so much to retain your empire, and your subjects to get rid of it, it were surely great baseness and cowardice in us who are still free not to try everything that can be tried, before submitting to your yoke.

ATHENIANS: Not if you are well advised, the contest not being an equal one, with honour as the prize and shame as the penalty, but a question of self-preservation and of not resisting those who are far stronger than you are. . . .

Of the gods we believe, and of men we know, that by a necessary law of their nature they rule wherever they can. And it is not as if we were the first to make this law, or to act upon it when made: we found it existing before us, and shall leave it to exist for ever after us; all we do is to make use of it, knowing that you and everybody else, having the same power as we have, would do the same as we do. . . . You will surely not be caught by that idea of disgrace, which in dangers that are disgraceful, and at the same time too plain to be mistaken, proves so fatal to mankind; since in too many cases the very men that have their eyes perfectly open to what they are rushing into, let the thing called disgrace, by the mere influence of a seductive name, lead them on to a point at which they become so enslaved by the phrase as in fact to fall wilfully into hopeless disaster, and incur disgrace more disgraceful as the companion of error, than when it comes as the result of misfortune. This, if you are well advised, you will guard against; and you will not think it dishonourable to submit to the greatest city in Hellas, when it makes you the moderate offer of becoming its tributary ally, without ceasing to enjoy the country that belongs to you; nor when you have the choice given you between war and security, will you be so blinded as to choose the worse. And it is certain that those who do not yield to their equals, who keep terms with their superiors, and are moderate towards their inferiors, on the whole succeed best. Think over the matter, therefore, after our withdrawal, and reflect once and again that it is for your country that you are consulting, that you have not more than one, and that upon this one deliberation depends its prosperity or ruin.

The Athenians now withdrew from the conference; and the Melians, left to themselves, came to a decision corresponding with what they had maintained in the discussion, and answered, 'Our resolution, Athenians, is the same as it was at first. We will not in a moment deprive of freedom a city that has been inhabited these seven hundred years; but we put our trust in the fortune by which the gods have preserved it until now, and in the help of men, that is, of the Lacedæmonians; and so we will try and save ourselves. Meanwhile we invite you to allow us to be friends to you and foes to neither party, and to retire from our country after making such a treaty as shall seem fit to us both. . . .'

The Athenian envoys now returned to the army; and the Melians showing no signs of yielding, the generals at once betook themselves to hostilities, and drew a line of circumvallation[3] round the Melians, dividing the work among the different states. Subsequently the Athenians returned with most of their army, leaving behind them a certain number of their own citizens and of the allies to keep guard by land and sea. The force thus left stayed on and besieged the place. . . .

Meanwhile the Melians attacked by night and took the part of the Athenian lines over against the market, and killed some of the men, and brought

---

3. **circumvallation:** ramparts and walls.

in corn and all else that they could find useful to them, and so returned and kept quiet, while the Athenians took measures to keep better guard in future.

Summer was now over. The next winter . . . the Melians again took another part of the Athenian lines which were but feebly garrisoned. Reinforcements afterwards arriving from Athens in consequence, under the command of Philocrates, son of Demeas, the siege was now pressed vigorously; and some treachery taking place inside, the Melians surrendered at discretion to the Athenians, who put to death all the grown men whom they took, and sold the women and children for slaves, and subsequently sent out five hundred colonists and inhabited the place themselves.

Source 3 from Aristotle, The Politics, *translated by T. A. Sinclair and revised by Trevor J. Saunders (Baltimore: Penguin, 1962, 1981), pp. 26–27, 31, 34, 50–53. Copyright © the estate of T. A. Sinclair, 1962; revised material copyright © Trevor J. Saunders, 1981. Reprinted with permission.*

3. From Aristotle, *The Politics*

We shall, I think, in this as in other subjects, get the best view of the matter if we look at the natural growth of things from the beginning. . . .

It was out of the association formed by men with these two, women and slaves, that the first household was formed; and the poet Hesiod was right when he wrote, "Get first a house and a wife and an ox to draw the plough." (The ox is the poor man's slave.) This association of persons, established according to the law of nature and continuing day after day, is the household. . . .

Now property is part of a household and the acquisition of property part of the economics of a household; for neither life itself nor the good life is possible without a certain minimum standard of wealth. Again, for any given craft the existence of the proper tools will be essential for the performance of its task. Tools may be animate as well as inanimate; a ship's captain uses a lifeless rudder, but a living man for watch; for the worker in a craft is, from the point of view of the craft, one of its tools. So any piece of property can be regarded as a tool enabling a man to live; and his property is an assemblage of such tools, including his slaves; and a slave, being a living creature like any other servant, is a tool worth many tools. . . .

The "slave by nature" then is he that can and therefore does belong to another, and he that participates in the reasoning faculty so far as to understand but not so as to possess it. For the other animals serve their owner not by exercise of reason but passively. The use, too, of slaves hardly differs at all from that of domestic animals; from both we derive that which is essential for our bodily needs. . . . It is clear then that in household management the people are

[63]

of greater importance than the material property, and their quality of more account than that of the goods that make up their wealth, and also that free men are of more account than slaves. About slaves the first question to be asked is whether in addition to their value as tools and servants there is some other quality or virtue, superior to these, that belongs to slaves. Can they possess self-respect, courage, justice, and virtues of that kind, or have they in fact nothing but the serviceable quality of their persons?

The question may be answered in either of two ways, but both present a difficulty. If we say that slaves have these virtues, how then will they differ from free men? If we say that they have not, the position is anomalous, since they are human beings and capable of reason. Roughly the same question can be put in relation to wife and child: Have not these also virtues? Ought not a woman to be self-respecting, brave, and just? Is not a child sometimes naughty, sometimes good? . . .

This mention of virtue leads us straightaway to a consideration of the soul; for it is here that the natural ruler and the natural subject, whose virtue we regard as different, are to be found. In the soul the difference between ruler and ruled is that between the rational and the nonrational. It is therefore clear that in other connexions also there will be natural differences. And so generally in cases of ruler and ruled; the differences will be natural but they need not be the same. For rule of free over slave, male over female, man over boy, are all natural, but they are also different, because, while parts of the soul are present in each case, the distribution is different. Thus the deliberative faculty in the soul is not present at all in a slave; in a female it is inoperative, in a child undeveloped. We must therefore take it that the same conditions prevail also in regard to the ethical virtues, namely that all must participate in them but not all to the same extent, but only as may be required by each for his proper function. The ruler then must have ethical virtue in its entirety; for his task is simply that of chief maker and reason is chief maker. And the other members must have what amount is appropriate to each. So it is evident that each of the classes spoken of must have ethical virtue. It is also clear that there is some variation in the ethical virtues; self-respect is not the same in a man as in a woman, nor justice, nor courage either, as Socrates thought; the one is courage of a ruler, the other courage of a servant, and likewise with the other virtues.

If we look at the matter in greater detail it will become clearer. For those who talk in generalities and say that virtue is "a good condition of the soul," or that it is "right conduct" or the like, delude themselves. Better than those who look for general definitions are those who, like Gorgias, enumerate the different virtues. So the poet Sophocles singles out "silence" as "bringing credit to a woman," but that is not so for a man. This method of assessing virtue according to function is one that we should always follow. Take the child: he is not yet fully developed and his function is to grow up, so we cannot speak of his virtue as belonging absolutely to him, but only in relation to the progress of his development and to whoever is in charge of him. So too with slave and master; we laid it down that a slave's function is to perform menial tasks; so the amount of virtue required will not be very great, only enough to ensure that he does not neglect his work through loose living or mere fecklessness.

Source 4 from B. K. Workman, editor and translator, They Saw It Happen in Classical Times *(New York: Barnes & Noble, 1964), pp. 32–34. Reprinted by permission of Littlefield, Adams & Company and Basil Blackwell, Publishers.*

4. An Unknown Author's View of Athenian Democracy

Insolent conduct of slaves and resident aliens is everywhere rife in Athens. You cannot strike a slave there, and he will not get out of your way in the street. There is good reason for this being the local custom. If the law allowed a free-born citizen to strike a slave, an alien, or a freedman, then you would often strike an Athenian citizen in the mistaken impression that he was a slave. For the common people dress as poorly as slaves or aliens and their general appearance is no better. . . .

The common people take no supervisory interest in athletic or aesthetic shows, feeling that it is not right for them, since they know that they have not the ability to become expert at them. When it is necessary to provide men to put on stageshows or games or to finance and build triremes,[4] they know that impresarios come from the rich, the actors and chorus from the people. In the same way, organizers and ship-masters are the rich, while the common people take a subordinate part in the games and act as oarsmen for the triremes. But they do at least think it right to receive pay for singing or running or dancing or rowing in the fleet, to level up the incomes of rich and poor. The same holds good for the law courts as well; they are more interested in what profit they can make than in the true ends of justice. . . .

Of the mainland cities in the Athenian Empire, the large ones are governed by fear, the small ones by want. For all states must import and export, and this they cannot do unless they remain subject to the mistress of the seas.

4. **trireme:** standard Greek warship, about 120 feet long and rowed by 150 to 175 men; a ram on the bow was the trireme's main weapon.

[65]

Source 5 from Julia O'Faolain and Lauro Martines, editors, Not in God's Image: Women in History from the Greeks to the Victorians *(New York: Harper & Row, 1973), pp. 20–22. Adapted from several translations. Copyright © 1973 by Julia O'Faolain and Lauro Martines. Reprinted with permission of HarperCollins Publishers, Inc.*

5. From Xenophon, *The Economist*

"Here's another thing I'd like to ask you," said I. "Did you train your wife yourself or did she already know how to run a house when you got her from her father and mother?"

"What could she have known, Socrates," said he, "when I took her from her family? She wasn't yet fifteen. Until then she had been under careful supervision and meant to see, hear, and ask as little as possible. Don't you think it was already a lot that she should have known how to make a cloak of the wool she was given and how to dole out spinning to the servants? She had been taught to moderate her appetites, which, to my mind, is basic for both men's and women's education."

"So, apart from that," I asked, "it was you, Ischomachus, who had to train and teach her her household duties?"

"Yes," said Ischomachus, "but not before sacrificing to the gods. . . . And she solemnly swore before heaven that she would behave as I wanted, and it was clear that she would neglect none of my lessons."

"Tell me what you taught her first. . . ."

"Well, Socrates, as soon as I had tamed her and she was relaxed enough to talk, I asked her the following question: 'Tell me, my dear,' said I, 'do you understand why I married you and why your parents gave you to me? You know as well as I do that neither of us would have had trouble finding someone else to share our beds. But, after thinking about it carefully, it was you I chose and me your parents chose as the best partners we could find for our home and our children. Now, if God sends us children, we shall think about how best to raise them, for we share an interest in securing the best allies and support for our old age. For the moment we only share our home. . . .'"

"My wife answered, 'But how can I help? What am I capable of doing? It is on you that everything depends. My duty, my mother said, is to be well behaved.'"

" 'Oh, by Zeus,' said I, 'my father said the same to me. But the best behavior in a man and woman is that which will keep up their property and increase it as far as may be done by honest and legal means.'"

" 'And do you see some way,' asked my wife, 'in which I can help in this?'"

" '. . . It seems to me that God adapted women's nature to indoor and man's to outdoor work. . . . As Nature has entrusted woman with guarding the household supplies, and a timid nature is no disadvantage in such a job, it has endowed woman with more fear than man. . . . It is more proper for a woman to stay in the house than out of doors and less so for a man to be indoors instead of out. If anyone goes against the nature given him by God and leaves his appointed post . . . he will be punished. . . . You must stay indoors and send out the servants whose work is outside and supervise those who work indoors, receive what is brought in, give out what is to be spent, plan ahead what should be stored and ensure that provisions for a year are not used up in a month. When the wool is brought in, you must see to it that clothes are made from it for whoever needs them and see to it that the corn is still edible. . . . Many of your duties will give you pleasure: for instance, if you teach spinning and weaving to a slave who did not know how to do this when you got her, you double her usefulness to yourself, or if you make a good housekeeper of one who didn't know how to do anything. . . .' Then I took her around the family living rooms, which are pleasantly decorated, cool in summer and warm in winter. I pointed out how the whole house faces south so as to enjoy the winter sun. . . . I showed her the women's quarters which are separated from the men's by a bolted door to prevent anything being improperly removed and also to ensure that the slaves should not have children without our permission. For good slaves are usually even more devoted once they have a family; but good-for-nothings, once they begin to cohabit, have extra chances to get up to mischief."

Source 6 from B. Jowett, translator, The Dialogues of Plato, *revised edition, vol. 3 (Oxford: Oxford University Press, 1895, revised 1924), pp. 58, 100–101, 103, 106, 140–142, 147–148, 151, 159.*

6. From Plato, *The Republic*

Is not the love of learning the love of wisdom, which is philosophy?

They are the same, he replied.

And may we not say confidently of man also, that he who is likely to be gentle to his friends and acquaintances, must by nature be a lover of wisdom and knowledge?

That we may safely affirm.

Then he who is to be a really good and noble guardian of the State will require to unite in himself philosophy and spirit and swiftness and strength?

Undoubtedly.

Then we have found the desired natures; and now that we have found them, how are they to be reared and educated? Is not this an enquiry which may be expected to throw light on the greater enquiry which is our final end—How do justice and injustice grow up in States?

Adeimantus thought that the enquiry would be of great service to us. . . .

Come then, and let us pass a leisure hour in storytelling, and our story shall be the education of our heroes.

By all means.

And what shall be their education? Can we find a better than the traditional sort?—and this has two divisions, gymnastic for the body, and music[5] for the soul.

True. . . .

Very good, I said; then what is the next question? Must we not ask who are to be rulers and who subjects?

Certainly.

There can be no doubt that the elder must rule the younger.

Clearly.

And that the best of these must rule.

That is also clear.

Now, are not the best husbandmen those who are most devoted to husbandry?

Yes.

And as we are to have the best of guardians for our city, must they not be those who have most the character of guardians?

Yes. . . .

Then there must be a selection. Let us note among the guardians those who in their whole life show the greatest eagerness to do what is for the good of their country, and the greatest repugnance to do what is against her interests.

Those are the right men.

And they will have to be watched at every age, in order that we may see whether they preserve their resolution, and never, under the influence either of force or enchantment, forget or cast off their sense of duty to the State. . . . And he who at every age, as boy and youth and in mature life, has come out of the trial victorious and pure, shall be appointed a ruler and guardian of the State; he shall be honoured in life and death, and shall receive sepulture[6] and other memorials of honour, the greatest that we have to give. But him who fails, we must reject. I am inclined to think that this is the sort of way in which our rulers and guardians should be chosen and appointed. I speak generally, and not with any pretension to exactness.

And, speaking generally, I agree with you, he said. . . .

Then let us consider what will be their way of life, if they are to realize our idea of them. In the first place, none of them should have any property of his own beyond what is absolutely necessary; neither should they have a private house or store closed against any one who has a mind to enter; their provisions should be only such as are required by trained warriors, who are men of temperance and courage; they should agree to receive from the citizens a fixed rate of pay, enough to meet the expenses of the year and no more; and they will go to mess and live together like soldiers in a camp. Gold and silver

5. By "music," the Athenians meant all that was sacred to the **muses**, the patron goddesses of the arts and sciences.

6. **sepulture:** a special burial ceremony.

we will tell them that they have from God; the diviner metal is within them, and they have therefore no need of the dross which is current among men, and ought not to pollute the divine by any such earthly admixture; for that commoner metal has been the source of many unholy deeds, but their own is undefiled. And they alone of all the citizens may not touch or handle silver or gold, or be under the same roof with them, or wear them, or drink from them. And this will be their salvation, and they will be the saviours of the State. But should they ever acquire homes or lands or moneys of their own, they will become housekeepers and husbandmen instead of guardians, enemies and tyrants instead of allies of the other citizens; hating and being hated, plotting and being plotted against, they will pass their whole life in much greater terror of internal than of external enemies, and the hour of ruin, both to themselves and to the rest of the State, will be at hand. For all which reasons may we not say that thus shall our State be ordered, and that these shall be the regulations appointed by us for our guardians concerning their houses and all other matters?

Yes, said Glaucon. . . .

The part of the men has been played out, and now properly enough comes the turn of the women. Of them I will proceed to speak, and the more readily since I am invited by you.

For men born and educated like our citizens, the only way, in my opinion, of arriving at a right conclusion about the possession and use of women and children is to follow the path on which we originally started, when we said that the men were to be the guardians and watchdogs of the herd.

True.

Let us further suppose the birth and education of our women to be subject to similar or nearly similar regulations; then we shall see whether the result accords with our design.

What do you mean?

What I mean may be put into the form of a question. I said: Are dogs divided into hes and shes, or do they both share equally in hunting and in keeping watch and in the other duties of dogs? or do we entrust to the males the entire and exclusive care of the flocks, while we leave the females at home, under the idea that the bearing and suckling of their puppies is labour enough for them?

No, he said, they share alike; the only difference between them is that the males are stronger and the females weaker.

But can you use different animals for the same purpose, unless they are bred and fed in the same way?

You cannot.

Then, if women are to have the same duties as men, they must have the same nurture and education?

Yes. . . .

My friend, I said, there is no special faculty of administration in a state which a woman has because she is a woman, or which a man has by virtue of his sex, but the gifts of nature are alike diffused in both; all the pursuits of men are the pursuits of women also, but in all of them a woman is inferior to a man.

Very true.

Then are we to impose all our enactments on men and none of them on women?

That will never do.

One woman has a gift of healing, another not; one is a musician, and another has no music in her nature?

Very true.

And one woman has a turn for gymnastic and military exercises, and another is unwarlike and hates gymnastics?

Certainly.

And one woman is a philosopher, and another is an enemy of philosophy; one has spirit, and another is without spirit?

That is also true.

Then one woman will have the temper of a guardian, and another not. Was not the selection of the male guardians determined by differences of this sort?

Yes.

Men and women alike possess the qualities which make a guardian; they differ only in their comparative strength or weakness.

Obviously.

And those women who have such qualities are to be selected as the companions and colleagues of men who have similar qualities and whom they resemble in capacity and in character?

Very true. . . .

The law, I said, which is the sequel of this and of all that has preceded, is to the following effect—"that the wives of our guardians are to be common, and their children are to be common, and no parent is to know his own child, nor any child his parent."

Yes, he said, that is a much greater wave [i.e. obstacle to be overcome] than the other; and the possibility as well as the utility of such a law are far more questionable. . . .

Both the community of property and the community of families, as I am saying, tend to make them more truly guardians; they will not tear the city in pieces by differing about "mine" and "not mine"; each man dragging any acquisition which he has made into a separate house of his own, where he has a separate wife and children and private pleasures and pains; but all will be affected as far as may be by the same pleasures and pains because they are all of one opinion about what is near and dear to them, and therefore they all tend towards a common end.

Certainly, he replied.

Source 7 adapted from Orestis B. Doumanis and Paul Oliver, editors, Shelter in Greece *(Athens: Architecture in Greece Press, 1974), p. 25.*

7. Floor Plan of a House from Olynthus, Fifth century B.C.

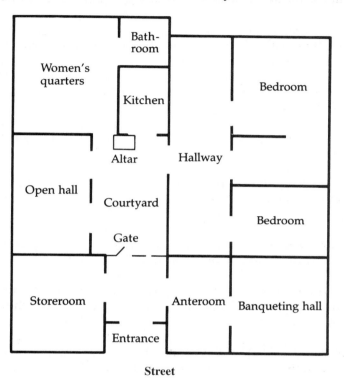

Street

QUESTIONS TO CONSIDER

Before you start to think about the questions in this section, you may want to turn to your text to read (or reread) the section on Athens during the classical period. This can give you more background on the authors and on the political events that might have affected what they wrote.

Though some of the written selections in this chapter clearly describe ideals and others reality, still others blend realism and idealism, creating an idealized view of actual persons or situations. Which selections would you put in this last category? Why would these authors describe reality in an idealized manner? (To answer this question, you need to think about both the purpose of each selection and whether the author truly thought that what he was describing actually existed—in other words, whether this was a conscious or unconscious alteration of reality.)

Once you have labeled the written sources as ideals, reality, and idealizations of reality, go back to your list of the personal qualities of Athenians. Which qualities would you put in each of these three categories? Now that you know you are describing only an ideal or real characteristic, would you add any further qualities? The next step is to divide your list into categories of persons, for it is clear that most of the authors make great distinctions between male and female, adult and child, slave and free. Do all the authors agree on the qualities important in an ideal man, woman, or slave? Which authors have opposing ideas? Why might this be so? Sometimes distinctions between categories are not clearly set out by the author; when Pericles, for instance, uses the words "person" and "people" in his funeral oration, one might think he was talking about all Athenians. Looking at your list divided into categories, of whom is Pericles speaking when he says "person" and "people"? Do any of the authors make distinctions between individuals of the same category based on such factors as wealth or education; for example, do they describe wealthy men differently than poor men, or set out different ideals for women who are interested in learning than for those who are not?

Turning from the individual to social units, what qualities should the ideal Athenian household possess? How might real households work to emulate these ideals? Judging from information in the selections and in your text about Athenian marriage patterns, family life, and social life in general, did real Athenian households approach the ideal at all? How did their beliefs about the way households should be run affect the way Athenians designed their houses? How did the layout of a house work to make reality correspond with those ideals?

The qualities of governments as presented in the selections may also be classified as real, ideal, or idealized. Were any of the words you used to describe the Athenian government after first reading Pericles included in your final list? Does his idealized view of Athens come closer to the realistic view provided in the Melian debate or to the purely ideal view of Plato? After reading all the selections, would you put the quality "democracy" into the real or the ideal column for Athens? How would Athenians define democracy? Do all the authors agree that democracy is a desirable form of government? Judging from information in your text about politics in Athens in the fifth century, why would authors disagree on this matter? If you put democracy in the ideal column, what changes in existing conditions would have been necessary for it to become a reality?

The selections you have read offer varying opinions on a great many subjects, including the benefits of wealth and private property, the relationship between dominant and dependent states and between dominant and dependent individuals, the reasons for the differences between men and women, the role of naval power in foreign policy, and the causes of imperialism. All these issues have both ideal and real components, and you may want to think about them before you draw your final conclusions about classical Athens. How well did Athens live up to the ideals it set for itself? How did

the different ideals held up for different categories of persons affect their participation in Athenian life?

EPILOGUE

We can find the ideals of the Athenians expressed not only in their philosophy, history, and architecture, as you have discovered here, but also in their drama, poetry, and sculpture. Indeed, most of the original sources we have from Athens are not realistic descriptions but either thoughts about ideals or idealizations of actual persons and episodes. That they are idealizations may be very clear to us as modern skeptical readers, but for a long time the statements in these sources were taken as literal truth. To give you an example, here is a quotation from Edith Hamilton, one of the foremost historians of Greece, published in 1930:

> For a hundred years Athens was a city where the great spiritual forces that war in men's minds flowed together along in peace; law and freedom, truth and religion, beauty and goodness, the objective and the subjective—there was a truce to their eternal warfare, and the result was the balance and clarity, the harmony and completeness, that the word Greek has come to stand for.[7]

Given what you have just read, would you agree with her? Do you

think everyone living in classical Athens would have agreed with her?

No matter how you have judged the relationship between ideal and reality in classical Athens, the ideals for the individual and state created there have significantly shaped the development of Western philosophy and social institutions. Roman philosophers closely studied Plato's *Republic,* and medieval philosophers were strongly influenced by Aristotle's *Politics.* Writers from the Renaissance to the present have invented ideal societies, "utopias" guided by wise leaders like Plato's guardians. Occasionally small groups of people have actually tried to set up working replicas of these ideal societies, frequently forbidding private property and the nuclear family as Plato did. Educational theorists have devised "perfect" school systems that, if not entirely successful when put into practice, have had their effect on real-life pedagogy. The Athenian ideal of government by the people is reflected in the constitutions of modern democratic states, with the category "people" now including groups unthinkable to Pericles.

In terms of Athenian history, democracy was an extremely short-lived phenomenon. Widespread revolt broke out in the Athenian empire, and Sparta ultimately defeated Athens, bringing the Peloponnesian War to a close after twenty-seven years. This did not end

7. Edith Hamilton, *The Greek Way* (New York: Norton, 1930), p. 206.

warfare in Greece, however, as the city-states continued to battle among themselves. Finally, in 338 B.C., Greece was conquered by Philip of Macedon, and Athens became simply one small part of a much larger empire. From that point on, Athenian ideals of individual behavior would be emulated in Western culture, but democratic government would not again be attempted as an experiment in the real world for another 2,000 years.

CHAPTER FOUR

THE ACHIEVEMENTS

OF AUGUSTUS

THE PROBLEM

For many centuries, the seat of power in Rome was the senate, a body of men drawn from the most powerful and prominent Roman families that made all major political and military decisions. Under the leadership of the senate, Rome had gradually taken control of the entire Italian peninsula. It then conquered southern France and much of Spain, and, after defeating Carthage in the Punic Wars, occupied northern Africa. These territorial conquests altered the nature of power in Rome, however, because the armies that conquered and held the new territories pledged loyalty to their military leaders and not to the senate. During the first century before Christ, several of these semi-independent armies challenged the senate's power, and civil war erupted in many parts of the Roman territory. The city itself was plundered several times by rival legions, and trade and communications were frequently disrupted. In 60 B.C., three army generals—Pompey, Crassus, and Julius Caesar—decided to form a political alliance, the triumvirate, leaving the senate intact but without much actual power.

All three of these generals were ambitious men who were unwilling to share power with anyone for very long. The senate was especially worried about Julius Caesar, who was gathering an increasingly larger army in Gaul (present-day France), and decided to put its trust in Pompey, whose base of power lay in Greece. (Crassus had meanwhile died in battle.) It ordered Caesar to disband his army and not to return to Rome, setting the Rubicon River near Ravenna in northern Italy as the line he must not cross. In 49 B.C., Caesar crossed the Rubicon (an expression we still use for an irrevocable decision), directly challenging the power of the senate and of Pompey. His armies quickly defeated those of the senate in Italy, and within a few months he held the entire Italian peninsula. From there Caesar turned his attention to Pompey's army, which his forces also defeated in 48 B.C., leaving him in control of all the Roman territory. Though he did not disband the senate, he did begin to shape the government to his liking, appointing officials and army officers and directly overseeing the administration of the provinces. He increased the size of the senate from 600 to 900 members by padding it with his followers, many of whom came from the provinces.

Caesar's meteoric and extralegal rise to power created great resentment among many Roman senators. Intensely proud of Roman traditions and of their own families' long-standing political power, they felt that Caesar was degrading the senate by adding unsophisticated rural representatives. A group of senators, led by Brutus and Cassius, decided to assassinate Caesar, which they did on the steps of the Roman senate on March 15, 44 B.C. The conspirators had not thought much beyond this act, however, and Caesar's death led not to peace but to a renewal of civil war. Some of the army was loyal to the assassins; some to Mark Antony, an associate of Caesar; and some to Caesar's nephew and adopted son, Octavian. At first Mark Antony and Octavian cooperated to defeat the assassins, but then they turned against each other. The war dragged on for over a decade, with Octavian's forces gradually gaining more territory. Octavian won the support of many Romans by convincing them that Antony was plotting with Cleopatra, queen of Egypt, and in 31 B.C. his forces decisively defeated those of Antony at the naval battle of Actium. Antony and his ally Cleopatra committed suicide, leaving Octavian sole ruler of the Mediterranean world.

The problem now facing Octavian was the same one Julius Caesar had confronted twelve years earlier: how to transform a state won by military force into a stable political system. Caesar's answer—personal, autocratic rule—had led to his assassination at the hands of disgruntled senators. This lesson was not lost on Octavian, who realized that directly opposing the strong republican tradition in Rome could be very dangerous.

This tradition had arisen from both political reality—the senate had held actual power for many generations—and Roman political theory. The Romans held that their form of government had been given to them by the gods, who had conferred authority on Romulus, the mythical founder of Rome. That authority was later passed on to the senate, whose original function was to consult the gods about actions Rome should take. The senate in turn passed on authority to the rest of the government bureaucracy and to male heads of household, for in Rome households were considered, as in Athens, the smallest unit of government. Only male heads of household could sit in the senate, for only such individuals were regarded as worthy enough to consult the gods on matters of great importance to the state. This meant that Roman society was extremely patriarchal, with fathers having (at least in theory) absolute control over their wives, children, and servants.

This divinely ordained authority could always be distributed downward as the political bureaucracy grew, but to do away with existing institutions was extremely dangerous. Any radical transformation of the structure of government, especially any change in the authority of the senate, would have been regarded as impious.

Octavian had himself grown up in this tradition and at least to some degree shared these ideas about authority and the divine roots of the Roman political system. He realized that he could be more effective—and probably would live longer—if he worked through, rather than against, existing political institutions. Moreover, serious problems existed that had to be faced immediately, and after years of civil war, the government bureaucracy

was no longer firmly in place to deal with them. Octavian needed to appoint officials and governors and reestablish law and order throughout Roman territory without offending the senate by acting like an autocrat or dictator.

In the eyes of many of his contemporaries, Octavian accomplished this admittedly difficult task very well. The senate conferred on him the name he is usually known by, Augustus, meaning "blessed" or "magnificent." Later historians regarded Augustus, rather than Julius Caesar, as the creator of the Roman Empire. Your task in this chapter will be to evaluate these judgments. How did Augustus transform the Roman republic into an empire? Why was he successful where Julius Caesar had not been?

SOURCES AND METHOD

As you think about these questions, you can see that they involve two somewhat different components: the process by which Augustus made changes and the results of these changes, or what we might term the "means" and the "ends." Both are important to consider in assessing the achievements of any political leader, and both have been used by the contemporaries of Augustus, later Roman writers, and modern historians in evaluating the first Roman emperor's reign.

One of the best sources for observing the process of political change is laws, especially basic laws such as constitutions that set out governmental

structure. Rome was a society in which law was extremely important and was explicitly written down, unlike many early societies, in which laws were handed down orally from generation to generation. As the Romans conquered Europe and the Mediterranean, they brought their legal system with them; consequently, Roman law forms the basis of most modern Western legal systems, with England and thus the United States the most notable exceptions.

We encounter some serious difficulties in using laws as our source material for the reign of Augustus, however. Given Roman ideas about authority and the strength of Roman tradition, would you expect him to have made major legal changes? Augustus, after all, described his aims and his actions as restoring republican government; if we use only the constitution of Rome as a source, we might be tempted to believe him. No new office was created for the emperor. Instead, he carefully preserved all traditional offices while gradually taking over many of them himself. Augustus was both a consul and a tribune, although the former office was usually reserved for a patrician and the latter for a plebeian. Later the senate appointed him *imperator,* or commander-in-chief of the army, and gave him direct control of many of the outlying provinces. These provinces furnished grain supplies essential to the people of Rome as well as soldiers loyal to Augustus rather than to the senate. The senate also gave him the honorary title of *princeps* (or "first citizen"), the title he preferred, which gradually lost its republican origins and gained the overtones of "monarch" evident in its modern English derivative, "prince." Augustus recognized the importance of religion to most Romans, and in 12 B.C. he had himself named *pontifex maximus,* or "supreme priest." He encouraged the building of temples dedicated to "Rome and Augustus," laying the foundations for the growth of a ruler cult closely linked with patriotic loyalty to Rome.

None of these innovations required any alteration in the basic constitution of Rome. What did change, however, was the tone of many laws, particularly those from the outlying provinces, where Augustus could be more open about the transformation he was working without bringing on the wrath of the senate. Our first two

selections, then, are decrees and laws from Roman territories, where we can perhaps see some hint of the gradual development of the republic into an empire.

Source 1 is a decree by Augustus himself, an inscription dated 4 B.C. from the Greek city of Cyrene. Like all laws, it was passed in response to a perceived problem. What problem does the decree confront? What procedure does it provide to solve this problem? What complications does it anticipate, and how does it try to solve them? You will notice that the decree itself is set within a long framework giving the reasons it was issued. This is true for many laws, including the American Constitution, which begins, "We the people of the United States, in order to form a more perfect union, establish justice, insure domestic tranquillity." Why does Augustus say he is passing this law? This framework can also give you clues to the relationship between Augustus and the senate. How is this relationship described, and what does Augustus's attitude appear to be?

The second law is an inscription dated A.D. 11 from an altar in the city of Narbonne in southern France. This law was passed by the local government, not the central Roman authorities. What does it order the population to do? Although the law itself does not state why it was passed, what might some reasons have been? What does the law indicate about attitudes toward Augustus and toward Roman authorities?

Another valuable source for examining the achievements of Augustus consists of the comments of his contemporaries and later Roman historians. Because Romans had such a strong sense of their own traditions, they were fascinated by history and were ever eager to point out how the hand of the gods operated in a way that allowed Rome to conquer most of the Western world. In the century before Augustus took over, it looked to many Romans as if the gods had forgotten Rome, leaving its citizens to kill each other in revolutions and civil wars. Augustus's military successes and political acumen seemed to show that he had the gods on his side, so writers delighted in extolling his accomplishments. Augustus's astuteness also extended to the world of literature and the arts, and he hired writers, sculptors, architects, and painters to glorify Rome, causing his own reputation no harm in the process. Many of the poems and histories are blatant hero worship, others communicate a more balanced view, and, because Augustus was not totally successful at winning everyone over to his side, some authors are openly critical.

Sources 3 through 6 are assessments by various Romans of Augustus's rule. As you read them, first try to gauge each author's basic attitude toward Augustus. What does he find to praise or blame? Does his judgment appear overly positive or negative? Does he sound objective? In answering these questions, you will need to pay attention not only to the content of the selection but also to the specific words each author chooses. What kinds of adjectives does he use to describe Augustus's person and political actions? Once you have

assessed the basic attitude of each author, identify what he regards as important in Augustus's reign. To what factors does he attribute Augustus's success? How does he describe the process by which the Roman republic was turned into an empire? What reasons does he give for Augustus's success and Julius Caesar's failure?

A bit of background on each of these selections will help you put them in better perspective. Source 3 was written by Horace, a poet living at the court of Augustus. This is an excerpt from his *Odes*, a literary rather than a primarily historical work. Source 4, an excerpt from Suetonius's biography of Augustus, was composed during the first half of the second century. Suetonius, private secretary to the emperor Hadrian, was keenly interested in the private as well as the public lives of the Roman emperors. Source 5 is taken from the long history of Rome by the politician and historian Dio Cassius (ca 150–235). Source 6 is drawn from the *Annals* of Tacitus, an orator and historian from a well-to-do Roman family. Sources 4 through 6 were written between one and two centuries after the events they present and are thus "history" as we know it, describing events after they happened.

Source 7 is a third type of evidence, namely, Augustus's own description of his rule. Usually called the *Res Gestae Divi Augusti*, it is an inscription he composed shortly before the end of his life. In this piece, following a long Roman tradition of inscriptions commemorating distinguished citizens, he describes the honors conferred on him as well as his accomplishments. Like

[79]

all autobiographical statements, it is intended not simply as an objective description of a ruler's deeds but specifically as a vehicle for all that Augustus most wanted people to remember about this reign. Even though it is subjective, the *Res Gestae* is unique and invaluable as a primary source because it gives us Augustus's own version of the transformations he wrought in Roman society. As you read it, compare Augustus's descriptions of his deeds with those of the historians you have just read. What does Augustus regard as his most important accomplishments?

Many of the best sources for Augustus, of course, as for all of ancient history, are not written but archaeological. In fact, two of the sources we have looked at so far, the decree issued by Augustus and the inscription from Narbonne (Sources 1 and 2), are actually archaeological as well as written sources because they are inscriptions carved in stone. Thus, unlike other texts from the ancient world, including such basic ones as Plato's *Republic,* we have the original text and not a later copy.

Inscriptions are just one of many types of archaeological evidence. As the Romans conquered land after land, they introduced not only their legal code but their monetary system as well. Roman coins have been found throughout all of Europe and the Near East, far beyond the borders of the Roman Empire. *Numismatics,* the study of coins, can thus provide us with clues available from no other source, for coins have the great advantage of being both durable and valuable. Though their value sometimes

works to render them less durable—people melt them down to make other coins or to use the metal in other ways—it also makes them one of the few material goods that people hide in great quantities. Their owners intend to dig them up later, of course, but die or forget where they have buried them, leaving great caches of coins for later archaeologists and historians.

Roman coins differ markedly from modern coins in some respects. Though the primary function of both is to serve as a means of exchange, Roman coins were also transmitters of political propaganda. One side usually displayed a portrait of the emperor, chosen very carefully by the emperor himself to emphasize certain qualities. The reverse side often depicted a recent victory, anniversary, or other important event, or the personification of an abstract quality of virtue such as health or liberty. Modern coins also feature portraits, pictures, and slogans, but they tend to stay the same for decades, and so we pay very little attention to what is on them. Roman emperors, on the other hand, issued new coins frequently, expecting people to look at them. Most of the people who lived in the Roman Empire were illiterate, with no chance to read about the illustrious deeds of the emperor, but they did come into contact with coins nearly every day. From these coins they learned what the emperor looked like, what he had recently done, or what qualities to associate with him, for even illiterate people could identify the symbols for such abstract virtues as liberty or victory. Over one hundred different portraits of Augustus have been found on coins, providing us with additional clues about the achievements he most wanted to emphasize.

Once you have read the written documents, look at the two illustrations of coins, Sources 8 and 9. On the first, issued in 2 B.C., the lettering reads CAESAR AUGUSTUS DIVI F PATER PATRIAE, or "Augustus Caesar, son of a God, Father of the Fatherland." (Julius Caesar had been deified by the senate after his assassination, which is why Augustus called himself "son of a God.") Augustus is crowned with what appears to be a wreath of wheat stalks; this crown was the exclusive right of the priests of one of Rome's oldest religious groups that honored agricultural gods. The second coin, issued between 20 and 16 B.C., shows Augustus alongside the winged figure of the goddess Victory in a chariot atop a triumphal arch that stands on top of a viaduct; the inscription reads QUOD VIAE MUN SUNT, "because the roads have been reinforced." Think about the message Augustus was trying to convey with each of these coins. Even if you could not read the words, what impression of the emperor would you have from coins like these?

Issuing coins was one way for an emperor to celebrate and communicate his achievements; building was another. As you will read in Augustus's autobiography, he had many structures—stadiums, marketplaces, and temples—built for various purposes. He, and later Roman emperors, also built structures that were purely symbolic, the most impressive of which were celebratory arches, built to commemorate an achievement or a military victory. The second coin shows Augustus standing on top of such an arch; Source 10 is a photograph of the arch of Augustus that still stands at Rimini. This arch was built at one end of the Flaminian Way, which Augustus reconstructed, as you will read in his autobiography; a similar arch was built at the other end in Rome. As you did when looking at the coins, think about the message such an arch conveys. It was put up with the agreement of the senate; does it give you a sense of republicanism or empire?

Roads are another prime archaeological source, closely related to the aqueducts we examined in Chapter 1. The Romans initially built roads to help their army move more quickly; once built, however, the road system facilitated trade and commerce as well. Roads are thus symbols of power as well as a means to maintain and extend it. Archaeologists have long studied the expansion of the Roman road system, and their findings can most easily be seen diagrammed on maps. Though maps do not have the immediacy of actual archaeological remains, they are based on such remains and enable us to detect patterns and make comparisons over time.

Selections 11 and 12 are maps of the major Roman roads existing before the reign of Augustus, those built or reconstructed during his reign, and the Roman road system at its farthest extent. Compare the first map with the information you have obtained from Augustus himself about his expansion of the frontiers of

Rome (Source 7, paragraph 26). Notice that he mentions only the western part of the Roman Empire; do the roads built during his reign reflect this western orientation? What do the later road-building patterns shown in Source 12 tell us about the goals and successes of later Roman emperors?

THE EVIDENCE

Sources 1 through 3 from Naphtali Lewis and Meyer Reinhold, editors and translators, Roman Civilization, *vol. 2,* The Empire *(New York: Columbia University Press, 1955), pp. 39–42; p. 62; p. 20. Reprinted with permission of Columbia University Press, 562 W. 113th St., New York, NY 10025, via Copyright Clearance Center, Inc.*

1. Decree Issued by Emperor Augustus, 4 B.C.

The Emperor Caesar Augustus, *pontifex maximus*, holding the tribunician power for the nineteenth year, declares:

A decree of the senate was passed in the consulship of Gaius Calvisius and Lucius Passienus, with me as one of those present at the writing. Since it affects the welfare of the allies of the Roman people, I have decided to send it into the provinces, appended to this my prefatory edict, so that it may be known to all who are under our care. From this it will be evident to all the inhabitants of the provinces how much both I and the senate are concerned that none of our subjects should suffer any improper treatment or any extortion.

DECREE OF THE SENATE

Whereas the consuls Gaius Calvisius Sabinus and Lucius Passienus Rufus spoke "Concerning matters affecting the security of the allies of the Roman people which the Emperor Caesar Augustus, our *princeps*, following the recommendation of the council which he had drawn by lot from among the senate, desired to be brought before the senate by us," the senate passed the following decree:

Whereas our ancestors established legal process for extortion so that the allies might more easily be able to take action for any wrongs done them and recover moneys extorted from them, and whereas this type of process is sometimes very expensive and troublesome for those in whose interest the law was enacted, because poor people or persons weak with illness or age are dragged from far-distant provinces as witnesses, the senate decrees as follows:

If after the passage of this decree of the senate any of the allies, desiring to recover extorted moneys, public or private, appear and so depose before one of the magistrates who is authorized to convene the senate, the magistrate—except where the extorter faces a capital charge—shall bring them before the senate as soon as possible and shall assign them any advocate they themselves request to speak in their behalf before the senate; but no one who has in accordance with the laws been excused from this duty shall be required to serve as advocate against his will. . . .

The judges chosen shall hear and inquire into only those cases in which a man is accused of having appropriated money from a community or from private parties; and, rendering their decision within thirty days, they shall order him to restore such sum of money, public or private, as the accusers prove was taken from them. Those whose duty it is to inquire into and pronounce judgment in these cases shall, until they complete the inquiry and pronounce their judgment, be exempted from all public duties except public worship. . . .

The senate likewise decrees that the judges who are selected in accordance with this decree of the senate shall pronounce in open court each his several findings, and what the majority pronounces shall be the verdict.

2. Inscription from the City of Narbonne, A.D. 11

In the consulship of Titus Statilius Taurus and Lucius Cassius Longinus, September 22. Vow taken to the divine spirit of Augustus by the populace of the Narbonensians in perpetuity: "May it be good, favorable, and auspicious to the Emperor Caesar Augustus, son of a god, father of his country, *pontifex maximus*, holding the tribunician power for the thirty-fourth year; to his wife, children, and house; to the Roman senate and people; and to the colonists[1] and residents of the Colonia Julia Paterna of Narbo Martius,[2] who have bound themselves to worship his divine spirit in perpetuity!"

The populace of the Narbonensians has erected in the forum at Narbo an altar at which every year on September 23—the day on which the good fortune of the age bore him to be ruler of the world—three Roman *equites*[3] from the populace and three freedmen shall sacrifice one animal each and shall at their own expense on that day provide the colonists and residents with incense and wine for supplication to his divine spirit. And on September 24 they shall likewise provide incense and wine for the colonists and residents. Also on January 1 they shall provide incense and wine for the colonists and residents. Also on January 7, the day on which he first entered upon the command of the world, they shall make supplication with incense and wine, and

---

1. The word "colonist" has a very specific meaning in Roman history. **Colonists** were Romans, often retired soldiers, who were granted land in the outlying provinces in order to build up Roman strength there. They were legally somewhat distinct from native residents, which is why this law uses the phrase "colonists and residents" to make it clear that both groups were required to follow its provisions.

2. The long phrase "Colonia Julia Pasterna of Narbo Martius" is the official and complete Roman name for the town of Narbo, which we now call Narbonne.

3. **equites:** cavalry of the Roman army.

shall sacrifice one animal each, and shall provide incense and wine for the colonists and residents on that day. And on May 31, because on that day in the consulship of Titus Statilius Taurus and Manius Aemilius Lepidus he reconciled the populace to the decurions,[4] they shall sacrifice one animal each and shall provide the colonists and residents with incense and wine for supplication to his divine spirit. And of these three Roman *equites* and three freedmen one . . . [The rest of this inscription is lost.]

3. From Horace, *Odes*

Thine age, O Caesar, has brought back fertile crops to the fields and has restored to our own Jupiter the military standards stripped from the proud columns of the Parthians;[5] has closed Janus' temple[6] freed of wars; has put reins on license overstepping righteous bounds; has wiped away our sins and revived the ancient virtues through which the Latin name and the might of Italy waxed great, and the fame and majesty of our empire were spread from the sun's bed in the west to the east. As long as Caesar is the guardian of the state, neither civil dissension nor violence shall banish peace, nor wrath that forges swords and brings discord and misery to cities. Not those who drink the deep Danube shall violate the orders of Caesar, nor the Getae, nor the Seres,[7] nor the perfidious Parthians, nor those born by the Don River. And we, both on profane and sacred days, amidst the gifts of merry Bacchus, together with our wives and children, will first duly pray to the gods; then, after the tradition of our ancestors, in songs to the accompaniment of Lydian flutes we will hymn leaders whose duty is done.

Source 4 from Suetonius, The Lives of the Twelve Caesars, *edited and translated by Joseph Gavorse (New York: Modern Library, 1931), p. 89.*

4. From Suetonius, *Life of Augustus*

The whole body of citizens with a sudden unanimous impulse proffered him the title of "father of his country"—first the plebs, by a deputation sent to

4. **decurion:** member of a town council.

5. The Parthians were an empire located in the region occupied by present-day Iraq. They had defeated Roman armies led by Mark Antony and had taken the Roman military standards, that is, the flags and banners of the army they defeated. Augustus recovered these standards, an important symbolic act, even though he did not conquer the Parthians.

6. This was a small temple in Rome that was ordered closed whenever peace reigned throughout the whole Roman Empire. During the reign of Augustus it was closed three times.

7. The Getae and the Seres were people who lived in the regions occupied by present-day Romania and Ukraine.

Antium, and then, because he declined it, again at Rome as he entered the theater, which they attended in throngs, all wearing laurel wreaths; the senate afterwards in the senate house, not by a decree or by acclamation, but through Valerius Messala. He, speaking for the whole body, said: "Good fortune and divine favor attend thee and thy house, Caesar Augustus; for thus we feel that we are praying for lasting prosperity for our country and happiness for our city. The senate in accord with the Roman people hails thee 'Father of thy Country.'" Then Augustus with tears in his eyes replied as follows (and I have given his exact words, as I did those of Messala): "Having attained my highest hopes, members of the senate, what more have I to ask of the immortal gods than that I may retain this same unanimous approval of yours to the very end of my life?"

Sources 5 through 7 from Naphtali Lewis and Meyer Reinhold, editors and translators, Roman Civilization, *vol. 2,* The Empire *(New York: Columbia University Press, 1955), pp. 4–8; p. 4; pp. 9–10, 12, 14–16, 17, 19. Reprinted with permission of Columbia University Press, 562 W. 113th St., New York, NY 10025, via Copyright Clearance Center, Inc.*

5. From Dio Cassius, *Roman History*

In this way the power of both people and senate passed entirely into the hands of Augustus, and from this time there was, strictly speaking, a monarchy; for monarchy would be the truest name for it, even if two or three men later held the power jointly. Now, the Romans so detested the title "monarch" that they called their emperors neither dictators nor kings nor anything of this sort. Yet, since the final authority for the government devolves upon them, they needs must be kings. The offices established by the laws, it is true, are maintained even now, except that of censor; but the entire direction and administration is absolutely in accordance with the wishes of the one in power at the time. And yet, in order to preserve the appearance of having this authority not through their power but by virtue of the laws, the emperors have taken to themselves all the offices (including the titles) which under the Republic possessed great power with the consent of the people—with the exception of the dictatorship. Thus, they very often become consuls, and they are always styled proconsuls whenever they are outside the *pomerium*.[8] The title *imperator* is held by them for life, not only by those who have won victories in battle but also by all the rest, to indicate their absolute power, instead of the title "king" or "dictator." These latter titles they have never assumed since they fell out of use in the constitution, but the actuality of those offices is secured to them by the appellation *imperator*. By virtue of the titles named, they secure the right to make levies, collect funds, declare war, make peace,

8. **pomerium:** the city limits of Rome.

[85]

and rule foreigners and citizens alike everywhere and always—even to the extent of being able to put to death both *equites* and senators inside the *pomerium*—and all the other powers once granted to the consuls and other officials possessing independent authority; and by virtue of holding the censorship they investigate our lives and morals as well as take the census, enrolling some in the equestrian and senatorial orders and removing others from these orders according to their will. By virtue of being consecrated in all the priesthoods and, in addition, from their right to bestow most of them upon others, as well as from the fact that, even if two or three persons rule jointly, one of them is *pontifex maximus*, they hold in their own hands supreme authority over all matters both profane and sacred. The tribunician power, as it is called, which once the most influential men used to hold, gives them the right to nullify the effects of the measures taken by any other official, in case they do not approve, and makes their persons inviolable; and if they appear to be wronged in even the slightest degree, not merely by deed but even by word, they may destroy the guilty party as one accursed, without a trial.

Thus by virtue of these Republican titles they have clothed themselves with all the powers of the government, so that they actually possess all the prerogatives of kings without the usual title. For the appellation "Caesar" or "Augustus" confers upon them no actual power but merely shows in the one case that they are the successors of their family line, and in the other the splendor of their rank. The name "Father" perhaps gives them a certain authority over us all—the authority which fathers once had over their children; yet it did not signify this at first, but betokened honor and served as an admonition both to them to love their subjects as they would their children; and to their subjects to revere them as they would their fathers. . . .

The senate as a body, it is true, continued to sit in judgment as before, and in certain cases transacted business with embassies and envoys from both peoples and kings; and the people and the plebs, moreover, continued to come together for the elections; but nothing was actually done that did not please Caesar. At any rate, in the case of those who were to hold office, he himself selected and nominated some; and though he left the election of others in the hands of the people and the plebs, in accordance with the ancient practice, yet he took care that no persons should hold office who were unfit or elected as the result of factious combinations or bribery.

Such were the arrangements made, generally speaking, at that time; for in reality Caesar himself was destined to have absolute power in all matters for life, because he was not only in control of money matters (nominally, to be sure, he had separated the public funds from his own, but as a matter of fact he spent the former also as he saw fit) but also in control of the army. At all events, when his ten-year period came to an end, there was voted him another five years, then five more, after that ten, and again another ten, and then ten for the fifth time, so that by the succession of ten-year periods he continued to be sole ruler for life. And it is for this reason that the subsequent monarchs, though no longer appointed for a specified period but for their whole life once for all, nevertheless always held a celebration every ten years, as if then renewing their sovereignty once more; and this is done even at the present day.

Now, Caesar had received many privileges previously, when the question of declining the sovereignty and that of apportioning the provinces were under discussion. For the right to fasten laurels to the front of the imperial residence and to hang the civic crown above the doors was then voted him to symbolize the fact that he was always victorious over enemies and savior of the citizens. The imperial palace is called Palatium, not because it was ever decreed that this should be its name but because Caesar dwelt on the Palatine and had his military headquarters there. . . . Hence, even if the emperor resides somewhere else, his dwelling retains the name of Palatium.

And when he had actually completed the reorganization, the name Augustus was at length bestowed upon him by the senate and by the people. . . . He took the title of Augustus, signifying that he was more than human; for all most precious and sacred objects are termed *augusta*. For which reason they called him also in Greek *sebastos* . . . meaning an august person.

6. From Tacitus, *Annals*

After the death of Brutus and Cassius, there was no longer any army loyal to the Republic. . . . Then, laying aside the title of triumvir and parading as a consul, and professing himself satisfied with the tribunician power for the protection of the plebs, Augustus enticed the soldiers with gifts, the people with grain, and all men with the allurement of peace, and gradually grew in power, concentrating in his own hands the functions of the senate, the magistrates, and the laws. No one opposed him, for the most courageous had fallen in battle or in the proscription. As for the remaining nobles, the readier they were for slavery, the higher were they raised in wealth and offices, so that, aggrandized by the revolution, they preferred the safety of the present to the perils of the past. Nor did the provinces view with disfavor this state of affairs, for they distrusted the government of the senate and the people on account of the struggles of the powerful and the rapacity of the officials, while the protection afforded them by the laws was inoperative, as the provinces were repeatedly thrown into confusion by violence, intrigue, and finally bribery. . . .

At home all was peaceful; the officials bore the same titles as before. The younger generation was born after the victory of Actium, and even many of the older generation had been born during the civil wars. How few were left who had seen the Republic!

Thus the constitution had been transformed, and there was nothing at all left of the good old way of life. Stripped of equality, all looked to the directives of a *princeps* with no apprehension for the present, while Augustus in the vigorous years of his life maintained his power, that of his family, and peace.

7. From Augustus, *Res Gestae Divi Augusti*

1. At the age of nineteen, on my own initiative and at my own expense, I raised an army by means of which I liberated the Republic, which was oppressed by the tyranny of a faction. For which reason the senate, with honorific decrees, made me a member of its order in the consulship of Gaius Pansa and Aulus Hirtius, giving me at the same time consular rank in voting, and granted me the *imperium*. It ordered me as propraetor, together with the consuls, to see to it that the state suffered no harm. Moreover, in the same year, when both consuls had fallen in the war, the people elected me consul and a triumvir for the settlement of the commonwealth.

2. Those who assassinated my father I drove into exile, avenging their crime by due process of law; and afterwards when they waged war against the state, I conquered them twice on the battlefield.

3. I waged many wars throughout the whole world by land and by sea, both civil and foreign, and when victorious I spared all citizens who sought pardon. Foreign peoples who could safely be pardoned I preferred to spare rather than to extirpate. . . . Though the Roman senate and people unitedly agreed that I should be elected soul guardian of the laws and morals with supreme authority, I refused to accept any office offered me which was contrary to the traditions of our ancestors. . . .

9. The senate decreed that vows for my health should be offered up every fifth year by the consuls and priests. In fulfillment of those vows, games were often celebrated during my lifetime, sometimes by the four most distinguished colleges of priests, sometimes by the consuls. Moreover, the whole citizen body, with one accord, both individually and as members of municipalities, prayed continuously for my health at all the shrines.

10. My name was inserted, by decree of the senate, in the hymn of the Salian priests. And it was enacted by law that I should be sacrosanct in perpetuity and that I should possess the tribunician power as long as I live. I declined to become *pontifex maximus* in place of a colleague while he was still alive, when the people offered me that priesthood, which my father had held. A few years later, in the consulship of Publius Sulpicius and Gaius Valgius, I accepted this priesthood, when death removed the man who had taken possession of it at a time of civil disturbance; and from all Italy a multitude flocked to my election such as had never previously been recorded at Rome. . . .

17. Four times I came to the assistance of the treasury with my own money, transferring to those in charge of the treasury 150,000,000 sesterces. And in the consulship of Marcus Lepidus and Lucius Arruntius I transferred out of my own patrimony 170,000,000 sesterces to the soldiers' bonus fund, which was

established on my advice for the purpose of providing bonuses for soldiers who had completed twenty or more years of service.

18. From the year in which Gnaeus Lentulus and Publius Lentulus were consuls, whenever the provincial taxes fell short, in the case sometimes of 100,000 persons and sometimes of many more, I made up their tribute in grain and in money from my own grain stores and my own patrimony. . . .

20. I repaired the Capitol and the theater of Pompey with enormous expenditures on both works, without having my name inscribed on them. I repaired the conduits of the aqueducts which were falling into ruin in many places because of age, and I doubled the capacity of the aqueduct called Marcia by admitting a new spring into its conduit. I completed the Julian Forum and the basilica which was between the temple of Castor and the temple of Saturn, works begun and far advanced by my father, and when the same basilica was destroyed by fire, I enlarged its site and began rebuilding the structure, which is to be inscribed with the names of my sons; and in case it should not be completed while I am still alive, I left instructions that the work be completed by my heirs. In my sixth consulship I repaired eighty-two temples of the gods in the city, in accordance with a resolution of the senate, neglecting none which at that time required repair. In my seventh consulship I reconstructed the Flaminian Way from the city as far as Ariminum,[9] and also all the bridges except the Mulvian and the Minucian. . . .

22. I gave a gladiatorial show three times in my own name, and five times in the names of my sons or grandsons; at these shows about 10,000 fought. Twice I presented to the people in my own name an exhibition of athletes invited from all parts of the world, and a third time in the name of my grandson. I presented games in my own name four times, and in addition twenty-three times in the place of other magistrates. On behalf of the college of fifteen, as master of that college, with Marcus Agrippa as my colleague, I celebrated the Secular Games[10] in the consulship of Gaius Furnius and Gaius Silanus. In my thirteenth consulship I was the first to celebrate the Games of Mars, which subsequently the consuls, in accordance with a decree of the senate and a law, have regularly celebrated in the succeeding years. Twenty-six times I provided for the people, in my own name or in the names of my sons or grandsons, hunting spectacles of African wild beasts in the circus or in the Forum or in the amphitheaters; in these exhibitions about 3,500 animals were killed.

9. Present-day Rimini, Italy.

10. The Secular Games were an enormous series of athletic games, festivals, and banquets that Augustus ordered held in 17 B.C. Though called "secular," they were held in honor of the gods and were directed by the College of Fifteen, a board that oversaw sacrifices to the gods. All adult Roman citizens were expected to view the games out of religious duty.

23. I presented to the people an exhibition of a naval battle across the Tiber where the grove of the Caesars now is, having had the site excavated 1,800 feet in length and 1,200 feet in width. In this exhibition thirty beaked ships, triremes or biremes, and in addition a great number of smaller vessels engaged in combat. On board these fleets, exclusive of rowers, there were about 3,000 combatants. . . .

26. I extended the frontiers of all the provinces of the Roman people on whose boundaries were peoples subject to our empire. I restored peace to the Gallic and Spanish provinces and likewise to Germany, that is, to the entire region bounded by the Ocean from Gades to the mouth of the Elbe River. I caused peace to be restored in the Alps, from the region nearest to the Adriatic Sea as far as the Tuscan Sea, without undeservedly making war against any people. My fleet sailed the Ocean from the mouth of the Rhine eastward as far as the territory of the Cimbrians,[11] to which no Roman previously had penetrated either by land or by sea. . . .

34. In my sixth and seventh consulships, after I had put an end to the civil wars, having attained supreme power by universal consent, I transferred the state from my own power to the control of the Roman senate and people. For this service of mine I received the title of Augustus by decree of the senate, and the doorposts of my house were publicly decked with laurels, the civic crown was affixed over my doorway, and a golden shield was set up in the Julian senate house, which, as the inscription on this shield testifies, the Roman senate and people gave me in recognition of my valor, clemency, justice, and devotion. After that time I excelled all in authority, but I possessed no more power than the others who were my colleagues in each magistracy.

35. When I held my thirteenth consulship, the senate, the equestrian order, and the entire Roman people gave me the title of "father of the country" and decreed that this title should be inscribed in the vestibule of my house, in the Julian senate house, and in the Augustan Forum on the pedestal of the chariot which was set up in my honor by decree of the senate. At the time I wrote this document I was in my seventy-sixth year.

11. Near present-day Hamburg, Germany.

Sources 8 and 9 from the American Numismatic Society, New York.

8. Roman Coin Issued 2 B.C.

9. Roman Coin Issued 20–16 B.C.

Source 10 from Alinari/Art Resource. Photo by Stab D. Anderson, 1931.

10. Arch of Augustus at Rimini

Source 11 adapted from sketches by Merry E. Wiesner.

11. Main Roman Roads, 31 B.C.–A.D. 14

Source 12 from Victor W. Von Hagen, The Roads That Led to Rome *(Cleveland and New York: World Publishing Co., © 1967 by George Weidenfeld and Nicolson, London), pp. 18–19.*

12. Main Roman Roads at Their Greatest Extent, A.D. 180

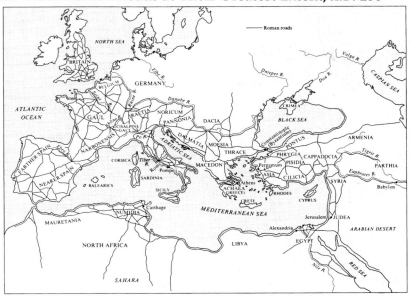

QUESTIONS TO CONSIDER

Now that you have examined various pieces of evidence, you need to put them together to arrive at a conclusion that you can support. Do not worry about not having all the evidence you need; no historian can ever discover "all" the facts about an event or person. He or she makes conclusions on the basis of the evidence available, alters those conclusions when new material is discovered, and uses those conclusions as a framework for further research. In this respect, historians operate just like physicists learning how the universe works. Do not worry if some of your sources disagree; ten people who witness an auto accident often come up with ten quite contradictory accounts of the event. Why might accounts of Augustus's rule be even more contradictory?

The sources have made you aware of the operation of Roman government on two levels: that of the formal constitution, which remained a republic, and that of the actual locus of power, which was increasingly the emperor. The changes that Augustus instituted thus took place at the second level, and in many areas we can ignore the formal constitution of Rome in describing the process of change. Comparing all the sources, how would you describe the means by which Augustus transformed the republic into a different type of government? Which steps were most important? Which observers seemed to have the clearer view of this process, Augustus himself and those living during his lifetime, or later historians?

In considering this last question, you need to think about the advantages and disadvantages of eyewitness reports versus later, secondary accounts.

The second question concerns results, not process: Why was Augustus successful? To answer this, we must consider not only the changes themselves, but people's perceptions of them. A ruler's place in history depends not only on real accomplishments but also on how these accomplishments are perceived and judged by later generations. Rulers perceived as good or successful are often given credit for everything good that happened during their reigns, even if they had nothing to do with it. Conversely, rulers regarded as unsuccessful, weak, or bad get blamed for many things that were not their fault. A reputation is generally based on actual achievements, but occasionally it is also determined by a ruler's successful manipulation of public opinion, and sometimes by that manipulation alone.

Augustus clearly recognized the importance of public opinion, which in Rome was tied to upholding tradition. How does he make use of Roman traditions in the laws and coins he issues? How do other observers judge his connection with tradition? Many of Rome's traditions were incorporated into public rituals and ceremonies. What sorts of ceremonies did Romans participate in or view? How did Augustus use these ceremonies to demonstrate his power or his personal connections with Roman tradition? Along with rituals, titles are also important demonstrations of power.

What does Augustus call himself and what do others call him, both in the written documents and on the coins? Why is there so much discussion of his accepting or not accepting various titles?

Now that you have considered the opinions of a range of commentators, assessed some actual legal changes and road-building patterns, examined some coins, and heard from

Augustus himself, you are ready to answer the questions: How did Augustus transform the Roman republic into an empire? Why was he successful? Once you have made your assessment, think about how you would use it to structure future research. What other evidence would be useful in supporting your conclusions? Where might you go to find that evidence?

EPILOGUE

Though Augustus said that his aim was a restoration of the republic, in reality he transformed Roman government into an empire ruled by one individual. His reign is generally termed the *Principate*, a word taken from Augustus's favorite title *princeps,* but the rulers of Rome after him did not hesitate to use the title *emperor.* Like him, they also retained the titles *pontifex maximus,* supreme priest, and *imperator,* commander-in-chief. It is interesting to see how many of our words denoting aspects of royal rule come from Augustus: not only "prince," "emperor," and "czar" (the Russian variant of "Caesar") but also "palace," from Palatine, the hill where Augustus had his house.

The emperors who came after Augustus built on his achievements, both literally and figuratively. They extended the borders of the Roman Empire even farther, so that at its largest it would stretch from Scotland to the Sudan and from Spain to Syria. The Roman road system was expanded to over 50,000 miles, longer

than the current interstate highway system in the United States; some of those roads are still usable today. Roman coins continued to be stamped with the emperor's picture and have been found as far away as southern India. Later emperors continued Augustus's building projects in Rome and throughout the empire. Vespasian built the Colosseum, which could seat 50,000 people; Trajan, the Forum with a number of different buildings and an enormous 125-foot column with his statue on top; Hadrian, the Pantheon and a wall dividing England and Scotland. The emperor Nero may have even ordered part of Rome burned to make room for his urban renewal projects.

Augustus's successors also continued his centralization of power. His stepson Tiberius stripped the assemblies of their right to elect magistrates, and later emperors took this power away from the senate as well. Bureaucrats appointed by the emperor oversaw the grain trade, the army, and the collection of taxes, with the senate gradually dwindling into a rubber stamp for the emperor's decisions. New territories were ruled directly by the emperor through governors and generals; in these jurisdictions, the senate did not have even the pretense of power.

The cult of ruler worship initiated somewhat tentatively in the provinces under Augustus grew enormously after his death, when, like Julius Caesar, he was declared a god. Though Romans officially deified only the *memory* of deceased emperors, some emperors were not willing to wait that long. Caligula declared himself a god at the age of twenty-five, spent much of his time in the temple of Castor and Pollux, and talked to the statue of Jupiter as an equal. Though Caligula was probably insane and later was stabbed to death, ruler worship in general was serious business for most Romans, closely linked as it was to tradition and patriotism. Groups like the Christians who did not offer sacrifices to the emperor or at least to the emperor's "genius" were felt to be unpatriotic, disloyal, and probably traitorous.

Thus in many ways Augustus laid the foundation for the success and durability of his empire. Historians have always been fascinated with the demise of the Roman Empire, but considering the fact that it lasted more than 400 years after Augustus in western Europe—and, in a significantly altered form, almost 1,500 years in eastern Europe—a more appropriate question might be why it lasted so long. Though the weaknesses that led to the empire's eventual collapse were also outgrowths of the reign of Augustus, the latter still represents a remarkable success story.

We must be careful of attributing too much to one man, however. As we have seen, Augustus had an extremely effective network of supporters and advisers, including Rome's most important men of letters. Their rendering of the glories of Roman civilization and the brilliance of Augustus has shaped much of what has been written about Rome since; you may only need to check the adjectives used in your text to describe Augustus to confirm this. Myths or exaggerations told about a ruler die hard, especially those that have been repeated for nearly 2,000 years.

CHAPTER FIVE

INVADING BARBARIANS

In surveying the world around them, the ancient Greeks often conceptualized things in dichotomies, or sets of opposites: light/dark, hot/cold, wet/dry, mind/body, male/female, and so on. One of their key dichotomies was Greek/non-Greek, and the Greeks coined the word "barbaros" for those whose native language was not Greek, because they seemed to the Greeks to be speaking nonsense syllables—*bar, bar, bar.* ("Bar-bar" is the Greek equivalent to "blah-blah" or "yada-yada.") *Barbaros* originally meant simply someone who did not speak Greek, but gradually it also implied someone who was unruly, savage, and more primitive than those in the advanced civilization of Greece. The word brought this meaning with it when it came into Latin and other European languages, and the Romans referred to those who lived beyond the northeastern boundary of Roman territory as "barbarians."

The Romans, and later others who lived along the Mediterranean, had many opportunities to talk about barbarians, because for at least a thousand years "invading barbarians" were a key feature of European history. From the first century through the eleventh, groups moving west and south migrated into, attacked, and sometimes conquered the more urbanized and densely populated areas near the Mediterranean. These barbarians challenged the armies, political institutions, and traditions of more settled states.

The first barbarians to prove a serious threat to Rome were peoples who spoke Germanic languages, often referred to as the "Germanic tribes." As they expanded their empire northward, the Romans built forts and walls as defenses against outsiders, but they also accepted non-Romans as recruits into the army. The population in the border areas became a mixture of Romans and various other groups, including many who spoke Germanic languages. In the middle of the third century, Germanic peoples under their own leaders moved across the Roman fortifications along the Rhine and Danube Rivers, meeting little resistance from Roman armies, whose soldiers were often Germanic already and whose leaders were frequently more interested in power struggles against other generals than in defending the border. Germanic groups were pushed by nomadic peoples moving westward across the Asian steppes, especially the Alans and the Huns, who also attacked the Roman Empire directly.

In the late third and early fourth centuries, the Roman emperors Diocletian and Constantine were able to reassert Roman power, to a large degree by dividing the empire into two parts to rule it more effectively. By the later fourth century, however, Germanic groups often known by tribal names such as Visigoths, Vandals, Suevi, Burgundians, Saxons, and Franks resumed their pulling apart of the Roman Empire, particularly its western half. They fought with each other as well, with Franks fighting Alamanni in Gaul, Visigoths fighting Vandals in the Iberian peninsula and across North Africa, Angles and Saxons fighting Celtic-speaking Britons in England, and Lombards fighting Ostrogoths in Italy. Under the leadership of their warrior-king Attila, the Huns swept into central Europe again, attacking Roman settlements in the Balkans and Germanic settlements along the Danube and Rhine Rivers. Various Germanic armies sacked the city of Rome several times during the fifth century—the word "vandalism" probably comes from the Vandals' plundering of Rome in 455—and in 476 one of their chieftains, Odoacer, deposed the weak emperor ruling in Rome, ending the Roman Empire in the west. The Germanic tribes established loose kingdoms in different parts of the western Roman Empire, though most of these were quite short-lived, with alliances frequently broken and renegotiated.

In the eastern half of the Roman Empire, later known as the Byzantine Empire, migrations and invasions of Germanic-speaking peoples were accompanied by similar movements of Slavic-speaking peoples from areas north of the Black Sea westward toward the Baltic and the Balkans, and northward into Russia and the Ukraine. These Slavic-speaking peoples later divided linguistically into groups such as Slovaks, Serbs, Poles, Croats, Czechs, Belorussians, and many others. In addition, Huns and other peoples from the central Asian steppes such as the Alans, Avars, Bulghars, and Khazars also raided the territory of the Byzantine Empire in the sixth century, at times approaching the walls of Constantinople. Despite these attacks, the Byzantine Empire survived until the fifteenth century, in part because the location and fortifications of Constantinople made the city almost impossible to capture, and in part because various emperors made strategic treaties with barbarian leaders. Germanic, Slavic, and various steppe peoples settled within the borders of the Byzantine Empire, often intermarrying; missionaries sent from Constantinople slowly converted them to Christianity.

In western Europe, the most successful Germanic kingdom was that of the Franks established in the sixth century, but in the ninth century the Frankish kingdoms themselves were threatened by new groups moving into western Europe from the north and east, just as the Roman Empire had been centuries earlier. These included Germanic

peoples who had been furthest from the Roman Empire during the previous period of migration, living in what is now Norway, Sweden, and Denmark. Like their earlier counterparts, these Germanic-speaking migrants, usually known as Vikings, first plundered and looted, stealing animals, precious metals, luxury goods, and people to be sold as slaves, but they then made alliances and established kingdoms in many places. Norwegian Vikings

[99]

moved further west than any Europeans had before, establishing permanent settlements on Iceland and short-lived settlements in Greenland and Newfoundland in what is now Canada. With fleets of more than one hundred highly maneuverable ships, Danish Vikings invaded northern France and were rewarded with land by the Frankish king Charles the Simple. They established the province of "Northmanland," or Normandy as it was later known, intermarrying with the local population and creating a distinctive Norman culture. From here they sailed around Spain and into the Mediterranean, eventually conquering Sicily from the Muslim Arabs in 1060, while other Normans crossed the English Channel, defeating Anglo-Saxon forces in 1066.

Swedish Vikings moved eastward, sailing up and down the rivers of Russia and portaging between them to the Black and Caspian Seas. They ultimately made it to Constantinople and cities along the southern shore of the Caspian Sea, which they raided and looted several times in the tenth century, taking booty and slaves. As in the west, raids for plunder gradually turned into trading missions, and the Vikings established settlements, intermarried, and assimilated with Slavic peoples. They formed a confederation of territories known as Rus with its capital at Kiev in modern-day Ukraine, which was at its most powerful in the late tenth and eleventh centuries. The word "Russia" comes from "Rus," though the origins of "Rus" are hotly debated, with some historians linking it with Swedish words and others with Slavic. Whatever the origins of

the word, Rus, like the western European Germanic kingdoms, did not last very long as a unified state.

Along with Vikings, central European steppe peoples known as Magyars also moved westward in Europe in the ninth century, crossing the Danube, attacking villages, gaining wealth, taking captives, and forcing leaders to pay tribute in an effort to prevent looting and destruction. Small groups of Magyars riding swift horses raided as far west as Spain and the Atlantic coast. Because of their skill with horses and their eastern origins, they were often identified with the earlier Huns by those they conquered, and so were called "Hungarians." Though the Magyars originated far west of the Mongolian homeland of the Huns and are probably unrelated ethnically, the name "Hungarians" stuck, and the state that developed in this area became known as Hungary. Like the Danish Vikings in Normandy and the Swedish Vikings in Rus, the Magyars intermarried with people already in the area, which included Germanic, Slavic, and other ethnic groups.

The invading barbarians have generally left little historical record themselves, but Roman and later other commentators had plenty to say about them. Your task in this chapter will be to use writings and visual evidence from nearly a thousand years to investigate portrayals of and attitudes toward barbarians coming from the north and east. What continuities and changes do you see in the depictions of barbarians written or drawn by people living in more settled areas to the south? How are these influenced by the author's or artist's own background and point of view?

SOURCES AND METHOD

The questions for this chapter ask you to assess various individuals' perceptions and attitudes, so you will be working in the realm of intellectual and cultural history. Since the sources that you will be using are descriptions and depictions of *people* rather than discussions of more abstract philosophical, religious, or cultural issues, they may be easier to understand than some sources in intellectual history. It is important to keep in mind, however, that we are always looking at *ideas* about those people: that is, at perceptions of barbarians in the minds of outsiders. All of the sources in this chapter were produced by educated men viewing barbarians coming from the north and east from the perspective of their own more established culture. Using a single type of source would be a problem if we were trying to learn all we could about a specific barbarian group, but our task here is different. In assessing continuities and change over time, it is important to have sources that are relatively comparable, for what might otherwise seem like a dramatic change may be due primarily to differences in source materials.

Your primary method in this chapter is careful reading and examination of the source materials. As you read the written sources, make a list of the words each author uses to describe the barbarians he encounters or has learned about. What qualities does he highlight? What seems to him to be particularly praiseworthy about

barbarian customs and practices? What disgusts or horrifies him? This list will serve as the basis for your comparisons, so the fuller it is, the better.

Source 1 is a selection from *Germania,* a description of the Germanic tribes written by the Roman lawyer, politician, and historian Tacitus (ca 56–ca 117). Tacitus never traveled in areas with a significant Germanic population, but he took his information from earlier writers who had, and perhaps from soldiers or merchants who had gone beyond the borders of the Roman Empire. The first part of *Germania* is a general description of Germanic laws and customs, and the second a more specialized discussion of different tribes, beginning with those closest to the Roman Empire and ending with those farthest away, about whom Tacitus had the least information. How does Tacitus describe the Germans physically? What character traits does he mention? How does he compare their actions while fighting and while not fighting? What does he say about the key qualities of their leaders? About the way leaders are chosen? About the ways young people are taught traditions and customs? What does he choose to highlight about the three different tribes, the Chatti, the Chauci, and the Fenni?

Source 2 is a selection from *The History,* written by Ammianus Marcellinus (ca 325–ca 391), a Roman military leader who fought in the armies of several emperors against Germanic tribes, steppe peoples, and Persians. On leaving active duty, he wrote a history of the Roman Empire from A.D. 96 to 378, though the first part of this

[101]

work has been lost. In the sections that survive, Ammianus Marcellinus describes different barbarian groups, many of whom he had met, and some of whom he had fought against. In this section, he discusses two groups of steppe peoples: the Huns, who probably originated in Mongolia, and the Alans, who came from somewhat further west in central Asia. What physical traits does he discuss? What does he think about their clothing and houses? About their qualities as warriors? About their child-rearing practices? What do the two tribes share, and on what points do they differ, in Ammianus Marcellinus's eyes?

Ammianus Marcellinus fought in what became the Byzantine Empire, which continued to experience attacks by various groups long after the fall of the Roman Empire in the west. Sources 3 and 4 offer Byzantine perspectives. Source 3 comes from *The Histories* written by the historian and poet Agathias in the mid-sixth century, describing recent encounters between forces of the Byzantine Emperor Justinian (r. 527–565) and various Germanic tribes in what is now Italy and Germany. In this section Agathias describes the Franks and the Alamanni. What does he find particularly worthy of praise in Frankish culture? Of blame in Alamanni? What practices does he find unusual in both groups? How do you think the fact that Agathias was a Christian influenced his opinions? How does he justify making comments about barbarian groups?

Source 4 comes from the *Manual of Strategy*, attributed to the Byzantine emperor Maurice (r. 582–602), who led campaigns himself against the Persians, Avars, and Slavs. In this handbook of military strategy written in common, everyday Greek, Maurice (or whoever actually wrote it) discusses battle formations, drills, tactics, supplies, and other practical matters. He also describes various groups that threatened Byzantium, including the Scythians (a term he uses to mean any of the steppe peoples such as Huns, Avars, Bulgars, Turks, and Khazars), the "light-haired people" such as Franks, Lombards, and other Germanic tribes, and the Slavs. What positive and negative qualities does Maurice choose to emphasize in these three groups? Which group appears to have gained his greatest respect? How does his position as a military commander shape his point of view?

Shortly after the rule of Emperor Maurice, the Byzantine Empire faced a threat that would be much more serious than the attacks of Germans, Slavs, and steppe peoples. Beginning in the 630s, Arabic forces inspired by the new religion of Islam swept out of the Arabian peninsula, conquering northern Africa, most of the Iberian peninsula, the eastern Mediterranean, and the Persian Empire centered on the Tigris and Euphrates valleys. Within a hundred years, Muslim leaders ruled much of what had been Roman territory and continued to attack Byzantine territories in Anatolia (modern-day Turkey). The Byzantines were able to prevent being completely overrun by allying with the "barbarian" Bulghars and also by the invention of "Greek fire," a burning chemical compound similar to napalm that could not be put out by water.

Western European and Byzantine attitudes toward the Muslims were extremely hostile, but they were somewhat different than their attitudes toward various barbarians, for the Muslims came from areas that included major cities and long-standing intellectual traditions, not from unsettled frontiers. As their states expanded, however, Muslims came into direct contact with the same groups that confronted the Romans and later the Byzantines: Germanic- and Slavic-speaking peoples and horse-riding steppe nomads. Like Roman and Byzantine historians and military leaders, merchants and travelers from the world of Islam frequently described the groups they encountered, in some cases providing the first written record of these peoples. Just as earlier Mediterranean writers had, they viewed these northern barbarians with a point of view shaped by their own more sophisticated, urbanized, and developed culture.

Sources 5 and 6 come from the Muslim world. In the 920s, the Muslim diplomat and missionary Ibn Fadlan was sent from the court of the caliph in Baghdad to the kingdom of the Bulghars on the upper Volga River (modern-day Tatarstan, a part of the Russian Federation). He traveled with trade caravans of merchants and described different groups he met on his journey, including Bulghars, Turkic-speaking tribes, and Rus. Source 5 is from Ibn Fadlan's eyewitness account of the Rus, written in Arabic. Scholars disagree about whether the Rus that Ibn Fadlan met were purely Swedish Vikings or a mixture of Swedes, Slavs, Finns, and others, but whatever their exact origin, they were certainly different from any people Ibn Fadlan had met before. How does he describe them? What does he think about their personal habits? What does the scene he describes at the cremation ceremony reveal?

In the 960s, Ibrahim Ibn Jakub, a highly educated Jew from the Muslim caliphate of Córdoba in Spain, traveled throughout northern Europe. Source 6 is from his report, written originally in Arabic and included as part of the Spanish Arab geographer and historian Abu Abdullah al-Bakri's *Book of Highways and of Kingdoms*. The first section comes from his description of the Christian kingdoms of northern Spain, and the second from his description of Cracow, in today's Poland. Ibn Jakub's comments on Cracow, and also on the Czech city of Prague, are the first written references to these cities in any language and thus some of the earliest documentary evidence about northern Slavs. How does he describe the inhabitants of northern Spain, who were primarily Frankish and other Germanic tribes? What does he see as praiseworthy, and what does he criticize? How does he describe the realm of the northern Slavs, ruled by Mesko (Mieszko in Polish)? What does he find worthy of comment?

Source 7 comes from the area in which Emperor Maurice fought and Ibn Fadlan traveled. It is a golden bottle with a picture of a Bulghar horseman holding a captive, found along with many other gold objects at

Nagyszentmiklós (today Sînicolaul Mare, Romania). The stash included objects with Greek, Turkish, and probably Viking inscriptions, and it seems to have been buried during a Hungarian invasion of the late ninth century. It is unclear exactly who made this or the rest of the gold objects, but it was clearly a very skilled goldsmith. What impression does the artist give of Bulghar horsemen on this bottle?

While Swedish Vikings traveled down the Volga, Norwegian Vikings traveled west. In 793, they attacked the isolated monastery on Lindisfarne Island off northern England. The English scholar and church official Alcuin of York, who came from an area near Lindisfarne but who was then living at Charlemagne's court on the continent, heard about this and commented, "Never before has such terror appeared in Britain. . . behold the church of St. Cuthbert [at Lindisfarne monastery] spattered with the blood of the priests of God, despoiled of all its ornaments." Source 8 is a fragment from a gravestone on Lindisfarne, depicting what is most likely a group of Viking warriors. As with Source 7, we do not know for sure who made this, but it dates from the time of the Viking raids. How does the stone-carver portray the Viking fighters?

By the late tenth century, Viking raids had turned into trading missions or campaigns of conquest, and Christian missionaries were active in the far north. Source 9, the final source in this chapter, comes from a history of the archbishops of Hamburg-Bremen (now in northern Germany) written in the 1070s by a learned author and cleric from southern Germany now generally called Adam of Bremen. Adam draws on some of the sources you have already read in this chapter—the first part of his history includes many long quotes from Tacitus's *Germania*—and also on his personal contacts in Bremen. Because the archbishops of Hamburg-Bremen were charged with converting Scandinavians and Slavs to Christianity, Adam was especially interested in what the people who lived farther north were like. To learn about them, he became acquainted with Sven Estrithson, the king of the Danes, who by this time had converted to Christianity. The section included here, on Swedes and Norwegians, thus involves many layers of looking northward, as it was written by a southern German, now living in northern Germany, relying on a Dane for information about people who lived still farther north. What does Adam see as noteworthy among the Swedes and Norwegians? How are these two groups alike, and how are they different, in Adam's opinion?

From your analysis of the evidence, you now have a very long list of words that different authors use to describe barbarians. To assess continuities, identify descriptive words that have come up again and again, creating an image of what we might call the stereotypical barbarian. In the minds of more sophisticated southerners, did male barbarians look a certain way? Did female? Did they dress or act a certain way? What differences do the authors see between northern barbarians, such as the Germanic tribes and Vikings, and eastern barbarians, such as the Huns and Avars? Or between barbarians that live closer to them and those that live further away? Do the various descriptions seem to fall into multiple patterns, what we might call the "good barbarians" and the "bad barbarians"? Once you have identified continuities, now turn to changes. What elements in these descriptions and depictions change significantly over the thousand years of the sources?

The second question asks you to consider the role that the author's or artist's point of view played in shaping his perception of barbarians. You can also think of this as a question about continuities and changes, that is, about similarities and differences among the authors. You already know some important similarities among the authors: they all come from urbanized cultures that had long traditions of written law and literature. They all saw themselves as different from barbarians, and they wrote in languages other than those spoken by the barbarians they were describing. In fact, probably none of them even *spoke* the language of the people they wrote about. How might the fact that the authors all saw a distinction between their own culture and that of the barbarians have shaped their impressions? What other similarities among the authors would have shaped their point of view?

The authors and artists were not exactly alike, of course. Sources 1 and 2 were produced by pagans, Sources 3, 4, 8, and 9 by Christians, Source 6 by a Jew, and Source 5 by a Muslim. (We have no way of knowing the religion of the artist who made Source 7.) How might these religious differences have influenced the qualities they chose to discuss? Ibn Fadlan and Adam of Bremen were both interested in converting pagan barbarians to their own monotheistic religions. How might this have shaped their opinions?

Another difference is the political setting in which the author or artist worked. Tacitus (Source 1) wrote at the height of the Roman Empire's power, Ammianus Marcellinus (Source 2) when the empire was under grave threats, Agathius and Maurice (Sources 3 and 4) when the western empire no longer existed. How might this have shaped their descriptions? How might the swiftness with which the Arabs had conquered North Africa and the eastern Mediterranean have affected the perceptions of Ibn Fadlan and Ibrahim Ibn Jakub (Sources 5 and 6)? How might the recent events at Lindisfarne have influenced the sculptor of the tombstone? The authors also differed in terms of occupation, which determined the setting in which they interacted with barbarians. Ammianus Marcellinus and Maurice were generals, Ibn Fadlan and Ibrahim Ibn Jakub were diplomats, Adam of Bremen was a cleric, and Tacitus was a lawyer and writer who never actually met the people he was describing. What difference might these factors have made? What other differences do you see among the authors, and how might these have affected their perceptions?

[105]

Source 1 from Tacitus, Agricola, Germany, and Dialogue on Orators, *translated by Herbert W. Benario. Copyright © 1967 by the Bobbs-Merrill Company, Inc. New edition copyright © 1991 by the University of Oklahoma Press, Norman, Publishing Division of the University. Reprinted by permission of Hackett Publishing Company, Inc., and the translator. All rights reserved.*

1. Tacitus, *Germania,* ca A.D. 100

I personally incline to the views of those who think that the peoples of Germany have not been polluted by any marriages with other tribes and that they have existed as a particular people, pure and only themselves. As a result, all have the same bodily appearance, as far as is possible in so large a number of men: fiery blue eyes, red hair, large bodies which are strong only for violent exertion. There is no comparable endurance of hardship and labors and they do not endure thirst and heat at all, but they have become accustomed to cold and hunger from their climate and soil. . . .

They pick their kings on the basis of noble birth, their generals on the basis of bravery. . . .[T]hey bear into battle certain images and emblems that have been removed from sacred groves; and, what is a particular incitement to bravery, neither chance nor a miscellaneous grouping brings about the cavalry or infantry formation, but families and clans; and close by are their dear ones, whence are heard the wailings of women and the crying of children. These are each man's most sacred witnesses, these are his greatest supporters: it is to their mothers and to their wives that they bring their wounds; and the women do not quake to count or examine their blows, and they furnish sustenance and encouragement to the fighters.

When they have come into battle, it is shameful for the chieftain to be excelled in valor, shameful for the entourage not to match the valor of the chieftain. Furthermore, it is shocking and disgraceful for all of one's life to have survived one's chieftain and left the battle: the prime obligation of the entourage's allegiance is to protect and guard him and to credit their own brave deeds to his glory: the chieftains fight for victory, the entourage for the chieftain. If the state in which they were born should be drowsing in long peace and leisure, many noble young men of their own accord seek those tribes which are then waging some war, since quiet is displeasing to the race and they become famous more easily in the midst of dangers, and one would not maintain a large retinue except by violence and war. . . .

Whenever they are not involved in wars, they devote little time to hunting, much more to leisure, with attention focused on sleep and food, all the bravest and most warlike men doing nothing, with the care of the home and household and fields assigned to the women and the old men and the most feeble of the family: they themselves lounge around, by an extraordinary contradiction of nature, since the same men so love inactivity and hate peace. . . .

[106]

They live with chastity secured, corrupted by no attractions of games, by no seductions of banquets. Men and women are alike ignorant of secret correspondence. Although their population is so great, there are very few cases of adultery....There no one laughs at vices, and corruption and being corrupted are not excused by invoking the "times." ...

In every home the young, naked and dirty, grow to possess these limbs, these bodies, which we admire. His own mother nurses each one, and the children are not handed over to servants or nursemaids. You would not distinguish master and slave by any niceties of upbringing: they live amidst the same animals and on the same ground until age sets the freeborn apart and valor recognizes them as her own. The young men experience love late, and for this reason their strength is not exhausted. Nor are the girls hurried into marriage; they have the same youthful vigor and similar stature: they are well matched in age and strength when they enter upon marriage, and the children reproduce the strength of their parents.

[Tacitus then describes different Germanic tribes.]

The Chatti tribe is distinguished by hardier bodies, sinewy limbs, a threatening countenance, and greater liveliness of mind. Inasmuch as they are Germans, they have considerable judgment and skill: they choose their commanders and obey them, know how to keep their ranks, recognize opportunities, delay their attacks, map out the day, entrench themselves at night, consider fortune doubtful but bravery sure. . . .

The following custom, rarely practiced by the other German peoples and dependent upon the personal daring of each individual, is general among the Chatti, namely to let their hair and beard grow long as soon as they have reached maturity and not to cut off the face's garb, which is vowed and owed to bravery, unless they have slain an enemy. They uncover their brows while standing over his bloody, despoiled corpse and claim that they have at last paid back the debt of their birth and have thus shown themselves worthy of country and parents. That shaggy filth remains for the cowardly and unwarlike. . . .

[The Chauci] are the noblest people among the Germans and of such character that they prefer to look out for their greatness with fair play. Without greed, without violent passion, quiet and off by themselves, they bring about no wars, lay no one waste by rapine or robbery. This is particular proof of their high character and strength, that they do not gain their superiority through aggression; nonetheless, all have their arms at hand and, if a situation demands it, there is an army, very powerful in men and horses; and they have the same renown when they are at peace. . . .

. . . The Fenni have astonishing savagery and squalid poverty: there are no arms, no horses, no household; herbs serve as their food, hides as their clothing, the ground as their bed; their only hopes are in their arrows, which they point with bones in the absence of iron. And the same hunt feeds men and women alike; for the latter accompany the men everywhere and claim their part in catching the spoil. The children have no other protection against wild animals and rains than being placed under some intertwined branches: to this hut the young men return, this is their refuge when they are old. But they think it a happier state than to groan over the working of fields, to struggle at homebuilding, to deal with their own fortunes and those of others with hope and fear: without concern in their relations with men as well as with gods, they have attained a most difficult thing, not to have the need even to express a wish.

Source 2 reprinted by permission of the publishers and the Trustees of the Loeb Classical Library ® from Ammianus Marcelenius: Volume I, Loeb Classical Library ® Volume 300, translated by John C. Rolfe, Cambridge, Mass.: Harvard University Press, Copyright © 1935, 1950 by the President and Fellows of Harvard College. The Loeb Classical Library ® is a registered trademark of the President and Fellows of Harvard College.

2. Ammianus Marcellinus, *The History*, ca A.D. 380

The people of the Huns, but little known from ancient records, dwelling beyond the Maeotic Sea near the ice-bound ocean, exceed every degree of savagery. Since there the cheeks of the children are deeply furrowed with the steel from their very birth, in order that the growth of hair, when it appears at the proper time, may be checked by the wrinkled sears, they grow old without beards and without any beauty, like eunuchs. They all have compact, strong limbs and thick necks, and are so monstrously ugly and misshapen, that one might take them for two-legged beasts or for the stumps, rough-hewn into images, that are used in putting sides to bridges. But although they have the form of men, however ugly, they are so hardy in their mode of life that they have no need of fire nor of savory food, but eat the roots of wild plants and the half-raw flesh of any kind of animal whatever, which they put between their thighs and the backs of their horses, and thus warm it a little. They are never protected by any buildings, but they avoid these like tombs, which are set apart from everyday use. For not even a hut thatched with reed can be found among them. But roaming at large amid the mountains and woods, they learn from the cradle to endure cold, hunger, and thirst. When away from their homes they never enter a house unless compelled by extreme necessity; for they think they are not safe when staying under a roof. They dress in linen cloth or in the skins of field-mice sewn together, and they wear the same clothing indoors and out. But when they have once put their necks into a faded tunic, it is not taken off or changed until by long wear and tear it has been reduced to rags and fallen from them bit by bit. They cover their heads with round caps and protect their hairy legs with goatskins; their shoes are formed upon no lasts, and so prevent their walking with free stop. For this reason they are not at all adapted to battles on foot, but they are almost glued to their horses, which are hardy, it is true, but ugly, and sometimes they sit them woman-fashion and thus perform their ordinary tasks. From their horses by night or day every one of that nation buys and sells, eats and drinks, and bowed over the narrow neck of the animal relaxes into a sleep so deep as to be accompanied by many dreams. And when deliberation is called for about weighty matters, they all consult as a common body in that fashion [on horseback]. They are subject to no royal restraint, but they are content with the disorderly government of their important men, and led by them they force their way through every obstacle. They also sometimes fight when provoked, and then they enter the battle drawn up in wedge-shaped masses, while their medley of voices makes a savage noise. And as they lightly equipped for swift motion, and unexpected in action, they purposely divide suddenly into scattered hands and attack, rushing about in disorder here and there, dealing terrific slaughter; and because of their extraordinary rapidity of movement they are never seen to attack a rampart or pillage an enemy's camp. And on this account you would not hesitate to call them the most terrible of all warriors, because they fight from a distance with missiles having sharp bone, instead of their usual [metal] points, joined to the shafts with wonderful skill; then they gallop over the intervening spaces and fight hand to hand with swords, regardless of their own lives; and while the enemy are guarding against wounds from the sabre-thrusts, they throw strips of cloth plaited into nooses over their opponents and so entangle them that they fetter their limbs and take from them the power of riding or walking. No one in their country ever plows a field or touches a plow-handle. They are all without fixed abode, without hearth, or law, or settled mode of life, and keep roaming from place to place, like fugitives, accompanied by the wagons in which they live; in wagons their wives weave for them their hideous garments, in wagons they cohabit with their husbands, bear children, and rear them to the age of puberty. None of their offspring, when asked, can tell you where he comes from, since he was conceived in one place, born far from there, and brought up still farther away. In truces they are faithless and unreliable, strongly inclined to sway to the motion of every breeze of new hope that presents itself, and sacrificing every feeling to the mad impulse of the moment. Like unreasoning beasts, they are utterly ignorant of the difference between right and wrong; they are deceitful and ambiguous in speech, never bound by any reverence for religion or for superstition. They burn with an infinite thirst for gold, and they are so fickle and prone to anger, that they often quarrel with their allies without provocation, more than once on the same day, and make friends with them again without a mediator.

This race of untamed men, without encumbrances, aflame with an inhuman desire for plundering others' property, made their violent way amid the rapine and slaughter of the neighbouring peoples as far as the Halani [Alans]. . . .

. . . [The Alans] have no huts and care nothing for using the plowshare, but they live upon flesh and an abundance of milk, and dwell in wagons, which they cover with rounded canopies of bark and drive over the boundless wastes. And when they come to a place rich in grass, they place their carts in a circle and feed like wild beasts. As soon as the fodder is used up, they place their cities, as we might call them, on the wagons and so convey them: in the wagons the males have intercourse with the women, and in the wagons their babes are born and reared; wagons form their permanent dwellings, and wherever they come, that place they look upon as their natural home. Driving their plow-cattle before them, they pasture them with their flocks, and they give particular attention to breeding horses. In that land the fields are always green, and here and there are places set thick with fruit trees. Hence, wherever they go, they lack neither food for themselves nor fodder for their cattle, because of the moist soil and the numerous courses of rivers that flow hard by them. Therefore, all those who through age or sex are unfit for war remain close by the wagons and are occupied in light tasks; but the young men grow up in the habit of riding from their earliest boyhood and regard it as contemptible to go on foot; and by various forms of training they are all skilled warriors. . . .

Moreover, almost all the Halani [Alans] are tall and handsome, their hair inclines to blond, by the ferocity of their glance they inspire dread, subdued though it is. They are light and active in the use of arms. In all respects they are somewhat like the Huns, but in their manner of life and their habits they are less savage. . . . Just as quiet and peaceful men find pleasure in rest, so the Halani delight in danger and warfare. There the man is judged happy who has sacrificed his life in battle, while those who grow old and depart from the world by a natural death they assail with bitter reproaches, as degenerate and cowardly; and there is nothing in which they take more pride than in killing any man whatever: as glorious spoils of the slain they tear off their heads, then strip off their skins and hang them upon their war-horses as trappings. . . . They choose as chiefs those men who are conspicuous for long experience as warriors.

Source 3 from Agathias—The Histories. Translated with an introduction and short explanatory notes by Joseph D. Frendo. Berlin Walter de Gruyter. Copyright © 1975. Reprinted by permission of Walter de Gruyter.

3. Agathias, *The Histories,*
ca A.D. 570

The Franks have a common frontier with Italy. They may reasonably be identified with the people who in ancient times were called "Germans," since they inhabit the banks of the Rhine and the surrounding territory, and though they occupy most of Gaul, it is a later acquisition since they did not previously live there. . . . But even now it does not seem to fall short at all of the dignity of its ancient inhabitants, for the Franks are not nomads, as indeed some barbarian peoples are, but their system of government, administration and laws are modelled more or less on the Roman pattern, apart from which they uphold similar standards with regard to contracts, marriage and religious observance. They are in fact all Christians and adhere to the strictest orthodoxy. They also have magistrates in their cities and priests and celebrate the feasts in the same way as we do, and, for a barbarian people, strike me as extremely well-bred and civilised and as practically the same as ourselves except for their uncouth style of dress and peculiar language. I admire them for their other attributes and especially for the spirit of justice and harmony which prevails amongst them. Although on many occasions in the past and even during my own lifetime their kingdom has been divided between three or more rulers they have never yet waged war against one another or seen fit to stain their country's honour by the slaughter of their kith and kin. And yet whenever great powers are seen to have reached a state of parity, arrogant and uncompromising attitudes are inevitably engendered and the logical outcome is rivalry, the lust for domination and a host of other passions that constitute a fertile breeding-ground for unrest and dissension. Nevertheless nothing of the kind occurs in their case no matter how many different kingdoms they are split up into. In the rare event of some dispute arising between their kings they draw themselves up ostensibly in battle formation and with the apparent object of deciding the issue by force of arms and then confront one another. But once the main body of the army on either side has come face to face they immediately lay aside all animosity, return to mutual understanding and enjoin their leaders to settle their differences by arbitration, or failing that by placing their own lives at stake in single combat. For it is not right, they say, or in keeping with ancestral precedent for the common good to suffer injury and upheaval on account of some personal feud of theirs. The immediate result is that they break their ranks and lay down their arms. Peace and quiet are restored, normal communications resumed and the horrors of war are forgotten. So law-abiding therefore and public spirited are the subject classes and so docile and amenable to reason, when need be, are their masters. It is for this reason that the basis of their power remains secure and their government stable and that they have not lost any of their territory but have actually increased it greatly. When justice and amity are second nature to a people then their state is guaranteed happiness and stability and rendered impregnable to enemy attack.

So, living this virtuous life, the Franks rule over their own people and their neighbors, the succession passing from father to son. . . .

. . . [I]t is the practice of the Frankish kings never to have their hair cut. It is never cut from childhood onwards and each individual lock hangs right down over the shoulders, since the front ones are parted on the forehead and hang down on either side. It is not, however, like that of the Turks and Avars, unkempt, dry and dirty and tied up in an unsightly knot. On the contrary they treat it with all kinds of soap and comb it very carefully. Custom has reserved this practice for royalty as a sort of distinctive badge and prerogative. Subjects have their hair cut all round, and are strictly forbidden to grow it any longer. . . .

. . . The Alamanni, if we are to take the word of Asinius Quadratus, an Italian who wrote an accurate account of German affairs, are a mixed and mongrel people. . . .

They have their own traditional way of life too, but in matters of government and public administration they follow the Frankish system, religious observance being the only exception. They worship certain trees, the waters of rivers, hills

[111]

and mountain valleys, in whose honour they sacrifice horses, cattle and countless other animals by beheading them, and imagine that they are performing an act of piety thereby. But contact with the Franks is having a beneficial effect and is reforming them in this respect too; already it is influencing the more rational among them and it will not be long, I think, before a saner view wins universal acceptance. For the irrationality and folly of their beliefs can hardly fail, I think, to strike even those who practise them, unless they happen to be complete fools, and as such can easily be eradicated. All those who do not attain to the truth merit pity rather than censure and fully deserve to be forgiven. It is not, after all, of their own accord that they fall into error, but in their search for moral goodness they form a wrong judgment, and there after cling tenaciously to whatever conclusions they have arrived at. Yet I am not sure that words are a sufficient remedy for the savagery and depravity of sacrificial worship, whether it be paid to groves as is indeed the case among barbarians, or to the so-called gods of antiquity as was the way with the rites of the Greeks. I am of the opinion that there is no being which delights in bloodstained altars and the brutal slaughter of animals. If there is a being capable of accepting such practices then it could not be beneficent and benign but would in all probability be a malignant, maniacal creature. . . . Some readers may consider that I have no business to make such remarks in a book of this kind, that they are uncalled for and irrelevant to my avowed intent. But for my part it gives me great pleasure to bring to light all the facts that come to my knowledge, to praise what is good about them, and to castigate openly and to expose their bad and unsatisfactory side. Indeed, if the writing of history were just a simple and uncritical narration of events without the redeeming feature of serving as a guide to life, then it might, perhaps, be rated scarcely any higher by some (I hope the expression is not too strong) than a collection of old wives' tales.

Source 4 from Maurices' Strategikon: Handbook of Byzantine Military Strategy, *translated by George T. Dennis pp. 116–121. Copyright © 1984. Reprinted by permission of the University of Pennsylvania Press.*

4. Maurice, *Strategikon,*
ca A.D. 600

DEALING WITH THE SCYTHIANS, THAT IS, AVARS, TURKS, AND OTHERS WHOSE WAY OF LIFE RESEMBLES THAT OF THE HUNNISH PEOPLES

The Scythian nations are one, so to speak, in their mode of life and in their organization, which is primitive and includes many people. Of these peoples only the Turks and the Avars concern themselves with military organization, and this makes them stronger than the other Scythian nations when it comes to pitched battles. The nation of the Turks is very numerous and independent. They are not versatile or skilled in most human endeavors, nor have they trained themselves for anything else except to conduct themselves bravely against their enemies. The Avars, for their part are scoundrels, devious, and very experienced in military matters.

These nations have a monarchical form of government, and their rulers subject them to cruel punishments for their mistakes. Governed not by love but by fear, they steadfastly hear labors and hardships. They endure heat and cold, and the want of many necessities, since they are nomadic peoples. They are very superstitious, treacherous, foul, faithless, possessed by an insatiate desire for riches. They scorn their oath, do not observe agreements, and are not satisfied by gifts. Even before they accept the gift, they are making plans for treachery and betrayal of their agreements. They are clever at estimating suitable opportunities to do this and taking prompt advantage of them. They prefer to prevail over their enemies not so much by force as by deceit, surprise attacks, and cutting off supplies. . . .

They prefer battles fought at long range, ambushes, encircling their adversaries, simulated retreats and sudden returns, and wedge-shaped formations, that is, in scattered groups. When they make their enemies take to flight, they put everything else aside, and are not content, as the Persians, the Romans, and other peoples, with pursuing them a reasonable distance and plundering their goods, but they do not let up at all until they have achieved the complete destruction of their enemies, and they employ every means to this end. . . .

They are seriously hurt by defections and desertions. They are very fickle, avaricious and, composed of so many as they are, they have no sense of kinship or unity with one another. If a few begin to desert and are well received, many more follow. . . .

DEALING WITH THE LIGHT-HAIRED PEOPLES, SUCH AS THE FRANKS, LOMBARDS, AND OTHERS LIKE THEM

The light-haired races place great value on freedom. They are bold and undaunted in battle. Daring and impetuous as they are, they consider any timidity and even a short retreat as a disgrace. They calmly despise death as they fight violently in hand-to-hand combat either on horseback or on foot. If they are hard pressed in cavalry actions, they dismount at a single prearranged sign and line up on foot. Although only a few against many horsemen, they do not shrink from the fight. They are armed with shields, lances, and short swords slung front their shoulders. They prefer fighting on foot and rapid charges.

Whether on foot or on horseback, they draw up for battle, not in any fixed measure and formation, or in regiments or divisions, but according to tribes, their kinship with one another, and common interest. Often, as a result, when things are not going well and their friends have been killed, they will risk their lives fighting to avenge them. In combat they make the front of their battle line even and dense. Either on horseback or on foot they are impetuous and undisciplined in charging, as if they were the only people in the world who are not cowards. They are disobedient to their leaders. They are not interested in anything that is at all complicated and pay little attention to external security and their own advantage. They despise good order, especially on horseback. They are easily corrupted by money, greedy as they are.

They are hurt by suffering and fatigue. Although they possess bold and daring spirits, their bodies are pampered and soft, and they are not able to bear pain calmly. In addition, they are hurt by heat, cold, rain, lack of provisions especially of wine, and postponement of battle. . . .

DEALING WITH THE SLAVS, THE ANTES, AND THE LIKE

The nations of the Slavs and the Antes live in the same way and have the same customs. They are both independent, absolutely refusing to be enslaved or governed, least of all in their own land. They are populous and hardy, bearing readily heat, cold, rain, nakedness, and scarcity of provisions.

They are kind and hospitable to travelers in their country and conduct them safely from one place to another, wherever they wish. If the stranger should suffer some harm because of his host's negligence, the one who first commended him will wage war against that host, regarding vengeance for the stranger as a religious duty. They do not keep those who are in captivity among them in perpetual slavery, as do other nations. But they set a definite period of time for them and then give them the choice either, if they so desire, to return to their own homes with a small recompense or to remain there as free men and friends.

They possess an abundance of all sorts of livestock and produce, which they store in heaps, especially common millet and Italian millet. Their women are more sensitive than any others in the world. When, for example, their husband dies, many look upon it as their own death and freely smother themselves, not wanting to continue their lives as widows.

They live among nearly impenetrable forests, rivers, lakes, and marshes, and have made the exits from their settlements branch out in many directions because of the dangers they might face. They bury their most valuable possessions in secret places, keeping nothing unnecessary in sight. They live like bandits and love to carry out attacks against their enemies in densely wooded, narrow, and steep places. They make effective use of ambushes, sudden attacks and raids, devising many different methods by night and by day. . . .

Owing to their lack of government and their ill feeling toward one another, they are not acquainted with an order of battle. They are also not prepared to fight a battle standing in close order, or to present themselves on open and level ground. If they do get up enough courage when the time comes to attack, they shout all together and move forward a short distance. If their opponents begin to give way at the noise, they attack violently; if not, they themselves turn around, not being anxious to experience the strength of the enemy at close range. They then run for the woods, where they have a great advantage because of their skill in fighting in such cramped quarters.

Source 5 from Ibn Fadlan and the Caliphal Mission through Inner Asia to the North: Voyaging the Volga. *Introduction and translation by James E. Montgomery. Reprinted with permission of James E. Montgomery.*

5. Ibn Fadlan's Account of His Travels to the Kingdom of the Bulghars 920s

I saw the Rūsiyyah when they has arrived on their trading expeditions and had disembarked at the River Āt.I. I have never seen more perfect physiques than theirs—they are like palm trees, are fair and reddish, and do not wear the *qurtaq* or the caftan. The man wears a cloak with which he covers one half of his body, leaving one of his arms uncovered. Every one of them carries an axe, a sword and a dagger and all of that which we have mentioned never parts from him. Their swords are Frankish, with broad, ridged blades. Each man, from the tip of his toes to his neck, is covered in dark [tatooed lines] trees, pictures and such like. Each woman has, on her breast, a small disc, tied [around her neck], made of either iron, silver, copper or gold, in relation to her husband's financial and social worth. Each disc has a ring to which a dagger is attached, also lying on her breast. Around their necks they wear hoops of gold and silver. . . . They are the filthiest of all Allāh's creatures: they do not purify themselves after excreting or urinating or wash themselves when in a state of ritual impurity [i.e., after coitus:] and do not [even] wash their hands after food. . . . They cannot, of course, avoid washing their faces and their heads each day, which they do with the filthiest and most polluted water imaginable. I shall explain. Every day the *jāriyah* [slave-girl] arrives in the morning with a large basin containing water which she hands to her master. He washes his hands and his face in the water, then he dips his comb in the water and brushes his hair, blow his nose and spits in the basin. There is no filthy impurity which he will not do in that water. When he no longer requires it, the *jāriyah* takes the basin to the man beside him and he goes through the same routine as his comrade. She continues to carry it from one man to the next until she has gone round everyone in the house, with each of them blowing his nose and spitting, washing his face and hair in the basin. . . .

It was said that when their chieftains die, the least thing they do is to burn [them], I was very keen to verify this, when I learned of the death of one of their great men. . . .

[Ibn Fadlan then watches a cremation, inn which the body of a chief and one of his slave girls are placed in a ship that is set on fire.]

Then the people came forward with sticks and firewood. Each one carried a stick the top of which he had set fire to and which he threw on top of the wood. The wood caught fire, and then the ship, the tent, the man, the *jāriyah* and all it contained. A dreadful wind arose and the flames of the fire grew in intensity and its blaze was fierce. One of the Rūsiyyah stood beside me and I heard him speaking to the interpreter who was with me. I quizzed him about that, and he replied, "He said, 'You Arab peoples are a foolish lot!'" So I said, "Why is that?" and he replied, "Because you purposely take him who is dearest to you and whom you hold in highest esteem and throw him in the soil, where he is eaten by the earth, by vermin and by worms, whereas we burn him in the fire there and then, so that he enters the Garden [Paradise] immediately and on the spot". Then he laughed loud and long. I quizzed him about that and he said. "Because of the love which my lord feels for him, he has sent the wind to take him away within an hour". In actual fact, it took scarcely an hour for the ship, the firewood, the *jāriyah* and her master to be burnt to an ash, then to a fine ash. Then they built something like a round hillock over the ship which they had pulled out of the water, and placed in the middle of it a large piece of wood, on which they wrote the name of the man and the name of the King of the Rūs. Then they left.

Source 6 from Christians and Moors in Spain, *Vol. 3, edited and translated by Charles Melville and Ahmad Ubaydli, pp. 53–54. Copyright © 1992. Reprinted by permission of Aris and Phillips, an imprint, of Oxbow Books.*

6. Ibrahim Ibn Jakub's description of Christian Spain and Poland, ca 960

The whole of Jilliqiyya [Christian Spain] is flat and most of the land is covered in sand. Their foodstuffs are mainly millet and sorghum and their normal drinks are apple cider and bushka, which is a drink made with flour (meal). The inhabitants are a treacherous people of depraved morals, who do not keep themselves clean and only wash once or twice a year in cold water. They do not wash their clothes once they have put them on until they fall to pieces on them, and assert that the filth that covers them thanks to their sweat is good for their bodies and keeps them healthy. Their clothes are very tight-fitting and have wide openings, through which most of their bodies show. They have great courage and do not contemplate flight when battle is joined, but rather consider death a lesser evil.

The lands of the Slavs stretch from the Syrian Sea to the Ocean in the north. . . . They comprise numerous tribes, each different from the other. . . . At present, there are four kings: the king of the Bulgars; Bojeslav, king of Faraga, Boiema and Karako; Mesko, king of the North; and Nakon on the border of the West. . . .

As far as the realm of Mesko is concerned, this is the most extensive of their lands. It produces an abundance of food, meat, honey, and fish. The taxes collected by the King from commercial goods are used for the support of his retainers. He keeps three thousand armed men divided into detachments. . . . and provides them with everything they need, clothing, horses, and weapons. . . . The dowry system is very important to the Slavs, and is similar to the customs of the Berbers. When a man possesses several daughters or a couple of sons, the former become a source of wealth, the latter a source of great prestige.

In general, the Slavs are violent, and inclined to aggression. If not for the disharmony amongst them, caused by the multiplication of factions and by their fragmentation into clans, no people could match their strength. They inhabit the richest limits of the lands suitable for settlement, and most plentiful in means of support. They are specially energetic in agriculture. . . . Their trade on land and sea reaches to the Ruthenians and to Constantinople. . . .

Their women, when married, do not commit adultery. But a girl, when she falls in love with some man or other, will go to him and quench her lust. If a husband marries a girl and finds her to be virgin, he says to her, 'If there were something good in you, men would have desired you, and you would certainly have found someone to take your virginity. Then he sends her back and frees himself from her.

The lands of the Slavs are the coldest of all. When the nights are moonlit and the days clear, the most severe frosts occur. . . . The wells and ponds are covered with a hard shell of ice as if made of stone. When people breathe, icicles form on their beards, as if made of glass. . . .

They have no bath-houses as such, but they do make use of wooden huts (for bathing). They build a stone stove, on which, when it is heated, they pour water. . . . They hold a bunch of grass in their hands, and waft the steam around. Then their pores open, and all excess matter escapes from their bodies. This hut is called al-istba.

Their kings travel in great carriages, on four wheels. From the corners of the carriage a cradle is slung on chains, so that the passenger is not shaken by the motion. They prepare similar carriages for the sick and injured. . . .

The Slavs wage war with the Byzantines, with the Franks and Langobards, and with other peoples, conducting themselves in battle with varying success.

[117]

Source 7 from Erich Lessing/Art Resource, New York.

7. Golden Bottle from Nagyszentmiklós, with Bulghar Horseman and Captive, late ninth century

Source 8 © Topham/The Image Works.

8. Lindisfarne Gravestone

Source 9 from History of the Archbishops of Hamburg-Bremen (Paper) *by Francis J. Tscahn, trans. Copyright 1959 by Columbia University Press. Reproduced with permission of Columbia University Press in the format Textbook via Copyright Clearance Center.*

9. Adam of Bremen, *History of the Archbishops of Hamburg-Bremen,* 1070s

The Swedish country is extremely fertile; the land is rich in fruits and honey besides excelling all others in cattle raising, exceedingly happy in streams and woods, the whole region everywhere full of merchandise from foreign parts. Thus you may say that the Swedes are lacking in none of the riches, except the pride that we love or rather adore. For they regard as nothing every means of vainglory; that is, gold, silver, stately chargers, beaver and marten pelts, which make us lose our minds admiring them. Only in their sexual relations with women do they know no bounds; a man according to his means has two or three or more wives at one time, rich men and princes an unlimited number. And they also consider the sons born of such unions legitimate. But if a man

[119]

knows another man's wife, or by violence ravishes a virgin, or spoils another of his goods, or does him an injury, capital punishment is inflicted on him. Although all the Hyperboreans[1] are noted for their hospitality, our Swedes are so in particular. To deny wayfarers entertainment is to them the basest of all shameful deeds, so much so that there is strife and contention among them over who is worthy to receive a guest. They show him every courtesy for as many days as he wishes to stay, vying with one another to take him to their friends in their several houses. These good traits they have in their customs. . . .

There are many Swedish peoples, excelling in strength and arms, besides being the best of fighters on horse as well as on ships. . . .

As Nortmannia is the farthest country of the world, so we properly place consideration of it in the last part of the book. By moderns it is called Norway. . . .

On account of the roughness of its mountains and the immoderate cold, Norway is the most unproductive of all countries, suited only for herds. They browse their cattle, like the Arabs, far off in the solitudes. In this way do the people make a living from their livestock by using the milk of the flocks or herds for food and wool for clothing. Consequently, there are produced very valiant fighters who, not softened by any overindulgence in fruits, more often attack others than others trouble them. Even though they are sometimes assailed—not with impunity—by the Danes, who are just as poor, the Norwegians live in terms of amity with their neighbors, the Swedes. Poverty has forced them thus to go all over the world and from piratical raids they bring home in great abundance the riches of the lands. In this way they bear up under the unfruitfulness of their own country. Since accepting Christianity, however, imbued with better teachings, they have already learned to love the truth and peace and to be content with their poverty.

1. **Hyperboreans:** northerners.

QUESTIONS TO CONSIDER

While the author's personal qualities and the historical circumstances shaped perceptions of barbarians in the written sources for this chapter, the purpose for which a source was produced also influenced its depiction of barbarians. Some of these purposes are very clear. Maurice, for example, wanted to provide practical advice for military leaders who would be fighting the groups he described in the near future. How might this have influenced what he included? Similarly, Adam of Bremen wanted to include information that would be useful for missionaries, and Ibrahim Ibn Jakub information that would be useful for merchants. How might this have shaped their descriptions? Several of the authors included their descriptions as part of longer histories, which they wrote in order to leave the story of a series of leaders to posterity: Ammianus Marcellinus described many of the Roman emperors, Agathias the most recent Roman emperors, and Adam of Bremen the archbishops of Hamburg-Bremen. How might this purpose have shaped their writing? Agathias says explicitly that he wants his history to serve "as a guide to life." How might this moral purpose have shaped what he included? Though he is not quite as open about it as Agathias, Tacitus also had a moral purpose; as you have read, he thought that Romans during his lifetime had grown "corrupted" by games and banquets, with men and women exchanging "secret correspondence" that led to adultery and laughing it all off. How does this criticism of his fellow Romans influence his discussion of Germanic peoples? The two visual sources were produced for very different purposes; one is a tombstone and the other a golden bottle, probably for serving oil or wine at banquets. How might these different purposes have shaped the way barbarians were portrayed on them?

As authors comment about barbarian culture, they often make explicit statements about their own. As we have just noted, Tacitus does this, as does Agathias, who says that the Frankish government administration and laws are modeled on the Roman pattern, and that the Franks celebrate feasts "the same way that we do." Maurice notes that Romans (of which he was one) pursue retreating enemies at "a reasonable distance" and just plunder their goods instead of destroying them completely as the

"Scythians" do. Adam of Bremen notes that his own people adore and take pride in riches, while Swedes do not. How do these comparisons shape their story? Do the barbarians more often seem better or worse?

The evidence includes explicit comparisons with the authors' own culture, but all of it is, of course, implicitly comparative, with author's highlighting ways in which barbarian cultures *differ* from their own. Their observations about barbarian habits and practices are thus comments on their own culture and can provide information about their own values even when they are not discussing these directly. What can you tell, for example, about standards of cleanliness in Muslim culture from the comments of Ibn Fadlan about the Rus and of Ibrahim Ibn Jakub about the Christians of northern Spain? About the importance of a permanent house in Roman culture from the comments of Tacitus about the Fenni and of Ammianus Marcellinus about the Huns and Alans? About Roman experiences with fighting on horseback from the comments of Ammianus Marcellinus and Maurice? Why do you think so many authors comment on barbarian marital and sexual practices, on hairstyles, and on the way cattle and other livestock are treated?

Keeping these considerations in mind, you are now ready to answer the central questions in this chapter: What continuities and changes do you see in the depictions of barbarians written or drawn by people living in more settled areas to the south? How are these influenced by the author's or artist's own background and point of view?

EPILOGUE

The Mediterranean was not the only area to experience "barbarian" invasions, for the peoples from the central Asian steppes moved in all directions. For many centuries during and after the Han dynasty in China (202 B.C.–A.D. 220), the Xiongnu were a threat along China's northwestern border. In the fourth century A.D., the White Huns crossed the Hindu Kush Mountains from central Asia into India; their attacks led to the disintegration of the prosperous Gupta Empire. In the ninth century, the Seljak Turks settled along the borders of the Abbasid Caliphate, the large Muslim state with its capital at Baghdad. Following the same pattern that the Germans had in the Roman Empire centuries earlier, Turks were recruited into Abbasid armies, took over military leadership, and eventually became the actual rulers. The most dramatic of these nomadic conquests was that of the Mongols under Genghis Khan, who in the thirteenth century established the largest land-based empire in history.

Learned writers in China, India, and Persia often described these steppe peoples in exactly the same sort of language the authors have in this chapter: as violent, unwashed, unattractive "hordes" with peculiar customs and unsophisticated habits. Such judgments were not limited to steppe nomads. Chinese and Japanese officials had the same opinion of the first Portuguese sailors who landed in East Asia in the sixteenth century, commenting frequently, just as many authors have here, on the extensive facial hair, foul smell, bad manners, and disgusting food of these *nanban*, or "southern barbarians." (The word *nanban* or *nanman*, which directly translates as "southern barbarian" or "southern outsider," was first used in China and Japan for people living in Southeast Asia; because Portuguese ships came from the south, it was later used for Europeans as well.)

As you have seen in this chapter, however, opinions about barbarians were not universally negative, and positive assessments also continued. The Turks converted to Islam, and religious leaders from more settled groups praised their expansion of the faith, just as Agathias had praised the Franks who had converted to Christianity. In the same way that Roman and Byzantine authors respected the military technology of the Huns, Japanese rulers respected (and adopted) the military technology of the Portuguese. In language that would not have surprised many of the authors in this chapter, the thirteenth-century Venetian merchant Marco Polo described Mongol women as "not excelled in the world for chastity and decency of conduct" and praised Genghis Khan as "one of approved integrity, great wisdom, commanding eloquence, and eminent for his valor."

CHAPTER SIX

THE DEVELOPMENT OF

THE MEDIEVAL STATE

The governments of medieval Europe are generally described as "feudal," a word that perhaps confuses more than it clarifies. The term "feudalism" was unknown in the Middle Ages; it was invented only later to describe the medieval system of landholding and government. Used correctly, *feudalism* denotes a system of reciprocal rights and obligations, in which individuals who fought (knights) promised their loyalty, aid, and assistance to a king or other powerful noble, becoming what were termed *vassals* of that lord. The lord in turn promised his vassals protection and material support, which in the Early Middle Ages was often board and room in the lord's own household. As their vassals became more numerous or lived farther away, lords increasingly gave them grants of land as recompense for their allegiance. This piece of land, termed a *fief* (*feudum* in Latin), theoretically still belonged to the lord, with the vassal obtaining only the use of it. Thus feudalism involved a mixture of personal and property ties. Unlike the systems of property ownership in the Roman Empire or most modern governments, it did not involve any ties to an abstract state or governmental system, but was simply a personal agreement between individuals.

Because this promise of allegiance and support could be made only by free individuals, the serfs who were tied to the land were not actually part of the feudal system. In the economic structure of medieval Europe, estates or *manors* of various sizes were worked by slaves, serfs, and free peasants. The whole economic system is termed *manorialism*. Fiefs were generally made up of manors and included the peasants who lived on them, but *manorialism* and *feudalism* are not synonymous.

Though serfs were not included in the feudal system, church officials were. Rulers rewarded church officials with fiefs for their spiritual services or promises of allegiance. In addition, the Church held pieces of land on its own, and granted fiefs in return for promises of assistance from knightly vassals. Abbots and abbesses of monasteries, bishops, and archbishops were either lords[1] or vassals in many feudal arrangements. In addition, both secular and clerical vassals further subdivided their fiefs, granting land to people who became their vassals, a process known as *subinfeudation*. Thus the same person could be a lord in one relationship and a vassal in another.

This system could easily become chaotic, particularly as it was easy to forget, once a family had held a piece of land for several generations, that the land actually belonged to the lord. This is more or less what happened from 700 until 1050, with political power becoming completely decentralized and vassals ruling their fiefs quite independently. About 1050 this began to change, however, and rulers started to manipulate feudal institutions to build up rather than diminish their power.

The rulers of England after the Norman Conquest in 1066 were particularly successful at manipulating feudal institutions to build up their own power. William the Conqueror (1066–1087) and Henry II (1154–1189) dramatically increased royal authority, as did later rulers of France, especially Philip II Augustus (1180–1223), and of Germany, especially

Frederick Barbarossa (1152–1190). Gradually the feudal system was transformed into one that is sometimes termed *feudal monarchy*. Because monarchs in the High Middle Ages had so much more power than they had had in the Early Middle Ages, however, some historians no longer term such governments feudal at all, but simply monarchies, and see in them the origins of the modern state.

In asserting their power, the rulers of western Europe had to suppress or limit the independent powers of two groups in medieval society—their noble vassals and church officials. The challenge provided by each group was somewhat different. Noble vassals often had their own armies, and the people living on their fiefs were generally more loyal to them than to any faraway ruler. During the period before the mid-eleventh century, vassals often supervised courts, which heard cases and punished crimes, and regarded themselves as the supreme legal authority in their fief. Though they were vassals of the ruler, church officials also owed allegiance to an independent, international power—the papacy in Rome. Throughout the Middle Ages, the pope and higher church officials claimed that all church personnel, down to village priests and monks, were not subject to any secular legal jurisdiction, including that of a ruler. They also argued that the spiritual hierarchy of Western Christianity, headed by the pope, was elevated by God over all secular hierarchies, so that every ruler was subject to papal authority.

---

1. Because abbesses and, in some parts of Europe, noblewomen who inherited land could grant fiefs and have vassals, the word "lord" in the context of feudalism did not always mean a man. It simply means "the person who holds the rights of lordship."

In this chapter we will be exploring the ways in which medieval monarchs asserted their authority over their vassals and the Church. We will use both visual and written evidence in answering the question, How did the rulers of the High Middle Ages overcome challenges to their power and begin the process of recentralization of power?

SOURCES AND METHOD

Traditionally, political history has been seen as the history of politics, and has used as its sources laws, decrees, parliamentary debates, and other written documents that give information about political changes. These are still important, but recently political history has been seen more broadly as the history not only of politics but of all relations involving power, and a wider range of sources is now used to understand the power relationships in past societies. Picking up techniques from anthropologists, political historians now use objects as well as written documents to explore the ways in which power is externally expressed and symbolized as well as the ways in which it is manipulated in relationships. The rulers of medieval western Europe were aware of the power of symbols, and along with actual military and legal moves to increase their authority, they also demonstrated that authority symbolically.

A symbol is basically something that stands for something else, that has a meaning beyond the actual object or words. Symbols can be used consciously or unconsciously, and can be interpreted differently by different observers or readers. Anthropologists have pointed out that symbols can often be read at many different levels, so understanding them in all their meanings can be very complicated. The symbols we will be looking at here are less complicated than many, however, because they were consciously employed by rulers and officials who wanted to be very sure that their correct meaning was understood. Since many of the observers were not highly educated or even literate, rulers chose simple symbols and repeated them so that their meaning would certainly be grasped. Because many of these symbols have much the same meaning to us today, you will find them easier to analyze than the symbols from unfamiliar cultures that are often the focus of anthropologists' studies. As we explore the ways in which rulers asserted their authority, then, we must keep in mind both the tactical and the symbolic impact of their actions.

The first four sources all provide evidence of one of the ways in which William the Conqueror and his successors gained power over the English nobility. Source 1 is from a history of England written in the early twelfth century by Ordericus Vitalis, a monk who was half Anglo-Saxon and half Norman. The author provides a relatively objective account of William's reign, and here describes how William subdued one of the many rebellions against him. Read the selection carefully. Rather than simply sending out armies, what does William do to establish royal power? Why does Ordericus feel this was effective in ending the rebellion?

Visual depictions of Norman castles may help you judge whether Ordericus's opinion about their importance was valid, so turn to the next three sources. Sources 2 and 3 are photographs of castles built by English kings. The first was begun at Richmond in 1089, and the second was built at Harlech between 1283 and 1290. Source 4 is a map of all the castles built in England by William the Conqueror during his reign, from 1066 to 1087. Many of these were wooden fortifications rather than the enormous stone castles shown in Sources 2 and 3, but William's successors expanded these simpler castles into larger stone ones as quickly as time and resources permitted. As you look at these, try to imagine yourself as a vassal or subject confronted by castles that looked like these in all the places you see on the map. What message would you get about the power of the king? What strategic value is gained by placing a castle on a hill? How would this also increase the castle's symbolic value? What other features of the castles depicted increase either their strategic value as fortresses or their symbolic value? The map indicates that the castles built by William were not evenly distributed. Given what your text tells you about the Norman Conquest and the problems that William faced, why

might he have built his castles where he did? Does this pattern of castle building surprise you? (A clue here is to keep in mind that castles are both symbols of power and a means to enforce that power, and that these castles may not all have been built for the same reason.)

Source 5 provides evidence of another way in which William and his successors both gained and demonstrated authority over their vassals. It is an excerpt from *The Anglo-Saxon Chronicle* describing William's requirement in 1086 that all vassals swear loyalty to him in what became known as the Salisbury Oath. Rulers such as William recognized that people regarded oaths as very serious expressions of their duties as Christians, and so they required their vassals to swear allegiance regularly in person in ceremonies of *homage* (allegiance) and *fealty* (loyalty). They expanded the ceremonies of knighthood, impressing on young knights their duties of obedience and loyalty. After you read this short selection, think about how the fact that the vassals had to leave their fiefs to swear the Oath might have also helped increase royal power.

After William, Henry II was the most innovative fashioner of royal power in medieval England. In 1166, he issued the Assize[2] of Clarendon (the location of the king's hunting lodge), which set up inquest juries to report to the king's sheriff or traveling judges the name of anyone suspected of having committed a major crime. Source 6 gives you some of the

2. **assize:** a decree made by an assembly.

clauses from the Assize of Clarendon. As you read it, note the ways in which the independent powers of the vassals in their territories are restricted. Who does it state is the ultimate legal authority? Who gains financially from these provisions?

Henry II directly limited not only the legal power of his vassals, but also that of the Church in England. Two years before the Assize of Clarendon, he issued the Constitutions of Clarendon, which purported to be a codification of existing practices governing relations between the Church and the state. Source 7 is an extract from this document. Read it carefully, noting first under whose authority Henry issues it. Who does he say has agreed to its provisions? How do these provisions limit the legal power of the Church over its own clergy? Over laypeople? What role is the king to play in the naming of church officials? In hearing cases involving clergy? How are church officials to be reminded of their duties as the king's vassals?

The Constitutions of Clarendon are perhaps the strongest statement of the power of a secular ruler over the Church to emerge from the Middle Ages, and, as we will see in the epilogue to this chapter, they were quickly opposed by the Church. This was not the only time a ruler asserted his power over the Church, however, for on the Continent German kings and emperors also claimed extensive powers over all aspects of church life up to and including the papacy. Source 8 gives an example of this assertion of power. It is a selection from the biography of the German emperor

Frederick Barbarossa (1152–1190), begun by Bishop Otto of Freising. Otto was Frederick's uncle, so although he was a bishop of the Church, he was quite favorably inclined toward the emperor. In this selection, Otto describes Frederick's coronation and some later responses by the emperor to papal ambassadors. What roles do church officials play in Frederick's coronation? What does Otto view as a further symbol of Frederick's right to rule? What role does Otto report that the pope claimed to have played in granting Frederick power? What, in contrast to this, does Frederick view as the source of his authority? What does he see to be his religious duties as emperor?

Along with actions such as constructing castles or requiring oaths of loyalty, both of which combined tactical with symbolic assertions of power, medieval rulers also demonstrated their power over vassals and the Church in purely symbolic ways. The final sources in this chapter provide examples of some of these. Source 9 is a description of the coronation ceremony of Richard the Lionhearted, Henry II's son, in 1189. More than the much shorter description of Frederick Barbarossa's coronation, which you have already read, it gives evidence of the way in which kings and other territorial rulers expanded their coronation ceremonies, turning them into long, spectacular celebrations of royal wealth and power. As you read it, look first for things that symbolize power relationships. What titles are used to describe the participants? What objects are used in the ceremonies?

[127]

Who is in attendance, and what roles do they play? What actions are required of the various participants, either during the ceremony or as part of their later duties?

Living in the media age as we do, we are certainly used to the manipulation of symbols to promote loyalty and allegiance. We may even be a bit jaded by flag-waving and military bands. Medieval people did not live in a world as full of visual stimulation, so the ceremonies surrounding a monarch were truly extraordinary.

Coronation ceremonies were rare events, and rulers also used symbols in more permanent visual demonstrations of their power, such as paintings and statuary, which they commissioned or which were designed in a way to gain their approval. The next three sources all depict rulers. Source 10 is a manuscript-illumination portrait of the German emperor Otto III (983–1002) seated on his throne. Source 11 is a section of the Bayeux tapestry showing on the left King Harold of England (1053–1066) seated on the throne. In the center, Englishmen acclaim him as king and point up to Halley's Comet (identified in the tapestry as a star). Because we no longer live in a world of royal authority, you may need some assistance in interpreting the meaning of the objects shown with the rulers, although medieval people would have understood them immediately. Many of these objects had both a secular and a religious meaning: the crown represented royal authority (the points symbolized the rays of the sun) and the crown of thorns worn by Jesus before the Crucifixion; the orb (the ball surmounted by a cross) represented the ruler's domination of the land and protection of the Church; the scepter also represented Church and state power by being ornamented with both religious and secular designs. Seeing a monarch in full regalia or a portrait of a monarch would impress on anyone that this was not just the greatest of the nobles, but also someone considered sacred, whose authority was supported by Scripture. Monarchs also demonstrated the sacred aspects of their rule with purely religious symbols, such as crosses and chalices.

Now look carefully at the pictures. What symbols are used to depict the sources of royal authority? How do these communicate the ruler's secular and religious authority? What types of individuals are shown with the ruler? What does this indicate about the relationship between lord and vassal, and between Church and state? Why might the appearance of the heavenly body that came to be known as Halley's Comet have been viewed as an appropriate symbol of monarchy?

You have now examined evidence of a number of ways in which rulers increased their own authority, decreased that of their noble vassals and church officials, and expressed their greater power symbolically. As you assess how all of these helped rulers overcome challenges to their authority, it will be useful to recognize that symbols are not just passive reflections of existing power relationships, but are actively manipulated to build up or decrease power. Therefore it is often difficult to separate what we might term the real or tactical effect of an action or legal change from the symbolic. As you answer the central question in this chapter, then, think about the ways in which symbols and real change are interwoven.

Source 1 from Ordericus Vitalis, The Ecclesiastical History of England and Normandy, *trans. Thomas Forester (London: Henry G. Bohn, 1854). This source taken from a reprint of this edition (New York: AMS Press, 1968), vol. 2, pp. 17–20.*

1. From Ordericus Vitalis's *The Ecclesiastical History of England and Normandy*

The same year [1068], Edwin and Morcar, sons of Earl Algar, and young men of great promise, broke into open rebellion, and induced many others to fly to arms, which violently disturbed the realm of Albion.[3] King William, however, came to terms with Edwin, who assured him of the submission of his brother and of nearly a third of the kingdom, upon which the king promised to give him his daughter in marriage. Afterwards, however, by a fraudulent decision of the Normans, and through their envy and covetousness, the king refused to give him the princess who was the object of his desire, and for whom he had long waited. Being, therefore, much incensed, he and his brother again broke into rebellion, and the greatest part of the English and Welsh followed their standard. The two brothers were zealous in the worship of God, and respected good men. They were remarkably handsome, their relations were of high birth and very numerous, their estates were vast and gave them immense power, and their popularity great. The clergy and monks offered continual prayers on their behalf, and crowds of poor daily supplications. . . .

At the time when the Normans had crushed the English, and were overwhelming them with intolerable oppressions Blethyn, king of Wales, came to the aid of his uncles, at the head of a large body of Britons. A general assembly was now held of the chief men of the English and Welsh, at which universal complaints were made of the outrages and tyranny to which the English were subjected by the Normans and their adherents, and messengers

3. **Albion:** England.

[129]

were dispatched into all parts of Albion to rouse the natives against their ene-mies, either secretly or openly. All joined in a determined league and bold conspiracy against the Normans for the recovery of their ancient liberties. The rebellion broke out with great violence in the provinces beyond the Humber. The insurgents fortified themselves in the woods and marshes, on the estuar-ies, and in some cities. York was in a state of the highest excitement, which the holiness of its bishop was unable to calm. Numbers lived in tents, disdaining to dwell in houses lest they should become enervated; from which some of them were called savages by the Normans.

In consequence of these commotions, the king carefully surveyed the most inaccessible points in the country, and, selecting suitable spots, fortified them against the enemy's excursions. In the English districts there were very few fortresses, which the Normans call castles; so that, though the English were warlike and brave, they were little able to make a determined resistance. One castle the king built at Warwick, and gave it into the custody of Henry, son of Roger de Beaumont.[4] Edwin and Morcar, now considering the doubt-ful issue of the contest, and not unwisely preferring peace to war, sought the king's favour, which they obtained, at least, in appearance. The king then built a castle at Nottingham, which he committed to the custody of William Peverell.

When the inhabitants of York heard the state of affairs, they became so alarmed that they made hasty submission, in order to avoid being compelled by force; delivering the keys of the city to the king, and offering him hostages. But, suspecting their faith, he strengthened the fortress within the city walls, and placed in it a garrison of picked men. At this time, Archill, the most pow-erful chief of the Northumbrians, made a treaty of peace with the king, and gave him his son as a hostage. The bishop of Durham, also being reconciled to King William, became the mediator for peace with the king of the Scots, and was the bearer into Scotland of the terms offered by William. Though the aid of Malcolm had been solicited by the English, and he had prepared to come to their succour with a strong force, yet when he heard what the envoy had to propose with respect to a peace, he remained quiet, and joyfully sent back am-bassadors in company with the bishop of Durham, who in his name swore fealty to King William. In thus preferring peace to war, he best consulted his own welfare, and the inclinations of his subjects; for the people of Scot-land, though fierce in war, love ease and quiet, and are not disposed to disturb themselves about their neighbours' affairs, loving rather religious exercises than those of arms. On his return from this expedition, the king erected castles at Lincoln, Huntingdon, and Cambridge, placing in each of them garrisons composed of his bravest soldiers.

4. **Roger de Beaumont:** a Norman noble.

Source 2 from the British Tourist Authority.

2. **Richmond Castle, begun in 1089**

Source 3: Photograph courtesy of the British Tourist Authority. Ground plan courtesy of the Ministry of Public Building and Works.

3. View and Ground Plan of Harlech Castle, Built by Edward I Between 1283 and 1290

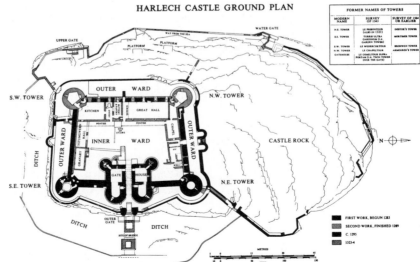

Source 4 adapted from map in H. C. Darby, Domesday England *(Cambridge: Cambridge University Press, 1977), p. 316.*

4. Major Royal Castles Built During the Reign of William the Conqueror, 1066–1087

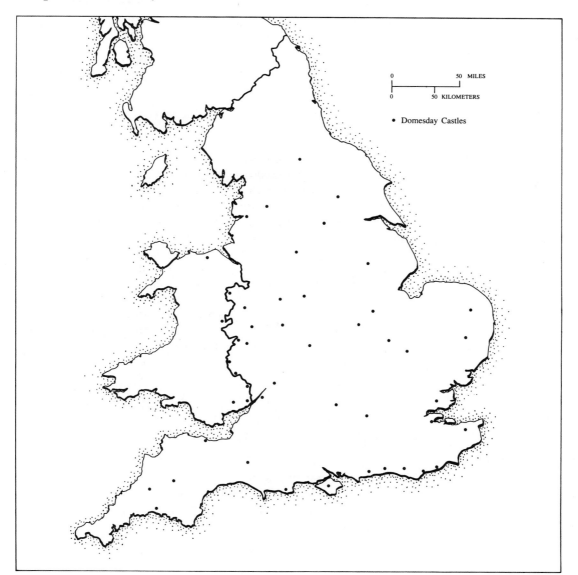

Source 5 from The Anglo-Saxon Chronicle *(London: Eyre and Spottiswoode, 1961, and New Brunswick, N.J.: Rutgers University Press), p. 162.*

5. From *The Anglo-Saxon Chronicle*

1086—In this year the king wore his crown and held his court at Winchester for Easter, and travelled so as to be at Westminster for Whitsuntide, and there dubbed his son, Henry, a knight. Then he travelled about so as to come to Salisbury at Lammas,[5] and there his councillors came to him, and all the people occupying land who were of any account all over England, no matter whose vassals they might be; and they all submitted to him and became his vassals, and swore oaths of allegiance to him, that they would be loyal to him against all other men. . . .

Sources 6 and 7 from Edward P. Cheyney, editor, "English Constitutional Documents," Translations and Reprints from the Original Sources of European History (Philadelphia: University of Pennsylvania, 1900), vol. 1, no. 6, pp. 22–25; pp. 26–30.

6. Assize of Clarendon

Here begins the Assize of Clarendon, made by King Henry II, with the assent of the archbishops, bishops, abbots, earls and barons of all England.

1. In the first place, the aforesaid King Henry, with the consent of all his barons, for the preservation of the peace and the keeping of justice, has enacted that inquiry should be made through the several counties and through the several hundreds,[6] by twelve of the most legal men of the hundred and by four of the most legal men of each manor, upon their oath that they will tell the truth, whether there is in their hundred or in their manor, any man who has been accused or publicly suspected of himself being a robber, or murderer, or thief, or of being a receiver of robbers, or murderers, or thieves, since the lord king has been king. And let the justices make this inquiry before themselves, and the sheriffs before themselves.

2. And let any one who has been found by the oath of the aforesaid to have been accused or publicly suspected of having been a robber, or murderer, or thief, or a receiver of them, since the lord king has been king, be arrested and go to the ordeal of water and let him swear that he has not been a robber, or murderer, or thief, or receiver of them since the lord king has been king, to the value of five shillings, so far as he knows. . . .

5. **Lammas:** the wheat-harvest festival, August 1.

6. **hundred:** a division of a county.

4. And when a robber, or murderer, or thief, or receiver of them shall have been seized through the above-mentioned oath, if the justices are not to come very soon into that country where they have been arrested, let the sheriffs send word to the nearest justice by some intelligent man that they have arrested such men, and the justices will send back word to the sheriffs where they wish that these should be brought before them; and the sheriffs shall bring them before the justices; and along with these they shall bring from the hundred and the manor where they have been arrested, two legal men to carry the record of the county and of the hundred as to why they were seized, and there before the justice let them make their law.

5. And in the case of those who have been arrested through the aforesaid oath of this assize, no one shall have court, or judgment, or chattels,[7] except the lord king in his court before his justices, and the lord king shall have all their chattels. In the case of those, however, who have been arrested, otherwise than through this oath, let it be as it has been accustomed and ought to be. . . .

17. And if any sheriff shall have sent word to any other sheriff that men have fled from his county into another county, on account of robbery or murder or theft, or the reception of them, or for outlawry or for a charge concerning the forest of the king, let him arrest them. And even if he knows of himself or through others that such men have fled into his county, let him arrest them and hold them until he shall have secured pledges from them.

18. And let all sheriffs cause a list to be made of all fugitives who had fled from their counties; and let them do this in the presence of their county courts, and they will carry the written names of these before the justices when they come first before these, so that they may be sought through all England, and their chattels may be seized for the use of the king. . . .

7. Constitutions of Clarendon

In the year of the incarnation of the Lord, 1164, of the papacy of Alexander, the fourth year, of the most illustrious king of the English, Henry II, the tenth year, in the presence of the same king, has been made this memorial or acknowledgment of a certain part of the customs and franchises and dignities of his predecessors, that is to say of King Henry, his grandfather, and of other kings, which ought to be observed and held in the kingdom. And on account of the discussions and disputes which have arisen between the clergy and the justices of our lord and king and the barons of the kingdom concerning the customs and dignities, this acknowledgment is made in the presence of the archbishops and bishops and clergy and earls and barons and principal men of the kingdom. And these customs, acknowledged by

---

7. **chattels:** all items of property and goods except land.

the archbishops and bishops and earls and barons, and by the most noble and ancient of the kingdom, Thomas, archbishop of Canterbury, and Roger, archbishop of York, . . . [plus 12 bishops and 38 named barons] and many others of the principal men and nobles of the kingdom, as well clergy as laity.

Of these acknowledged customs and dignities of the realm, a certain part is contained in the present writing. Of this part the heads are as follows:

1. If any controversy has arisen concerning the advowson[8] and presentation of churches between laymen and ecclesiastics, or between ecclesiastics, it is to be considered or settled in the courts of the lord king.

2. Churches of the fee of the lord king cannot be given perpetually without his assent and grant.

3. Clergymen charged and accused of anything, when they have been summoned by a justice of the king shall come into his court, to respond there to that which it shall seem good to the court of the king for them to respond to, and in the ecclesiastical court to what it shall seem good should be responded to there; so that the justice of the king shall send into the court of holy church to see how the matter shall be treated there. And if a clergyman shall have been convicted or has confessed, the church ought not to protect him otherwise.

4. It is not lawful for archbishops, bishops, and persons of the realm to go out of the realm without the permission of the lord king. And if they go out, if it please the lord king, they shall give security that neither in going nor in making a stay nor in returning will they seek evil or loss to the king or the kingdom. . . .

7. No one who holds from the king in chief, nor any one of the officers of his demesnes shall be excommunicated, nor the lands of any one of them placed under an interdict, unless the lord king, if he is in the land, first agrees, or his justice, if he is out of the realm, in order that he may do right concerning him. . . .

8. Concerning appeals, if they should occur, they ought to proceed from the archdeacon to the bishop, from the bishop to the archbishop. And if the archbishop should fail to show justice, it must come to the lord king last, in order that by his command the controversy should be finally terminated in the court of the archbishop, so that it ought not to proceed further without the assent of the lord king. . . .

10. If any one who is of a city or a castle or a borough or a demesne manor of the lord king has been summoned by the archdeacon or the bishop for any offence for which he ought to respond to them, and is unwilling to make answer to their summons, it is fully lawful to place him under an interdict, but he ought not to be excommunicated before the principal officer of the lord

8. **advowson:** the right to recommend candidates for vacant church positions that carried with them capital assets.

king for that place agrees, in order that he may adjudge him to come to the answer. And if the officer of the king is negligent in this, he himself will be at the mercy of the lord king, and afterward the bishop shall be able to coerce the accused man by ecclesiastical justice.

11. Archbishops, bishops, and all persons of the realm, who hold from the king in chief, have their possessions from the lord king as a barony, and are responsible for them to the justices and officers of the king, and follow and perform all royal rules and customs; and just as the rest of the barons ought to be present at the judgment of the court of the lord king along with the barons, at least till the judgment reaches to loss of limbs or to death.

12. When an archbishopric or bishopric or abbacy or priorate of the demesne of the king has become vacant, it ought to be in his hands, and he shall take thence all its rights and products just as demesnes. And when it has come to providing for the church, the lord king ought to summon the more powerful persons of the church, and the election ought to be made in the chapel of the lord king himself, with the assent of the lord king and with the agreement of the persons of the realm whom he has called to do this. And there the person elected shall do homage and fealty to the lord king as to his liege lord, concerning his life and his limbs and his earthly honor, saving his order, before he shall be consecrated. . . .

This acknowledgment of the aforesaid royal customs and dignities has been made by the aforesaid archbishops, and bishops, and earls, and barons, and the more noble and ancient of the realm, at Clarendon, on the fourth day before the Purification of the Blessed Mary, perpetual Virgin, Lord Henry being there present with his father, the lord king. There are, however, many other and great customs and dignities of holy mother church and of the lord king, and of the barons of the realm, which are not contained in this writing. These are preserved to holy church and to the lord king and to his heirs and to the barons of the realm, and shall be observed inviolably forever.

8. Coronation of Emperor Frederick Barbarossa, 1152

[*From* Gesta Friderici]

In the year . . . 1152, after the most pious King Conrad had died in the spring . . . in the city of Bamberg . . . there assembled in the city of Frankfort from the vast expanse of the transalpine kingdom [Germany], marvellous to tell, the whole strength of the princes, not without certain of the barons from Italy, in one body, so to speak. Here, when the primates were taking counsel about the prince to be elected—for the highest honour of the Roman Empire claims this point of law for itself, as if by special prerogative, namely, that the kings do not succeed by heredity but are created by the election of the princes—finally Frederick, duke of Swabia, son of Duke Frederick, was desired by all, and with the approval of all, was raised up as king. . . .

When the king had bound all the princes who had assembled there in fealty and homage, he, together with a few whom he had chosen as suitable, having dismissed the others in peace, took ship with great joy on the fifth day and, going by the Main and Rhine, he landed at the royal palace of Sinzig. There, taking horse, he came to Aachen on the next Saturday; on the following day, Sunday [March 9th] . . . led by the bishops from the palace to the church of the blessed Virgin Mary, and with the applause of all present, crowned by Arnold, archbishop of Cologne, assisted by the other bishops, he was set on the throne of the Franks, which was placed in the same church by Charles the Great. Many were amazed that in such a short space of time not only so many of the princes and nobles of the kingdom had assembled but also that not a few had come even from western Gaul, where, it was thought, the rumour of this event could not yet have penetrated. . . .

Nor should I pass over in silence that on the same day in the same church the bishop-elect of Münster, also called Frederick, was consecrated as bishop by the same bishops who had consecrated the king; so that in truth the highest king and the priest believed this to be a sort of prognostication[9] in the present joyfulness that, in one church, one day saw the unction[10] of two persons, who

9. **prognostication:** prophecy.
10. **unction:** anointing.

alone are anointed sacramentally with the institution of the old and new dispensations and are rightly called the anointed of Christ. . . .

[*From "The Deeds of Frederick Barbarossa"*]

In the middle of the month of October (1157) the emperor set out for Burgundy to hold a diet at Besançon. . . . We must speak of the ambassadors of the Roman pontiff, Hadrian. . . . The personnel of the embassy consisted of Roland, cardinal priest of the title of St. Mark and chancellor of the Holy Roman Church, and Bernard, cardinal priest of the title of St. Clement, both distinguished for their wealth, their maturity of view, and their influence, and surpassing in prestige almost all others in the Roman Church. . . . When this letter had been read and carefully set forth by Chancellor Rainald in a faithful interpretation, the princes who were present were moved to great indignation, because the entire content of the letter appeared to have no little sharpness and to offer even at the very outset an occasion for future trouble. But what had particularly aroused them all was the fact that in the aforesaid letter it had been stated, among other things, that the fullness of dignity and honor had been bestowed upon the emperor by the Roman pontiff, that the emperor had received from his hand the imperial crown, and that he would not have regretted conferring even greater benefits (*beneficia*) upon him. . . . And the hearers were led to accept the literal meaning of these words and to put credence in the aforesaid explanation because they knew that the assertion was rashly made by some Romans that hitherto our kings had possessed the imperial power over the City, and the kingdom of Italy, by gift of the popes, and that they made such representations and handed them down to posterity not only orally but also in writing and in pictures. . . .

They returned without having accomplished their purpose, and what had been done by the emperor was published throughout the realm in the following letter (October, 1157):

"Whereas the Divine Sovereignty, from which is derived all power in heaven and on earth, has entrusted unto us, His anointed, the kingdom and the empire to rule over, and has ordained that the peace of the churches is to be maintained by the imperial arms, not without the greatest distress of heart are we compelled to complain to Your Benevolence that from the head of the Holy Church, on which Christ has set the imprint of his peace and love, there seem to be emanating causes of dissentions and evils, like a poison, by which, unless God avert it, we fear the body of the Church will be stained, its unity shattered, and a schism created between the temporal and spiritual realms. . . . And since, through election by the princes, the kingdom and the empire are ours from God alone, Who at the time of the passion of His Son Christ subjected the world to dominion by the two swords, and since the apostle Peter taught the world this doctrine: 'Fear God, honor the king,' whosoever says that we received the imperial crown as a benefice (*pro beneficio*) from the lord

[139]

pope contradicts the divine ordinance and the doctrine of Peter and is guilty of a lie. . . ."

Source 9 from J. A. Giles, translator and editor, Roger of Wendover's Flowers of History *(London: H. G. Bohn, 1849), vol. 2, pp. 79–81.*

9. Coronation of Richard the Lionhearted, 1189

Duke Richard, when all the preparations for his coronation were complete, came to London, where were assembled the archbishops of Canterbury, Rouen, and Treves, by whom he had been absolved for having carried arms against his father after he had taken the cross. The archbishop of Dublin was also there, with all the bishops, earls, barons, and nobles of the kingdom. When all were assembled, he received the crown of the kingdom in the order following: First came the archbishops, bishops, abbots, and clerks, wearing their caps, preceded by the cross, the holy water, and the censers, as far as the door of the inner chamber, where they received the duke, and conducted him to the church of Westminster, as far as the high altar, in a solemn procession. In the midst of the bishops and clerks went four barons carrying candlesticks with wax candles, after whom came two earls, the first of whom carried the royal sceptre, having on its top a golden cross; the other carried the royal sceptre, having a dove on its top. Next to these came two earls with a third between them, carrying three swords with golden sheaths, taken out of the king's treasury. Behind these came six earls and barons carrying a chequer,[11] over which were placed the royal arms and robes, whilst another earl followed them carrying aloft a golden crown. Last of all came Duke Richard, having a bishop on the right hand, and a bishop on the left, and over them was held a silk awning. Proceeding to the altar, as we have said, the holy Gospels were placed before him together with the relics of some of the saints, and he swore, in presence of the clergy and people, that he would observe peace, honour, and reverence, all his life, towards God, the holy Church and its ordinances: he swore also that he would exercise true justice towards the people committed to his charge, and abrogating all bad laws and unjust customs, if any such might be found in his dominions, would steadily observe those which were good. After this they stripped him of all his clothes except his breeches and shirt, which had been ripped apart over his shoulders to receive the unction. He was then shod with sandals interwoven with gold thread, and Baldwin archbishop of Canterbury anointed him king in three places, namely, on his head, his shoulders, and his right arm, using prayers

11. **chequer:** a small table.

composed for the occasion: then a consecrated linen cloth was placed on his head, over which was put a hat, and when they had again clothed him in his royal robes with the tunic and gown, the archbishop gave into his hand a sword wherewith to crush all the enemies of the Church; this done, two earls placed his shoes upon his feet, and when he had received the mantle, he was adjured by the archbishop, in the name of God, not to presume to accept these honours unless his mind was steadily purposed to observe the oaths which he had made: and he answered that, with God's assistance, he would faithfully observe everything which he had promised. Then the king taking the crown from the altar gave it to the archbishop, who placed it upon the king's head, with the sceptre in his right hand and the royal wand in his left; and so, with his crown on, he was led away by the bishops and barons, preceded by the candles, the cross and the three swords aforesaid. When they came to the offertory of the mass, the two bishops aforesaid led him forwards and again led him back. At length, when the mass was chanted, and everything finished in the proper manner, the two bishops aforesaid led him away with his crown on, and bearing in his right hand the sceptre, in his left the royal wand, and so they returned in procession into the choir, where the king put off his royal robes, and taking others of less weight, and a lighter crown also, he proceeded to the dinner-table, at which the archbishops, bishops, earls, and barons, with the clergy and people, were placed, each according to his rank and dignity, and feasted splendidly, so that the wine flowed along the pavement and walls of the palace.

Source 10 © Bettman/CORBIS.

10. Portrait of Emperor Otto III

Source 11 from Giraudon/Art Resource, New York.

11. Portion of the Bayeux Tapestry Showing King Harold Seated on the Throne of England, with Halley's Comet Above

QUESTIONS TO CONSIDER

The power relationships we have been investigating involve three main groups in medieval society: the nobles, the Church, and the rulers. To understand changes in the balance of power among them, you will need to extract information from each of the sources about them, and then compare your findings.

Take the nobles first. How would you compare the role of the nobles in the ceremonies of homage such as the Salisbury Oath with their role in the coronation ceremonies? How is their relationship to the ruler expressed in the pictures of Otto III and Harold? How does this compare with the way this relationship is expressed in the Assize of Clarendon? What differences do you see in the role of the nobles in Germany and those in England, as expressed in the coronation accounts?

Turning to the Church, what types of religious objects appear in the ceremonies and depictions of rulers? Do they serve to express the power of the Church as an institution or of someone else? What do they reveal to you about medieval religious beliefs and practices? What do the pictures of Otto III and Harold indicate about the relationship between the ruler and church officials? How does this compare with the expression of this relationship in the Constitutions of Clarendon?

The claim of rulers such as Henry II and Frederick Barbarossa to religious authority was accompanied in the High Middle Ages by changes in the theory underlying kingship. In the Early Middle Ages, the king was viewed as simply the greatest of the nobles, whose power derived from the agreements he had made with his vassals. This idea continued into the High Middle Ages, but alongside it developed the idea that the king got his power from God as well. Rulers were increasingly viewed not only as the apex of a pyramid of vassals, but also as the representative to God for their entire kingdom. They were not regarded as divine in the way that ancient rulers such as the Egyptian pharaohs and Roman emperors had been, for Christianity would not allow this, but they were considered sacred in some ways. What evidence of this new idea of kingship can you find in either the Constitutions of Clarendon or the statements of Frederick Barbarossa? The two coronation ceremonies, Sources 8 and 9, are from the period of the building up of the monarchy. What evidence do you see in them of both the older idea of the king as the greatest of the nobles, and the newer idea of the king as ordained by God?

Remember that most literate people in the Middle Ages were clerics, so that all of the documents included here were probably written by priests or monks. How might this have affected their account of the events? Given what you have read and looked at here, what actions would you now regard as most significant in the creation of the medieval state?

EPILOGUE

The moves undertaken by rulers to increase their power during the High Middle Ages did not go unchallenged. The Constitutions of Clarendon were immediately opposed by church officials, including Henry II's friend Thomas Becket, whom Henry had made the Archbishop of Canterbury. The controversy between them grew very bitter, and ended with Becket's murder by several of Henry's nobles. After this the Constitutions were officially withdrawn, but Henry continued to enforce many of their provisions anyway.

In the area ruled by the German emperors, the Church was better able to assert its independent power; in fact, constant disputes with the pope were one of the reasons that the German emperors were not successful at establishing a unified country. Church officials patterned themselves after secular rulers and began in the twelfth century to demand regular oaths of homage and loyalty. They made sure that church power was clearly symbolized in any royal ceremony and in all ceremonies of knighthood. As rulers built castles, they built cathedrals, permanent monuments in stone to both the glory of God and the authority of the Church. The consecrations of churches and cathedrals rivaled the coronations of monarchs in splendor and pomp. The Church was fortunate in this regard, for opportunities for special ceremonies and celebrations were much more frequent than they were for secular rulers. Even the regular mass could be used to convey the Church's might to all who observed it. The king may have had sacred authority, but church officials wanted to make sure that everyone knew that they did as well.

Nobles in England also opposed the growth of royal power, and were more effective than the Church in enforcing limits to royal authority. The most famous of these was the Magna Carta in 1215, which King John was forced to sign at a meeting in Runnymede, giving the higher nobles of England the right to participate in government. This document said nothing about the rights of the vast majority of English people, but it is still unusual in its limitation of the power of the king, though John immediately refuted it once he left Runnymede.

Despite opposition, however, the expansion of royal power at the expense of the nobles and Church continued, for this expansion had only begun during the High Middle Ages. Monarchs in the later Middle Ages, the Renaissance, and the early modern period continued to build up their power, devising new methods of taxation to raise revenue, creating a centralized legal system under firm royal control, reducing the role of or doing away with feudal assemblies of nobles, hiring middle-class lawyers and bureaucrats as their advisers and officials, and forbidding the nobles to maintain their own armies while building up royal armies led by generals whom they chose for loyalty.

This expansion of royal power was made easier in many countries in the sixteenth century because of the Protestant Reformation. Many rulers, such as Henry VIII of England, resented any independent power of the Church; they thus found Protestant theology, which declared the papacy to be evil and the ruler the proper source of all religious authority, very attractive. Some rulers became Protestant out of sincere religious conviction, but for others the chance to take over church property and appoint church officials was the strongest motivation.

The growth of actual royal power was accompanied, as you would expect after working through this chapter, by changes in the theory underlying kingship and in the symbols used to portray the king. Political theorists developed the idea of the divine right of kings, whereby kings got their power directly and pretty much only from God, and so were not answerable to their subjects for their behavior. You can see this idea beginning in the documents you have just read, and it would be developed to its furthest extent in seventeenth-century absolutism.

Centralized monarchy did not develop in all parts of Europe, however. Germany and Italy remained divided, and in fact did not become unified nations until the late nineteenth century, just a little over a hundred years ago. From the description of Frederick Barbarossa's coronation, you can see one reason for this, the fact that the emperorship was elected rather than hereditary. The lack of strong central governments in Germany and Italy was one reason for their decreasing political importance in the early modern period. The rulers of western Europe had much greater financial resources, and so could field larger armies and encourage economic development. After the voyages of the Portuguese and Spanish revealed new lands and new ways to the East, these rulers also supported exploration and colonization, which further increased royal and national power. Some type of feudal structure existed in most parts of western Europe in the High Middle Ages, but it was the rulers of France, England, and Spain who were most successful at manipulating both actual power and the symbols of that power to build up their own authority and end the feudal system.

CHAPTER SEVEN

LIFE AT A

MEDIEVAL UNIVERSITY

THE PROBLEM

In Europe during the classical period, education was handled by private tutors and small schools, and during the Early Middle Ages most education was carried out by monasteries and convents, which gave children basic training in Latin. Some monasteries provided more advanced education for the few individuals who would become leaders in the Church or administrators for secular rulers. Beginning in the eleventh century, schools attached to cathedrals in some cities also began offering more advanced subjects and developed a curriculum based on the works of Christian and classical authors. These cathedral schools took in boys and young men who had learned their Latin in monasteries or through tutors. One of the earliest cathedral schools was that in Paris, where students were drawn by excellent teachers such as Peter Abelard. Because only an official of the bishop, called the *scholasticus* or chancellor, had the authority to issue licenses to teach, students and

teachers clustered around the cathedral of Notre Dame, located on an island in the Seine. This educational community soon grew so large that it required additional housing on the left bank of the river, which came to be known as the "Latin Quarter" after the official academic language. Special residence halls for students, called *colleges*, were opened, though the teachers themselves had no classrooms and simply rented rooms on their own for lecturing.

As the number of students in Paris increased, the teachers joined together into a "universal society of teachers," or *university* for short. Believing that the chancellor often either granted the right to teach to unqualified parties or simply sold licenses outright, they began to require that prospective teachers pass an examination set by the university besides getting the chancellor's approval. This certificate to teach was the earliest form of academic degree, granting the holder one of the titles, *master* or *doctor*, that we still use today. (Bachelor's degrees were to come later.) Most of the students studied theology, and Paris became the model for later universities such as Oxford and Cambridge in England and Heidelberg in Germany.

Colleges at many universities changed their character over the centuries. Originally no more than residence halls, the colleges gradually began to sponsor lectures and arrange for courses, and the university became simply the institution that granted degrees. This process was especially noticeable at the English universities of Oxford and Cambridge. When colleges were first established in the United States, they generally modeled themselves on the colleges of Oxford and Cambridge; because they were not part of larger universities, the colleges also granted degrees themselves. Thus modern U.S. colleges may be either completely independent institutions or part of a university, such as the College of Engineering or the College of Letters and Science found at many universities. In most cases, colleges that are part of modern universities have completely lost their original function as residences.

The University of Bologna had somewhat different roots and a different emphasis. Bologna was located at the crossing of the main trade routes in northern Italy, and so was a center of commerce and trade. In the late eleventh century, a manuscript of the Roman emperor Justinian's law code was discovered in the area. Scholars studying the text realized that Roman law provided better ways of handling complex business transactions than did existing customary law, and they began teaching Roman law at professional schools for lawyers, notaries, and merchants

in Bologna. The university developed from these professional schools, and consequently the students were older and more sophisticated than those at Paris. Here, the students themselves banded into a university; they determined the fees teachers would be paid, the hours of classes, and the content of lectures. The most important course of study at Bologna was law, though other subjects were added later. Bologna became the model for European universities such as Orleans or Padua, where students have retained their traditional power through modern times.

Because all those associated with the universities were literate, a great many records survive detailing every aspect of university life, both inside and outside the classroom. We can observe the process by which universities were established, read the rules students were required to live by, and learn what they were supposed to be studying (as well as what they actually spent time doing!). Much of medieval university life will seem familiar to us, for modern colleges and universities have inherited a great deal from their medieval predecessors. Indeed, most of the universities that had their beginning in the Middle Ages are still thriving today, making universities one of the few medieval institutions we can evaluate to some extent as insiders, rather than the outsiders we are when we look at such vanished social forms as serfdom or feudalism.

Because of the many parallels between medieval and modern universities, your task in this chapter will be twofold. First, you will be asked to use a variety of records to answer this question: What was life like for students at a medieval university? You can then use this description and your own experiences as a student to answer the second question: How would you compare medieval with modern student life, and what factors might account for the differences?

SOURCES AND METHOD

You will be using four types of sources in this chapter. The first type (Sources 1 through 4) consists of rules for university or college life issued by the founders. These are prescriptive documents, setting forth standards of functioning and behavior. The second type (Sources 5 through 8), written by teachers at medieval universities, describes their methods of teaching or presents the area on which they concentrated. The third type (Source 9) is a critique of university teaching by an individual outside the university structure. These sources provide us with information about how and what students studied or were supposed to study and so have both prescriptive and descriptive qualities. Selections of the fourth type (Sources 10 through 13) describe actual student life or were written by students themselves. These sources are thus fully descriptive, recounting real events or the problems and desires of real students.

As you read each selection, keep in mind the identity of its author and his position in the university. (No women were allowed to attend medieval universities in any capacity, so we can be sure that all authors, even anonymous students, were male.) Then as now, the perspective of administrators, those who established and ran the universities, was very different from that of students and faculty. It is also important to identify the source as prescriptive or descriptive. Prescriptive rules were often written in response to real problems, but the standards they laid down should never be mistaken for reality.

Begin your analysis of medieval university life with a careful reading of Sources 1 through 4. Source 1 describes privileges granted to the students at the University of Paris by the king of France in 1200. Though the University of Paris was originally started by the teachers themselves, the king took the scholars under his special protection and guaranteed them certain extraordinary rights. What privileges are they granted in this document?

Source 2 consists of the statutes issued for the University of Paris by Cardinal Robert Courçon in 1215. Courçon, a representative of Pope Innocent III, took a special interest in the university and approved rules governing academic life. Innocent had been a student at Paris himself and wanted to ensure the university's tradition of theological orthodoxy and high levels of scholarship and behavior. As you read the selection, note the restrictions placed on those allowed to teach the arts. What restrictions are placed on teachers of theology? Why would Innocent be stricter about theology? What other areas did he believe important to regulate? What matters were the masters and students allowed to decide for themselves?

Source 3 contains further statutes issued for the University of Paris by Pope Gregory XI in 1231. What rules did he set for the chancellor's granting of teaching licenses? What issues was the university permitted to decide for itself? What special legal protections did students and teachers have? As pope, Gregory was particularly concerned with the manner in which theology was taught. What special restrictions did he lay down for students and teachers of theology? How would you compare these rules with the earlier ones established by Innocent III?

Source 4 is a series of rules governing life in one of the residential colleges, not the university as a whole. They were issued by Robert de Sorbon, the chaplain of King Louis IX, who established the college in the thirteenth century. This college was originally a residence hall for students of theology. By the sixteenth century, however, the word *Sorbonne* was used to describe the faculty of theology; since the nineteenth century the entire University of Paris has been called the Sorbonne.

As you can see from Source 4, Sorbon's establishment was simply a residence hall, with none of the broader functions that colleges later assumed. What aspects of student life did he regulate? What qualities did he attempt to encourage in the students living at his college?

By reading these four prescriptive sources, you have gained some information about the structure of one university (Paris), the hierarchy of authority, special student privileges, daily life in a residential college, and the handling of rule infractions. You have also learned something about the ideals held by authorities and patrons, for the popes and Sorbon established these rules because they held certain beliefs about how students should behave. What qualities would their ideal student exhibit? What did they see as the ultimate aim of the university? You can also use these sources to assess how church and secular leaders reacted to scholars, students, and the university in general. How would you describe their attitude—patronizing, respectful, hostile? How might their opinions about members of the university community have influenced other citizens of these university towns?

Besides informing us of standards, rules can also expose real-life problems because those who set the regulations were often responding to events in their environment. Which rules were specifically aimed at halting acts that were already taking place? Which rules seem most likely to have been a response to actual behavior? What kinds of acts did the authorities appear most upset about? Why do you think they believed these acts were important? Judging by the information in these sources, how would you describe relations between university students and the other residents of Paris? Before you go on to the next selections, write a brief description of medieval university life as you now see it. What types of sources would help you test whether your assumptions at this point are correct?

You have probably realized that so far you do not know very much about what or how students actually studied, other than those writings the popes recommended or forbade. The next four selections provide specific academic information. Sources 5 and 6 were written by teachers of theology and philosophy at Paris; Sources 7 and 8, by teachers of law at Bologna. Source 5 is the introduction to Peter Abelard's *Sic et Non,* a philosophical treatise introducing students and other readers to the *scholastic method* of inquiry, which applied logic to Christian theology. Source 6 is a demonstration of the scholastic method by one philosopher, Anselm of Canterbury, to prove the existence of God. If you are not familiar with philosophical works, you will need to read these excerpts very carefully, with special attention to the author's main points and the way in which logic is used to advance arguments. Because scholastic philosophers regarded logic as the most important aid to human understanding, it is fair for you to be critical if you see any flaws in their own logic. In making this analysis, you will be engaging in an activity that students in medieval universities both did themselves and were encouraged to do.

Begin with Abelard's introduction. How did he suggest to students that they read the works of the church fathers? How were they to handle seeming contradictions? Was all literature to be treated in this way? What,

for Abelard, was the most important quality a student could possess? How was education supposed to strengthen this quality? Proceed to Anselm's proof, which you may need to read a number of times. Do you see any flaws in the logic? If you were a student disputing his proof, where would you begin?

Source 7 is an announcement of lectures in law by Odofredus, a teacher at the University of Bologna, written about 1255. Although later in the thirteenth century the city of Bologna began to pay teachers in order to control the university faculty more closely, at this point teachers were still paid directly by their students, and so Odofredus did not simply announce his course, he advertised it in a way that would make it attractive. What did he see as the positive qualities of his teaching method? How did he propose to handle a text? What specific skills was he trying to teach his students?

Source 8 is the introduction to the *Digest,* the main part of the collection of laws and commentaries made by the Emperor Justinian in the sixth century and one of the basic legal texts taught by Odofredus and his colleagues at Bologna. Like many textbooks, it opens with definitions of what would be taught. What distinctions among types of law does it present? What is the ultimate aim of legal education to be? Return to the description of university life you wrote after reading the first group of sources. What can you now add about the way teachers approached their subjects or the way in which material was taught? What do you now know about the content of courses in medieval universities?

Though teachers of theology and law used both logic and reason as means of analysis, there were some thinkers in the Middle Ages who questioned their value, particularly in matters of theology. Source 9 is an excerpt from two letters of St. Bernard of Clairvaux (1090–1153), a very influential French abbot, mystic, and adviser to the papacy. What does Bernard object to in Abelard's teaching? Why does he view Abelard's ideas as dangerous? What is his opinion of the scholastic method being developed at that time in the universities?

Students did not spend all their time studying, nor did they always behave in the ways popes or patrons hoped they would. The final group of sources come from students themselves or describe what might be termed their extracurricular activities. Source 10 is an anonymous account of a riot in Oxford in 1298, and Source 11 is a description of student life at Paris written by Jacques de Vitry, a high-minded scholar and historian who had studied at Paris himself. Source 12 consists of two letters, one from a student at Oxford to his father and another from a father to his son, a student at Orleans; Source 13 contains three anonymous short poems written originally in Latin by twelfth-century students.

The account of the riot is relatively straightforward and objective, like a story you might read in a newspaper today. What does this incident indicate about the relations between university scholars and townspeople? Whom did the two sets of disputants ask to decide the matter?

The other selections are more subjective than this account, so you must keep the point of view and the intent of the authors in mind as you read them. What kind of language does Vitry use to describe students? With what authority did he criticize their actions? How would you describe his general opinion of university life? How would you compare his critique of logic and the philosophers who used it with Bernard's? What tactics did the student use to convince his father to send money? How would you compare the father's attitude with Vitry's?

Most medieval student poetry was written by young scholars who wandered from university to university and took much longer at their studies than normal, if they ever finished at all. It is important when reading from this genre to remember that the authors were not describing the daily grind but celebrating their wild escapades, in the same way you might talk about an academic year in terms of homecoming parties, weekend bashes, and early morning cramming for exams. This does not mean that we should reject their poetry as a valid historical source; rather, we must simply be aware of its intent and limitations. Keeping this in mind, how do the poets describe themselves and their problems? How does this description of student life reinforce or change what you have learned so far?

Return to your original description of university life. What would you add now?

THE EVIDENCE

Sources 1 through 3 from Dana Carleton Munro, editor and translator, Translations and Reprints from the Original Sources of European History, *vol. 2, no. 3 (Philadelphia: University of Pennsylvania Press, no date), pp. 4–5; pp. 12–15; pp. 7–11.*

1. Royal Privileges Granted to the University of Paris by the King of France, 1200

In the Name of the sacred and indivisible Trinity, amen. Philip, by the grace of God, King of the French. . . .

Concerning the safety of the students at Paris in the future, by the advice of our subjects we have ordained as follows: we will cause all the citizens of Paris to swear that if any one sees an injury done to any student by any layman, he will testify truthfully to this, nor will any one withdraw in order not to see [the act]. And if it shall happen that any one strikes a student, except in self-defense, especially if he strikes the student with a weapon, a club or a stone, all laymen who see [the act] shall in good faith seize the malefactor or malefactors and deliver them to our judge; nor shall they withdraw in order not to see the act, or seize the malefactor, or testify to the truth. Also, whether the malefactor is seized in open crime or not, we will make a legal and full examination through clerks or laymen or certain lawful persons; and our count and our judges shall do the same. And if by a full examination we or our judges are able to learn that he who is accused, is guilty of the crime, then we or our judges shall immediately inflict a penalty, according to the quality and nature of the crime; notwithstanding the fact that the criminal may deny the deed and say that he is ready to defend himself in single combat, or to purge himself by the ordeal by water.

Also, neither our provost nor our judges shall lay hands on a student for any offence whatever; nor shall they place him in our prison, unless such a crime has been committed by the student, that he ought to be arrested. And in that case, our judge shall arrest him on the spot, without striking him at all, unless he resists, and shall hand him over to the ecclesiastical judge, who ought to guard him in order to satisfy us and the one suffering the injury. And if a serious crime has been committed, our judge shall go or shall send to see what is done with the student.

2. Statutes for the University of Paris Issued by Robert Courçon, 1215

R., servant of the cross of Christ, by the divine mercy cardinal priest of the title of St. Stephen in Monte Celio and legate of the apostolic seat, to all the masters and scholars at Paris—eternal safety in the Lord.

Let all know, that having been especially commanded by the lord pope to devote our energy effectively to the betterment of the condition of the students at Paris, and wishing by the advice of good men to provide for the tranquillity of the students in the future, we have ordered and prescribed the following rules:

No one is to lecture at Paris in arts before he is twenty-one years old. He is to listen in arts at least six years, before he begins to lecture. He is to promise that he will lecture for at least two years, unless he is prevented by some good reason, which he ought to prove either in public or before the examiners. He must not be smirched by any infamy. When he is ready to lecture, each one is to be examined according to the form contained in the letter of lord P. bishop of Paris (in which is contained the peace established between the chancellor and the students by the judges appointed by the lord pope, approved and confirmed namely by the bishop and deacon of Troyes and by P., the bishop, and J., the chancellor of Paris).

The treatises of Aristotle on logic, both the old and the new, are to be read in the schools in the regular and not in the extraordinary courses. The two Priscians,[1] or at least the second, are also to be read in the schools in the regular courses. On the feast-days nothing is to be read except philosophy, rhetoric, *quadrivialia*,[2] the Barbarism, the Ethics, if they like, and the fourth book of the Topics. The books of Aristotle on Metaphysics or Natural Philosophy, or the abridgements of these works, are not to be read, nor the writings of Master David of Dinant, the heretic Amauri, or the Spaniard Mauricius.[3]

In the promotions and meetings of the masters and in the confutations or arguments of the boys or youths there are to be no festivities. But they may call in some friends or associates, but only a few. We also advise that donations of garments and other things be made, as is customary or even to a greater extent, and especially to the poor. No master lecturing in arts is to

1. **Priscian:** a Roman grammarian whose two works presented models of correct letters and legal documents.

2. *quadrivialia:* the four more advanced fields of study within the seven liberal arts: arithmetic, geometry, astronomy, and music.

3. Aristotle's treatises on metaphysics and natural philosophy were forbidden by the pope because they stated that the world was eternal (rather than created by God) and that the human soul was not immortal. The last three authors the Church regarded as heretics.

wear anything except a cope,[4] round and black and reaching to the heels—at least, when it is new. But he may well wear a pallium.[5] He is not to wear under the round cope embroidered shoes and never any with long bands.

If anyone of the students in arts or theology dies, half of the masters of arts are to go to the funeral one time, and the other half to the next funeral. They are not to withdraw until the burial is completed, unless they have some good reason. If any master of arts or theology dies, all the masters are to be present at the vigils, each one is to read the psalter or have it read. Each one is to remain in the church, where the vigils are celebrated, until midnight or later, unless prevented by some good reason. On the day when the master is buried, no one is to lecture or dispute.

We fully confirm to them the meadow of St. Germain in the condition in which it was adjudged to them.

Each master is to have jurisdiction over his scholars. No one is to receive either schools or a house without the consent of the occupant, if he is able to obtain it. No one is to receive a license from the chancellor or any one else through a gift of money, or furnishing a pledge or making an agreement. Also, the masters and students can make among themselves or with others agreements and regulations, confirmed by a pledge, penalty or oath, about the following matters: namely, if a student is killed, mutilated or receives some outrageous injury—if justice is not done; for fixing the prices of lodgings; concerning the dress, burial, lectures and disputations; in such a manner, however, that the university is not scattered or destroyed on this account.

We decide concerning the theologians, that no one shall lecture at Paris before he is thirty-five years old, and not unless he has studied at least eight years, and has heard the books faithfully and in the schools. He is to listen in theology for five years, before he reads his own lectures in public. No one of them is to lecture before the third hour on the days when the masters lecture. No one is to be received at Paris for the important lectures or sermons unless he is of approved character and learning. There is to be no student at Paris who does not have a regular master.

3. Statutes for the University of Paris Issued by Pope Gregory XI, 1231

Gregory, the bishop, servant of the servants of God, to his beloved sons, all the masters and students of Paris—greeting and apostolic benediction. . . .

4. **cope:** a long cloak or cape.
5. **pallium:** a white stole usually worn by popes and archbishops as a symbol of their authority. In this case, a master teacher was allowed to wear one as an indication of his level of academic achievement and its corresponding institutional authority; the pallium thus served a function similar to the master's or doctoral hood.

Concerning the condition of the students and schools, we have decided that the following should be observed: each chancellor, appointed hereafter at Paris, at the time of his installation, in the presence of the bishop, or at the command of the latter in the chapter at Paris—two masters of the students having been summoned for this purpose and present in behalf of the university—shall swear that, in good faith, according to his conscience, he will not receive as professors of theology and canon law any but suitable men, at a suitable place and time, according to the condition of the city and the honor and glory of those branches of learning; and he will reject all who are unworthy without respect to persons or nations. Before licensing anyone, during three months, dating from the time when the license is requested, the chancellor shall make diligent inquiries of all the masters of theology present in the city, and of all other honest and learned men through whom the truth can be ascertained, concerning the life, knowledge, capacity, purpose, prospects and other qualities needful in such persons; and after the inquiries, in good faith and according to his conscience, he shall grant or deny the license to the candidate, as shall seem fitting and expedient. The masters of theology and canon law, when they begin to lecture, shall take a public oath that they will give true testimony on the above points. The chancellor shall also swear, that he will in no way reveal the advice of the masters, to their injury; the liberty and privileges being maintained in their full vigor for the canons at Paris, as they were in the beginning. Moreover, the chancellor shall promise to examine in good faith the masters in medicine and arts and in the other branches, to admit only the worthy and to reject the unworthy.

In other matters, because confusion easily creeps in where there is no order, we grant to you the right of making constitutions and ordinances regulating the manner and time of lectures and disputations, the costume to be worn, the burial of the dead; and also concerning the bachelors,[6] who are to lecture and at what hours, and on what they are to lecture; and concerning the prices of the lodgings or the interdiction of the same; and concerning a fit punishment for those who violate your constitutions or ordinances, by exclusion from your society. And if, perchance, the assessment of the lodgings is taken from you, or anything else is lacking, or an injury or outrageous damage, such as death or the mutilation of a limb, is inflicted on one of you; unless through a suitable admonition satisfaction is rendered within fifteen days, you may suspend your lectures until you have received full satisfaction. And if it happens that any one of you is unlawfully imprisoned, unless the injury ceases on a remonstrance from you, you may, if you judge it expedient, suspend your lectures immediately.

We command, moreover, that the bishop of Paris shall so chastise the excesses of the guilty, that the honor of the students shall be preserved and evil

---

6. **bachelor:** a student who had his first degree and could teach beginning-level subjects.

deeds shall not remain unpunished. But in no way shall the innocent be seized on account of the guilty; nay rather, if a probable suspicion arises against anyone, he shall be detained honorably and on giving suitable bail he shall be freed, without any exactions from the jailors. But if, perchance, such a crime has been committed that imprisonment is necessary, the bishop shall detain the criminal in his prison. The chancellor is forbidden to keep him in his prison. We also forbid holding a student for a debt contracted by another, since this is interdicted by canonical and legitimate sanctions. Neither the bishop, nor his official, nor the chancellor shall exact a pecuniary penalty for removing an excommunication or any other censure of any kind. Nor shall the chancellor demand from the masters who are licensed an oath, or obedience, or any pledge; nor shall he receive any emolument[7] or promise for granting a license, but be content with the above-mentioned oath.

Also, the vacation in summer is not to exceed one month, and the bachelors, if they wish, can continue their lectures in vacation time. Moreover, we prohibit more expressly the students from carrying weapons in the city, and the university from protecting those who disturb the peace and study. And those who call themselves students but do not frequent the schools, or acknowledge any master, are in no way to enjoy the liberties of the students.

Moreover, we order that the masters in arts shall always read one lecture on Priscian, and one book after the other in the regular courses. Those books on natural philosophy which for a certain reason were prohibited in a provincial council, are not to be used at Paris until they have been examined and purged of all suspicion of error. The masters and students in theology shall strive to exercise themselves laudably in the branch which they profess; they shall not show themselves philosophers, but they shall strive to become God's learned. And they shall not speak in the language of the people, confounding the sacred language with the profane. In the schools they shall dispute only on such questions as can be determined by theological books and the writings of the holy fathers.

It is not lawful for any man whatever to infringe this deed of our provision, constitution, concession, prohibition and inhibition or to act contrary to it, from rash presumption. If anyone, however, should dare to attempt this, let him know that he incurs the wrath of almighty God and of the blessed Peter and Paul, his apostles.

Given at the Lateran, on the Ides of April [April 13], in the fifth year of our pontificate.

7. **emolument:** fee.

Source 4 from University Records and Life in the Middle Ages *by Lynn Thorndike, ed. Copyright © 1944 Columbia University Press. Reprinted with permission of the publisher.*

4. Robert de Sorbon's Regulations for His College, before 1274

I wish that the custom which was instituted from the beginning in this house by the counsel of good men may be kept, and if anyone ever has transgressed it, that henceforth he shall not presume to do so.

No one therefore shall eat meat in the house on Advent, nor on Monday or Tuesday of Lent, nor from Ascension Day to Pentecost.

Also, I will that the community be not charged for meals taken in rooms. If there cannot be equality, it is better that the fellow eating in his room be charged than the entire community.

Also, no one shall eat in his room except for cause. If anyone has a guest, he shall eat in hall. If, moreover, it shall not seem expedient to the fellow to bring that guest to hall, let him eat in his room and he shall have the usual portion for himself, not for the guest. If, moreover, he wants more for himself or his guest, he should pay for it himself. . . .

Also, the fellows should be warned by the bearer of the roll that those eating in private rooms conduct themselves quietly and abstain from too much noise, lest those passing through the court and street be scandalized and lest the fellows in rooms adjoining be hindered in their studies. . . .

Also, the rule does not apply to the sick. If anyone eats in a private room because of sickness, he may have a fellow with him, if he wishes, to entertain and wait on him, who also shall have his due portion. What shall be the portion of a fellow shall be left to the discretion of the dispenser. If a fellow shall come late to lunch, if he comes from classes or a sermon or business of the community, he shall have his full portion, but if from his own affairs, he shall have bread only. . . .

Also, all shall wear closed outer garments, nor shall they have trimmings of vair or grise [8] or of red or green silk on the outer garment or hood.

Also, no one shall have loud shoes or clothing by which scandal might be generated in any way.

Also, no one shall be received in the house unless he shall be willing to leave off such and to observe the aforesaid rules.

Also, no one shall be received in the house unless he pledges faith that, if he happens to receive books from the common store, he will treat them carefully as if his own and on no condition remove or lend them out of the

---

8. **vair:** squirrel fur. **grise:** any type of gray fur.

house, and return them in good condition whenever required or whenever he leaves town.

Also, let every fellow have his own mark on his clothes and one only and different from the others. And let all the marks be written on a schedule and over each mark the name of whose it is. And let that schedule be given to the servant so that he may learn to recognize the mark of each one. And the servant shall not receive clothes from any fellow unless he sees the mark. And then the servant can return his clothes to each fellow. . . .

Also, for peace and utility we propound that no secular person living in town—scribe, corrector, or anyone else—unless for great cause eat, sleep in a room, or remain with the fellows when they eat, or have frequent conversation in the gardens or hall or other parts of the house, lest the secrets of the house and the remarks of the fellows be spread abroad.

Also, no outsider shall come to accountings or the special meetings of the fellows, and he whose guest he is shall see to this.

Also, no fellow shall bring in outsiders frequently to drink at commons, and if he does, he shall pay according to the estimate of the dispenser.

Also, no fellow shall have a key to the kitchen.

Also, no fellow shall presume to sleep outside the house in town, and if he did so for reason, he shall take pains to submit his excuse to the bearer of the roll. . . .

Also, no women of any sort shall eat in the private rooms. If anyone violates this rule, he shall pay the assessed penalty, namely, sixpence.[9] . . .

Also, no one shall form the habit of talking too loudly at table. Whoever after he has been warned about this by the prior shall have offended by speaking too loudly, provided this is established afterwards by testimony of several fellows to the prior, shall be held to the usual house penalty, namely two quarts of wine.

The penalty for transgression of statutes which do not fall under an oath is twopence, if the offenders are not reported by someone, or if they were, the penalty becomes sixpence in the case of fines. I understand "not reported" to mean that, if before the matter has come to the attention of the prior, the offender accuses himself to the prior or has told the clerk to write down twopence against him for such an offence, for it is not enough to say to the fellows, "I accuse myself."

9. This was a substantial amount for most students to pay.

Source 5 from James Harvey Robinson, editor and translator, Readings in European History, *vol. 1 (Boston: Ginn, 1904), pp. 450–452.*

5. Introduction to Peter Abelard's *Sic et Non,* ca 1122

There are many seeming contradictions and even obscurities in the innumerable writings of the church fathers. Our respect for their authority should not stand in the way of an effort on our part to come at the truth. The obscurity and contradictions in ancient writings may be explained upon many grounds, and may be discussed without impugning the good faith and insight of the fathers. A writer may use different terms to mean the same thing, in order to avoid a monotonous repetition of the same word. Common, vague words may be employed in order that the common people may understand; and sometimes a writer sacrifices perfect accuracy in the interest of a clear general statement. Poetical, figurative language is often obscure and vague.

Not infrequently apocryphal works are attributed to the saints. Then, even the best authors often introduce the erroneous views of others and leave the reader to distinguish between the true and the false. Sometimes, as Augustine confesses in his own case, the fathers ventured to rely upon the opinions of others.

Doubtless the fathers might err; even Peter, the prince of the apostles, fell into error; what wonder that the saints do not always show themselves inspired? The fathers did not themselves believe that they, or their companions, were always right. Augustine found himself mistaken in some cases and did not hesitate to retract his errors. He warns his admirers not to look upon his letters as they would upon the Scriptures, but to accept only those things which, upon examination, they find to be true.

All writings belonging to this class are to be read with full freedom to criticise, and with no obligation to accept unquestioningly; otherwise the way would be blocked to all discussion, and posterity be deprived of the excellent intellectual exercise of debating difficult questions of language and presentation. But an explicit exception must be made in the case of the Old and New Testaments. In the Scriptures, when anything strikes us as absurd, we may not say that the writer erred, but that the scribe made a blunder in copying the manuscripts, or that there is an error in interpretation, or that the passage is not understood. The fathers make a very careful distinction between the Scriptures and later works. They advocate a discriminating, not to say suspicious, use of the writings of their own contemporaries.

In view of these considerations, I have ventured to bring together various dicta of the holy fathers, as they came to mind, and to formulate certain questions which were suggested by the seeming contradictions in the statements. These questions ought to serve to excite tender readers to a zealous inquiry into truth and so sharpen their wits. The master key of knowledge is, indeed, a persistent and frequent questioning. Aristotle, the most clear-sighted of all the philosophers, was desirous above all things else to arouse this questioning spirit, for in his *Categories* he exhorts a student as follows: "It may well be difficult to reach a positive conclusion in these matters unless they be frequently discussed. It is by no means fruitless to be doubtful on particular points." By doubting we come to examine, and by examining we reach the truth.

[*Abelard provides arguments for and
against 158 different philosophical or
theological propositions. The following are
a few of the questions he discusses.*]

Should human faith be based upon reason, or no?
Is God one, or no?
Is God a substance, or no?
Does the first Psalm refer to Christ, or no?
Is sin pleasing to God, or no?
Is God the author of evil, or no?
Is God all-powerful, or no?
Can God be resisted, or no?
Has God free will, or no?
Was the first man persuaded to sin by the devil, or no?
Was Adam saved, or no?
Did all the apostles have wives except John, or no?
Are the flesh and blood of Christ in very truth and essence present in the
    sacrament of the altar, or no?
Do we sometimes sin unwillingly, or no?
Does God punish the same sin both here and in the future, or no?
Is it worse to sin openly than secretly, or no?

Source 6 from Roland H. Bainton, The Medieval Church *(Princeton, N.J.: D. VanNostrand,
1962), pp. 128–129.*

6. St. Anselm's Proof of the Existence of God, from His *Monologium,* ca 1070

I sought if I might find a single argument which would alone suffice to demonstrate that God exists. This I did in the spirit of faith seeking understanding. . . . Come now, O Lord my God, teach my heart where and how it may seek Thee. O Lord, if Thou art not here where shall I seek Thee absent, and if Thou art everywhere why do I not see Thee present? Surely Thou dwellest in light inaccessible. When wilt Thou enlighten our eyes? I do not presume to penetrate Thy profundity but only in some measure to understand Thy truth, which my heart believes and loves, for I seek not to understand that I may believe, but I believe in order that I may understand.

Now the fool will admit that there can be in the mind something than which nothing greater can be conceived. This, being understood, is in the mind, but it cannot be only in the mind, because it is possible to think of something which exists also in reality and that would be greater. If, therefore, that than which nothing greater can be conceived is only in the mind, that than which a greater cannot be conceived is that than which a greater can be conceived and this certainly cannot be. Consequently, without doubt, that than which nothing greater can be conceived exists both in the mind and in reality. This, then, is so sure that one cannot think of its not being so. For it is possible to think of something which one cannot conceive not to exist which is greater than that which cannot be conceived can be thought not to exist, it is not that a greater than which cannot be conceived. But this does not make sense. Therefore, it is true that something than which a greater cannot be conceived is not able to be conceived as not existing. This art Thou, O Lord, my God.

Source 7 from Lynn Thorndike, editor and translator, University Records and Life in the Middle Ages *(New York: Columbia University Press, 1944), pp. 66–67. Reprinted with permission of Columbia University Press, 562 W. 113th St., New York, NY 10025, via Copyright Clearance Center, Inc.*

7. Odofredus Announces His Law Lectures at Bologna, ca 1255

If you please, I will begin the *Old Digest*[10] on the eighth day or thereabouts after the feast of St. Michael[11] and I will finish it entire with all ordinary and extraordinary, Providence permitting, in the middle of August or thereabouts. The *Code*[12] I will always begin within about a fortnight of the feast of St. Michael and I will finish it with all ordinary and extraordinary, Providence permitting, on the first of August or thereabouts. The extraordinary lectures used not to be given by the doctors. And so all scholars including the

10. **Old Digest:** the first part of the *Digest,* the emperor Justinian's collation of laws, commentaries, and interpretations of laws by Roman jurists.

11. **feast of St. Michael:** September 29.

12. *Code:* another part of Justinian's collation of laws reflecting the additions to Roman law that came about after Christianity became the official religion of the empire.

unskilled and novices will be able to make good progress with me, for they will hear their text as a whole, nor will anything be left out, as was once done in this region, indeed was the usual practice. For I shall teach the unskilled and novices but also the advanced students. For the unskilled will be able to make satisfactory progress in the position of the case and exposition of the letter; the advanced students can become more erudite in the subtleties of questions and contrarieties. I shall also read all the glosses, which was not done before my time. . . .

For it is my purpose to teach you faithfully and in a kindly manner, in which instruction the following order has customarily been observed by the ancient and modern doctors and particularly by my master, which method I shall retain. First, I shall give you the summaries of each title before I come to the text. Second, I shall put forth well and distinctly and in the best terms I can the purport of each law. Third, I shall read the text in order to correct it. Fourth, I shall briefly restate the meaning. Fifth, I shall solve conflicts, adding general matters (which are commonly called *brocardica*) and subtle and useful distinctions and questions with the solutions, so far as divine Providence shall assist me. And if any law is deserving of a review by reason of its fame or difficulty, I shall reserve it for an afternoon review.

Source 8 from Anders Piltz, The World of Medieval Learning, *translated by David Jones (Totowa, N.J.: Barnes & Noble, 1981), p. 97.*

8. Introduction to *Digest* of Emperor Justinian, sixth century

Public law is the legislation which refers to the Roman state, *private law* on the other hand is of value to the individual. Common law contains statutes about sacrifices, the priesthood and civil servants. Private law can be divided into three parts: it comprises regulations based on natural law and regulations governing the intercourse of nations and of individuals. *Natural law* is what is taught to all living creatures by nature itself, laws which apply not only to mankind but to every living creature on the earth, in the heavens or in the seas. It is this that sanctions the union of man and woman, which is called marriage, and likewise the bearing and upbringing of children: we can see that other living creatures also possess understanding of this law. *International law* is the [commonly recognized set of] laws applied by every nation of the world. As can be seen it differs from natural law in that the latter is the same for all living creatures whereas the former only concerns human intercourse. . . . *Civil law* does not deviate completely from natural law but neither is it subordinate to it . . . . It is either written or unwritten . . . . Its

[163]

sources are laws, popular decisions, decisions of the senate, the decrees of princes and the opinions of jurists.... *Justice* is the earnest and steadfast desire to give every man the rights he is entitled to. The injunctions of the law are these: live honestly, do no man injury, give to every man what he is entitled to.

Jurisprudence is knowledge of divine and human things, the study of right and wrong.

Source 9 from The Letters of St. Bernard of Clairvaux, *translated by Bruno Scott James (Chicago: Henry Regnery Co. 1953), pp. 321, 328.*

9. Extracts from *The Letters of St. Bernard of Clairvaux*, 1140

Master Peter Abelard is a monk without a rule, a prelate without responsibility.... He speaks iniquity openly. He corrupts the integrity of the faith and the chastity of the Church. He oversteps the landmarks placed by our Fathers in discussing and writing about faith, the sacraments, and the Holy Trinity; he changes each thing according to his pleasure, adding to it or taking from it. In his books and in his works he shows himself to be a fabricator of falsehood, a coiner of perverse dogmas, proving himself a heretic not so much by his error as by his obstinate defence of error. He is a man who does not know his limitations, making void the virtue of the cross by the cleverness of his words. Nothing in heaven or on earth is hidden from him, except himself.... He has defiled the Church; he has infected with his own blight the minds of simple people. He tries to explore with his reason what the devout mind grasps at once with a vigorous faith. Faith believes, it does not dispute. But this man, apparently holding God suspect, will not believe anything until he has first examined it with his reason. When the Prophet says, "Unless you believe, you shall not understand," this man decries willing faith as levity, misusing that testimony of Solomon: "He that is hasty to believe is light of head." Let him therefore blame the Blessed Virgin Mary for quickly believing the angel when he announced to her that she should conceive and bring forth a son. Let him also blame him who, while on the verge of death, believed those words of One who was also dying: "This day thou shalt be with me in Paradise."

Source 10 from Cecil Headlam, The Story of Oxford *(London: Dent, 1907), pp. 234–235.*

10. Anonymous Account of a Student Riot at Oxford, 13th century

They [the townsmen] seized and imprisoned all scholars on whom they could lay hands, invaded their inns, made havoc of their goods and trampled their books under foot. In the face of such provocation the Proctors[13] sent their bedels[14] about the town, forbidding the students to leave their inns. But all commands and exhortations were in vain. By nine o'clock next morning, bands of scholars were parading the streets in martial array. If the Proctors failed to restrain them, the mayor was equally powerless to restrain his townsmen. The great bell of S. Martin's rang out an alarm; oxhorns were sounded in the streets; messengers were sent into the country to collect rustic allies. The clerks,[15] who numbered three thousand in all, began their attack simultaneously in various quarters. They broke open warehouses in the Spicery, the Cutlery and elsewhere. Armed with bows and arrows, swords and bucklers, slings and stones, they fell upon their opponents. Three they slew, and wounded fifty or more. One band, led by Fulk de Neyrmit, Rector of Piglesthorne, and his brother, took up a position in High Street between the Churches of S. Mary and All Saints', and attacked the house of a certain Edward Hales. This Hales was a longstanding enemy of the clerks. There were no half measures with him. He seized his crossbow, and from an upper chamber sent an unerring shaft into the eye of the pugnacious rector. The death of their valiant leader caused the clerks to lose heart. They fled, closely pursued by the townsmen and country-folk. Some were struck down in the streets, and others who had taken refuge in the churches were dragged out and driven mercilessly to prison, lashed with thongs and goaded with iron spikes.

Complaints of murder, violence and robbery were lodged straight-way with the King by both parties. The townsmen claimed three thousand pounds' damage. The commissioners, however, appointed to decide the matter, condemned them to pay two hundred marks, removed the bailiffs, and banished twelve of the most turbulent citizens from Oxford. Then the terms of peace were formally ratified.

---

13. **proctor:** university official who maintained order and supervised examinations.
14. **bedel:** assistant to the proctor.
15. **clerks:** here, students and teachers.

Source 11 from Dana Carleton Munro, editor and translator, Translations and Reprints from the Original Sources of European History, *vol. 2, no. 3 (Philadelphia: University of Pennsylvania Press, no date), pp. 19–21.*

11. Jacques de Vitry's Description of Student Life at Paris, ca 1225

Almost all the students at Paris, foreigners and natives, did absolutely nothing except learn or hear something new. Some studied merely to acquire knowledge, which is curiosity; others to acquire fame, which is vanity; others still for the sake of gain, which is cupidity and the vice of simony. Very few studied for their own edification, or that of others. They wrangled and disputed not merely about the various sects or about some discussions; but the differences between the countries also caused dissensions, hatreds and virulent animosities among them, and they impudently uttered all kinds of affronts and insults against one another.

They affirmed that the English were drunkards and had tails; the sons of France proud, effeminate and carefully adorned like women. They said that the Germans were furious and obscene at their feasts; the Normans, vain and boastful; the Poitevins, traitors and always adventurers. The Burgundians they considered vulgar and stupid. The Bretons were reputed to be fickle and changeable and were often reproached for the death of Arthur. The Lombards were called avaricious, vicious and cowardly; the Romans, seditious, turbulent and slanderous; the Sicilians, tyrannical and cruel; the inhabitants of Brabant, men of blood, incendiaries, brigands and ravishers; those of Flanders, fickle, prodigal, gluttonous, yielding as butter, and slothful. After such insults, from words they often came to blows.

I will not speak of those logicians, before whose eyes flitted constantly "the lice of Egypt," that is to say, all the sophistical subtleties, so that no one could comprehend their eloquent discourses in which, as says Isaiah, "there is no wisdom." As to the doctors of theology, "seated in Moses' seat," they were swollen with learning, but their charity was not edifying. Teaching and not practicing, they have "become as sounding brass or a tinkling cymbal," or like a canal of stone, always dry, which ought to carry water to "the bed of spices." They not only hated one another, but by their flatteries they enticed away the students of others; each one seeking his own glory, but caring not a whit about the welfare of souls.

Having listened intently to these words of the Apostle, "If a man desire the office of a bishop, he desireth a good work," they kept multiplying the prebends,[16] and seeking after the offices; and yet they sought the work

16. **prebends:** that part of church revenues paid as a clergyman's salary.

decidedly less than the preëminence, and they desired above all to have "the uppermost rooms at feasts and the chief seats in the synagogue, and greetings in the market." Although the Apostle James said, "My brethren, be not many masters," they on the contrary were in such haste to become masters, that most of them were not able to have any students, except by entreaties and payments. Now it is safer to listen than to teach, and a humble listener is better than an ignorant and presumptuous doctor. In short, the Lord had reserved for Himself among them all, only a few honorable and timorous men, who had not stood "in the way of sinners," nor sat down with the others in the envenomed seat.

Sources 12 and 13 from Charles Homer Haskins, The Rise of Universities *(Ithaca, N.Y.: Cornell University Press, 1957), pp. 77–80; pp. 85–87.*

12. Two Letters, thirteenth century

B. to his venerable master A., greeting. This is to inform you that I am studying at Oxford with the greatest diligence, but the matter of money stands greatly in the way of my promotion,[17] as it is now two months since I spent the last of what you sent me. The city is expensive and makes many demands; I have to rent lodgings, buy necessaries, and provide for many other things which I cannot now specify. Wherefore I respectfully beg your paternity that by the promptings of divine pity you may assist me, so that I may be able to complete what I have well begun. For you must know that without Ceres and Bacchus Apollo[18] grows cold.

To his son G. residing at Orleans P. of Besançon sends greetings with paternal zeal. It is written, "He also that is slothful in his work is brother to him that is a great waster." I have recently discovered that you live dissolutely and slothfully, preferring license to restraint and play to work and strumming a guitar while the others are at their studies, whence it happens that you have read but one volume of law while your more industrious companions have read several. Wherefore I have decided to exhort you herewith to repent utterly of your dissolute and careless ways, that you may no longer be called a waster and your shame may be turned to good repute.

17. **promotion:** that is, attaining his degree.
18. **Ceres:** Roman god of grain. **Bacchus:** god of wine. **Apollo:** god of wisdom.

13. Three Anonymous
Student Poems, twelfth century

I, a wandering scholar lad,
  Born for toil and sadness,
Oftentimes am driven by
  Poverty to madness.

Literature and knowledge I
  Fain would still be earning,
Were it not that want of pelf[19]
  Makes me cease from learning.

These torn clothes that cover me
  Are too thin and rotten;
Oft I have to suffer cold,
  By the warmth forgotten.

Scarce I can attend at church,
  Sing God's praises duly;
Mass and vespers both I miss,
  Though I love them truly.

Oh, thou pride of N——,
  By thy worth I pray thee
Give the suppliant help in need,
  Heaven will sure repay thee.

Take a mind unto thee now
  Like unto St. Martin;
Clothe the pilgrim's nakedness,
  Wish him well at parting.

So may God translate your soul
  Into peace eternal,
And the bliss of saints be yours
  In His realm supernal.

———————

We in our wandering,
Blithesome and squandering,
  Tara, tantara, teino!

Eat to satiety,
Drink with propriety;
  Tara, tantara, teino!

Laugh till our sides we split,
Rags on our hides we fit;
  Tara, tantara, teino!

Jesting eternally,
Quaffing infernally:
  Tara, tantara, teino!
                    etc.

———————

Some are gaming, some are drinking,
Some are living without thinking;
And of those who make the racket,
Some are stripped of coat and jacket;
Some get clothes of finer feather,
Some are cleaned out altogether;
No one there dreads death's invasion,
But all drink in emulation.

19. **pelf:** a contemptuous term for money.

QUESTIONS TO CONSIDER

You have now examined medieval universities and colleges from four points of view—those of the authorities who established them, the teachers who taught in them, the church officials who criticized them, and the students who attended them. In refining your description of university life, think first about points on which a number of sources agree. What role did religious and secular authorities play in the universities, both in their founding and in day-to-day operations? What privileges were extended to teachers and students, and how did these benefits affect their relationship with townspeople? Given these privileges along with student attitudes and actions, what opinion would you expect townspeople to have of students? Which of Sorbon's rules would you expect to have been frequently broken? What qualities did authorities and teachers alike see as vital to effective teaching? What qualities did both try to encourage in students? Would students have agreed about any of these? What problems did the authorities, teachers, and students all agree were most pressing for students?

Now turn to points on which you have contradictory information. How would you compare Abelard's beliefs about the role of logic in education with those of Bernard and de Vitry? How might Bernard and de Vitry have viewed Anselm's attempt to prove the existence of God through reason? Would Abelard have believed that the rules for students set out in Sources 1 through 4 helped or hindered the learning process? What suggestions for educational improvements might a philosopher like Abelard have made? A churchman like Bernard? Would Anselm and Odofredus have agreed about the proper methods and aims of education?

De Vitry's critique and the student poetry have pointed out that the rules for student life set out in Sources 1 through 4 were not always followed. The consequences of St. Bernard's criticism similarly demonstrate that Abelard's assertion of the need for free discussion of all topics was an ideal and not always the reality in medieval universities. In 1140, St. Bernard convinced the church leadership at the Council of Sens to condemn Abelard's teachings. Abelard appealed to the pope, who upheld the council's decision, and Abelard retired to a monastery, never to teach again. What does this incident indicate about where the ultimate authority in the university lay? Does this assertion of papal authority contradict any of the ideas expressed in other sources for this chapter besides Abelard's writings?

Some of the contradictions you have discovered are inherent in the highly different points of view of the four groups and are irreconcilable. You must, however, make some effort to resolve those contradictions that involve conflicting points of *fact* rather than simply conflicting *opinions*. Historians resolve contradictions in their sources by a variety of methods: by assessing the authors' intent and possible biases, giving weight to evidence that is likely to be most objective; by judging each source as partially valid, speculating on how each author's point of view might have affected his or her description; by trying to find additional information confirming one side or the other. At this point you can use the first two methods in your own thinking: Which observers do you judge to be most objective? Why did the students, teachers, and officials have different viewpoints in the first place? (You can also think about the third method historians use to resolve contradictions in their evidence: What other types of sources would you examine to confirm what you have discovered here?) Once you have made these judgments, you can complete your description of medieval university life.

Now move on to the second part of your task in this chapter, which is to compare medieval and modern university life. Some of the more striking contrasts have probably already occurred to you, but the best way to proceed is to think first about your evidence. What types of sources would give you the information for modern universities that you have unearthed for medieval ones? What are the modern equivalents of the medieval rules and ordinances? Of descriptions of student actions? Of student poetry? Of course announcements? Of philosophical treatises? Besides such parallel sources, where else can you find information about modern universities? What types of sources generated from modern universities,

or from their students and teachers, have no medieval equivalent?

After considering these points of similarity and difference in sources, we are ready to make a specific comparison of university life in medieval and modern times. Because higher education in the United States is so diverse—some colleges and universities are public and some private, some religious and some nonsectarian, some residential and some commuter—it would be best if you compared your own institution with the more generalized description of medieval universities that you have developed. Do you see any modern equivalents to the privileges granted students by popes and kings? To the frequent clashes between universities and their surrounding communities? To the pope's restriction of "academic freedom" in the case of Abelard? How would you compare the relationship between religious and political authorities in medieval universities and in your own institution? The concern of authorities for the methods and content of higher education? How would you compare student residential life? Student problems? The students themselves? Relations between students and their parents? How would you compare the subjects taught? The method of teaching? The status of the faculty? Relations between students and teachers? Teachers' and students' views of the ultimate aims of education?

Once you have drawn up your comparison, you will need to perform what is often the most difficult task of any historical inquiry, which is to suggest reasons for what you have discovered. In doing this, you need to speculate not only about why some things have changed, but also about why others have remained the same. In your view, what is the most important difference between medieval and modern universities, and why?

EPILOGUE

The pattern set by Paris and Bologna was a popular one; by 1500, more than eighty universities were in existence throughout Europe. Students often traveled from university to university in search of the best teachers or most amenable surroundings; because there were no admission forms or credits required for graduation, transferring from school to school was much easier in the Middle Ages than it is today.

As you have deduced from the sources, medieval students and teachers were criticized for all the seven deadly sins: greed, sloth, pride, lust, gluttony, envy, and anger. Toward the end of the Middle Ages, the university system itself came under increasing attack for being too remote from worldly concerns, providing students only with useless philosophical information that would never help them in the real world of politics and business. Especially in Italy, independent teachers of speech and writing began to offer young men who wanted an education an alternative to universities, setting up academies to teach practical rhetorical and literary skills for those who planned to engage in commerce, banking, or politics. This new program of study, called *humanism,* emphasized language and literature rather than theology and philosophy.

Though the universities initially opposed the humanist curriculum, by the sixteenth century a considerable number, especially the newer ones, began to change their offerings. They established endowed chairs for teachers of Latin, Greek, and Hebrew, particularly because students who had trained at humanist secondary schools demanded further language training.

The gradual introduction of humanism set a pattern that universities were to follow when any new body of knowledge or subject matter emerged. Innovative subjects and courses were at first generally taught outside the universities in separate academies or institutes, then slowly integrated into the university curriculum. In the seventeenth and eighteenth centuries, natural science was added in this way; in the nineteenth century, the social sciences and modern languages; and in the twentieth, a whole range of subjects, such as agriculture, engineering, and the fine arts. Thus, even though the university has survived since the Middle Ages, Peter Abelard or Robert de Sorbon might have difficulty recognizing the institution in its present-day form.

CHAPTER EIGHT

INFIDELS AND HERETICS: CRUSADES

OF THE HIGH MIDDLE AGES

The collapse of the Roman Empire in the West in the fifth century created a power vacuum, and the Christian church headed by the bishop of Rome emerged as a strong political and economic as well as religious institution. It owned a great deal of land, developed its own court system, and collected taxes. The bishop of Rome (later called the pope) gradually assumed more authority than any church official had earlier, transforming the Church into a clear hierarchy. Popes sent out missionaries throughout western, northern, and central Europe, called councils to decide church doctrine, appointed officials when positions became vacant, and established close relationships with kings and emperors. By the late eleventh century, Christianity was the primary religion in all of Europe, except for the southern part of Spain, which was under Muslim rule, and small Jewish communities in some towns and cities. Even in northern Sweden and Finland, the last areas to become Christianized, churches were being built and people baptized and buried in Christian ceremonies.

Under the leadership of a series of reforming popes beginning with Leo IX (pontificate 1049–1054), the western church announced its independence from secular rulers and its power over them, and it established authority over rulers and commoners alike in a wide array of disputes. Pope Gregory VII (pontificate 1073–1085) declared that all papal orders were orders of God and that he had the right to declare any ruler who opposed him a tyrant whose subjects could legitimately rebel. Under the leadership of Innocent III (pontificate 1198–1216), who became the most powerful pope in history, the Church in Rome declared itself to be supreme, united and *catholic* (worldwide), and responsible for the earthly well-being and eternal salvation of all citizens of Christendom. Innocent pushed the kings of France, Portugal, and England to do his will, and in 1215 he called together the Fourth Lateran Council, which gave ordained priests the power to transform bread and wine during church ceremonies into the body and blood of Christ (a change termed *transubstantiation*). This power was possessed by no other group in society, not even kings. Priests were now the mediators between everyone and God, and this papal doctrine set the spiritual hierarchy of the Church above the secular hierarchies of kings and other rulers.

The power and reach of the Roman church were thus substantial; nevertheless, both external and internal enemies threatened the Church's power. Papal claims to supreme worldwide authority were disputed by the leaders of the Christian church in what had been the eastern half of the Roman Empire. In this area—known as the Byzantine Empire, or Byzantium—the empire had not collapsed (though it did slowly shrink over the centuries), and the emperor maintained some authority over religious as well as political matters. Both the emperors and church leaders in Byzantium and elsewhere in eastern Europe did not accept the pope's claims, and they viewed the Christian churches in eastern Europe—generally termed "Orthodox"—as free of papal control.

Christianity also faced a challenge from Islam. During the life of the Prophet Muhammad (ca 570–632), the founder of Islam, Arabic Muslims began to conquer areas that had been Christian, first in the eastern Mediterranean and then across North Africa.

After Muhammad's death, Muslim forces crossed the Straits of Gibraltar and conquered most of the Iberian peninsula (present-day Spain and Portugal), and also pushed further north into Asia Minor (present-day Turkey). They did not force Christians to convert—though over the centuries many did—but they did order them to pay higher taxes than their Muslim subjects.

For many centuries Christians and Muslims maintained relatively calm relations with one another; Christian pilgrims were free to travel through Muslim lands to Jerusalem, and Muslims and Christians lived near one another in Spain and parts of Italy. This changed in the later eleventh century when the Seljuk Turks, who had recently converted to Islam, conquered Syria and most of Asia Minor from the Byzantine Empire and took over control of Jerusalem from the more tolerant Abbasid Muslims. They began to bar pilgrims and to make life more difficult for Christians and Jews living in their territories. At the same time, Christian armies began slowly conquering Muslim holdings in central Spain and Sicily. The pope sponsored groups of soldiers in both of these campaigns, and Pope Gregory VII asserted that any land conquered from the Muslims belonged to the papacy because it had been territory held by *infidels,* a word meaning "unbeliever" that Christians and Muslims both came to use to describe the other.

A third challenge to the power of the Roman church came from individuals and groups within western Europe who disagreed with papal teachings on

Chapter 8

Infidels and

Heretics:

Crusades of the

High Middle

Ages

various topics but still understood themselves to be Christians. Christianity arose from the teachings of Jesus of Nazareth (ca 5 B.C.–A.D. 29), whom his followers believed to be divine. The sayings of Jesus and the accounts of his preaching were often enigmatic, however, and so were used to support widely differing ideas and practices. This diversity was troubling to many Christian leaders, and they thus began to declare certain ideas *orthodox,* that is, acceptable or correct, and others *heretical,* that is, unacceptable or incorrect.[1] Church councils, philosophers, and officials debated various points of belief and practice—such as the relationship between the divine and human in Jesus, or whether believers should be baptized when they are children or adults, or whether humans have free will—and on many issues gradually drew a line between heresy and orthodoxy. Incorrect belief would lead, in orthodox opinion, to damnation, and heretics might also "infect" others with their beliefs, which would then endanger the salvation of others as well.

"Heresy" and "orthodoxy" are, of course, relative terms. Only those who don't accept a belief label it as a heresy; to those who accept it, the others are the heretics. Official rulings on

certain points of belief and practice were frequently ignored by groups or individuals whose opinions differed, and church leaders had to decide whether and how to respond.

During the eleventh century, especially in northern Italy and southern France, large numbers of people were attracted by ideas that the Church judged heretical.

One group, called by their enemies the Cathars or the Albigensians (from Albi, a town in southern France), asserted that the material world was created not by the good god of the New Testament, but by a different evil god of the Old Testament. The idea that there are two gods, one good and one evil, is generally termed *dualism* and is found in many cultures and historical periods worldwide. Dualistic ideas emerged first in Christianity in the eastern church, becoming especially strong in the area that would later be Bulgaria; exactly how and when they were transported to southern France is not clear. What is clear is that by the twelfth century many people, including prominent nobles and wealthy townspeople, had accepted them and no longer supported the Roman church, which they viewed as founded by the evil god. Understandably, the Roman church saw dualism—the Cathars—as heretics.

The Cathars, who called themselves simply "good people," especially denounced the materialism of the Church. They emphasized the statements of Christ and the apostles in the New Testament about the evils of material goods, and contrasted these with the wealth and power of

---

1. To avoid confusion, when referring to beliefs that are judged acceptable, "orthodox" is spelled with a small *o,* and when referring to the Christianity in eastern Europe, "Orthodox" is spelled with a capital letter. Christians in eastern Europe thus regard their beliefs as both Orthodox and orthodox. The Christian church in western Europe is generally referred to as the Roman church or, since the sixteenth century, as the Roman Catholic Church.

the Roman church. For Cathars it was not a ritual of ordination that gave a man priestly power, but living an ascetic life. They rejected the authority, hierarchy, and sacraments of the Roman church and began setting up their own bishoprics.

Thus although in some ways the western church in the High Middle Ages was very powerful, external and internal enemies clearly challenged that power, and the church hierarchy had to decide on an appropriate response. Pope Gregory VII considered leading an army in person into the Byzantine Empire to reunite both eastern and western churches under papal control, and he encouraged Norman military campaigns against Byzantium. His successor Urban II (pontificate 1088–1099) was more interested in diplomatic methods of healing the split, as was the new emperor of Byzantium, Alexius I Comnenus (r. 1081–1118), and relations between the eastern and western churches improved. Alexius saw this as a good time to enlist western help in his campaign to retake Asia Minor from the Seljuk Turks, and he sent an ambassador to Pope Urban II in 1095 asking him for assistance in recruiting soldiers. Urban II decided to go much further than this, however, and at a council of French bishops at Clermont in November 1095 urged a military campaign not simply to help the Byzantines against the Turks in Asia Minor, but to take Jerusalem as well. Thus Urban II rejected a direct military solution to the split between the western and eastern churches, but advocated one in the conflict between Christianity and Islam. About one

hundred years later, in 1208, Pope Innocent III decided that similar measures were needed against the Cathars, and he called for a military campaign to wipe out heresy and take back southern France for the Church. The leader of this crusade, Simon of Montfort, was a northern French noble who had himself been a crusader to the Holy Land on the Fourth Crusade in 1202–1203. (For more on the Fourth Crusade, see the Epilogue.) He was joined by other northern French nobles, who saw this as an opportunity to gain wealth and glory, and the whole enterprise was supported by the king of France, who saw it as an opportunity to gain territory.

In both of these campaigns, the pope called on Christian fighters to oppose the enemy, in what has since come to be termed a "crusade." (The word *crusade* did not appear in English until the late sixteenth century, and it means literally "taking the cross," from the cross that soldiers sewed on their garments as a Christian symbol; people going off to fight simply said they were taking "the way of the cross" or "the road to Jerusalem.") One of these enemies was external—Muslim infidels—and one of them was internal—Cathar heretics—but both threatened the power of the western Christian church.

The crusades against the Muslims have been the subjects of History Channel series, network primetime specials, websites, popular and scholarly books, and even video games. The crusades against the Cathars have received much less attention, but in significant ways they were very similar to those against the Muslims. Both

Chapter 8

Infidels and

Heretics:

Crusades of the

High Middle

Ages

crusades were initiated by the pope, included sieges of cities held by the enemy, and involved mass movements of troops and the people who supplied them; participants in both of them produced written descriptions and explanations of what happened and recorded deeds of bravery and treachery. Both campaigns arose within the context of the split between the eastern and western churches, which, as we will see, interwove in various, sometimes tragic, ways with the battles against Muslims and Cathars. Your job in this chapter will be to use letters, chronicles, and reports to compare and contrast aspects of the two crusades.

(Because there was no official crusade against the eastern church, the documents in this chapter do not deal directly with that split, but focus on the campaigns against Muslims and Cathars.) How did the western church in the High Middle Ages encourage people to respond to external and internal threats to its power and vision of salvation? How did people actually respond? In the minds of those who called for or went on crusades, how were infidels and heretics similar, and how were they different? Along with the authority of the Church, what other aims and values of high medieval culture do the records of the crusades reveal?

SOURCES AND METHOD

Most of the sources in this chapter were written by men who participated in the Crusades on the side of the Roman church. In some instances they were eyewitnesses to the events they describe, and in others they reported what people who had actually been there told them. The sources thus do not present all sides of these campaigns; for this we would need Muslim and Cathar documents. However, because our focus in this chapter is on the ideas, words, and actions of western church officials and those who went on crusades, documents written by individuals sympathetic to those crusades are appropriate sources. We are looking for aspects of *their* point of view as they confronted different types of challenges.

In order to compare the two crusades, you might take your notes on the readings in two side-by-side columns. As you read, pay close attention to the language used by their authors and the individuals they quote. Some issues to think about for your comparison include the words used to describe the enemies of the Church; the aims the popes set for the campaigns they proposed; the reward offered for those who followed the call; the way the participants and the battles are described; and the role (in the mind of the chronicler) of divine intervention.

Source 1 is from the *Chronicle of the First Crusade* by Fulcher of Chartres (1059–1127), a French priest who attended the Council of Clermont in 1095 and who was inspired to join the forces setting off to conquer Jerusalem. He moved between the armies commanded by different northern French nobles, and he stayed on in the crusader kingdoms founded after the fall of Jerusalem until his death in 1127. He was quite learned and well read, though he was not a nobleman or a high church official, and among chroniclers of this first crusade he is regarded as generally reliable. The section reproduced here includes Fulcher's version of Urban's decree at the Council of Clermont and his description of the impact of Urban's words. (Other chronicles have slightly different versions, and there is no official record of this from Urban's own hand.) Read Source 1 carefully. What does Urban exhort his listeners to do? What sort of people does he envision accepting his invitation? What kind of language does Urban use to describe the Turks? What does he promise as a reward for taking up his call? How does Fulcher describe the scenes when the fighters left their homes?

Source 2 is from another chronicle of the Crusades, *The Deeds of the Franks and Other Pilgrims to Jerusalem,* written by an anonymous author who was a vassal of Bohemond, the Norman ruler of southern Italy. The author was a layman and a knight, and he—or members of his family—may have taken part in Norman campaigns during the 1080s against the Muslims in Sicily or the Byzantine Empire. The chronicle covers the period from 1095 to 1099, and appears to have been written by 1101; it was widely known, frequently recopied, and heavily used by later authors of chronicles, who often repeat many of its sections verbatim without mentioning their source. (In the manuscript culture of the Middle Ages, plagiarism was seen as a sign of respect for someone's work.) Because the author is a layman, not a cleric, he has a slightly different perspective from Fulcher. The section included here picks up the story after Clermont, describes the author's journey toward Jerusalem, and discusses the battle for the city of Nicaea in Asia Minor, the first major battle fought by the European armies. What words does the author use to describe his lord Bohemond and the knights on his side? What is the response of this army when they encounter dualist heretics on their way to Jerusalem? What factors does he see as important in the successful overtaking of Nicaea? How does he summarize the results of the battle?

Sources 3 and 4 are letters written by noblemen who responded to the pope's call. Source 3 is a letter written in 1098 from Stephen, count of Blois and Chartes, to his wife Adele back in France. In this, Stephen picks up the story after the capture of Nicaea and describes the long siege of Antioch. Source 4 is a letter from three other participants in the crusade—Daimbert, the archbishop of Pisa, Duke Godfrey of Bouillon, and Count Raymond of St. Gilles—written in the name of the whole army and addressed to the pope, the bishops, and "the whole Christian people." It summarizes the long siege of Antioch and the very brief siege of Jerusalem, and discusses a second major battle in defense of crusader holdings in the Holy Land. What aspects of the battles do the authors highlight? How do they portray the military ability

Chapter 8

Infidels and

Heretics:

Crusades of the

High Middle

Ages

and tactics of the crusaders' opponents? How do they see the hand of God working in their battles? How do the authors describe their own goals? Source 4 ends with a series of specific requests from the crusaders; what rewards do they hope to achieve?

With Source 5, we turn to the material on the Cathar crusade. Source 5 includes several sections from *The History of the Albigensian Crusade* by Peter of Les Vaux-de-Cernay, a Cistercian monk from an abbey near Paris. Peter's uncle Guy, the abbot there, went to the south of France first to preach against Cathar heretics and in 1212 to be part of the crusade against them, taking Peter along on his second trip. Abbot Guy later became bishop of Carcassone, a city in the heart of Cathar territory, and was close friends with Simon of Montfort. Peter admired Simon greatly, and his account is clearly written from a pro-crusade perspective. It is nevertheless valuable in its eyewitness reports and proximity to the events, as it was probably written during the period 1213–1215. The first part of Source 5 is a letter from Pope Innocent III to the nobles of central France in which the pope describes the murder of Peter of Castelnau, a Cistercian monk he had sent to preach against the heretics, and then calls for a crusade against them. In contrast to Urban II's call for a crusade, which was delivered orally and which only exists in reports from people who heard it or heard about it, this is the actual papal letter, of which there are many official copies. Peter of Les Vaux-de-Cernay clearly had access to one of these copies, since he repeats the

letter here verbatim. How does Urban describe Peter of Castelnau? What sort of language does he use to describe Count Raymond of Toulouse, whom he viewed as a protector of heretics and perhaps one himself? Who is to avenge the murder and fight against heresy? What is to be done to heretics and those who protect them? How will the crusaders be rewarded? How should this crusade compare with those against Muslims, in Innocent's opinion? The second part of Source 5 describes Simon of Montfort's siege in 1211 of Lavaur, a fortified town and stronghold of Catharism. What sort of words does Peter use to describe the heretics? What actions of theirs does he use to justify his opinion of them? How does he describe the crusaders who died? How does he describe the battle? To what does he ascribe victory?

Source 6 is from a second chronicle, *The Song of the Cathar Wars,* begun by William of Tudela, who describes himself as a member of the clergy native to Navarre (in present-day northern Spain). William began writing this work in 1210; an anonymous author finished it. It was written in verse in Occitan, the language of southern France, and was to be sung as entertainment, but it is largely a reliable account of the events it relates. The selection included here is from the part written by William, who clearly supported the papacy, and tells the story of the beginning of the crusade. How does he describe the response of the pope and the bishops to the murder of Peter of Castelnau? How does he describe the group that gathered to fight the heretics?

Source 7, the final source in this chapter, is a papal letter from Innocent III to Arnold Amalric of Cîteaux (the same Arnold of Source 6), who was the pope's official representative in southern France. During 1211 and 1212 the crusaders under Simon of Montfort had been very successful, so successful that Peter II, the king of Aragon whose territories bordered the lands now held by Simon of Montfort, became worried about Simon's power. He persuaded the pope that Simon was using the crusade to enhance his personal power and that the crusade should be halted. In this letter, what does the pope order Arnold Amalric to do? How does he justify this? How does he compare the threat posed by the heretics with that posed by Muslims?

THE EVIDENCE

Source 1 from Fulcher of Chartes, Chronicle of the First Crusade, *translated by Martha Evelyn McGinty (Philadelphia: University of Pennsylvania Press, 1941), pp. 15–18, 23–24.*

1. From Fulcher of Chartes, *Chronicle of the First Crusade*

POPE URBAN'S DECREE AT THE COUNCIL OF CLERMONT

2. "Now that you, O sons of God, have consecrated yourselves to God to maintain peace among yourselves more vigorously and to uphold the laws of the Church faithfully, there is work to do, for you must turn the strength of your sincerity, now that you are aroused by divine correction, to another affair that concerns you and God. Hastening to the way, you must help your brothers living in the Orient, who need your aid for which they have already cried out many times.[2]

3. "For, as most of you have been told, the Turks, a race of Persians,[3] who have penetrated within the boundaries of Romania[4] even to the Mediterranean to that point which they call the Arm of Saint George,[5] in occupying more and more of the lands of the Christians, have overcome them, already victims of seven battles, and have killed and captured them, have overthrown churches, and have laid waste God's kingdom. If you permit this supinely for very long, God's faithful ones will be still further subjected.

---

2. Alexius I Comnenus had asked Urban II twice for help.

3. The Seljuk Turks were not Persians, but came from central Asia.

4. Fulcher is here using "Romania" to describe both Europe and the territory of the Byzantine Empire in Asia Minor. The Seljuk Turks called this territory Rum.

5. **Arm of Saint George:** the Bosporus, the strait that separates present-day Greece from Turkey.

Chapter 8

Infidels and

Heretics:

Crusades of the

High Middle

Ages

4. "Concerning this affair, I, with suppliant prayer—not I, but the Lord—exhort you, heralds of Christ, to persuade all of whatever class, both knights and footmen, both rich and poor, in numerous edicts, to strive to help expel that wicked race from our Christian lands before it is too late.

5. "I speak to those present, I send word to those not here; moreover, Christ commands it. Remission of sins will be granted for those going thither, if they end a shackled life either on land or in crossing the sea, or in struggling against the heathen. I, being vested with that gift from God, grant this to those who go.

6. "O what a shame, if a people, so despised, degenerate, and enslaved by demons would thus overcome a people endowed with the trust of almighty God, and shining in the name of Christ! O how many evils will be imputed to you by the Lord Himself, if you do not help those who, like you, profess Christianity!

7. "Let those . . . who are accustomed to wage private wars wastefully even against Believers, go forth against the Infidels in a battle worthy to be undertaken now and to be finished in victory. Now, let those, who until recently existed as plunderers, be soldiers of Christ; now, let those, who formerly contended against brothers and relations, rightly fight barbarians; now, let those, who recently were hired for a few pieces of silver, win their eternal reward. Let those, who wearied themselves to the detriment of body and soul, labor for a twofold honor. Nay, more, the sorrowful here will be glad there, the poor here will be rich there, and the enemies of the Lord here will be His friends there.

8. "Let no delay postpone the journey of those about to go, but when they have collected the money owed to them and the expenses for the journey, and when winter has ended and spring has come, let them enter the crossroads courageously with the Lord going on before."

IV

THE BISHOP OF PUY AND THE EVENTS AFTER THE COUNCIL

1. After these words were spoken, the hearers were fervently inspired. Thinking nothing more worthy than such an undertaking, many in the audience solemnly promised to go, and to urge diligently those who were absent. There was among them one Bishop of Puy, Ademar by name,[6] who afterwards, acting as vicar-apostolic, ruled the whole army of God wisely and thoughtfully, and spurred them to complete their undertaking vigorously. . . .

3. Many, one after another, of any and every occupation, after confession of their sins and with purified spirits, consecrated themselves to go where they were bidden.

4. Oh, how worthy and delightful to all of us who saw those beautiful crosses, either silken or woven of gold, or of any material, which the pilgrims sewed on the shoulders of their woolen cloaks or cassocks by the command of the Pope, after taking the vow to go. To be sure, God's soldiers, who were making

---

6. Ademar de Monteil, bishop of Puy in France, was the first to respond to Urban's exhortation.

themselves ready to battle for His honor, ought to have been marked and forti-fied with a sign of victory. And so by embroidering the symbol [of the cross] on their clothing in recognition of their faith, in the end they won the True Cross it-self. They imprinted the ideal so that they might attain the reality of the ideal. . . .

10. What more shall I tell? The islands of the seas and all the kingdoms of the earth were so agitated that one believed that the prophecy of David was ful-filled, who said in his Psalm: "All nations whom Thou hast made shall come and worship before Thee, O Lord";[7] and what those going all the way there later said with good reason: "We shall worship in the place where His feet have stood."[8] We have read much about this in the Prophets which it is tedious to repeat.

11. Oh, how much grief there was! How many sighs! How much sorrow! How much weeping among loved ones when the husband left his wife so dear to him, as well as his children, father and mother, brothers and grandparents, and possessions however great!

12. But however so many tears those remaining shed for those going, these were not swayed by such tears from leaving all that they possessed; without doubt believing that they would receive an hundredfold what the Lord promised to those loving him.

13. Then the wife reckoned the time of her husband's return, because if God permitted him to live, he would come home to her. He commended her to the Lord, kissed her, and promised as she wept that he would return. She, fearing that she would never see him again, not able to hold up, fell senseless to the ground; mourning her living beloved as though he were dead. He, having compassion, it seems, neither for the weeping of his wife, nor feeling pain for the grief of any friends, and yet having it, for he suffered severely, unchanging, went away with a determined mind.

14. Sadness to those remaining, however, was joy to those going away. What, then, can we say? "This is the Lord's doing; it is marvelous in our eyes."[9]

Source 2 from Rosalind Hill, editor, The Deeds of the Franks and Other Pilgrims to Jerusalem *(London: Thomas Nelson and Sons Ltd., 1962), pp. 7, 8, 14–15, 17.*

2. From *The Deeds of the Franks and other Pilgrims to Jerusalem*

As for Bohemond, that great warrior, he was besieging Amalfi[10] when he heard that an immense army of Frankish[11] crusaders had arrived, going to the Holy

7. Psalms 86:9.
8. Psalms 132:7.
9. Psalms 118:23.
10. **Amalfi:** a port town in southern Italy that Bohemond was attempting to make part of the Nor-man kingdom.
11. **Frankish:** here, a generic term for all crusaders.

Chapter 8

Infidels and

Heretics:

Crusades of the

High Middle

Ages

Sepulchre and ready to fight the pagans. So he began to make careful inquiries as to the arms they carried, the badge which they wore in Christ's pilgrimage and the war-cry which they shouted in battle. He was told, 'They are well-armed, they wear the badge of Christ's cross on their right arm or between their shoulders, and as a war-cry they shout all together "God's will, God's will, God's will!"' Then Bohemond, inspired by the Holy Ghost, ordered the most valuable cloak which he had to be cut up forthwith and made into crosses, and most of the knights who were at the siege began to join him at once, for they were full of enthusiasm, so that Count Roger[12] was left almost alone, and when he had gone back to Sicily he grieved and lamented because he had lost his army. My lord Bohemond went home to his own land and made careful preparations for setting out on the way to the Holy Sepulchre. Thereafter he crossed the sea with his army. . . .

Then we set out and travelled through very rich country from one village to another, and from one city to another and from one castle to another, until we came to Castoria,[13] where we held the feast of Christmas and stayed for some days trying to buy provisions, but the inhabitants would sell us none, because they were much afraid of us, taking us to be no pilgrims but plunderers come to lay waste the land and to kill them. So we seized oxen, horses and asses, and anything else we could find, and leaving Castoria we went into Palagonia,[14] where there was a castle of heretics.[15] We attacked this place from all sides and it soon fell into our hands, so we set fire to it and burnt the castle and its inhabitants together. . . .

Eventually we came to Nicea, which is the capital of Rum, on Wednesday the sixth of May, and there we encamped. Before my lord the valiant Bohemond came to us we were so short of food that a loaf cost twenty or thirty pence, but after he came he ordered plenty of provisions to be brought to us by sea, so goods poured in both by land and sea, and all Christ's army enjoyed great abundance.

[viii] On Ascension Day[16] we began to lay siege to the town, and to build siege-engines and wooden towers by means of which we could knock down the towers on the wall. We pressed the siege so bravely and fiercely for two days that we managed to undermine the wall of the city, but the Turks who were inside sent messengers to the others who had come to their help, telling them that they might come and enter, fearlessly and safely, by way of the south gate, for there was no-one there to stand in their way or attack them. This gate, however, was blocked on that very day (the Saturday after Ascension Day) by the count of St. Gilles and the bishop of Le Puy. The count, who came from the

---

12. Roger Guiscard, Bohemond's uncle.

13. **Castoria:** Kastoria, a town in central Greece.

14. **Palagonia:** now Bitola, a town in present-day Macedonia.

15. Probably dualistic heretics, since there were many in this area.

16. May 14, 1097.

other side of the city with a very strong army, trusting in God's protection and glorious in his earthly weapons, found the Turks coming towards the gate against our men. Protected on all sides by the sign of the Cross, he made a fierce attack upon the enemy and defeated them so that they took to flight and many of them were killed. . . .

We besieged this city for seven weeks and three days, and many of our men suffered martyrdom there and gave up their blessed souls to God with joy and gladness, and many of the poor starved to death for the Name of Christ. All these entered Heaven in triumph, wearing the robe of martyrdom which they have received, saying with one voice, 'Avenge, O Lord, our blood which was shed for thee, for thou art blessed and worthy of praise for ever and ever. Amen.'

Sources 3 and 4 from Translations and Reprints from the Original Sources of European History *(Philadelphia: University of Pennsylvania Department of History, 1897), pp. 5–12.*

3. Letter from Stephen, Count of Blois and Chartes, to His Wife Adele

Count Stephen to Adele, his sweetest and most amiable wife, to his dear children, and to all his vassals of all ranks—his greeting and blessing.

You may be very sure, dearest, that the messenger whom I sent to give you pleasure, left me before Antioch safe and unharmed, and through God's grace in the greatest prosperity. And already at that time, together with all the chosen army of Christ, endowed with great valor by Him, we had been continuously advancing for twenty-three weeks toward the home of our Lord Jesus. You may know for certain, my beloved, that of gold, silver and many other kind of riches I now have twice as much as your love had assigned to me when I left you. For all our princes, with the common consent of the whole army, against my own wishes, have made me up to the present time the leader, chief and director of their whole expedition.

You have certainly heard that after the capture of the city of Nicaea we fought a great battle with the perfidious Turks and by God's aid conquered them. Next we conquered for the Lord all Romania.[17] . . . Hastening with great joy to the . . . city of Antioch, we besieged it and very often had many conflicts there with the Turks; and seven times with the citizens of Antioch and with the innumerable troops coming to its aid, whom we rushed to meet, we fought with the fiercest courage, under the leadership of Christ. And in all these seven battles, by the aid of the Lord God, we conquered and most assuredly killed an innumerable host of them. In those battles, indeed, and in very many attacks made upon the city, many of our brethren and followers were killed and their souls were borne to the joys of paradise.

17. **Romania:** modern-day Turkey.

Chapter 8

Infidels and

Heretics:

Crusades of the

High Middle

Ages

We found the city of Antioch very extensive, fortified with incredible strength and almost impregnable. In addition, more than 5,000 bold Turkish soldiers had entered the city, not counting the Saracens, Publicans, Arabs, Turcopolitans, Syrians, Armenians and other different races of whom an infinite multitude had gathered together there. In fighting against these enemies of God and of our own we have, by God's grace, endured many sufferings and innumerable evils up to the present time. Many also have already exhausted all their resources in this very holy passion. Very many of our Franks, indeed, would have met a temporal death from starvation, if the clemency of God and our money had not succoured them. Before the above-mentioned city of Antioch indeed, throughout the whole winter we suffered for our Lord Christ from excessive cold and enormous torrents of rain. What some say about the impossibility of bearing the heat of the sun throughout Syria is untrue, for the winter there is very similar to our winter in the west. . . .

I love to tell you, dearest, what happened to us during Lent. Our princes had caused a fortress to be built before a certain gate which was between our camp and the sea. For the Turks daily issuing from this gate, killed some of our men on their way to the sea. The city of Antioch is about five leagues' distance from the sea. For this reason they sent the excellent Bohemond and Raymond, count of St. Gilles, to the sea with only sixty horsemen, in order that they might bring mariners to aid in this work. When, however, they were returning to us with those mariners, the Turks collected an army, fell suddenly upon our two leaders and forced them to a perilous flight. In that unexpected flight we lost more than 500 of our foot-soldiers—to the glory of God. Of our horsemen, however, we lost only two, for certain.

On that same day truly, in order to receive our brethren with joy, and ignorant of their misfortunes, we went out to meet them. When, however, we approached the above-mentioned gate of the city, a mob of horsemen and foot-soldiers from Antioch, elated by the victory which they had won, rushed upon us in the same manner. Seeing these, our leaders sent to the camp of the Christians to order all to be ready to follow us into battle. In the meantime our men gathered together and the scattered leaders, namely, Bohemond and Raymond, with the remainder of their army came up and narrated the great misfortune which they had suffered.

Our men, full of fury at these most evil tidings, prepared to die for Christ and, deeply grieved for their brethren, rushed upon the sacrilegious Turks. They, enemies of God and of us, hastily fled before us and attempted to enter their city. But by God's grace the affair turned out very differently; for, when they wanted to cross a bridge built over the great river *Moscholum*, we followed them as closely as possible, killed many before they reached the bridge, forced many into the river, all of whom were killed, and we also slew many upon the bridge and very many at the narrow entrance to the gate. I am telling you the truth, my beloved, and you may be very certain that in this battle we killed thirty emirs, that is princes, and three hundred other Turkish nobles, not counting the remaining

Turks and pagans. Indeed, the number of Turks and Saracens killed is reckoned at 1,230, but of ours we did not lose a single man. . . .

These which I write to you, are only a few things, dearest, of the many which we have done, and because I am not able to tell you, dearest, what is in my mind, I charge you to do right, to carefully watch over your land, to do your duty as you ought to your children and your vassals. You will certainly see me just as soon as I can possibly return to you. Farewell.

4. Letter to the Pope and Bishops from the Archbishop of Pisa, Godfrey of Bouillon, and Raymond of St. Gilles

To lord Paschal, pope of the Roman church, to all the bishops, and to the whole Christian people, from the archbishop of Pisa, duke Godfrey, now, by the grace of God, defender of the church of the Holy Sepulchre,[18] Raymond, count of St. Gilles, and the whole army of God, which is in the land of Israel, greeting.

Multiply your supplications and prayers in the sight of God with joy and thanksgiving, since God has manifested His mercy in fulfilling by our hands what He had promised in ancient times. For after the capture of Nicaea, the whole army, made up of more than three hundred thousand soldiers, departed thence. And, although this army was so great that it could have in a single day covered all Romania and drunk up all the rivers and eaten up all the growing things, yet the Lord conducted them amid so great abundance that a ram was sold for a penny and an ox for twelve pennies or less. Moreover, although the princes and kings of the Saracens[19] rose up against us, yet, by God's will, they were easily conquered and overcome. Because, indeed, some were puffed up by these successes, God opposed to us Antioch, impregnable to human strength. And there He detained us for nine months and so humbled us in the siege that there were scarcely a hundred good horses in our whole army. God opened to us the abundance of His blessing and mercy and led us into the city, and delivered the Turks and all of their possessions into our power.

Inasmuch as we thought that these had been acquired by our own strength and did not worthily magnify God who had done this, we were beset by so great a multitude of Turks that no one dared to venture forth at any point from the city. Moreover, hunger so weakened us that some could scarcely refrain from eating human flesh. It would be tedious to narrate all the miseries which we suffered in that city. But God looked down upon His people whom He had

18. Godfrey was made the ruler of Jerusalem after it was conquered, but he was given the title "defender of the church of the Holy Sepulchre," not "king," to show that he was under the authority of the pope; he died within a year.
19. **Saracens:** Muslims.

Chapter 8

Infidels and

Heretics:

Crusades of the

High Middle

Ages

so long chastised and mercifully consoled them. Therefore, He at first revealed to us, as a recompense for our tribulation and as a pledge of victory, His lance which had lain hidden since the days of the apostles.[20] Next, He so fortified the hearts of the men, that they who from sickness or hunger had been unable to walk, now were endued with strength to seize their weapons and manfully to fight against the enemy.

After we had triumphed over the enemy, as our army was wasting away at Antioch from sickness and weariness and was especially hindered by the dissensions among the leaders, we proceeded into Syria, stormed Barra and Marra, cities of the Saracens, and captured the fortresses in that country. And while we were delaying there, there was so great a famine in the army that the Christian people now ate the putrid bodies of the Saracens. . . . Therefore, with the Lord's companionship and aid, we proceeded thus as far as Jerusalem.

And after the army had suffered greatly in the siege, especially on account of the lack of water, a council was held and the bishops and princes ordered that all with bare feet should march around the walls of the city, in order that He who entered it humbly in our behalf might be moved by our humility to open it to us and to exercise judgment upon His enemies. God was appeased by this humility and on the eighth day after the humiliation He delivered the city and His enemies to us. It was the day indeed on which the primitive church was driven thence, and on which the festival of the dispersion of the apostles is celebrated. And if you desire to know what was done with the enemy who were found there, know that in Solomon's Porch and in his temple our men rode in the blood of the Saracens up to the knees of their horses.

Then, when we were considering who ought to hold the city, and some moved by love for their country and kinsmen wished to return home, it was announced to us that the king of Babylon had come to Ascalon[21] with an innumerable multitude of soldiers. His purpose was, as he said, to lead the Franks, who were in Jerusalem, into captivity, and to take Antioch by storm. But God had determined otherwise in regard to us.

Therefore, when we learned that the army of the Babylonians was at Ascalon, we went down to meet them, leaving our baggage and the sick in Jerusalem with a garrison. When our army was in sight of the enemy, upon our knees we invoked the aid of the Lord, that He who in our other adversities had strengthened the Christian faith, might in the present battle break the strength of the Saracens and of the devil and extend the kingdom of the church of Christ from sea to sea, over the whole world. There was no delay; God was

---

20. Several crusaders reported visions of St. Andrew and St. Peter telling them the lance that had been used to pierce Christ's side was buried in a church at Antioch; it was later dug up at this site. Though Fulcher and other authors suspected it had been planted there, most of the army regarded it as authentic, and their interest in fighting was renewed.

21. **Ascalon:** a city near Jerusalem.

present when we cried for His aid, and furnished us with so great boldness, that one who saw us rush upon the enemy would have taken us for a herd of deer hastening to quench their thirst in running water. It was wonderful, indeed, since there were in our army not more than 5,000 horsemen and 15,000 foot-soldiers, and there were probably in the enemy's army 100,000 horsemen and 400,000 foot-soldiers. Then God appeared wonderful to His servants. For before we engaged in fighting, by our very onset alone, He turned his multitude in flight and scattered all their weapons, so that if they wished afterwards to attack us, they did not have the weapons in which they trusted. There can be no question how great the spoils were, since the treasures of the king of Babylon were captured. More than 100,000 Moors perished there by the sword. Moreover, their panic was so great that about 2,000 were suffocated at the gate of the city. Those who perished in the sea were innumerable. Many were entangled in the thickets. The whole world was certainly fighting for us, and if many of ours had not been detained in plundering the camp, few of the great multitude of the enemy would have been able to escape from the battle.

And although it may be tedious, the following must not be omitted: On the day preceding the battle the army captured many thousands of camels, oxen and sheep. By the command of the princes these were divided among the people. When we advanced to battle, wonderful to relate, the camels formed in many squadrons and the sheep and oxen did the same. Moreover, these animals accompanied us, halting when we halted, advancing when we advanced, and charging when we charged. The clouds protected us from the heat of the sun and cooled us. . . .

Therefore, we call upon you of the catholic church of Christ and of the whole Latin church to exult in the so admirable bravery and devotion of your brethren, in the so glorious and very desirable retribution of the omnipotent God, and in the so devoutly hoped-for remission of all our sins through the grace of God. And we pray that He may make you—namely, all bishops, clerks and monks who are leading devout lives, and all the laity—to sit down at the right hand of God, who liveth and reigneth God for ever and ever. And we ask and beseech you in the name of our Lord Jesus, who has ever been with us and aided us and freed us from all our tribulations, to be mindful of your brethren who return to you, by doing them kindnesses and by paying their debts, in order that God may recompense you and absolve you from all your sins and grant you a share in all the blessings which either we or they have deserved in the sight of the Lord. Amen.

Chapter 8

Infidels and

Heretics:

Crusades of the

High Middle

Ages

Source 5 from Peter of Les Vaux-de-Cernay, The History of the Albigensian Crusade, *translated by W. A. and M. D. Sibly (Woodbridge: Boydell Press, 1998), pp. 31–33, 36–38, 111–112, 115–118.*

5. Peter of Les Vaux-de-Cernay, *The History of the Albigensian Crusade*

'Innocent, servant of the servants of God, sends greetings and his apostolic blessing to his beloved children, the noble counts and barons and all the people of the provinces of Narbonne, Arles, Embrun, Aix and Vienne.

'News has reached us of a cruel deed which must surely bring grief on the whole Church. Brother Peter of Castelnau of blessed memory, monk and priest, a man surely renowned amongst righteous men for the conduct of his life, his learning and his high reputation, was sent by us with others to the South to preach peace and support the faith. He had performed the tasks entrusted to him in distinguished fashion, and was indeed still doing so, since all that he taught he had learnt in the school of Christ, and by holding fast to arguments which were faithful to the true doctrine he could both encourage his hearers with wholesome teaching and confute objectors. He was always ready to give an answer to every man who questioned him, as a man Catholic in faith, experienced in the law and eloquent in speech. Against him the Devil roused his minister, the Count of Toulouse.[22] This man had often incurred the censure of the Church for the many grave outrages he had committed against her [i.e., the Church], and often—as might be expected of a person who was crafty and cunning, slippery and unreliable—had received absolution under the guise of feigned penitence. At last he could not hold back the hatred he had conceived against Peter—since indeed in Peter's mouth the word of God was not restrained from executing vengeance upon the nations and punishments upon the people; hatred the stronger because the Count himself was so richly deserving of punishment for his great crimes. He then summoned Peter and his fellow papal legate to the town of Saint-Gilles, promising to give complete satisfaction on every heading under which he was accused. When they came to the town the Count at one moment seemed truthful and compliant and promised to carry out all the salutary instructions given to him; at the next he became deceitful and obdurate and absolutely refused to do so, with the result that the legates at last decided to quit the town. Thereupon the Count publicly threatened them with death, vowing to keep a close watch on their departure whether they went by land or water. He immediately matched his words with actions and dispatched his accomplices to lay a carefully chosen ambush. His insane fury could not be

22. Raymond VI, the count of Toulouse, protected Cathars, though he never became one himself; he preferred diplomacy to direct confrontation and probably did not approve the murder of Peter of Castelnau, as Peter of Les Vaux-de-Cernay claims here.

calmed either by the prayers of our beloved son, the Abbot of Saint-Gilles, or by the remonstrances of the consuls and townsmen; so the latter escorted the legates—against the Count's wishes and indeed to his great annoyance—under the protection of an armed guard to the banks of the Rhône. As night fell the legates settled down to rest, unaware that encamped with them were some of the Count's attendants who, as events proved, intended to seek their blood.

'Early the next morning, after Mass had been celebrated in the customary manner, as the innocent soldiers of Christ were preparing to cross the river, one of those attendants of Satan, brandishing his lance, wounded Peter from behind the ribs—Peter who stood with immovable firmness on the Rock of Christ,[23] unguarded against such treachery. Then—good confronting evil—Peter faced his attacker and, following as did St Stephen[24] the example of Christ his teacher, said to him: "May God forgive you, even as I forgive you," repeating these words of pious forbearance again and again. Then injured though he was, the hope of heavenly things allowed him to forget the bitterness of the wound he had suffered, and even though the moment of his precious death was now approaching, he continued discussing with his fellow priests what needed to be done to further the cause of the faith and peace; until at last after many prayers he went happily to rest in Christ.

'So he shed his blood in the cause of the faith and peace—surely no more praiseworthy cause for martyrdom can be imagined. . . .[Thus] it will be permitted to any Catholic person—provided the rights of the superior lord are respected—not only to proceed against the Count in person, but also to occupy and possess his lands, in the expectation that the right thinking of the new occupier may purge those lands of the heresy which has hitherto so foully defiled them in consequence of the Count's villainy. Indeed, since his hand is now raised against all men, it is fitting that all men's hands should oppose him.

'If this vexation fails to lead him to understanding, we shall make it our business to step up our action against him. However, if he at any time promises to give satisfaction, then for sure he will have to give clear proofs of his repentance; he must expel the followers of heresy from the whole of his dominions, and he must devote himself to the cause of reconciliation and fraternal peace. It was chiefly because of the faults he is known to have committed in these two respects that the Church's condemnation was pronounced against him—although if the Lord were to mark all his iniquities, he would be hard put to it to give suitable satisfaction whether for himself or for the host of others he has brought to the net of damnation. . . .

23. Both Christ and the apostle Peter are described as rocks in Christian Scripture. Peter's name in Greek is similar to the word meaning "rock," so when Christ calls him the rock on which he will build his church, this is to some degree a play on words. The western church regarded Peter as the first bishop of Rome, and later papal claims to power were based on Christ's statement giving Peter "the keys of the kingdom of heaven" (Matthew 16:18–19).

24. Stephen was the first Christian martyr; his death is recorded in Acts 7:54–60.

Chapter 8

Infidels and

Heretics:

Crusades of the

High Middle

Ages

'Forward then soldiers of Christ! Forward, brave recruits to the Christian army! Let the universal cry of grief of the Holy Church arouse you, let pious zeal inspire you to avenge this monstrous crime against your God! Remember that your Creator had no need of you when He created you; but now, although He does not truly need your support, nevertheless—acting as if through your help He were less wearied in achieving His will, and His Omnipotence were in fact the less through needing your obedience—He has at this time given you an opportunity of serving Him in a way that is acceptable to Him. After the murder of that just man the Church in the South sits without a comforter in sadness and grief. We are told that faith has vanished, peace has perished, that the plague of heresy and the madness of our enemies have gone from strength to strength, and it is clear that potent help must be provided for the ship of the Church in that area in this unprecedented storm if she is not to founder almost totally. We therefore advise and urge you all most strongly (confidently enjoining you at this most critical time in the name of Christ, and supporting our request with our promise of remission of sins): do not delay in opposing these great evils. In the name of the God of peace and love, apply yourselves vigorously to pacifying those nations. Work to root out perfidious heresy in whatever way God reveals to you. Attack the followers of heresy more fearlessly even than the Saracens— since they are more evil—with a strong hand and a stretched out arm. As to the Count of Toulouse who, like one who has made a covenant with Death, gives no thought to his own death—if his punishment starts to turn him to understanding, if his face, filled with shame, begins to seek the name of the Lord, continue by the added weight of your threats to drive him to give satisfaction to ourselves and the Church and indeed God; expelling him and his supporters from the towns of the Lord and seizing their lands, where Catholic inhabitants will take over from the displaced heretics and will serve before God in holiness and righteousness according to the tenets of the true faith which you follow.

'Given at the Lateran on 10 March 1208 in the eleventh year of our papacy.'. . .

Seige of Lavaur

Lavaur was a very noteworthy and extensive [fortified town] situated by the River Agout and about five leagues from Toulouse.[25] In Lavaur were the traitor Aimeric, who had been the lord of Montréal, and numerous other knights, enemies of the cross, up to eighty in number, who had entered the place and fortified it against us. The Dame of Lavaur was a widow named Giraude, a heretic of the worst sort and sister to Aimeric.

On their arrival, our soldiers laid siege to the [town] on one side only, since they had insufficient strength to surround it entirely. After a few days siege-engines were erected and our men began to attack the [town] in the usual manner, whilst the enemy defended as best they could. Indeed the place contained a huge force and was excellently equipped for defence; in fact the defenders almost

25. Five leagues = 20 miles.

outnumbered the attackers. I should add that when our army first arrived the enemy made a sortie and captured one of our knights, whom they took inside and killed instantly. Even though we were laying siege on one side only, the army was split into two parts and so disposed that if the need arose neither division could help the other without hazard. However, not long afterwards the Bishop of Lisieux, the Bishop of Bayeux and the Count of Auxerre arrived from France with a large force of crusaders, and the siege was then extended to another side of the [town]; further, a wooden bridge was built across the River Agout which our men crossed so that they now completely surrounded the town. . . .

. . . [O]ur men were labouring without respite in their efforts to take the place. Our opponents, as befitted their arrogance, defended themselves vigorously. I must mention that they rode along the walls on horses fully protected by armour, to show their contempt for our side and demonstrate that the walls were substantial and well fortified. What arrogance!

A Matter Worthy of Record

One day our men had built a wooden fortification near the walls of the [town], and on top of it Christ's knights had placed the sign of the Cross. Our opponents concentrated fire from their engines on the Cross and broke one of the arms, whereupon the shameless dogs started howling and cheering as if breaking the cross was a famous victory. But He who sanctified the cross avenged this wrong miraculously and for all to see: soon afterwards (most marvellous to relate) it came about that the enemies of the cross, who had rejoiced in destroying the Cross, were captured on the day of the feast of the Cross.[26] So the Cross avenged the injuries it had suffered—as will be shown later in my narrative.

Whilst this was happening our men built a siege-engine of the type commonly called a "cat."[27] When it was ready they dragged it to the ditch surrounding Lavaur. Then with a great effort they brought up wood and branches which they tied into bundles and threw into the ditch to fill it. Our enemies, with their usual cunning, dug an underground passage reaching as far as our engine; they went along the passage by night, took the bundles which our men had thrown into the ditch and carried them into the town. Moreover some of them got close to the cat and under cover of silence made treacherous efforts to drag our men to them by catching them with iron hooks as they strove unceasingly to fill the ditch under the protection of the engine. Also, one night they came out by the underground passage and tried to set fire to the cat by hurling large quantities of lighted darts, fire, tow, fat and anything else that would burn. However, two German counts who were with our army were keeping

26. May 3.
27. **cat:** a covered wagon mounted on wheels that could be dragged up to the walls of a besieged town or castle to provide cover for troops attempting to fill a moat or dig out under a wall.

Chapter 8

Infidels and

Heretics:

Crusades of the

High Middle

Ages

guard round the cat that night. The alarm was raised amongst our soldiers who hurriedly armed themselves and rushed to protect the siege-engine. The two German counts and the other Germans with them saw that they could not reach the enemy in the ditch from where they were, courageously and at great risk threw themselves into the ditch, and attacked the enemy boldly; they thrust them back into the [town] having first killed some of them and wounded many more. . . .

Whilst our men were thus devoting their every effort to the siege, the bishops present and the venerable Abbot of the Cistercian monastery of La Cour-Dieu, who were with the army and had been instructed by the papal legates to act in their stead, gathered together with all the other clergy and with the utmost fervour began to sing the *Veni Creator Spiritus*.[28] When they saw and heard this, our enemies—so God disposed—became stupefied and almost lost their powers of resistance; to the extent that—as they later admitted—they feared those who sang more than those who fought, those who recited the psalms more than those who attacked them, those who prayed more than those who sought to wound. So the wall was penetrated, our men entered Lavaur and our adversaries, no longer able to resist, gave themselves up. Through the will of God, who came in His mercy to our aid, Lavaur was taken on the feast of the Invention of the Holy Cross.

Soon Aimeric, the former lord of Montréal, of whom we spoke above, was led out of Lavaur with up to eighty other knights. The noble Count proposed that they should all be hanged from fork-shaped gibbets. However, after Aimeric, who was taller than the others, had been hanged, the gibbets started to fall down, since through excessive haste they had not been properly fixed in the ground. The Count realised that to continue would cause a long delay and ordered the rest to be put to the sword. The crusaders fell to this task with great enthusiasm and quickly slew them on the spot. The Count had the Dame of Lavaur, sister of Aimeric and a heretic of the worst sort, thrown into a pit and stones heaped on her. Our crusaders burnt innumerable heretics, with great rejoicing.[29] . . .

I must not pass over a miracle at Lavaur which I heard about from a reliable source. By some mischance the cloak of a crusader knight caught fire; by God's miraculous judgment it came about that it was all burnt except the part where the cross was stitched on, which survived without being touched by the flames.

28. *Veni Creator Spiritus:* "Come Creating Spirit," a hymn attributed to Charlemagne.
29. Other chroniclers note that 300 to 400 people were killed.

Source 6 from William of Tudela, The Song of the Cathar Wars: A History of the Albigensian Crusade, *translated by Janet Shirley (Aldershot: Scolar Press, 1996), pp. 13, 15, 17.*

6. From William of Tudela, *The Song of the Cathar Wars*

Murder of Peter of Castelnau, 14 January 1208

At this time Peter of Castelnau was travelling out of Provence on his pacing mule. He reached the Rhône at St Gilles, and there he excommunicated the count of Toulouse for supporting the mercenaries who were ravaging the countryside. Thereupon an evil-hearted squire, hoping to win the count's approval, stepped like a traitor behind the legate, drove his sharp sword into his spine and killed him. The man fled at once on his fast horse to his home town of Beaucaire, where he had kinsmen.

Yet the legate raised his hands to heaven before he died and in the sight of all those present asked God to forgive this wicked man. This was while he was receiving communion at about cockcrow. Then he died, just as the day was dawning. His soul went to God the Father and they buried him at St Gilles with many a *Kyrie eleison* sung and many candles burning.

A Crusade Is Decided On

You can be sure the pope was not pleased when he heard of his legate's death. He grasped his chin in anger and called on St James of Compostela and on St Peter of Rome who lies in the chapel there. He spoke his anathema and then dashed out the candle. Brother Arnold of Cîteaux was present, and so too were Master Milo, that fine Latinist, and the twelve cardinals all in a circle. There it was they made the decision that led to so much sorrow, that left so many men dead with their guts spilled out and so many great ladies and pretty girls naked and cold, stripped of gown and cloak. From beyond Montpellier as far as Bordeaux, any that rebelled were to be utterly destroyed. This was told me by Master Pons of Mela, who was present on behalf of the king who holds Tudela, lord of Pamplona and Estella, the best knight who ever sat a horse.[30] (Miramelis, commander of the heathen, felt his strength! Castile and Aragon were there too; side by side their kings rode and fought.[31] I intend to make a good new song about this, and shall write it out on fair parchment.)

---

30. The author is here referring to Sancho VIII, king of Navarre (r. 1194–1234).

31. Sancho VIII, along with the kings of Castile and Aragon, defeated the emir of Morocco (whose title is given here as "Miramelis") at the battle of Las Navas de Tolosa in 1212. The author is referring to this battle here, and saying he will write a song about that battle later.

Chapter 8

Infidels and

Heretics:

Crusades of the

High Middle

Ages

The abbot of Cîteaux, however, sat with his head bent. Then he rose and, standing by a marble column, said to the pope:

"By St Martin, my lord, this talking is a waste of time! Come, have your letters written in good Latin, and then I can set off. Send them to France, to the Limousin, to Poitou, the Auvergne and Périgord; have the indulgence proclaimed here too and all over the world as far as Constantinople. Proclaim that any man who does not take the cross shall drink no wine, shall not eat off a cloth morning or night, shall wear neither linen nor hemp and when he dies shall lie unburied like a dog." He fell silent, and his advice seemed right to all who were there.

Everyone greatly respected the abbot of Cîteaux (who later became archbishop of Narbonne, the best who ever wore mitre there), and when he had spoken, no one said a word. Then the pope, looking thoroughly unhappy, spoke as follows:

"Go to Carcassonne, brother, and to great Toulouse on the Garonne and lead the armies against the ungodly. Cleanse the troops from their sins in the name of Christ, and in my name preach to them and exhort them to drive the heretics out from amongst the virtuous." After that, at about the hour of nones, the abbot left the town and spurred hard on his way, accompanied by the archbishop of Tarragona, by the bishops of Lerida, of Barcelona and of Maguelonne near Montpellier and, from beyond the Spanish passes, those of Pamplona, Burgos and Tarazona. All these rode with the abbot of Cîteaux.

The Crusade Is Preached

As soon as they had taken leave, the abbot mounted and rode to Cîteaux, where all the white monks who wore mitres had gathered for the chapter-general on the feast of the Holy Cross in summer,[32] as is their custom. In the presence of the whole assembly he sang mass and after that he preached to them and showed every one of them his letter and explained that they were to go here and there about the world, over the whole length and breadth of holy Christendom.

Recruits Flock In

Then, once they knew that their sins would be forgiven, men took the cross in France and all over the kingdom. Never in my life have I seen such a gathering as that one they made against the heretics and clog-wearers![33] The duke of Burgundy took the cross there and so did the count of Nevers and many great men. What they must have cost, those gold embroidered crosses and bands of

---

32. September 14.

33. **clog-wearers:** a nickname given to Waldensians, another group that rejected material wealth and so wore sandals or clogs instead of fancier shoes.

silk which they displayed on the right breast! Nor shall I try to tell you how they were armed, equipped and mounted, nor about the iron-clad horses and their emblazoned trappings, for God has made never a clerk or a scholar clever enough to tell you the half of it, nor to list all the abbots and priests gathered there in the host that lay on the plains outside Béziers. . . .

God be my witness, it was an enormous force. It contained twenty thousand knights all fully armed and more than two hundred thousand villeins and peasants, not counting clergy and citizens.[34] They came from the whole length and breadth of the Auvergne, from Burgandy, from France, from the Limousin, from the whole world—north and south Germans, Poitevins, Gascons, men from the Rouergue and Saintonge. God made never a clerk who could write them all down, however hard he tried, not in two months or three. Provence was there in full and so was Vienne; from the Lombardy passes all the way to Rodez every man came flocking because the pardon offered to crusaders was so generous. They rode in close array with banners raised. . . .

Source 7 from Patrologiae. . . Latina, *edited by J.-P. Migne et al. (Paris, 1844–1864), vol. 216, pp. 744–745, translated by W. A. and M. D. Sibly and included in Peter of Les Vaux-de-Cernay,* The History of the Albigensian Crusade *(Woodbridge: Boydell Press, 1998), p. 308.*

7. Letter from Pope Innocent III to the Legate Arnold Amalric, January 15, 1213

In the South, which had been infested with the poison of heresy and oppressed by disastrous war, the little foxes that were spoiling the vines of the Lord God of Hosts have been taken, so that with God's help the business of the faith has by now sufficiently prospered. A more urgent cause is now at hand, and it is right that the hands of Christians should turn to it. We have heard that the King of the Saracens is preparing everywhere for battle, his resolve to attack followers of the Christian faith compounded by the severity of his fall at the hands of Christians—or rather at the hands of Christ who exercised a propitious judgment on our behalf. The Holy Land, which is a portion of our inheritance from the Lord, is greatly in need of help and looks to receive the support of Christians. Often, very often, efforts concentrated on a single end have led to success—the opposite, to failure, and the less we are

34. These numbers are far too high; historians estimate that the crusade probably included about 5,000 horsemen and 10,000 to 15,000 others.

Chapter 8

Infidels and

Heretics:

Crusades of the

High Middle

Ages

engaged on other matters, the more we will be able to attend effectively to the general and special business of Christian believers in opposing the faithless race of Saracens. We therefore hereby enjoin you, our dear brother, to devote your earnest attention to negotiating treaties for peace and a truce with our dearest son in Christ, Peter the illustrious King of Aragon, and counts and barons and other men of good sense whom you think should be involved, so that you may through such treaties provide a secure and lasting peace for the whole of the South. You should thus cease to call Christians to arms, or weary them through the indulgences granted by the Apostolic See for the fight against the heretics, until or unless you receive a specific instruction on this matter from the Apostolic See.

QUESTIONS TO CONSIDER

Your task in this chapter is to evaluate and compare the words and actions of church leaders and others involved with crusades against infidels and heretics. When considering the way church leaders, particularly the popes and bishops, encouraged people into action, you will need to think about both the words they used—what we might now call propaganda—and the rewards offered for such action. As you look at your notes on the descriptions of those who chose to go on a crusade, you will probably find words like "shining," "worthy," "delightful," "pious," and "saints," and their campaign described as "just," "marvelous," "brave," and "fierce." As you look at words to describe Muslims or Cathars, you find words and phrases like "wicked," "despised," "degenerate," "enslaved by demons," "horrible," "crafty," "cunning," and "ministers of deceit." How might such language have encouraged people to depart, despite the grief of their wives and families? How, in fact, might the scene of family grief at a crusader's departure in Source 1 have encouraged others to go? What impact might the scenes of the crusaders sewing crosses on their clothes have had on readers of these texts or on those who heard about these events?

Sources 3 and 4 were written by people who did respond to the pope's call. What motives do they give, or suggest, for their actions? Were their motives entirely spiritual, or were there other, more practical benefits to joining a crusade? How do these compare to the spiritual and practical benefits offered by the crusade against the Cathars, as described in Source 5?

Look carefully at the language used to describe what are quite similar actions on all sides, military combat and the massacre of opponents either after a defeat or as an ambush. How does the language of the letters and chronicles differ depending on who is doing the killing? How did they justify the slaughter of their enemies? Do you see any differences between the two crusades in this? Among the chroniclers themselves?

In some cases, such as the words of Innocent III in Sources 5 and 7, you have explicit statements within one source comparing Muslims and Cathars; in Source 2, the army stops off on its way to Jerusalem and kills heretics. What do these direct comparisons indicate? In most cases your comparisons are between sources: How would you compare the words used to describe infidels and heretics? How would you compare the descriptions of actual battles and of the virtues of the Christian fighters in them? How would you compare the descriptions of those who died in these campaigns?

The final question asks you about the chroniclers' aims and values, and your evaluation of the chroniclers' language has certainly given you some sense about these. What words would they use to describe the ideal crusading leader? The ideal crusading soldier? The ideal priest or church official? The accounts of battles describe siege machines and siege tactics at some length. What does this indicate about the values of the authors? They also describe miracles that either inspired the troops or improved their chances for victory.

How do the authors balance human ingenuity and divine intervention when exploring the reasons for crusader victories? The crusades against Muslims have traditionally been seen as blending central and yet somewhat contradictory elements of medieval European culture: piety, bloodthirstiness, greed, fanaticism, and military idealism. Does your reading of crusader chronicles support this view? Would this also be a valid characterization of the crusades against the Cathars? To what extent might this characterization be the result of the type of sources you have read, which describe military campaigns and the sacking of cities?

You are now ready to answer the questions in this chapter: How did the western church in the High Middle Ages encourage people to respond to external and internal threats to its power? How did people actually respond? In the minds of those who called for or went on crusades, how were infidels and heretics similar, and how were they different. Along with the authority of the Church, what other aims and values of high medieval culture do the records of crusaders reveal?

EPILOGUE

Neither of the crusades discussed in this chapter was very successful. Though the crusaders did take Jerusalem, the military leaders described in such glorious detail in the chronicles fought among themselves, and

Muslim forces reorganized and fought back. The battles described here became part of what was known as the First Crusade, and there were many that followed for the next two hundred years. In 1187 the Muslims under Saladin retook Jerusalem, and before he called for a crusade against Cathar heretics, Innocent III also sent

Chapter 8

Infidels and

Heretics:

Crusades of the

High Middle

Ages

out preachers calling on Christian knights to retake Jerusalem. Those who responded decided that going by sea would be better than going by land, and they stopped off in Constantinople for supplies. The supplies never materialized, and in 1204 the crusaders decided to capture and sack Constantinople instead. Though he initially forbade these attacks on eastern Christians by western Christians, after the city was looted and the Byzantine emperor overthrown, Innocent noted that this development might heal the split between the two churches and bring about eastern acceptance of papal authority. It did not, and it obviously had no effect on Muslim successes, which may be why Innocent by 1213 had become more worried about Muslims than about heretics, as we saw in Source 7.

Innocent's suspension of the crusade against the Cathars in 1213 did not end the fighting in southern France, which eventually involved troops of the king of Navarre and the king of France. Ultimately Simon of Montfort was killed; in 1229 the leaders in southern France agreed to terms of peace that left the king of France the primary beneficiary. The end of the war did not mean an end to Catharism, but the papacy decided that education and investigations would be more effective ways to combat heresy than military campaigns. The pope founded the University of Toulouse, which he hoped would promote knowledge and combat ignorance, error, and incorrect belief. In the 1230s and 1240s the papacy established the

papal Inquisition, sending out inquisitors with the power to seek out suspected heretics, question them in private without revealing who had denounced them, and sentence them to punishments ranging from penance to life imprisonment; heretics who did not repent were handed over to the secular government to be burned, and their property was confiscated. These measures were very successful, and the last Cathar leaders were burned in the 1320s, though the beliefs did not die out completely.

Recently, in fact, people in the United States and Canada have developed a Christian church based on what they view as Cathar values, the Assembly of Good Christians.

In this chapter, you have evaluated and compared the responses of Roman Christians to what they regarded as internal and external threats, but the western church is not the only medieval institution for which such a comparison is possible. Islam was also deeply divided internally and threatened from the outside; as in Christianity, reactions on the part of officials and individuals varied. The writings by Sunni and Shi'ite clerics about each other, and by Muslim authors about Christian crusaders, provide interesting parallels with the sources in this chapter and offer the opportunity for other lines of comparison. Such comparisons do not need to be limited to the Middle Ages, of course, for responses to internal and external challenges reveal a great deal about the aims and values of any culture.

CHAPTER NINE

CAPITALISM AND CONFLICT

IN THE MEDIEVAL CLOTH TRADE

During the Early Middle Ages, western Europe was largely a rural society. Most of the cities of the Roman Empire had shrunk to villages, and the roads the Romans had built were allowed to fall into disrepair. Manors and villages were relatively self-sufficient in basic commodities such as grain and cloth, and even in times of famine they could not import the food they needed because the cost of transportation was too high. Much local trade was carried out by barter, and any long-distance trade that existed was handled by Jews, Greeks, and Syrians, who imported luxury goods like spices, silks, and perfumes from the Near East. These extremely expensive commodities were purchased only by nobles and high-ranking churchmen. The lack of much regional trade is reflected in the almost complete absence of sources about trade before the tenth century. Commercial documents are extremely rare, and both public and private records testify to the agrarian nature of early medieval society.

This situation began to change in the tenth century, when Vikings in the north and Italians in the south revived long-distance European commerce. The Vikings initially raided and plundered along the coasts of northern Europe, but they soon turned to trading with the very people whose lands they had threatened. At the same time, merchants from the cities of Genoa, Pisa, and Florence were taking over former Muslim trade routes in the western Mediterranean. These Italian merchants began to keep increasingly elaborate records of their transactions and devised new methods of bookkeeping to keep track of their ventures. They developed new types of partnerships to share the risks and found ways to get around the medieval Christian church's prohibition of the lending of money at interest (termed *usury*). These changes, combined with the growth in trade, led to a transformation of the European economy often called the *Commercial Revolution*.

Once western European merchants began to trade more extensively with the East, particularly after the Crusades in the twelfth century, it became clear that the balance of trade favored the East; Eastern luxuries such as spices and silks were paid for primarily in gold. Gradually, however, western European merchants began to add high- and medium-quality woolen cloth, with Italian merchants trading cloth made in Flanders (modern-day Belgium and northeast France) to Asia and Africa, carrying it all the way to the court of Genghis Khan. They also shipped increasing quantities of cloth to other locations in Europe, eventually importing raw wool from England to supply the Flemish cloth-makers and handling both long-distance and regional trade.

The reinvigoration of trade in the Commercial Revolution came with, and was one of the causes of, a rebirth of town life. Especially in Italy and the Low Countries, but in many other parts of Europe as well, towns began to spring up around cathedrals, monasteries, and castles or at locations favorable for trade, such as ports or major crossroads. Many of these became cloth-producing centers, as weavers and other artisans involved in the many stages of cloth production gathered together to manufacture goods for regional and long-distance traders. Cloth merchants in these towns—sometimes in combination with the merchants of other types of products—joined together to form a merchants' guild that prohibited non-members from trading in the town. These same merchants often made up the earliest town government, serving as mayors and members of the city council, so that a town's economic policies were determined by its merchants' self-interest. Acting through the city council, the merchants' guilds determined the hours that markets would be open, decided which coins would be accepted as currency, and set prices on imported and local goods. Foreign affairs were also guided by the merchants, and cities formed alliances, termed *hanses,* with other cities to gain trading benefits.

From its beginnings, the trade in fine cloth was organized as a capitalist enterprise. Cloth merchants, called *drapers,* purchased raw materials, hired workers for all stages of production, and then sold the finished cloth; they rarely did any production themselves, and in some parts of Europe they were actually forbidden to do so. Some stages of production might be carried out in drapers' homes or in buildings that they owned, but more often production was carried out in the houses of those that they hired, who were paid by the piece rather than by the hour or day; these workers, especially those who wove cloth, might in turn hire several people to weave alongside them.

Cloth went through many stages from sheep to finished cloth. Once the sheep were sheared, the wool was sorted, beaten, and washed; it was then carded and spun by women using either hand spindles or, after the thirteenth century, spinning wheels. Next, the thread was prepared for weaving by *warpers,* who wound the long threads for the warp (warp threads are those that run lengthwise on a piece of cloth), and by *spoolers,* who wound woof threads (woof threads are those that run crosswise). The prepared thread went to the weavers, who used horizontal treadle looms. After the cloth was woven, it went to *fullers,* who stamped the cloth with their feet in troughs full of water, alkaline earth, and urine to soften it and fill in the spaces between the threads. (In the thirteenth century in some parts of Europe, fulling began to take place in water-powered fulling mills.) The cloth was then cleaned, hung to dry on wooden frames called *tenters,* and stretched to the correct width. The cloth was finished by repeatedly brushing it with thistle-like plants called *teasles* set in rows on a frame and then shearing the resulting fuzz off with large shears. It could be dyed at any stage in this process, as wool, thread, or whole cloth.

Some of these processes, such as dyeing, weaving, and shearing, required great skill and were usually reserved for men; others, such as spinning, sorting, and stretching on the tenter, called for less skill and were often carried out by women or young people. Once the cloth had been sheared for the final time, it went to the drapers, who monopolized all cutting of bolts of cloth and, thus, all retail sales. In areas where merchants organized production on a huge scale, such as Florence, there was a distinction between merchants and drapers, with the major merchants doing no actual cloth cutting themselves but simply hiring drapers; in most parts of Europe, however, merchants cut as well as sold, and were often called merchant-drapers.

Especially in Flanders and Florence, the merchants who controlled the cloth trade attempted to regulate everything down to the smallest detail. They set up precise standards of quality with severe penalties for those who did not meet them, regulated the length of the workday and the wages of all workers, and sent out inspectors regularly to enforce the ordinances and handle disputes. At first there was little opposition, but, beginning in the twelfth and thirteenth centuries in many areas, cloth workers challenged the merchants' control through strikes and revolts, and attempted to form their own organizations, called *craft guilds.* (At the same time, those who produced or handled many other sorts of products, such as shoemakers, butchers, and blacksmiths, were also forming separate craft guilds.) In some areas, such as Florence, the cloth merchants were successful at stopping all organizing and suppressing all rebellions, but in others, such as many cities in Flanders, the merchants lost, and the wool workers were able to form their own guilds and even become part of the city government for at least a short period of time. In some places, those artisans who were highly skilled and who owned some of their own equipment, such as weavers, fullers, dyers, and shearers, were able to form guilds, whereas the less-skilled spinners and sorters were not.

In periods during which they were able to form independently, the craft guilds took over the regulation of production from the merchant guilds. They set quality standards for their particular product and regulated the size of workshops, the training period, and the conduct of members. In most cities, individual guilds, such as those of weavers or dyers, achieved a monopoly in the production of one particular product, forbidding non-members to work. The craft guild then chose some of its members to act as inspectors and set up a court to hear disputes between members, although the city court remained the final arbiter, particularly in cases involving conflict between merchants and artisans or between members of craft guilds and those who were not members.

Each guild set the pattern by which members were trained. If one wanted to become a dyer, for instance, one spent four to seven years as an apprentice and then at least that long as a journeyman, working in the shop of a master dyer, after which one could theoretically make one's masterpiece. If the masterpiece was approved by the other master dyers and if they thought the market in their town was large enough to allow for another dyer, one could then become a master and start a shop. Though the amount of time a candidate had to spend as an apprentice and a journeyman varied slightly from guild to guild, all guilds—both those in the cloth industry and those in other sorts of production—followed this same three-stage process. The apprentices and journeymen generally lived with the master and his family, and were often forbidden to marry. Conversely, many guilds required that masters be

married, as they believed a wife was absolutely essential to the running of the shop and the household, and also felt that married men were likely to be more stable and dependable.

The master's wife assisted in running the shop, often selling the goods her husband had produced. Their children, both male and female, also worked alongside the apprentices and journeymen; the sons were sometimes formally apprenticed, but the daughters generally were not, since many guilds limited formal membership to males. Most guilds did allow a master's widow to continue operating a shop for a set period of time after her husband's death, for they recognized that she had the necessary skills and experience. Such widows paid all guild dues but did not vote or hold office in the guilds because they were not considered full members. The fact that women were not formally guild members did not mean that they did not work in guild shops, however, for alongside the master's wife and daughters, female domestic servants often performed the less-skilled tasks. In addition, there were a few all-female guilds in several European cities, particularly Cologne and Paris, in which girls were formally apprenticed in the same way boys were in regular craft guilds.

Both craft and merchants' guilds were not only economic organizations but also systems of social support. Though they were harsh against outsiders, they were protective and supportive of their members. They took care of elderly masters who could no longer work, and often supported masters' widows and orphans. They maintained an altar at a city church, and provided for the funerals of members and baptisms of their children. Guild members marched together in city parades, and reinforced their feelings of solidarity with one another by special ceremonies and distinctive dress.

Whether workers were able to form separate craft guilds or not, conflicts between merchants and workers over the cloth trade were a common feature of medieval town life in the major centers of cloth production. These conflicts often disrupted cloth production from a certain area, allowing other areas to expand their trade. In the late fourteenth century, for example, mass rebellions in Florence and Flanders benefited English weavers, who began to turn a greater percentage of English wool into cloth rather than exporting it as raw wool to the Continent. Government policy in England also helped the English weavers, as the crown in 1347 imposed a 33 percent tariff on the export of raw wool, while setting only a 2 percent tariff on the export of finished cloth. The crown also ordered people to wear English cloth (a provision that was very difficult to enforce) and encouraged Flemish cloth-makers

displaced by unrest in their own towns to settle in England. Flemish cloth-makers also migrated to many towns in Germany, and by the sixteenth century the production of wool cloth was more dispersed throughout Europe than it had been several centuries earlier.

Often the change from the medieval to the modern economy is described as "the rise of capitalism," a change accompanied by "the rise of the middle class." Though specialists in the period disagree about many aspects of the development of capitalism, they agree that cloth production and trade was the earliest and most important capitalist enterprise in medieval Europe. Thus we can see in the cloth trade many of the issues that would emerge later in other parts of the economy, and that are still issues facing business and governments today. Your task in this chapter will be to use a variety of sources regarding cloth production from several parts of Europe to answer these questions: What were the key economic and social goals of governments, merchant-capitalists, and artisans regarding the cloth trade, and how did they seek to achieve these aims? What economic and social conflicts emerged as the cloth trade grew and changed?

SOURCES AND METHOD

In analyzing the development of the cloth trade, historians have a wide variety of documents at their disposal. Because cloth was regarded by city

and national governments as so important, their records include many laws that refer to the cloth trade, and often describe royal or municipal actions that encouraged cloth production. Some of the earliest attempts by governments to gather statistical information also refer to wool and cloth. The merchants' and later craft guilds themselves kept records—both regulations and ordinances, and records of judgments against those who broke these ordinances. Private business documents and personal documents such as contracts also often refer to aspects of the cloth trade.

In general, these sources can be divided into two basic types, a division that holds equally for sources from many other historical periods. The first type is *prescriptive*—laws, regulations, and ordinances that describe how the cloth trade was supposed to operate and how the guild or government officials who wrote the ordinances hoped things would be. These documents do not simply describe an ideal, however; they were generally written in response to events already taking place, so they can tell us about real problems and the attitudes of guilds and officials toward these problems. It is sources such as these that will allow us to answer the first of our questions, for they tell us specifically about goals and efforts to achieve them. What they cannot tell us is if any of these efforts worked, or what problems these efforts might have caused. For this we need to turn to a second type of primary evidence, *descriptive* documents such as court records and statistical information. Through these records we can observe how regulations were actually enforced, and assess—to a limited degree, because medieval statistics must always be used very carefully—the results of government and guild efforts to build up the cloth trade. As you are reading the sources, then, the first question you have to ask yourself is whether the record is prescriptive or descriptive, for confusing the two can give a very skewed view of medieval economic and social issues. (This kind of discrimination must be applied to any historical source, of course, and is not always an easy task. Sometimes even prominent historians have built a whole pyramid of erroneous theories about the past by assuming that prescriptive sources accurately described reality.)

The first three selections are all laws regarding the wool trade issued by territorial rulers. Source 1 comes from what are termed the laws of King Edward the Confessor of England (though they were written after his reign, sometime after 1115), setting out what were termed the "Liberties of London," or what we would term the rights accorded the citizens of London by the king. Source 2 is a similar law of the count of Holland regarding the city of Dortrecht. Read each of these carefully. What special privileges were granted to the citizens of these towns by their rulers? Source 3 is a proclamation of the countess of Flanders in 1224. What extra inducement did she offer to encourage wool production in the town of Courtrai? At this point you may want to begin a three-column list or chart, one column for the goals stated either explicitly or implicitly in the sources, a second for the actions taken to achieve those goals, and a third for the conflicts alluded to or discussed.

The next three sources are regulations regarding those who worked in cloth production issued by merchants' guilds or by the city councils, which were usually dominated by the merchants. Source 4 is from the English town of Winchester, Source 5 from the German town of Stendal, and Source 6 from the Flemish town of Arras. Read each of these sources carefully and add the information there to your three-column list. What were the most important aims of the merchants? What punishments did they set for those who broke the regulations, and how did they otherwise enforce their rules? Do the kinds of distinctions they make between groups—citizens and foreigners; those who make cloth and those who cut and sell it; members of artisans' families and nonmembers; masters, journeymen, and apprentices in a shop—suggest or perhaps contribute to social conflicts? What other types of conflicts are mentioned explicitly? (In all of these sources, the word "guest" or "foreigner" is used for someone who comes from a different town or village, and not necessarily from a different country.)

Though in many cities we do not have complete records of how well the provisions set forth in the ordinances were actually carried out, we can get glimpses from court records and similar sources from some cities. Through these we can see some instances of the enforcement of regulations and of the conflicts that this could cause. Sources 7 through 10 are examples of actual cases involving disputes in the cloth trade; Sources 7 and 8 are from fourteenth-century Flanders, and Sources 9 and 10 from sixteenth-century Germany. In Source 7, what is Jacquemars des Mares's aim? That of the cloth inspectors and the city

council? How well do the actions of the city councils in Sources 7, 8, and 9 reinforce the aims of the merchants as set out in Sources 4, 5, and 6? Though the ultimate decisions of the city council in Source 10 are not known, from the supplication itself we can get a good idea of actions taken by members of the weavers' guild. Do these fit with the aims of the merchants, or are the aims of these artisans somewhat different? Why might women have appealed to the city council, made up largely of merchants, to rectify actions taken against them by artisans?

Along with government records, private records can give us additional information about the cloth trade. Most private business documents are primarily descriptive in nature, although they can also contain information about the aims of those who drew them up. Source 11 contains two apprenticeship contracts from the thirteenth century. What were the aims of the parents involved and of the master weavers? Can we get any hints of potential conflicts that arose in apprenticeships? Source 12 contains several insurance contracts for wool and cloth shipments from a fourteenth-century Italian merchant. Why would wool traders have wanted to enlist his services? How does their using an insurer fit with their other actions?

The final sources for this chapter are statistical and rely on both official and private records. Source 13 consists of two charts of the total number of cloths produced in Florence and Ypres in Flanders, based on guild records. Source 14 consists of two charts of the export of raw wool and wool cloth from England, based on customs records that began after customs duties were imposed in 1347. These records do not include cloth made for use in England and report *only* exports that went through the customs office (there was a great deal of smuggling, so they may significantly underreport the total amounts exported), but we can use them in conjunction with the charts of Source 13 to ascertain general trends. How would you compare the trends in cloth production for the three areas? How would you assess the success of English government policies that encouraged weaving? How might the decline in the amount of raw wool exported from England have affected weaving in Florence, Ypres, and other areas, despite the efforts there of governments or merchants?

THE EVIDENCE

Source 1 from Benjamin Thorpe, Ancient Laws and Institutes of England *(London: Eyre and Spottiswoode, 1840), p. 462.*

1. Laws Regarding Foreign Merchants Under King Edward the Confessor of England, after 1115

And after he has entered the city, let a foreign merchant be lodged wherever it please him. But if he bring dyed cloth, let him see to it that he does not sell his merchandise at retail, but that he sell not less than a dozen pieces at a time. And if he bring pepper, or cumin, or ginger, or alum, or brasil wood, or resin, or incense, let him sell not less than fifteen pounds at a time. But if he bring belts, let him sell not less than a thousand at a time. And if he bring cloths of silk, or wool or linen, let him see that he cut them not, but sell them whole.

Also a foreign merchant may not buy dyed cloth, nor make the dye in the city, nor do any work which belongs by right to the citizens.

Source 2 from C. Gross, The Gild Merchant *(Oxford: Clarendon, 1890), vol. 1, p. 293.*

2. Law Regarding Cloth Cutting Under the Count of Holland, 1200

I, Theodore, by the grace of God, Count of Holland, and Adelaide, Countess of Holland, my wife, wish it to be known to all, both present and future, that we decree that our townsmen of Dortrecht may enjoy in their own right the following freedom in the said town, namely, that it is permitted to no one in Dortrecht to cut cloth for retail sale except to those who are designated by this trade, being called cutters of cloth, and except they be in the hanse[1] and fraternity of the townsmen belonging to Dortrecht. And that this charter, instituted by us, may forever be secure and intact, we corroborate it by affixing our seals thereto, and the signatures of witnesses.

These are the witnesses. . . .

Source 3 from Roy C. Cave and Herbert H. Coulson, A Source Book for Medieval Economic History *(New York: Biblo and Tannen, 1965), p. 374.*

3. Proclamation Regarding Taxes by the Countess of Flanders, 1224

I, Joan, Countess of Flanders and Hainault, wish it to be known to all both now and in the future, that I and my successors cannot and ought not to take any tax or payment from the fifty men who shall come to live at Courtrai, for as long as they remain here, to work in the woolen industry from this day on. But their heirs, after the decease of their parents, shall serve me just as my other burgesses do. Given at Courtrai, in the year of the Lord 1224, on the feast of St. Cecilia.

1. **hanse:** in this instance, the merchants' guild.

Source 4 from Beverley Town Documents, *edited by A. F. Leach, Publications of the Selden Society, vol. 14 (London: Selden Society, 1900), appendix II, pp. 134–135.*

4. City Ordinances Regarding Weavers in Winchester, England, ca 1209

This is the law of the Fullers and Weavers of Winchester: Be it known that no weaver or fuller may dry or dye cloth nor go outside the city to sell it. They may sell their cloth to no foreigner, but only to merchants of the city. And if it happens that, in order to enrich himself, one of the weavers or fullers wishes to go outside the city to sell his merchandise, he may be very sure that the honest men of the city will take all his cloth and bring it back to the city, and that he will forfeit it in the presence of the aldermen and honest men of the city. And if any weaver or fuller sell his cloth to a foreigner, the foreigner shall lose his cloth, and the other shall remain at the mercy of the city for as much as he has. Neither the weaver nor the fuller may buy anything except for his trade but by making an agreement with the mayor. No free man[2] can be accused by a weaver or a fuller, nor can a weaver or a fuller bear testimony against a free man. If any of them become rich, and wish to give up his trade, he may forswear it and turn his tools out of the house, and then do as much for the city as he is able in his freedom.

Sources 5 and 6 from Roy C. Cave and Herbert H. Coulson, A Source Book for Medieval Economic History *(New York: Biblo and Tannen, 1965), pp. 246–248; pp. 250–252.*

5. City Ordinances Regarding Guilds in Stendal, Germany, 1231 and 1233

We make known . . . that we, . . . desiring to provide properly for our city of Stendal, have changed, and do change, for the better, the laws of the gild [*sic*] brethren, and of those who are called cloth-cutters, so that they might have the same laws in this craft as their gild brethren the garment-cutters in Magdeburg have been accustomed to observe in the past.

These are the laws:

1. No one shall presume to cut cloth, except he be of our craft; those who break this rule will amend to the gild with three talents.[3]

2. **free man:** a citizen of Winchester. The weavers and fullers were not fully citizens at this point, but probably came from outside Winchester.
3. **talents, denarii, solidi:** different coins in circulation in Stendal. A mark was worth about 160 denarii; a solidus was worth about 25 denarii. The value of a talent varied widely.

2. Thrice a year there ought to be a meeting of the brethren, and whoever does not come to it will amend according to justice.

3. Whoever wishes to enter the fraternity whose father was a brother and cut cloth will come with his friends to the meeting of the brethren, and if he conduct himself honestly, he will be able to join the gild at the first request on payment of five solidi, and he will give six denarii to the master. And if he be dishonest and should not conduct himself well, he should be put off until the second or third meeting. But any of our citizens who wish to enter the gild, if he be an honest man, and worthy, will give a talent to the brethren on entry into the gild, and will present a solidus to the master. But if a guest who is an honest man should decide to join our fraternity, he will give thirty solidi to the gild on his entry, and eighteen denarii to the master. . . . But if any brother should make cloth against the institutions of the brethren, and of their decrees, which he ought on the advice of the consuls to observe, he will present to the consuls by way of emendation one talent for each offense or he will lose his craft for a year.

4. But if any one be caught with false cloth, his cloth will be burned publicly, and verily, the author of the crime will amend according to justice. . . .

9. If any one should marry a widow whose husband was of the craft, he will enter the fraternity with three solidi.

6. Shearers' Charter from Arras, Flanders, 1236

Here is the Shearers' Charter, on which they were first founded.

This is the first ordinance of the shearers, who were founded in the name of the Fraternity of God and St. Julien, with the agreement and consent of those who were at the time mayor and aldermen.

1. Whoever would engage in the trade of a shearer shall be in the Confraternity of St. Julien, and shall pay all the dues, and observe the decrees made by the brethren.

2. That is to say: first, that whoever is a master shearer shall pay 14 solidi to the Fraternity. And there may not be more than one master shearer working in a house. And he shall be a master shearer all the year, and have arms for the need of the town.

3. And a journeyman shall pay 5 solidi to the Fraternity.

4. And whoever wishes to learn the trade shall be the son of a burgess or he shall live in the town for a year and a day; and he shall serve three years to learn this trade.

5. And he shall give to his master 3 *muids*[4] for his bed and board; and he ought to bring the first *muid* to his master at the beginning of his apprenticeship, and another *muid* a year from that day, and a third *muid* at the beginning of the third year.

6. And no one may be a master of this trade of shearer if he has not lived a year and a day in the town, in order that it may be known whether or not he comes from a good place. . . .

9. And whoever does work on Saturday afternoon, or on the Eve of the Feast of Our Lady, or after Vespers on the Eve of the Feast of St. Julien, and completes the day by working, shall pay, if he be a master, 12 denarii, and if he be a journeyman, 6 denarii. And whoever works in the four days of Christmas, or in the eight days of Easter, or in the eight days of Pentecost, owes 5 solidi. . . .

11. And an apprentice owes to the Fraternity for his apprenticeship 5 solidi. . . .

13. And whoever does work in defiance of the mayor and aldermen shall pay 5 solidi. . . .

16. And those who are fed at the expense of the city shall be put to work first. And he who slights them for strangers owes 5 solidi: but if the stranger be put to work he cannot be removed as long as the master wishes to keep him. . . . And when a master does not work hard he pays 5 solidi, and a journeyman 2 solidi. . . .

18. And after the half year the mayor and aldermen shall fix such wages as he ought to have. . . .

20. And whoever maligns the mayor and aldermen, that is while on the business of the Fraternity, shall pay 5 solidi. . . .

23. And if a draper or a merchant has work to do in his house, he may take such workmen as he wishes into his house, so long as the work be done in his house. And he who infringes this shall give 5 solidi to the Fraternity. . . .

25. And each master ought to have his arms when he is summoned. And if he has not he should pay 20 solidi. . . .

32. And if a master does not give a journeyman such wage as is his due, then he shall pay 5 solidi.

33. And he who overlooks the forfeits of this Fraternity, if he does not wish to pay them when the mayor and aldermen summon him either for the army or the district, then he owes 10 solidi, and he shall not work at the trade until he has paid. Every forfeit of 5 solidi, and the fines which the mayor and aldermen command, shall be written down. All the fines of the Fraternity ought to go for the purchase of arms and for the needs of the Fraternity.

4. **muid:** a silver coin in circulation in Arras.

34. And whatever brother of this Fraternity shall betray his confrère for others shall not work at the trade for a year and a day. . . .

36. And should a master of this Fraternity die and leave a male heir he may learn the trade anywhere where there is no apprentice.

37. And no apprentice shall cut to the selvage[5] for half a year, and this is to obtain good work. And no master or journeyman may cut by himself because no one can measure cloth well alone. And whoever infringes this rule shall pay 5 solidi to the Fraternity for each offense.

38. Any brother whatsoever who lays hands on, or does wrong to, the mayor and aldermen of this Fraternity, as long as they work for the city and the Fraternity, shall not work at his trade in the city for a year and a day.

And if he should do so, let him be banished from the town for a year and a day, saving the appeal to Monseigneur the King and his Castellan. . . .

Sources 7 and 8 from Carolly Erickson, The Records of Medieval Europe, *translated by Carolly Erickson (Garden City, N.Y.: Anchor, 1971), p. 238.*

7. Judgment Against a Draper in Flanders, mid-14th century

When Jacquemars des Mares, a draper, brought one of his cloths to the great cloth hall of Arras and sold it, the aforesaid cloth was examined by the *espincheurs*[6] as is customary, and at the time they had it weighed, it was half a pound over the legal weight. Then, because of certain suspicions which arose, they had the cloth dried, and when it was dry, it weighed a half pound less than the legal weight. The *espincheur* brought the misdeed to the attention of the Twenty;[7] Jacquemars was fined 100 shillings.

8. Dispute Between Master Fullers and Their Apprentices in Flanders, 1345

A point of discussion was mooted between the apprentice fullers on the one hand, and the master fullers on the other. The apprentices held that, as they laid out in a letter, no one could have work done in his house without taking apprentices. . . . For they complained of fulling masters who had their children work in their houses, without standing [for jobs] in the public square like the other apprentices, and they begged that their letter be answered. The fulling masters

5. **selvage:** very edge of the cloth.
6. **espincheur:** cloth inspector.
7. **Twenty:** court of twenty men, made up of members of the city council.

stated certain arguments to the contrary. The aldermen sent for both parties and for the Twenty also and asked the masters if indeed they kept their children as apprentices; each master said he did. It was declared by the aldermen that every apprentice must remain in the public square, as reason demanded.

Done in the year of 1344 [1345], in the month of February, and through a full sitting of the aldermen.

Source 9 from Merry E. Wiesner, translator, unpublished decisions in Nuremberg Stadtarchiv, Quellen zur Nürnbergische Geschichte, Rep. F5, no. 68/I, fol. 58 (1577).

9. Decision by the Nuremberg City Council, 1577

The honorable city council has decided to deny the request of Barbara Hansmesser that she be allowed to dye wool because the blanketweavers' guild has so adamantly opposed it. Because her husband is not a citizen, they are both ordered to get out of the city and find work in some other place, with the warning that if they are found in the vicinity of this city, and are doing any work here, work will be taken from them and the yarn cut to pieces. They can count on this.

Source 10 from Merry E. Wiesner, translator, unpublished supplications in Frankfurt Stadtarchiv, Zünfte, Ugb. C-32, R, no. 1.

10. Widow's Supplication to the Frankfurt City Council, late sixteenth century

Most honorable and merciful gentlemen, you certainly know what a heavy and hard cross God has laid on me, and in what a miserable situation I find myself, after the much too early death of my late husband, with my young children, all of them still minors and some still nursing. This unfortunate situation is well known everywhere.

Although in consideration of my misfortune most Christian hearts would have gladly let me continue in my craft and occupation, and allowed me to earn a little piece of bread, instead the overseers of the woolweavers' guild came to me as soon as my husband had died, in my sorrow and even in my own house. Against all Christian charity, they began to order changes in my workshop with very harsh and menacing words. They specifically ordered that my apprentice, whom I had raised and trained at great cost and who had just come to be of use to me in the craft, leave me and go to them, which would be to their great advantage but my greater disadvantage. They ordered this on the pretense that there was no longer a master here so he could not finish his training.

Honorable sirs, I then humbly put myself under the protection of the lord mayors here, and asked that the two journeymen and the apprentice be allowed to continue on in their work as they had before unimpeded until a final judgment was reached in the matter. Despite this, one of the weavers began to shout at my journeymen whenever he saw them, especially if there were other people on the street. In his unhindered and unwarranted boldness, he yelled that my workshop was not honorable, and all journeymen who worked there were thieves and rascals. After doing this for several days, he and several others came into my workshop on a Saturday, and, bitter and jealous, pushed my journeymen out. They began to write to all places where this craft is practiced to tell other masters not to accept anyone who had worked in my workshop.

I now humbly beg you, my honorable and gracious sirs, protect me and my hungry children from such abuse, shame, and insult. Help my journeymen, who were so undeservedly insulted, to regain their honor. I beg you, as the protector of humble widows, to let my apprentice stay with me, as apprentices are allowed to stay in the workshops of widows throughout the entire Holy Roman Empire, as long as there are journeymen, whether or not there is a master present. Protect me from any further insults of the woolweavers' guild, which does nothing to increase the honor of our city, which you, honorable sirs, are charged to uphold. I plead with you to grant me my request, and allow me to continue my workshop.

Source 11 from Roy C. Cave and Herbert H. Coulson, A Source Book for Medieval Economic History *(New York: Biblo and Tannen, 1965), pp. 256–257.*

11. Two Apprenticeship Contracts, thirteenth century

Be it known to present and future aldermen that Ouede Ferconne apprentices Michael, her son, to Matthew Haimart on security of her house, her person, and her chattels,[8] and the share that Michael ought to have in them, so that Matthew Haimart will teach him to weave in four years, and that he (Michael) will have shelter, and learn his trade there without board. And if there should be reason within two years for Michael to default she will return him, and Ouede Ferconne, his mother, guarantees this on the security of her person and goods. And if she should wish to purchase his freedom for the last two years she may do so for thirty-three solidi, and will pledge for that all that has been stated. And if he should not free himself of the last two years let him return, and Ouede Ferconne, his mother, pledges this with her person and her goods. And the said Ouede pledges that if Matthew Haimart suffers either loss or damage through Michael, her son, she will restore the loss and damage on the security of herself and all her goods, should Michael do wrong.

8. **chattels:** personal property.

[213]

April the ninth. I, Peter Borre, in good faith and without guile, place with you, Peter Feissac, weaver, my son Stephen, for the purpose of learning the trade or craft of weaving, to live at your house, and to do work for you from the feast of Easter next for four continuous years, promising you by this agreement to take care that my son does the said work, and that he will be faithful and trustworthy in all that he does, and that he will neither steal nor take anything away from you, nor flee nor depart from you for any reason, until he has completed his apprenticeship. And I promise you by this agreement that I will reimburse you for all damages or losses that you incur or sustain on my behalf, pledging all my goods, etc.; renouncing the benefit of all laws, etc. And I, the said Peter Feissac, promise you, Peter Borre, that I will teach your son faithfully and will provide food and clothing for him.

Done at Marseilles, near the tables of the money-changers. Witnesses, etc.

Source 12 from Robert S. Lopez and Irving W. Raymond, editors and translators, Medieval Trade in the Mediterranean World *(New York: Columbia University Press, 1955), pp. 263–265, no. 138.*

12. Insurance Contracts from Pisa, 1384

This is a book of Francesco of Prato and partners, residing in Pisa, and we shall write in it all insurances we shall make in behalf of others. May God grant us profit from these and protect us from dangers.

[*Seal of Francesco son of Marco*]

A memorandum that on September 7, 1384, in behalf of Baldo Ridolfi and partners we insured for 100 gold florins wool in the ship of Guilhem Sale, Catalan, [in transit] from Peñiscola to Porto Pisano. And from the said 100 florins we received 3 gold florins in cash, and we insured against all risks, as is evident by a record by the hand of Gherardo d'Ormanno which is undersigned by our hand.

Said ship arrived safely in Porto Pisano and unloaded on . . . October, 1384, and we are free from the insurance.

A memorandum that on September 10 in behalf of Ambrogio, son of Bino Bini, we insured for 200 gold florins Milanese cloth in the ship of Bartolomeo Vitale, [in transit] from Porto Pisano to Palermo. And from the said 200 florins we received 8 gold florins, charged to the debit account of Ambrogio on *c.* 174, and no other record appears [written] by the hand of any broker.

Arrived in Palermo safely.

First graph in Source 13 from R. S. Lopez, "Hard Times and Investment in Culture," The Renaissance: Medieval or Modern *(Boston: D. C. Heath, 1959); second graph from H. van Werveke, "De omgang van de Ieperse lakenproductie in de veertiende eeuw,"* Medelelingen, K. Vlaamse Acad. voor Wetensch., Letteren en schone Kunsten van Belgie *(1947). Both reprinted in Harry A. Miskimin,* The Economy of Early Renaissance Europe, 1300–1460 *(Englewood Cliffs, N.J.: Prentice Hall, 1969), p. 94.*

13. Trends in the Cloth Trade in Florence and Ypres

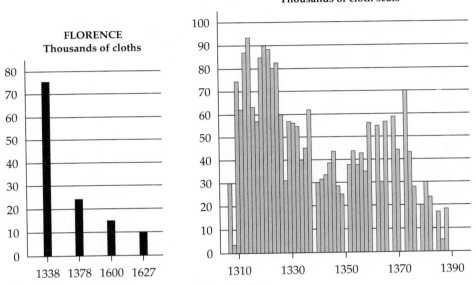

*The drapers' guild attached a seal to each cloth that it handled.

Table in Source 14 from A. R. Bridbury, Economic Growth: England in the Later Middle Ages *(London: G. Allen and Unwin, 1962), p. 32. Used by permission of the author; graphs adapted from H. C. Darby, editor,* A New Historical Geography of England *(Cambridge, England: Cambridge University Press, 1973), p. 219. Reprinted with permission of Cambridge University Press.*

14. English Exports of Raw Wool and Cloth, Based on Customs Records, ca 1350–1550

Years	Raw wool (sacks)	Woollen cloths (as equivalent to sacks of raw wool)
1361–70	28,302	3,024
1371–80	23,241	3,432
1381–90	17,988	5,521
1391–1400	17,679	8,967
1401–10	13,922	7,651
1411–20	13,487	6,364
1421–30	13,696	9,309
1431–40	7,377	10,051
1441–50	9,398	11,803
1471–80	9,299	10,125
1481–90	8,858	12,230
1491–1500	8,149	13,891

1   Raw Wool Exports

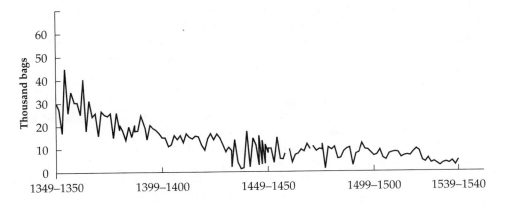

2   Cloth Exports

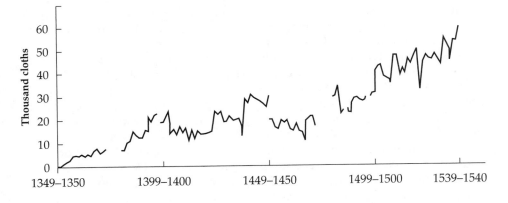

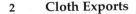

QUESTIONS TO CONSIDER

The records you have read shed some light on a wide variety of issues in the medieval cloth trade, as well as providing information on other social and economic matters. To draw some general conclusions and answer the questions for this chapter, you will need to go back to your list of goals, actions, and conflicts, and put together the information from the various sources. Because our focus here is on cloth production and sales, you will also need to leave aside what you have learned about other issues, though this may be very interesting to you. Investigating social and economic questions often involves not only uncovering sources that deal with your problem directly, but also extracting small bits of information from sources that cover a great many other areas, such as the city council records of Sources 9 and 10. Being a social historian requires that you discipline yourself to stick to the topic; though it may be fascinating to read every entry about every issue, this will not help with the completion of your research project.

Go back, then, to your list: How would you describe the key aims of territorial rulers regarding the cloth trade? Of local ruling bodies such as city councils? Do the sources you have read here lead you to support the thesis that city ordinances generally reflect the aims of cloth merchants? How might the aims of territorial rulers and merchants come into conflict? (For one example, how might cloth merchants or artisans already working in cloth production in Courtrai feel about the tax breaks that the Countess of Flanders gave to immigrants into the city in Source 3? What might cloth merchants do in response to this to maintain their monopoly on the cloth trade? For another, how might merchants in raw wool have regarded the changing nature of English exports as traced in Source 14 and the government tariff policies that were responsible for this?) In addition to shaping government policies, what private actions do you find merchants engaging in to achieve their goals?

Turning to the relationship of the merchants—or the city councils, usually dominated by merchants—to the artisans: What actions by artisans are explicitly prohibited in city ordinances or guild charters? (See Sources 4, 5, and 6.) How do these prohibitions

reflect merchant aims? How would you describe the attitudes of merchants toward artisans—suspicious, friendly, hostile, paternalistic, fraternal? How did groups or individuals use the conflicts between these two to their own advantage? (The best examples here are the supplication quoted in Source 10 and the dispute recorded in Source 8. To whom did the widow and the apprentices turn for help, and about which groups were they complaining? In the widow's supplication, what sort of language does she use to persuade authorities to help her?)

Turning to the workplace itself: How would you characterize the atmosphere in the houses of most woolworkers—collegial and friendly, or divided and somewhat hostile? As you have no doubt noticed, ordinances regulated not simply individual workers, but their families as well. What special privileges were given to members of the master's family? Who objected to these privileges, and why? How did the guilds treat widows of their members? Do you see any discrepancy in the discussion of widows in the ordinances and in the actual treatment of a member's widow in Source 10? How do the guilds react to women working who were not the wives or widows of guild members? Would you regard the guilds as generally helpful to families or helpful to only certain types of families? Along with the privileges accorded to the master's family members, what other sources of dispute between masters and journeymen, and between masters and apprentices, are mentioned in the sources? How might the goals of the craft guild masters and those of the merchants come into conflict in the handling of these disputes?

You are now ready to answer the questions posed by this chapter: What were the key economic and social goals of governments, merchant-capitalists, and artisans regarding the cloth trade, and how did they seek to achieve these aims? What economic and social conflicts emerged as the cloth trade grew and changed?

EPILOGUE

Because of its capitalist organization and complex division of labor, the medieval cloth trade is often seen as a harbinger of modern economic developments. As you have read the sources for this chapter, you have probably discovered other areas in which there are parallels between the medieval cloth trade and the modern economy. Many of the goals of governments, merchants, and artisans that we have seen expressed in the medieval sources are shared by modern governments, corporations, and unions: the expansion of domestic production, the maintenance of order in the workplace, the limitation of risk, the highest level of profit, steady wages and job security, protection from foreign competition, the replacement of exports of raw materials with exports of manufactured products. As they were in the Middle Ages, these goals are often contradictory, if not mutually exclusive.

Many of the actions taken by medieval authorities and individuals continue to appear on the evening news as it reports economic developments: protectionist legislation, tax breaks to promote the development of industry and job creation, preferential treatment for certain groups, the transfer of jobs to places where wages are lower or workers are less likely to strike, immigration policies that promote the immigration of workers with specific skills, fraud and falsification of merchandise in an attempt to increase profits.

Many of the conflicts we have seen here still beset workplaces in the twentieth century: disputes over wage levels and the right to work; disagreements between labor and management over who controls certain aspects of the workplace; conflicts between older and younger workers, now often expressed as issues of seniority; and demands that employers pay more attention to the family responsibilities of their employees and make the workplace more "family friendly." Methods of enforcing aims and resolving conflicts that were tried in the Middle Ages are still often tried today, such as the use of outside authorities or arbitrators, revolts and strikes, and blacklisting and fines.

Though in the contemporary economy production of many types of goods often faces conflicts—automobiles, electronic and computer equipment, and agricultural products usually gain the most headlines—cloth and clothing production is still an important issue for many nations, corporations, and unions. Many of the commercials promoting the retail giant Wal-Mart's policy of buying products made in the United States highlight cloth and clothing manufacturers. The attempts by U.S. immigration authorities to make employers responsible for making sure their foreign-born employees have the necessary work permits have targeted sportswear makers in New York and California who hire undocumented aliens. Lawsuits by U.S. companies charging copyright infringement are often brought against foreign manufacturers of such items as T-shirts and beach towels. Just as cloth production in the Middle Ages was a harbinger of trends and conflicts in the modern economy, cloth production in the early twenty-first century may also be a harbinger of the future. The internationalization of the marketplace and work force that it points to perhaps would not seem so strange to the countess of Flanders or Francesco of Prato, nor would the difficulties that can result from this seem so strange to the woolworkers of Florence or Ypres.

CHAPTER TEN

LIFE IN AN ENGLISH VILLAGE

IN THE HIGH MIDDLE AGES

Since the development of agriculture and the domestication of animals, most of the world's population have been farmers or herders, living in family units in small settlements. Despite their great numbers, however, rural men and women left relatively little historical record until the twentieth century. They were largely illiterate, and the groups that were literate in their societies—priests, scribes, government officials, chroniclers—were generally uninterested in the lives of people in the countryside. They often looked down on rural residents, dismissing them as hicks or *hoi polloi*, an expression that comes from the Greek words for "the many." In some cultures, the literate elite wrote materials *for* common people, such as sermons and moral guides, but only during times of crisis, such as famines, natural disasters, or war, did they write much *about* them. Even then, their comments might only refer to number of dead or complaints about crops that were not being harvested or animals that were not being tended.

Today we are often much more interested in the lives of ordinary rural people of the past than were their better-educated and wealthier contemporaries. There are now thousands of book-length studies from around the world on rural people, as well as specialized journals such as *Peasant Studies* and *Agricultural History*. Other historical periodicals, such as the *Journal of Social History* or the *Journal of Women's History*, frequently include articles about rural people. The problem of sources has not gone away, but historians are using many different types of evidence to explore the lives of people who themselves left neither writing nor an extensive visual record. At the same time, however, modern farming methods and the fact that most of us live in cities or suburbs make the day-to-day existence of rural people in earlier eras increasingly foreign. Thus before we can carry out analyses of peasant revolts, agricultural innovations, popular religion, family structure, or other aspects of rural life that might interest us, we often need to get a firmer grasp of exactly what people were doing as they raised crops and animals throughout the year.

For many rural societies, sources about everyday life are exactly what is lacking, but by the thirteenth century, records from some parts of England begin to provide more extensive information. The vast majority of people in medieval England were peasants who lived in small family groups in villages and made their living predominantly by raising crops and animals. Villages were under the jurisdiction of lords, members of the nobility or gentry who might live in a large house in the village but often lived elsewhere. The territory controlled by a lord is generally termed a *manor*, and it might consist of one village, a number of villages, or even only part of a village.

Within each manor, lords and peasants developed customs that set out the terms of their mutual dependence. Peasants owed lords services, rents, and taxes, and they received in return customary rights to hold pieces of land, raise their families, and pass these rights on to their children. Lords occasionally took surveys, termed *extents* or *custumals*, that listed the land and obligations of each household. Some of these extents are very brief, but others describe in great detail all of the tasks that peasants were expected to perform as part of their obligations, thus providing a glimpse of the normal yearly round of work. Since lords relied on the villagers' sworn testimony regarding landholdings, dues, and services owed when drawing up

these custumals, they derive directly from the villagers' experience. Lords generally appointed officials such as *stewards* or *bailiffs* to oversee the legal and business operations of their manors, and they sometimes appointed lower officials as well. By the thirteenth century, treatises describing the proper management of manors spelled out the duties of such officials over the course of the agricultural year, explaining how estates would ideally be run.

The lord often held some of the land of the manor directly—called the *demesne* (pronounced "domain")—but in many villages peasant families held most fields and decided what would be planted in each field, rotating the crops according to tradition and need. In many parts of England (and elsewhere in northern Europe) the fields of the village were farmed in what is termed *open-field agriculture*, a pattern that differs sharply from modern farming practices. Some fields would be planted in crops such as wheat or rye for human consumption, some in oats or other crops for both animals and humans, and some would be left unworked or *fallow* to allow the soil to rejuvenate. The exact pattern of this rotation varied from location to location, but in most areas with open-field agriculture the holdings farmed by any one family did not consist of a whole field but of strips in many fields. Village land also included meadows and woods held by the village as a whole, called the *commons*, where villagers could let their animals graze.

Decisions about the open-field system and many other local issues were largely handled by the villagers them- selves, who also appointed officials in addition to those appointed by the lord, including reeves, constables, and ale-tasters. We often do not know ex- actly how officials were chosen or elected, but we do know that they were always adult men and generally heads of households.

Several times a year and in some places even more often, the villagers gathered for court proceedings during which the legal and financial affairs of both the lord and village were han- dled. Anyone with a debt or agreement to record, a case against a fellow vil- lager, or a charge to answer would be present, so these were often crowded and noisy events. In the thirteenth century these courts began keeping formal records on pieces of parchment that were stitched end to end and then rolled up. Such *court rolls* were generally made while the court was in session, not written up afterward, and were sometimes kept by reeves or other officials chosen from among the village men. The courts often went be- yond enforcing rules and issued new ordinances, which historians now term *by-laws*, to regulate activities in the village or its fields and woods. Gener- ally these by-laws were passed not out of theoretical reflection but because people were already carrying out the activities they discuss, and officials or village leaders judged such activities harmful. Thus both court records and by-laws provide information about day-to-day life in rural villages.

Each male villager over the age of twelve was expected to enroll in a *frankpledge* or *tithing*, a unit of ten or so men who were responsible for one an- other's behavior. Each tithing was headed by a *capital* or *chief pledge*, usu- ally a villager from a more prominent family who also often acted as a juror on cases brought before the manorial court. *Jurors* were men who held land in the village and who were charged with knowing what had gone on since the last time the court met. Since mano- rial courts relied more on the collective memory of village traditions and cus- toms than on written laws, jurors were often asked to decide issues by simply talking among themselves or to others who might know. For example, they might decide who had the rights to a certain piece of land. For this reason, jurors were chosen from among those most likely to know the facts of the case, the opposite of modern jury selec- tion. Both plaintiff and defendant often brought in others who would swear to their view of the case or their good character, and in particularly contested cases the jurors would ask the whole village to back their judgment. Punish- ments were generally fines or occasion- ally banishment; imprisonment and corporal punishments were quite rare. (Serious criminal cases were not han- dled by the manorial courts but by the royal courts.) Often individuals were required to have someone else pledge that they would actually pay the fine assessed. Villagers were expected to bring cases against each other to court, and they could be fined if the jurors learned about things such as debt or trespass that they had not brought to court.

The medieval village had no police as we know them, so if villagers saw a crime or infraction, they were expected to chase the perpetrator themselves and yell to others to join in, in what was termed *raising the hue and cry*. They could be fined for not doing this, and also fined for doing this if it was unwarranted.

Village juries also carried out inquests into cases of sudden or suspicious death, including homicides, suicides, and accidents (termed "misadventure"). In 1194, the king established the office of coroner, and four men were elected in each county from among the knights and gentry for this office. Coroners held inquests, found witnesses and suspects, heard confessions and appeals, and held property that might later be forfeited. Villagers who witnessed a death or found a dead body were required to summon a coroner, who examined the body, convened a group of villagers as a jury, and recorded the details of each case. In cases of accidental death, the coroner also assessed the value of the item that had caused the death; the item was sold, and the proceeds went to the king as a special tax. (Since earlier the money

had been used to pay for prayers for the soul of the deceased, this amount was called the *deodand*, or gift to God.) Thousands of coroners' inquests survive for several English counties in the thirteenth and fourteenth centuries, and they can tell us a great deal about patterns of violence. In particular, those that concern accidental deaths can also provide information about day-to-day life, because that is when "misadventure" happened.

By the late thirteenth century, then, a variety of records begin to appear in England that allow us to gain an understanding of everyday rural life. Your task in this chapter will be to use different types of sources from the late thirteenth and early fourteenth centuries to answer the following questions: What were the primary activities carried out over the year as people raised crops and animals, including activities that were approved and those that were viewed as problematic? What do the sources suggest about relations within a village, both among ordinary people and between villagers and their superiors?

SOURCES AND METHOD

Many of the types of documents that survive from medieval English villages are *prescriptive* sources; that is, they set out the way that things were supposed to be, not the way they actually were—the taxes and labor services villagers *should* pay, the duties officials *should* perform, the laws

people *should* follow. Within such prescriptive sources, however, we can also find a great deal of information about many aspects of actual rural life, information that can be enhanced through *descriptive* sources, such as records of actual court proceedings. For this chapter, you will be using five types of sources: manorial extents and custumals, village by-laws, treatises of manorial management, court records, and coroners' inquests. Your method will be to read the sources carefully, taking notes and analyzing them as you gather information to answer the first question; then you can reflect on this information to answer the second.

Source 1 is a custumal describing the labor services, money rents, and products owed throughout the agricultural year to the lord of the village of Bureton by Robert Tac, one of the villagers. As you read, jot down the various tasks that Robert is to do. What activities associated with grain production is he to do in spring? In summer? In autumn? In winter? What is he to do in terms of caring for animals? What other types of work are expected of him at various times of the year? Source 2 is an extent from the village of Alwalton in 1279, which sets out a much shorter list of obligations for each head of household, with the villagers divided into free tenants, villeins (serfs), and cotters (cottagers), who were poor villagers holding very small pieces of land. What activities do the villeins perform for the lord? The cotters? Many of the cotters hold only one or one-half rood of land, that is, a quarter or an eighth of an acre, not much more than a city lot. (A half-rood would be a square about twenty-five yards on a side.) Would you expect them to be able to live from the produce of their land? Do the sources so far provide hints about what else they might be doing to make a living? Source 3 is a section of an extent from the manor of Bernehorne in 1307 describing the rents and services owed by a villager named John of Cayworth and listing the meals he is to receive while working at

various tasks. What activities is John to perform throughout the year? The extent also sets a monetary value on the work and on the food provided; what do these items indicate about the price of labor relative to that of food?

With Source 4, we turn from rules set by manorial lords to rules set by villagers themselves, called by-laws; here instead of lists of obligations, we have lists of prohibitions. By-laws were issued because certain activities had created problems in a village; you can thus generally use them as evidence that the actions they prohibit were going on. As you did for Sources 1 through 3, jot down the various activities discussed directly or by implication in the by-laws. You can see that "there shall be no carting by night" or "no one shall gather straw in the fields unless it be each from his own land" are direct references to work activities. What tasks are suggested in the statement that "everyone shall see that his stiles and lanes . . . are so kept that neither the lord nor any of his tenants incur damage because of the lack of such maintenance"? Many of the villagers' concerns are easy to understand: they don't want animals wandering the fields, especially when the grain is still growing; they don't want people harvesting grain or other crops that do not belong to them (a particularly easy thing to do in an open-field system, where each field contained strips farmed by many families); they don't want grain taken directly from the field as payment for work because it was difficult to judge how much was being taken; they don't want any work done at night, when the opportunities for deception increased. One common issue is probably less familiar: concerns over gleaning, which was part of the harvesting process. People who gleaned picked up small bits of grain that had fallen from the stalks as they were cut, generally keeping the kernels that they gathered. As you can see in the by-laws, villages generally reserved gleaning for poor people who were for some reason unable to carry out the main tasks of harvesting, which generally meant the elderly, small children (especially orphans), and those who were weak, ill, or handicapped. Why do you think they limited gleaning in this way? Why do you think people were so concerned about "strangers" and "outsiders" who gleaned?

Source 5 is a different type of prescriptive source. This is an extract from *Seneschaucie*, an anonymous treatise written in Norman French in the 1270s describing the role of officials and workers on a manor. The author may have been trained in law and was perhaps a manorial official himself, though his identity was unknown even in his own day. The chief official on the idealized manor set out here was the steward—*seneschal* in French, from which the work gets its title—who was also the audience for a work such as this. Under his direction were reeves, haywards, ploughmen, waggoners, shepherds, dairymaids, and other officials, whose tasks the steward was to understand and oversee. Read the whole document through carefully and take notes on the activities of each type of person. What sorts of expertise and knowledge were

expected of the various officials? To what extent did they operate independently of the lord and his officials on a daily basis? As in the by-laws in Source 4, certain activities are prohibited; what are these, and why do you think they were forbidden?

Sources 6 and 7 are records of the actual manorial courts preserved as court rolls, and are thus descriptive rather than prescriptive sources. These will allow you to assess what villagers and officials were actually doing and how their activities fit with expectations set out in custumals, by-laws, and management treatises. Before you begin reading them, it might be helpful to reread the last part of the Problem section to refresh your memory about how manorial courts operated.

Source 6 is the entire court roll for one day, November 17, 1288, for the village of Broughton. As you will see, this was a very busy day. Some of the matters brought up do not pertain directly to the questions for this chapter, but reading the document in its entirety can give you a good idea of all the matters that could come before a court and broaden your understanding of medieval village life. The court roll begins with a listing of the chief pledges and jurors and then goes on with the day's business; fines and other punishments are listed in the text and summarized in a column on the left. As you read the document, you will find many issues that are not much different from what you might find at a local court today: people not showing up for work, disputes over who owned certain land or things, unpaid debts, insults exchanged among neighbors, animals running loose, people (in this case a brewer and a miller) charging too much for their services, interpersonal violence. What activities appear to be common problems or issues of concern for villagers or the lord? How do the interests of the lord and those of the villagers emerge in the court proceedings? All of the chief pledges and the jurors are male, but women appear quite often in this document. What do these court proceedings reveal about women's activities and position in the village? What sense do you get of the individuality of men and women in the village? At the end of the document, various officials are fined for not doing things they were supposed to; what do these clauses indicate about the expectations set out for manorial officials?

Source 7 is another court roll, from February 2, 1314, on the manor of Addington, held by a noble widow. (This is "the lady" referred to in the source.) As you will see, various people are fined for different activities that went against manorial rules, much like in Source 6. One individual, however, a certain Thomas Cubbel, accounted for most of the actions of the court. As you read this document, note down the various cases in which he was involved: What does he accuse Gervase le Leche, Robert Russel, and Robert Cros of doing? What does the court decide to do in these cases? What is Thomas himself accused of doing concerning the "bedripsilver"? What did he neglect to do regarding William Prelly? Based on just this one court record, what can you speculate about the type of person Thomas Cubbel was? About relations between him and his neighbors? What does this suggest

about relations among neighbors, at least in this village? At the very end of document, what is the whole population of the village accused of doing? Why do you think they did this, and what might this mean in terms of relations between villagers and their lord (who was in this case a lady)?

Source 8 presents six short cases from coroners' inquests concerning accidental deaths or homicides. In Source 8a, what is Alfred of Ravensden doing when he dies of "falling sickness"? In Source 8b, where are William and Muriel Blanche working when their daughters die? In Source 8c, what is the twelve-year-old John doing when he drowns? In Source 8d, what is Amice doing when she is killed? In Source 8e, what is Henry Wymer doing when he dies? In Source 8f, what is Ralph doing when he discovers the dead body? In all of these cases, how are villagers involved in the coroners' inquests?

Source 9 is one final coroner's inquest concerning the activities of a certain John, who was the hayward—one of the officials—in the village of Houghton. You will need to read this case closely to figure out what is happening, as it is action-packed. What is John accused of doing? What does he confess to doing, and what is the punishment set? Then what does he do? What does the village do to him in the end? What does this suggest about relations between villagers and village officials? This case occurred in the 1270s, the same period when the anonymous author was writing *Seneschaucie*. How does this real hayward fit with the idealized one described in the treatise?

THE EVIDENCE

Source 1 from Nathaniel J. Hone, The Manor and Manorial Records *(London: Methuen, 1906), pp. 227–230.*

1. Custumal of Village of Bureton, ca 1250

These are the rents and customs owing yearly to the lord Abbot of Glastonbury from the vill of Bureton.

Robert Tac holds 1 virgate[1] of land and pays of gavol [*i.e.* money rent] yearly 4^s[2] at four annual terms, to wit, at each term 12^d[3], and for a gift to the larderer at the feast of St Martin 2^n, [April 13] and a cock and hen for cherset[4] on St Martin's day. And he owes to be at the lord's bedrip[5] for 2 days, to wit, at the winter bed rip with as many oxen as he has and with his plough and horse or mare if he have one, and the lord shall find him in food [i.e., provide food for him] to wit, one day in bread, meat, pottage and beer in sufficient and good quality and the next day in bread, cheese, pottage and beer. And he owes also to be at the lord's bedrip in Lent [the 40 days before Easter] with his plough and horse if he have one, and with as many oxen as he has for one day. And he ought to have from the lord for each plough 1^d and for each harrow 1 farthing.[6] And he owes to be at the lord's bedrip in summer, to wit, to work at the fallow one day with his plough if he have one, and with as many oxen as he has, and the lord shall find him in bread and cheese. And he owes to come one day with one man to weed the lord's corn [i.e., grain], and shall find him in bread and cheese once in the day, and after that day he shall come every day after Pentecost [49 days after Easter] with one man until the lord's corn shall be weeded except feast days and Saturdays, until the lord's field shall be reaped. And he shall weed daily till terce,[7] and shall have nothing. And he owes to come with one reaping hook to reap the seven meadows of the lord of which three meadows are at Burton and four meadows at Niweton. And he and his fellows shall have half a measure of corn and a ram or 12^d at the will of the lord and 1 cheese of the best cheeses that are made at the lord's hall, so that it do not exceed the price of 5^d. And he owes to toss [stack mown hay] the said meadows with his fellows, and they have nothing. And if

1. **virgate:** a measure of land, above 25–30 acres.
2. **4^s:** 4 shillings.
3. **12^d:** 12 pence, abbreviated "d" for *denarius*, the Latin word for penny. 12 pence = 1 shilling.
4. **cherset:** a church tax, paid in goods or money.
5. **bedrip:** service owed the lord.
6. **farthing:** one-quarter of a penny.
7. **terce:** 9 A.M.

he rides to Niweton on his beast to move the said meadows, he shall give his beast while he is mowing there of the grass which he mows for his fodder and he owes to find one man and the third part of a wain [a cart] to carry the lord's hay and corn as long as necessary both at Niweton and at Burton and each wain should have from the lord's wood one [tree-]trunk which is called wenbote. And these trunks they ought to have when they begin to move, and when they carry the hay they shall have nothing. Also he owes to work every day from the feast of St Peter ad Vincula to the feast of St Michael, [August 2 to September 29] excepting feast days and Saturdays. And when he reaps he owes to reap 1 acre and he shall have nothing. And he owes to reap a bedrip at Burton twice, to wit 2 acres of corn one day, and another day 2 acres of oats. And when he collects brushwood (coopertionem) he owes to collect ten heaps, and in each heap, ten armfuls, to wit, in the first week after autumn and in the second week nine heaps and in the third week eight heaps, since at each solemn feast the need of it decreases until at feast of St Michael, they collect but one heap. And when he threshes he owes to thresh a sixth part of one measure and to winnow [separate grain from its husks] the same and to have nothing. And when he collects fencewood, he owes to collect two bundles of thorns and carry them to the court but not to make the fence, or one bundle of thorns and one bundle of rods, and to make the fence. And he owes to thresh 1 measure of corn at Mow-thrash (mughythreses) and to have the straw. And he shall have such measure which he may sell at Sherburn or St Edward's [Shaftesbury] less 2^d, or he can drink a scot-ale of the lord for ½^d. Also if the lord's court shall be injured by wind or tempest he shall help with the other neighbours to put the lord's buildings in good repair. And every year he owes with his neighbours to separate the ox-shed [*i.e.* to weed out the weak stock] of the lord if there is need. And he owes for the whole year to carry the lord's corn with his beast, as well from Niweton as Burton to Glastonbury or elsewhere at the lord's will. And he should have when he carries to Glastonbury, to wit, for each horse 1 loaf,[8] and if he carries the lord's corn to market to be sold, for each horse he should have a quarter. Also for every cart when they carry the corn in autumn he shall have daily 3 sheaves and the man who is in the grange to stack the lord's corn from the carts 3 sheaves a day to wit, from the last cart. Also he owes with his other neighbours to cut down a trunk once a year and to help place it on the cart, or prepare it for firewood against the lord's coming. And he ought, he and another holder of a yardland, to have a log at Christmas from the lord's wood which is called woodtale (wdetale), and the lord to find him in food on Christmas Day, to wit, in bread, cheese, pottage and two dishes of meat. And he shall take with him a plate, mug and napkin if he wishes to eat off a cloth, and he shall bring a bundle of brushwood to cook his food, unless he would have it raw. And if he have a young ox calved, he can sell it before he shall have yoked it, but after he has yoked it,

---

8. That is, he receives one loaf of bread to eat for each horse that carries the lord's grain to Glastonbury.

he cannot without licence of the lord's bailiffs. And if he have a male foal foaled, he can sell him without licence whilst he is being suckled, but after he is weaned not at all. And if he have porkers he can sell them at will before the Nativity of the Blessed Virgin [8th Sept.], but after that day not at all, unless he gives pannage[9] to the lord, nor can he marry his daughter to any except upon the lord's land without licence, but upon the lord's land well. Also he owes to harrow[10] the lord's land in winter daily, until he can use the lord's ploughs and in Lent similarly to harrow the oats. And the lord ought to have a draught beast to carry the seed and to harrow his land after it has been harrowed until plough time. Also he ought to have housebote and haybote[11] from the lord's wood. Also he owes to help with his neighbours every year to well enclose the Holpulemetle. Also he owes one feast day in autumn to gather nuts in the lord's wood for the use of the lord, and he owes to enclose the lord's park at Pilton, and he owes to carry, if necessary, great timber to the lord's hall with his neighbours, if the lord wishes to build there. And the said Robert, and every tenant that keeps pigs, shall have a sow free of pannage.

Sources 2 and 3 from Translations and Reprints from the Original Sources of European History, *vol. 3, no. 5 (Philadelphia: University of Pennsylvania Department of History, 1897), pp. 4–7; pp. 10–11.*

2. Extent of Village of Alwalton, 1279

Free tenants

The abbot of Peterborough holds the manor of Alwalton and vill from the lord king directly. . . . Thomas le Boteler holds a messuage[12] with a court yard which contains 1 rood,[13] and 3 acres of land, by charter, paying thence yearly to the said abbot 14s. . . .

Villeins

Hugh Miller holds 1 virgate of land in villenage by paying thence to the said abbot 3s. 1d. Likewise the same Hugh works through the whole year except. 1 week at Christmas, 1 week at Easter, and 1 at Whitsuntide that is in each

9. **pannage:** a fee paid to the lord for the right to pasture swines on his land.
10. **harrow:** to break up earth with a tool with sharp tines, also called a harrow.
11. **housebote and haybote:** the right of villagers to take wood from the lord's land to repair their houses or fences.
12. **messuage:** land surrounding a house.
13. **rood:** one-fourth acre.

week 3 days, each day with 1 man, and in autumn each day with 2 men, performing the said works at the will of the said abbot as in plowing and other work. Likewise he gives 1 bushel of wheat for benseed and 18 sheaves of oats for foddercorn. Likewise he gives 3 hens and 1 cock yearly and 5 eggs at Easter. Likewise he does carrying to Peterborough and to Jakele and no where else, at the will of the said abbot. Likewise if he sells a brood mare in his court yard for 10s. or more, he shall give to the said abbot 4d., and if for less he shall give nothing to the aforesaid. He gives also merchet[14] and heriot,[15] and is tallaged [taxed] at the feast of St. Michael, at the will of the said abbot. There are also there 17 other villeins, viz. John of Ganesoupe, Robert son of Walter, Ralph son of the reeve, Emma ate Pertre, William son of Reginald, Thomas son of Gunnilda, Eda widow of Ralph, Ralph Reeve, William Reeve, William son of William Reeve, Thomas Flegg. Henry Abbott, William Hereward, Serle son of William Reeve, Walter Palmer, William Abbot, Henry Serle; each of whom holds 1 virgate of land in villenage, paying and doing in all things, each for himself, to the said abbot yearly just as the said Hugh Miller....

Cotters

Henry, son of the miller, holds a cottage with a croft which contains 1 rood, paying thence yearly to the said abbot 2s. Likewise he works for 3 days in carrying bay and in other works at the will of the said abbot, each day with 1 man and in autumn 1 day in cutting grain with 1 man.

Likewise Ralph Miller holds a cottage with a croft which contains a rood, paying to the said abbot 2s; and he works just as the said Henry....

Likewise Sara, widow of William Miller, holds a cottage and a croft which contains half a rood, paying to the abbot 4d.; and she works just as the said Henry....

[*Eight other men and three other women, all widows, hold similar amounts of land with similar obligations.*]

Likewise William Drake holds a cottage with a croft which contains half a rood, paying to the abbot 6d.; and he works just as the said Henry.

There are there also 6 other cotters, viz. William Drake Jr., Amycia the widow, Alice the widow, Robert son of Eda, William Pepper, William Coleman, each of whom holds a cottage with a croft which contains half a rood, paying and doing in all things, each for himself, just as the said William Drake.

Likewise each of the said cottagers, except the widows, gives yearly after Christmas a penny which is called head-penny.

14. **merchet:** a payment collected by the lord of the manor, usually from the father of a girl on her marriage, but also frequently from widows remarrying, and even from men of villein status on their marriage.

15. **heriot:** a payment to the lord at the villager's death.

Chapter 10
Life in an
English Village
in the High
Middle Ages

3. Extent of Manor of
Bernehorne, 1307

John of Cayworth holds a house and 30 acres of land and owes yearly 2s. at Easter and Michaelmas; and he owes a cock and two hens at Christmas, of the value of 4d.

And he ought to harrow for 2 days at the Lenten sowing with one man and his own horse and his own harrow, the value of the work being 4d.; and he is to receive from the lord on each day 3 meals, of the value of 5d., and then the lord will be at a loss of 1d. Thus his harrowing is of no value to the service of the lord.

And he ought to carry the manure of the lord for 2 days with one cart, with his own 2 oxen, the value of the work being 8d.: and he is to receive from the lord each day 3 meals of the price as above. And thus the service is worth 3d. clear.

And he shall find one man for 2 days for mowing the meadow of the lord, who can mow, by estimation 1 acre and a half, the value of the mowing of an acre being 6d.: the sum is therefore 9d. and he is to receive each day 3 meals of the value given above; and thus that mowing is worth 4d. clear.

And he ought to gather and carry that same hay which he has cut, the price of the work being 3d.

And he shall have from the lord 2 meals for 1 man, of the value of 1½d. Thus the work will be worth 1½d. clear.

And he ought to carry the hay of the lord for 1 day with a cart and 3 animals of his own, the price of the work being 6d. And he shall have from the lord 3 meals of the value of 2½d. And thus the work is worth 3½d. clear.

And he ought to carry in autumn beans or oats for 2 days with a cart and 3 animals of his own, the value of a work being 12d. And he shall receive from the lord each day 3 meals of the value given above: and thus the work is worth 7d. clear.

And he ought to carry wood from the woods of the lord as far as the manor [-house] for two days in summer with a cart and three animals of his own the value of the work being 9d. And he shall receive from the lord each day 3 meals of the price given above, and thus the work is worth 4d. clear.

And he ought to find 1 man for 2 days to cut heath [for fuel], the value of the work being 4d. and he shall have 3 meals each day of the value given above; and thus the lord will lose, if he receives the service, 3d. Thus that mowing is worth nothing to the service of the lord.

And he ought to carry the heath which he has cut, the value of the work being 5d. And he shall receive from the lord 3 meals at the price of 2½d. And thus the work will be worth 2½d. clear.

And he ought to carry to Battle [a nearby town] twice in the summer season, each time half a load of grain, the value of the service being 4d. And he shall receive in the manor each time 1 meal at the value of 2d. And thus the work is worth 2d. clear.

The total of the rents, with the value of the hens is 2s. 4d.

The total of the values of the works is 2s, 3½d.; owed from the said John yearly.

Source 4 from Warren O. Ault, Open Field Farming in Medieval England: a Study of Village By-laws *(London: George Allen and Unwin, 1972), pp. 82–83, 85, 86, 89, 155–159.*

4. Village By-laws, 1286.

1286

NEWINGTON

It is granted by the whole court that no one in this manor shall harbour any stranger who is a wrongdoer especially in autumn time under pain of 2s. 6d. to the lord.

And that no one in the aforesaid time shall accept any one as a gleaner who is capable of doing the work of a reaper.

1287

WELWYN RECTORY MANOR

It is ordered by a judgment of the whole court that men and women who are able to reap be distrained not to glean after the fashion of paupers and that those who harbour them be punished and whatever [they] the gleaners have gathered be siezed. . . .

1290

NEWTON LONGVILLE

It is granted and ordered by the community of the town that no one henceforth shall gather herbage in another's grain.

Item that no one who holds land of the lord shall gather peas, beans or vetches in the fields except on land that they have sown. . . .

Item that no one shall allow his calves to be in the fields in the growing grain [*infra segetem*] before the other animals. . . .

Item that no one be allowed to glean who is able to earn a penny a day with food or two pence without food if he finds anyone who wished to hire him.

Item that no outsider be allowed to glean unless he who harbours him is willing to answer for his deeds.

Item that no pauper be allowed to gather beans between the selions [ridges within a field] but only at the ends and dividing lines. And if he shall do otherwise he shall lose what he has gathered and he shall not be allowed to enter the fields thenceforth to gather beans.

Item that there shall be no carting by night.

[233]

Item that everyone shall see that his stiles and lanes, those nearest his neighbours, are so kept that neither the lord nor any of his tenants incur damage because of the lack of such maintenance.

Item that no one shall have his beasts depasture in any cultivated area until one land [*terra*] is lying wholly cleared [of grain]. . . .

Item that no one shall have his beasts depasture in the growing grain in the night time.

Item that no one shall . . . [gather] peas nor shall any grain be taken from the fields by night . . . [illegible].

And if any one shall be found [doing the] contrary he shall give the lord 6d. And if any one shall be found to be delinquent in the premises by night he shall give the lord 12d. . . .

1295

NEWTON LONGVILLE

All the lord's tenants, free and customary, agree to observe all the statutes of autumn which were ordained at the court held on the Saturday next after the Feast of the Apostles Peter and Paul in the eighteenth year of King Edward,[16] and Hugh Robard, John Hervy, John Bouere, Henry Simcan, Ralph Robyns [and] Henry Hakene are elected to see that these statutes are observed and to present [offenders]. . . .

1306

GREAT HORWOOD

It is granted by the whole township that no one shall accept any outsider as a gleaner in autumn nor any man or woman to glean who is able to earn a penny a day with food.

Nor shall anyone pay in the field with sheaves, only handfuls.

Nor shall anyone reap or cart except by day.

Nor shall anyone allow [his] calves or foals to go into the common [fields of] grain.

Nor shall anyone gather straw in the fields unless [it be] each from his own land.

And if anyone be found guilty in respect of the aforesaid provisions in any way, as often as he is found guilty he shall pay the lord 4d.

And to maintain the aforesaid conservators are chosen, namely, Hannole Bret, William le Frankelyn, Robert Saundres and Ralph Margery. . . .

1319

GREAT HORWOOD

A grant by the community of the town. It is granted and ordered by the whole homage of the town of Great Horwood in the presence of the lord that no one

---

16. These statutes are the by-laws issued in 1290 listed above.

among them male or female be allowed to glean who can earn [his] food and a penny a day for his work.

And also that no one of them shall accept any outsider to glean among them.

And that none of them shall have his grain carted from the field by night.

And that none of them shall pay any one with grain in the field.

And that none of them shall allow his workers to carry any grain from the field as their wages etc.

And that each one of them shall have all openings of all their tenements toward the fields in such a state of repair that wrongdoers cannot enter a field in any part of the town except by the king's highways or the common roads.

And they grant all these on pain of three pence to be paid to the lord for each default etc.

Source 5 from Walter of Henley's Husbandry, *edited by Elizabeth Lamond (London: Longmans, 1890), pp. 85–103, 111–119.*

5. From *Seneschaucie*, 1270s

HERE BEGINS THE BOOK OF THE OFFICE OF SENESCHAL

The seneschal of lands ought to be prudent and faithful and profitable, and he ought to know the law of the realm, to protect his lord's business and to instruct and give assurance to the bailiffs who are beneath him in their difficulties. He ought two or three times a year to make his rounds and visit the manors of his stewardship, and then he ought to inquire about the rents, services, and customs, hidden or withdrawn, and about franchises of courts, lands, woods, meadows, pastures, waters, mills, and other things which belong to the manor and are done away with without warrant, by whom, and how: and if he be able let him amend these things in the right way without doing wrong to any, and if he be not, let him show it to his lord, that he may deal with it if he wish to maintain his right.

The seneschal ought, at his first coming to the manors, to cause all the demesne lands of each to be measured by true men. . . .

The seneschal ought, on his coming to each manor, to see and inquire how they are tilled, and in what crops they are, and how the cart-horses and avers [draft-horses], oxen, cows, sheep, and swine are kept and improved. And if there be loss or damage from want of guard, he ought to take fines from those who are to blame, so that the lord may not lose. . . .

The seneschal ought, on his coming to the manors, to inquire how the bailiff bears himself within and without, what care he takes, what improvement he makes, and what increase and profit there is in the manor in his office, because of his being there. And also of the provost, and hayward, and keeper of cattle, and all other offices, how each bears himself towards him, and thereby he can be more sure who make profit and who harm. Also he ought to provide that there should be no waste or destruction on any manor, or overcharge of anything belonging to the manor. He ought to remove all those that are not necessary for the lord, and all the servants who do nothing, and all overcharge in the dairy, and other profitless and unreasonable offices which are called wrong outlays, without profit. . . .

. . . And he ought to see that the horses and oxen and all the stock are well kept, and that no other animals graze in, or eat their pasture. . . .

THE OFFICE OF REEVE

The reeve ought to be elected and presented by the common consent of the township, as the best husbandman and the best farmer among them. And he must see that all the servants of the court rise in the morning to do their work, and that the ploughs be yoked in time, and the lands well ploughed and cropped, and turned over, and sown with good and clean seed, as much as they can stand. . . .

. . . The reeve ought to see that the corn is well and cleanly threshed, so that nothing is left in the straw to grow in thatches, nor in manure to sprout. . . . And the reeve must take care that no thresher or winnower shall take corn to carry it away in his bosom, or in tunic, or boots, or pockets, or sacks or sacklets hidden near the grange. . . .

. . . And the reeve ought often to see that all the beasts are well provided with forage and kept as they ought to be, and that they have enough pasture without overcharge of the other beasts, and he ought to see that the keepers of all kinds of beasts do not go to fairs, or markets, or wrestling-matches, or taverns, by which the beasts aforesaid may go astray without guard. . . .

THE OFFICE OF HAYWARD

The hayward ought to be an active and sharp man, for he must, early and late, look after and go round and keep the woods, corn, and meadows and other things belonging to his office, . . . And he ought to sow the lands, and be over the ploughers and harrowers at the time of each sowing. And he ought to make all the boon-tenants and customary-tenants who are bound and accustomed to come, do so, to do the work they ought to do. And in haytime he ought to be over the mowers, the making, the carrying, and in August assemble the reapers and the boon-tenants and the labourers and see that the corn be properly and cleanly gathered; and early and late watch so that nothing be stolen or eaten by beasts or spoilt. . . .

THE OFFICE OF PLOUGHMEN

The ploughmen ought to be men of intelligence, and ought to know how to sow, and how to repair and mend broken ploughs and harrows, and to till the land well, and crop it rightly, and they ought to know also how to yoke and drive the oxen, without beating or hurting them, and they ought to forage them well, and look well after the forage that it be not stolen nor carried off; and they ought to keep them safely in meadows and several pastures, and other beasts which are found therein they ought to impound. And they and the keepers must make ditches and build and remove the earth, and ditch it so that the ground may dry and the water be drained. And they must not flay any beast until some one has inspected it, and inquired by what default it died. And they must not carry fire into the byres for light, or to warm themselves, and have no candle there, or light unless it be in a lantern, and for great need and peril. . . .

THE OFFICE OF COWHERD

The cowherd ought to be skilful, knowing his business and keeping his cows well, and foster the calves well from time of weaning. And he must see that he has fine bulls and large and of good breed pastured with the cows, to mate when they will. . . . And every night the cowherd shall put the cows and other beasts in the fold during the season, and let the fold be well strewed with litter or fern, as is said above, and he himself shall lie each night with his cows. . . .

THE OFFICE OF SHEPHERD

Each shepherd ought to find good pledges to answer for his doings and for good and faithful service. . . . And he must cover his fold and enclose it with hurdles and mend it within and without, and repair the hurdles and make them. And he ought to sleep in the fold, he and his dog; and he ought to pasture his sheep well, and keep them in forage, and watch them well, so that they be not killed or destroyed by dogs or stolen or lost or changed, nor let them pasture in moors or dry places or bogs, to get sickness and disease for lack of guard. No shepherd ought to leave his sheep to go to fairs, or markets, or wrestling matches, or wakes, or to the tavern, without taking leave or asking it, or without putting a good keeper in his place to keep the sheep, that no harm may arise from his fault. . . .

THE OFFICE OF DAIRYMAID

The dairymaid ought to be faithful and of good repute, and keep herself clean, and ought to know her business and all that belongs to it. She ought not to allow any under-dairymaid or another to take or carry away milk, or butter, or cream, by which the cheese shall be less and the dairy impoverished. And she ought to know well how to make cheese and salt cheese, and she ought to save and keep the vessels of the dairy, that it need not be necessary to buy new ones every year. And she ought to know the day when she begins to make cheese and of what weight, and when she begins to make two cheeses a day, of how much and of what weight, and then the bailiff and the provost ought to inspect the dairy often and the cheeses, when they increase and decrease in weight, and that no harm be done in the dairy, nor any robbery by which the weight shall be lessened. . . .

The dairymaid ought to help to winnow the corn when she can be present, and she ought to take care of the geese and hens and answer for the returns and keep and cover the fire, that no harm arise from lack of guard.

Source 6 from Warren O. Ault, Open Field Farming in Medieval England: A Study of Village, By-laws *(London: George Allen and Unwin, 1972), pp. 82–83, 85, 86, 89, 155–159.*

200 BROUGHTON [HUNTS.] DAY OF ST HUGH, BISHOP OF LINCOLN, IN THE SIXTEENTH YEAR OF KING EDWARD AND THE THIRD YEAR OF ABBOT JOHN. [NOVEMBER 17, 1288]

Names of the chief pledges John Joceline John Aspelaon, William son of John at the Bridge, John Le Bon, Alexander the Woodward, Ralph the Clerk, John Hobbe, Ralph Euerard, Alexander of Bluntysham, William Henry, John Randolph, John Gere and Henry at the Gate

6d. 8d. Names of the jurors Elias Carpenter, John Baldry, Simon Crane, Simon the Smith, John Nunne, Andrew Onty, Simon Edward, Richard of Broughton, John Nel, William the Cooper, Alan the Horseman, and Alan son of John son of Hugh. They pay 6s. 8d. chevage.

From Simon le Bond because he spoke ill of the beer of Robert Curteys from whence the said Robert suffered damage in the amount of 6d. He is poor, pledge Henry son of John, and by the same pledge he shall make satisfaction to the said Robert for the damage as above and they [the pence] are granted to the clerk.

2d. Thomas Cobbe plaintiff and John de Ely defendant are in agreement and John puts himself in mercy, 2d., pledge Richard de Balliol.

Ordered William de Broughton, William de Lond', John Cook and Ralph Norreys are distrained to answer at the next [court] because they made default at the first boon day[17] of autumn.

From Richard de Camera because he made default at the first boon day of autumn, a mass[18] remitted.

12d. And John Nuncium le Mung 12d. because he did not send to the first boon day of the lord as many men as he had at his own work, remitted, pledge John Wylymot.

6d. It is found by the injury of neighbours that Walter Grave said opprobrious [shameful] things to John Bennett at a work [day] for the

---

17. **boon day:** unpaid day of service owned by a peasant to a lord.

18. The fine in this case was set at the amount normally paid to have a mass said by a priest, though it was remitted, or canceled.

lord in autumn therefore he shall make satisfaction to him in respect of his damages which are taxed at 1d. and for the trespass he is in mercy 6d., pledge Simon Grune.

Distraint William de Broughton is distrained to answer at the next court for the damage done by his two horses in the lord's peas.

From Richard de Broughton because he did not come to work for the lord in ditching at Wyrlewyk, forgiven, pledge William Carpenter.

From William le Cupere for damage done by his horse by night in the lord's peas, forgiven, pledge Richard de Broughton.

6d.
12d. From Richard at the well for damage done by his beasts in the lord's grain. From Robert the reeve for the same, pledge each other. Fine of both 6d.

Distraint
6d. Alice Robynes is distrained[19] for her geese damaging the lord's grain.

From Richard the parson for damage done by his geese in the lord's grain. From Richard de Broughton for the same. Pledge each the other. Fine of both 6d.

From Simon Grave for his mainpast[20] wrongfully gleaning the lord's grain in autumn 6d., pledge John Wylymot.

Henry the miller and Thomas le Hund plaintiffs offer themselves against John le Tynkere who was attached [fined] by two rings of wheat in the hands of John le boteler and John Roger who when John le Tynkere did not come [*sic*]. Therefore let him be better distrained.

The reeve and the beedle must be queried concerning the produce of an acre and a half which John Robert leased to John Stoke and which they should have taken to the lord's use but because the said John Stoke took away the produce against the prohibition of the said reeve and beedle by the warrant of John Roger who was not able to warrant [this he] is in mercy 6d. pledges Richard the parson and William son of Ralph and by the same pledge he shall make satisfaction to the said reeve and beedle for the aforesaid produce for which they were at first charged. The produce is estimated at 3 rings, 3 bushels and a half of rye and 2 rings, 3 bushels of peas.

John Roger acknowledges that he had warranted John Stoke the pasture of an acre and a half when he was not able to warrant this. Therefore he is in mercy, a mass, pledge John de Wistowe.

Thomas Prat acknowledges that he is in debt to Agnes Gylot for goods to the value of 6d. Therefore he shall make satisfaction to her for the aforesaid 6d. and for the detention he is in mercy, a mass, pledge Edward Edeline. Day of payment on the Purification of the Blessed Mary.

Andrew Onty was attached to answer for that he carried away the produce of half an acre of land which John Gere rented from the

19. **distrain:** compel, usually by confiscating something.
20. **mainpast:** person for whom another is guardian.

said Andrew but because it was witnessed by William Nuncium that he had leave he is quit thereof.

The tasters namely Alexander the Woodward and Richard de Hyrst say that the wife of Elias Carpenter broke the assize of beer.[21] Therefore she is in mercy 2s., pledge Geoffrey the Marshal.

Ordered The chief pledges say that the bailiff of the lord abbot made two pits in the town, to its nuisance. Therefore the bailiff and the reeve are ordered to put them right.

And they say that William Russel harboured a certain Nicholas de Eton' who is outside the assize.[22] Therefore he is in mercy, a mass, pledge John the Beedle.

6d. And they say that Hugh Knyt harboured a strange woman who is not profitable to the town, 6d., pledge John Gore.

And they say that John son of Agnes Matheu is not at all faithful and he withdrew himself [left the village]. Therefore let him be taken if he shall come within this liberty.

And they say that John the Tynekere made an assault in the home of Thomas le Hund and wounded him. Therefore let him be attached by his body. And let it be remembered that 2 rings of wheat are in the lord's possession, wherefore let them be kept.

6d.
1 capon
1 capon
4d.

And they say that John Robert is a tanner of leather but he gives 6d. per annum. From Robert Curteys for the same, one capon. From Thomas Colbe for the same, one capon. And they say that John Robert is a tanner of leather but he gives the lord 4d. per annum.

6d. And they say that Henry the Miller took false tolls in the mill. Therefore he is in mercy 6d. pledge Walter the Miller.

12d. And they say that Robert Strypling pastured the grain of the neighbours by night. Therefore he is in mercy, a mass, pledge John Ballard. From Henry son of John for the same with his beasts 6d., pledge John le Bon.

12d. And they say that the wife of Thomas le Hund was a gleaner against the common statute of the town. Therefore she is in mercy pledge the reeve. From Mariota Gylbert for the same, pledge the beadle. From Alice daughter of Robert Matheu for the same, pledge the same John. From Johanna, daughter of Ralph Eureard for the same, pledge the reeve. From Robert Strypling because he took sheaves out of the field, pledge the reeve. From Felicia daughter of John le Straker because she gleaned contrary to the statue, pledge Hugh the Stalkere. Fine of all of them 12d. The jurors say that Richard le Camera made a pit in the royal way across from Simon Crane which is a nuisance. Therefore let it be amended.

21. **assize of beer:** ordinances setting the quality and price of beer and ale.

22. **outside the assize:** here, outside the law.

And they say that Reginald Gylbert surcharged the pasture with twenty sheep. Therefore he is in mercy 6d., pledge William Kepline. And they say that William Kepline paid with sheaves in the field in autumn contrary to the common statute of the township. Therefore he is in mercy 12d., pledge the reeve.

Emma, daughter of Robert le Clerk, complains of William Gylbert for that while she was harrowing in the field of Broughton on the land of Agnes Gylbert on Wednesday next before the Purification of the Blessed Mary in the sixteenth year of the reign of King Edward [February 3, 1288] the said William came and threw her to the ground and by force and violence raped her and drew blood against the peace of the lord king, etc. And the said William being present denied force, violence and the shedding of blood and said that he did not rape the said Emma but that for the past three years he had known the same Emma by her own free will whenever he wished and he asked, and the said Emma likewise, that this be enquired by the thirteen chief pledges and the twelve jurors whose names are at the top of this view. Who came and say that the said William did not rape the said Emma on the day specified nor did he know her against her will as she charged but in the way he was used to knowing her nor did he shed her blood. Therefore the said William is quit and the said Emma for her false claim is in mercy. She is poor.

Richard de Broughton, clerk, complains of Alexander Bluntysham, William Ketline and John of Broughton for that they pastured their lambs on half an acre of growing wheat at Haycroft to his damage 2s. etc. And the aforesaid Alexander, William and John came and acknowledged it all and asked an assessment of the damage, and

18d.   they were taxed at one ring of wheat with which they should recompense the said Richard and for their trespass they are in mercy 18d., pledge each other.

Ordered   From John de Boteler for unlawful detention of 6d. from Johanna Euererad, a mass, pledge his father. And by the same pledge he shall pay the said Joanna the said money. . . .

From the reeve and the beadle because they did not have the book for charging the jury as is proper, forgiven. . . .

From Absalom the reeve because he did not have the roll of the halmote of the last court so that it could be looked through and the

6d.   pleas carried forward, 6d.

From the chief pledges because they did not present Richard de Camera who made a pit in the royal road nor Roger Gilbert who surcharged the pasture with his sheep, and from the jury who concealed John son of Agnes Matheu who has withdrawn himself for the time being and from the whole township for not keeping

10s.   watch in due form, 10s.

Chapter 10

Life in an
English Village
in the High
Middle Ages

From Alexander Woodward and Richard de Hyrst tasters for many concealments of the trespasses of the brewsters and because they did not do their office in due form in tasting the beer of the brewsters and for other trespasses, fine of both 12d.

12d.

Source 7 from Nathaniel J. Hone, The Manor and Manorial Records *(London: Methuen, 1906) pp. 150–153.*

7. Court Roll from Manor of Addington, 1314

Thomas Cubbel plaintiff opposes himself against Gervase le Leche in a plea of trespass. And it is commanded to distrain the aforesaid Gervase whereupon he answers that nothing can be found upon him and the said plea still stands, let him be distrained at the next court to answer the said Thomas in the plea aforesaid. And it is commanded to attach John son of Chichelotes to answer concerning a trespass made on the heath. . . .

Thomas Cubbel is summoned because he has concealed [hidden away] 2½d of bedripsilver[23] forthcoming of a certain tenement which is called le popeland and has detained the said 2½d for 7 years past and still detains it. . . .

John Shad in mercy for a trespass made in Howelotesfeld with his draught cattle, pledge John atte Welle, fine 3d.

Thomas Fox for a trespass made in the wood, also Hugh Gibbe in mercy for the same 3d.

Rose Neuman for a trespass made with her sheep in the grass, pledge Thomas fox 3d.

John Wolward in mercy for his oxen in the wood, pledge W. Fox 3d.

Richard Sanneye for his sheep, in . . . pledge Roger Sanneye 3d.

John Shad because he has taken away furze [shrubs] in Howelcotesfeld, pledge Allan Russel 6d.

Dionis atte hamme for his draught cattle in Howelcotesfeld, pledge John atte hamme.

Sabina Tampun in mercy because she has taken furze in Howelotesfeld, by gage of 1 plough—pardoned because she is poor.

Thomas Cubbel in mercy because he hath not William Prelly for whom he was pledge. And it is commanded to distrain the aforesaid William to show how he came into the lord's fee 6d.

Roger Sannaye in mercy for his sheep in the pasture, pledge Walter in ye Lane 6d.

Thomas Cubbel and John Seynclere have agreed by licence of the lord, and the aforesaid John has put himself in mercy, pledge Walter the clerk and William Chaunter 6d.

23. **bedripsilver:** payment made by peasants instead of doing boon day service.

Thomas Cubbel opposes himself against Robert Russel in a plea of trespass which said Robert is not here, therefore let him be attached to answer the aforesaid Thomas at the next court. And the aforesaid Thomas may have a day. And upon this comes John de Bures and asks the court for a sow of aforesaid Robert of which he is not yet attached, and he hath a day till next court that he may better certify and show for himself why he ought to have the same. And John de Bures was distrained for a horse for relief, and he does not justify himself . . . pledge a water mill.

Thomas Cubbel opposes himself against Robert Cros who is not as yet attached. And it is commanded to attach the aforesaid Robert to answer the aforesaid Thomas in a plea of trespass, and aforesaid Thomas thereupon hath a day. . . . The whole vill are charged to acknowledge that they are wrongdoers, because they have maliciously tied together the feet of the lady's swine. And they ask thereof a day at the next court, and they have it.

Sum 7^s 9^d and 1^d of increased rent which is included in the total sum.

Sources 8 and 9 from Select Cases from the Coroners' Rolls A.D. *1265–1413, edited by* Charles Gross *(London: Selden Society, 1896), pp. 3, 6, 12–13, 28, 30, 37, 59.*

8. Coroners' Inquests, 1266–1301

8A. 1266

It happened in a field in a certain place called Nomansland on Monday next before the feast of St. Peter's chair that Alfred of Ravensden went after dinner to sow his land, and when he came to the said place, he had the falling sickness [epilepsy] which caused him to fall to the ground, and he suddenly died by misadventure. Isabel, daughter of John of Ravensden, who first found him, produced pledges: Walter, son of Alfred of Ravensden, and Arnulph Argent of the same place.

Inquest was made before Simon Read, the coroner, by four neighbouring townships, Ravensden, Renhold, Wilden, Bolnhurst, and Goldington; they say that, as far as they know, death was due to misadventure, as is aforesaid.

8B. 1267

It happened in the vill of Barford on Friday next before the Assumption of the Blessed Mary in the fifty-first year of King Henry at the house of William Blanche that Muriel, his daughter, who was almost six years old, and Beatrice, her sister, who was almost three years old [were in the house] while the said William and Muriel, his wife, were in the fields, and a fire broke out in the said house and burned it, together with Beatrice, William's infant daughter.

Inquest was made by four neighbouring townships, Wilden, Renhold, Barford, Roxton; they say that, as far as they know, it was a misadventure, as is aforesaid.

8C. 1269

It happened in the vill of Wilden after the hour of vespers on Wednesday next before the feast of the Apostles Philip and James in the fifty-third year that John, son of William White of Wilden, who was twelve years of age, was watching his father's lambs in a yard which formerly belonged to Thomas Tirel of Wilden. And at the said hour John took off his clothes and entered a certain stream in the said yard to bathe, and he was drowned by misadventure. Adam Saucer, who first found him, produced pledges: Simon Sprott and Nicholas Albric of Wilden.

Inquest was made before Simon Read, the coroner.

8D. 1270

Amice daughter of William le Lorimer of Bedford went into 'Wilputtesburne' in Cardington field by Cardington wood to gather corn. Thunder and lightning occurred and she was struck and fell and immediately died. Maud daughter of Nicholas de Augul first found her and found pledges, Robert Holdebert and William Budell.

Inquest before the same coroner by Willington, cardington, Cople and East-cotts: a misadventure.

8D. 1301

It happened at Titchmarsh on Monday next before the feast of St. James the Apostle in the twenty-ninth year of King Edward that a certain Henry Wymer of Titchmarsh, so it is said, tied up his cart which was loaded with hay, [when] by misadventure he fell to the ground, broke his neck, and died forthwith. Inquest was made before G. of Luddington by four neighbouring townships, to wit, Titchmarsh, Thrapston, Thorpe Achurch, and Clapton. They say as above; they suspect nobody ; it was merely a misadventure. The cart with the harness was worth 2s. 8d., the hay 18d., the mare 4s., and for these the township of Titchmarsh will account.[24]

8F. 1271

It happened in the vill of Roxton early in the morning on Sunday next before the feast of St. Margaret that Ralph, son of William Shepherd of Roxton, was going along the western part of the wood of Sir Humphrey of Barford, having charge of certain cows and heifers. One heifer would [not] go into the wood, and Ralph entered a ditch of the wood to turn the heifer back [to its mates], and in that ditch he found the dead body of a certain man, a stranger, who had a wound four inches long on the head above the left ear, and the brains had ex-uded from it. [Ralph] raised the hue, and the hue was pursued. He produced pledges: Roger Beer of Roxton and William of Barford.

24. The cart, harness, hay, and horse were regarded as having "caused" the accident; they were sold for the amounts listed, and the money paid by the village of Titchmarsh to the lord as the *deodand*.

Inquest was made before Ralph of Goldington, the coroner, by four neighbouring townships, Roxton, Barford, Wilden, and Coldsden and Chawston as one township; they say on their oath that they know nothing about the slain man, nor do they know when or where he was killed, nor whence he came, but they well know that he was not killed there, nor can they find or obtain knowledge of any tracks made by him in coming there. . . .

9. Coroner's Inquest, 1276

It happened at Houghton on Monday next before the feast of St. Mark the Evangelist in the fourth year of King Edward that John, son of William of Westfield, of the vill of Winring in the county of Hertford, was hayward in the vill of Houghton, and he was arrested on suspicion of larceny [theft] and was imprisoned by the township of Houghton . . ., and he escaped from the prison of that township and fled to the church of Houghton. . . .[25] On the following Monday he abjured the king's realm,[26] according to the custom of the kingdom, before P. Loring, the coroner, and four neighbouring townships, Houghton, Totternhoe, Tilsworth, Chalgrave, and before the king's bailiff, and the port of Dover was assigned to him;[27] for he confessed before the coroner and the four townships that he was a thief, and that he had robbed Sir William of Gorham at Westwick in Hertfordshire, and he would not submit to the king's peace.[28] On the same day [of his abjuration] he came forth [from sanctuary] and proceeded on his way [toward Dover]. He fled from the highway,[29] and was followed by William of Houghton; and on the hue and the suit of the whole vill he was beheaded by the township of Houghton.

QUESTIONS TO CONSIDER

Some of the sources in this chapter were intentionally written to present information about rural life. Manorial extents and custumals (Sources 1 through 3), for example, were produced to describe landholding patterns and peasants' obligations as they actually existed, and treatises of manorial management (Source 5) were written to lay out the duties of officials in clear and explicit language. Other sources were produced for very different purposes and provide information about rural life somewhat incidentally. Village courts did not draft by-laws intentionally to give information about agricultural activities or relations between villagers, nor did coroners keep records of their inquests to allow us to see what people were doing when they died. All historians

25. Churches offered sanctuary, for suspects could not be arrested there.
26. **abjured the king's realm:** swore that he would leave England.
27. He was required to go straight to Dover to sail from England.
28. He chose banishment rather than leaving the Church and standing trial.
29. He left the road to Dover.

use information gathered from documents that are often primarily about something else, and sometimes they describe their methods with a word taken from the activities you have read about here—*gleaning*. Like gleaners in village fields, historians pick up small bits that have been overlooked by those who have already gone through; these bits may prove extremely valuable, allowing the historian to understand an issue much more fully.

As you read through the sources, you no doubt gleaned information that interested you but that did not relate directly to the questions of the chapter. You may have noted how much work children and adolescents were doing, or the fact that very young children were left home alone. You may also have noticed the way that time was reckoned according to Christian feast days, not by day and month. You may have noted the differences and similarities in the types of work men and women were doing, or been surprised at how often widows are listed as landholders. In reading about widows, you might have wondered why no man is described as a widower. You may have noticed people's leisure activities as well as their work, and you may have wondered about crime and violence, as the sources include cases of murder, rape, and robbery.

Several of the sources include lists of people, which may have led you to note the wide variety in names. Widows are usually simply listed as "the widow" or "widow of so-and-so," but other people are identified in many different ways. They are linked to a specific location ("of Cayworth"), their father and sometimes grandfather ("Emma, daughter of Robert," "Alan son of John son of Hugh"), or their occupation ("the reeve"). Some of them have clear last names ("Simon Read the coroner"), but for others, including millers and carpenters, it is difficult to tell whether the identifier is an occupation or a name. Some of the names are Norman French, such as "John le Bon". Thus these sources provide information about the gradual development of last names in England, though this is certainly not something their authors intended to do when they wrote them.

Almost every historical source, not simply those in this chapter, includes information on a variety of issues. Historians often set out on new lines of inquiry based on something they have discovered when investigating a completely different topic. If they follow every interesting lead, however, no project is ever finished, so scholars often shelve a topic of interest for years—or sometimes decades—before having the time to return to explore it. You must similarly focus your efforts for this chapter and return to the original questions: What were the primary activities carried out over the year as people raised crops and animals, including activities that were approved and those that were viewed as problematic? What do the sources suggest about relations within a village, both among ordinary people and between villagers and their superiors? In developing your answer, you will need to weave together the different types of sources—manorial extents, village by-laws, treatises of manorial management, court records, and coroners' inquests—in order to form a more complete picture of the village and the people who lived in it.

EPILOGUE

The sources in this chapter all come from a relatively short period of time and from villages that are quite similar to one another, and the central questions ask you to present a sort of snapshot of village activities and relations. They focus on activities that continue across many centuries or even millennia of European history: plowing, planting, harvesting, caring for animals, carting, preserving food, repairing fences, worrying about strangers, keeping an eye on one's neighbors, and fulfilling obligations to one's superiors.

Along with continuities, the sources also contain information about processes of historical change in medieval villages. Historians have generally found the origins of the modern economy in the activities of merchants that you explored in Chapter 9, but similar developments can be found in very "traditional" villages as well. Though villagers often paid their obligations in labor, you have seen that as early as the thirteenth century many taxes, rents, and fees were paid in cash, and officials were aware of the market value of various labor services. Commercial relations were thus evident in medieval villages long before the "rise of capitalism" that is often seen as a mark of the "modern" economy. In the sixteenth and seventeenth centuries, much land in England was transformed from open fields for growing grain to enclosed pastures for sheep, because landlords decided that this would bring a greater profit. Concerns about profit are also often viewed as a hallmark of the modern economy, but medieval landowners considered such issues as well. In Source 5, for example, the seneschal is instructed to pay careful attention to profit and loss, and to end unprofitable enterprises.

Wage labor is another feature of the "modern" economy, but the sources provide evidence of landlords paying peasants in exchange for their labor and of wealthier peasants hiring poor cotters, or "finding a man" for mowing hay or cutting heath, in the language of Source 3. Thus there was income-producing work available in medieval villages, not simply in commercial cities.

Along with aspects of the modern economy, medieval villages also exhibited other features we often view as "modern." Sources clearly present rural people as distinct individuals, identified by name, not as a uniform group. Medieval elites may have viewed villagers as unsophisticated yokels, and people since then have seen them as oppressed and conformist, but we can certainly wonder whether medieval villagers themselves would have shared these views.

[247]

CHAPTER ELEVEN

THE RENAISSANCE

MAN AND WOMAN

The age we know as the Renaissance had its beginnings in the fourteenth century as a literary movement among educated, mostly upper-class men in northern Italian cities, notably Florence. Such writers as Petrarch attempted to emulate as closely as possible the literary figures of ancient Rome, believing that these men, especially Cicero, had attained a level of style and a command of the Latin language that had never since been duplicated. Petrarch's fascination with antiquity did not stop with language, however, but also included an interest in classical architecture and art; he spent long hours wandering around the large numbers of Roman ruins remaining in Italy. His obsession with the classical past also led him to reject the thousand-year period between his own time and that of Rome, viewing this as a "dark," "gothic," or at best "middle" age—a deep trough between two peaks of civilization.

Though Petrarch himself did not call his own period the *Renaissance*—a word that means "rebirth"—he clearly believed he was witnessing the dawning of a new age.

Writers and artists intending to recapture the glory that was Rome would have to study Roman models, and Petrarch proposed an appropriate course of study or curriculum termed the *studia humanitates,* or simply "liberal studies" or the "liberal arts." Like all curricula, it contained an implicit philosophy, a philosophy that came to be known as *humanism.* Humanism was not a rigorous philosophical system like Aristotelianism, or an all-encompassing belief system like Christianity, but what we might better call an attitude toward learning and toward life.

This new attitude had a slow diffusion out of Italy, with the result that the Renaissance "happened" at very different times in different parts of Europe. Because it was not a single historical event in the same sense as the French Revolution or the

[248]

Peloponnesian War, the Renaissance is difficult to date. Roughly, we can say it began in Italy in the fourteenth century; spread to France, Germany, and Spain by the end of the fifteenth century; to England by the early part of the sixteenth century; and not until the seventeenth century to Scandinavia. Thus the Renaissance preceded the Reformation—which *was* an event—in most of Europe, took place at the same time as the Reformation in England, and came after the Reformation in Scandinavia. Shakespeare, for example, is considered a "Renaissance" writer even though he lived 250 years after Petrarch.

Though the chronology may be somewhat confusing, there are certain recurring features of humanism through the centuries. One of these is a veneration of the classical past. Petrarch concentrated primarily on Latin and ancient Rome, but during the mid-fifteenth century humanists also began to emphasize Greek language, art, architecture, philosophy, and literature. Though they disagreed about the relative merits of the classical philosophers and writers, all agreed that classical philosophy and literature were of paramount importance to their own culture.

Another feature of humanism is its emphasis on individualism. Medieval society was corporate—that is, oriented toward, and organized around, people acting in groups. Medieval political philosophy dictated that the smallest component of society was not the individual but the family. An individual ruler stood at the top of medieval society, but this ruler was regarded as tightly bound to the other nobles by feudal alliances and, in some ways, as simply the greatest of the nobles. Workers banded together in guilds; pious people formed religious confraternities; citizens swore an oath of allegiance to their own city. Even art was thought to be a group effort, with the individual artist feeling no more need to sign a work than a baker did to sign each loaf of bread. (We know the names of some medieval artists from sources such as contracts, bills of sale, and financial records, but rarely from the paintings or sculptures themselves.)

Christianity encouraged this sense of community as well. Though Christians were baptized and participated in most other sacraments as individuals, the priest represented the whole community when he alone drank wine at communion, and Christ was believed to have embodied all of Christianity when he died. Christians were encouraged to think of themselves as part of one great "Christendom" and to follow the example of Christ by showing humility and meekness rather than the self-assurance that draws attention to the individual.

These attitudes began to shift during the Renaissance. The family, the guild, and other corporate groups remained important social forces, but some individuals increasingly viewed the group as simply a springboard to far greater individual achievement that could be obtained through talent or hard work. Rather than defining themselves primarily within the context of the group, some prized their own sense of uniqueness and individuality, hiring artists to paint or sculpt their portraits and writers to produce verbal likenesses. Caught up in this new individualism, artists and writers themselves began to paint their own self-portraits and write autobiographies. Visual artists, believing that their skill at painting or sculpture was a result not simply of good training but of individual genius, began to sign their works. Rather than the vices they were to medieval Christians, self-confidence and individualism became virtues for many people. Humanists wrote not only biographies of prominent individuals but also treatises that described the attributes of the ideal person. In their opinion, that person should be well rounded and should also exhibit the quality of *virtù*—a word that does not mean "virtue" but rather the ability to make an impact in one's chosen field of endeavor.

The notion of individualism includes a belief that the people and objects of this world are important, at least important enough to warrant a picture or a verbal description. This belief, usually called *secularism,* is also a part of humanism. "Secularism" is a highly charged word in modern American political jargon—even more so when expanded to "secular humanism"—and may be too strong a term to apply to Renaissance thinkers. No one in the Renaissance denied the existence of God or the central importance of religion in human life. What they did reject was the idea that it was necessary to forsake the material world and retire to a life of contemplation in order to worship God. God had created this world full of beauty, including the human body, to be appreciated. The talents of each person should be developed to their fullest through education and then displayed to the world because those talents came from God. Studying pre-Christian philosophers such as Plato or Aristotle could enhance an understanding of Christianity because God could certainly have endowed these thinkers with great wisdom even though they were not Christian.

The basis for all these features of humanism—classicism, individualism, secularism—was learning, and humanists all agreed on the importance of education, not just for the individual but also for society as a whole. During the mid-fifteenth century many humanists, such as Leonardo Bruni, began to stress that a proper liberal education was based on training for service to society as well as on classical models. Medieval education had been primarily an organ of the Church, oriented to its needs. Church and cathedral schools trained students to read and write so that they could copy manuscripts, serve as church lawyers, and write correspondence. Monks, priests, and nuns also used their education to honor the glory of God by reciting prayers, studying the Bible and other religious works, composing and singing hymns, or simply speculating on the nature of God. In the Middle Ages the ultimate aim of human life was to *know,* and particularly to know God, so medieval education was often both inwardly directed and otherworldy, helping individuals to come to a better understanding of God. The Renaissance humanists, on the other hand, believed the ultimate aim of human life was to *act*, so humanist education was resoundingly outwardly directed and this-worldly, emphasizing practical skills such as public speaking and writing that would benefit any politician, diplomat, military leader, or businessman. This education was not to be used in a monastery where only God could see it, but in the newly expanding cities and towns of northern Italy, cities that were growing steadily richer thanks to the development of trade we examined in Chapter 9. The primarily classical humanism of the fourteenth century was gradually transformed into civic humanism as humanists took employment as city secretaries and historians and as merchants and bankers sent their sons to humanist schools.

Humanism underwent a further transformation in the sixteenth century, when the governing of the cities of northern Italy was taken over by powerful noblemen. These rulers hired humanists as secretaries, tutors, diplomats, and advisers, and they established humanist academies in their capital cities. Unlike medieval rulers, who saw themselves primarily as military leaders, Renaissance rulers saw themselves as the leaders of all facets of life in their territories. Thus they supported poets and musicians as well as generals, learned several languages, and established their court as the cultural as well as political center of the territory.

Reflecting this new courtly milieu, humanists began to write biographies of rulers and to reflect on the qualities that were important in the ideal ruler and courtier. The trait of *virtù*, so vital in an individual, was even more critical in a ruler. For a ruler, *virtù* meant the ability to shape society as a whole and leave an indelible mark on history. Humanists held up as models worthy of emulation such classical rulers as Alexander the Great and Julius Caesar.

In many ways, then, Renaissance thinkers broke with the immediate medieval past in developing new ideals for human behavior. For one group, however, this break was not so complete. When humanists described the ideal woman, she turned out to be much more like her medieval counterpart than the "Renaissance man" was. The problem of female education was particularly perplexing for humanists. Medieval women, like medieval men, had been educated to serve and know God. Renaissance men were educated to serve the city or the state, which no humanist felt was a proper role for women. If women were not to engage in the type of public activities felt to be the proper arena for displaying talent and education, why should they be educated at all? Should the new virtues of self-confidence and individualism be extended to include women? Or should women be the link with the older Christian virtues of modesty and humility? How could women properly show *virtù*— a word whose roots lie in the word *vir*, which meant "man"—when to do so required public actions? Should women, perhaps, be even more encouraged to remain within the private

[251]

sphere of home and family, given the opinions of classical philosophers such as Aristotle (which we saw in Chapter 3) about the proper role of women? In their consideration of the proper "Renaissance woman," humanists often exhibited both the tension between, and their attempts to fuse, the pagan classical and medieval Christian traditions.

In this chapter, you will examine the writings of several humanists describing the ideal educational program for boys and girls, the ideal male and female courtier, and the ideal ruler. In addition, you will read one short section from the autobiography of a humanist and another from the biography of a ruler written by a humanist; you will also look at several portraits. How do these authors describe the ideal man, woman, and ruler? How were these ideals expressed in written descriptions and visual portraits of actual Renaissance people?

SOURCES AND METHOD

The written sources in this chapter are primarily prescriptive; in other words, they present ideals that their humanist authors hoped people would emulate. Our questions and methodology are those of intellectual historians, who are interested in the development of ideas as well as in how those ideas relate to other types of changes. Intellectual history is an especially important dimension of the Renaissance, which was primarily an intellectual rather than a political or social movement. The questions you need to keep most in mind, then, relate to the ideas set forth here: What qualities was the ideal man, woman, or ruler supposed to possess? How were these qualities to be inculcated in young people? On the basis of these qualities, what did humanists think was most important in human existence? How did authors and artists portraying real people—in biographies, autobiographies, or portraits—express similar ideas?

Whenever we use prescriptive literature as our historical source, we must first inquire into the author's motives. Why did our Renaissance writers believe that people had to be instructed in matters of behavior? Were they behaving badly, or were they confronting new situations in which they would not know how to act? The intentions of these humanist authors were fairly straightforward because they believed themselves to be living in a new age, a rebirth of classical culture. In their minds, people needed to be informed about the values of this new age and instructed in the means for putting these values into practice. The humanist authors were thus attempting to mold new types of people to fit a new world, not simply correcting attitudes and behavior they felt were wrong or misguided. Consequently, humanist prescriptive literature concentrates on the positive, telling people what to do rather than what not to do (unlike much other prescriptive literature, such as the Ten Commandments).

Before you read the written selections, look at the three portraits. The first is a self-portrait by the German artist Albrecht Dürer; the second a portrait of an Italian woman known simply as Simonetta, by the Italian artist Sandro Botticelli or a member of his workshop; the third a sculpture of the Venetian general Bartolommeo Colleoni by Andrea del Verrocchio. How would you describe the expressions of the subjects in each of these portraits? Do any of them exhibit the qualities prized by the humanists—individualism, *virtù,* self-confidence? What other traits did the artist choose to emphasize? What differences do you see in the portrait of the woman compared with those of the two men? Now proceed to the written evidence.

Sources 4 and 5 are letters from humanists to members of the nobility. The first, discussing the proper education for men, is from Peter Paul Vergerius to Ubertinus, the son of the ruler of Padua, Italy; the second, discussing the proper education for women, is from Leonardo Bruni to Lady Baptista Malatesta, the daughter of the Duke of Urbino. As you read them, note both the similarities and the differences in the two courses of study. What factors might account for this? What is the ultimate purpose of the two educational programs?

Sources 6 and 7 are taken from one of the most popular advice manuals ever written, Baldassare Castiglione's *The Courtier.* Castiglione was himself a courtier in Urbino, Mantua, and Milan, and he wrote this discussion of the perfect courtier and court lady in the form of a dialogue between noblemen. As you did for Sources 4 and 5, compare the qualities prescribed for men and women, respectively. How do these relate to the educational program discussed in Sources 4 and 5?

Source 8 comes from one of the most widely read pieces of political advice ever written, Machiavelli's *The Prince.* Like Castiglione, Niccolo Machiavelli had served various governments and had watched rulers and states rise and fall in late-fifteenth- and early-sixteenth-century Italy. What does he believe is the most critical factor or factors in the training of a prince? What qualities should a ruler possess to be effective and display *virtù*?

The first five documents are all straightforward prescriptive literature, as the authors' frequent use of such words as "ought" and "should" indicates. This was not the only way humanists communicated their ideals, however; biographies of real people also expressed these ideals. To use biographies as a source of ideas, we must take a slightly more subtle approach, identifying those personal characteristics the author chose to emphasize, those that might have been omitted, and the way in which each biographer manipulated the true personality of his subject to fit the humanist ideal. These are points to consider as you read the next two documents. Source 9 is from the autobiography of Leon Battista Alberti, which you will note is written in the third person. How does Alberti describe himself? How did his life reflect the new humanist ideals? Why might he have chosen to write in the third person instead of saying "I"? Source 10 is Polydore Vergil's description of Henry VII of England, who ruled from 1485 to 1509. What does it tell us about Renaissance monarchs and also about the author?

Once you have read the written selections, return to the portraits. Do you find anything there that you did not see before?

THE EVIDENCE

Source 1 from German Information Center.

1. Albrecht Dürer, *Self-Portrait in a Fur Coat,* 1500

Source 2 from Staatliche Museen zu Berlin—Preussischer Kulturbesitz Gemaldegalerie. Photograph: Jorg P. Anders.

2. Workshop of Botticelli (ca 1444–1510), So-called *Simonetta*

Source 3 from Venice (Alinari/Art Resource, New York).

3. Andrea del Verrocchio (ca 1435–1488), Sculpture of General Bartolommeo Colleoni

Sources 4 and 5 from W. H. Woodward, editor and translator, Vittorino da Feltre and Other Humanist Educators *(London: Cambridge University Press, 1897), pp. 102, 106–107, 109, 110; pp. 126–129, 132, 133.*

4. Peter Paul Vergerius, Letter to Ubertinus of Padua, 1392

3. We call those studies *liberal* which are worthy of a free man; those studies by which we attain and practice virtue and wisdom; that education which calls forth, trains, and develops those highest gifts of body and of mind which ennoble men, and which are rightly judged to rank next in dignity to virtue only. For to a vulgar temper gain and pleasure are the one aim of existence, to a lofty nature, moral worth and fame. It is, then, of the highest importance that even from infancy this aim, this effort, should constantly be kept alive in growing minds. . . .

We come now to the consideration of the various subjects which may rightly be included under the name of "Liberal Studies." Amongst these I accord the first place to History, on grounds both of its attractiveness and of its utility, qualities which appeal equally to the scholar and to the statesman. Next in importance ranks Moral Philosophy, which indeed is, in a peculiar sense, a "Liberal Art," in that its purpose is to teach men the secret of true freedom. History, then, gives us the concrete examples of the precepts inculcated by Philosophy. The one shows what men should do, the other what men have said and done in the past, and what practical lessons we may draw therefrom for the present day. I would indicate as the third main branch of study, Eloquence, which indeed holds a place of distinction amongst the refined arts. By philosophy we learn the essential truth of things, which by eloquence we so exhibit in orderly adornment as to bring conviction to differing minds. And history provides the light of experience—a cumulative wisdom fit to supplement the force of reason and the persuasion of eloquence. For we allow that soundness of judgment, wisdom of speech, integrity of conduct are the marks of a truly liberal temper. . . .

4. The principal "Disciplines" have now been reviewed. It must not be supposed that a liberal education requires acquaintance with them all: for a thorough mastery of even one of them might fairly be the achievement of a lifetime. Most of us, too, must learn to be content with modest capacity as with modest fortune. Perhaps we do wisely to pursue that study which we find most suited to our intelligence and our tastes, though it is true that we cannot rightly understand one subject unless we can perceive its relation to the rest. The choice of studies will depend to some extent upon the character of individual minds. . . .

Respecting the general place of liberal studies, we remember that Aristotle would not have them absorb the entire interests of life: for he kept steadily in view the nature of man as a citizen, an active member of the State. For the man who has surrendered himself absolutely to the attractions of Letters or of speculative thought follows, perhaps, a self-regarding end and is useless as a citizen or as prince.

5. Leonardo Bruni, Letter to Lady Baptista Malatesta, ca 1405

There are certain subjects in which, whilst a modest proficiency is on all accounts to be desired, a minute knowledge and excessive devotion seem to be a vain display. For instance, subtleties of Arithmetic and Geometry are not worthy to absorb a cultivated mind, and the same must be said of Astrology. You will be surprised to find me suggesting (though with much more hesitation) that the great and complex art of Rhetoric should be placed in the same category. My chief reason is the obvious one, that I have in view the cultivation most fitting to a woman. To her neither the intricacies of debate nor the oratorical artifices of action and delivery are of the least practical use, if indeed they are not positively unbecoming. Rhetoric in all its forms—public discussion, forensic argument, logical fence, and the like—lies absolutely outside the province of women.

What Disciplines then are properly open to her? In the first place she has before her, as a subject peculiarly her own, the whole field of religion and morals. The literature of the Church will thus claim her earnest study. Such a writer, for instance, as St. Augustine affords her the fullest scope for reverent yet learned inquiry. Her devotional instinct may lead her to value the help and consolation of holy men now living; but in this case let her not for an instant yield to the impulse to look into their writings, which, compared with those of Augustine, are utterly destitute of sound and melodious style, and seem to me to have no attraction whatever.

Moreover, the cultivated Christian lady has no need in the study of this weighty subject to confine herself to ecclesiastical writers. Morals, indeed, have been treated of by the noblest intellects of Greece and Rome. What they have left to us upon Continence, Temperance, Modesty, Justice, Courage, Greatness of Soul, demands your sincere respect. . . .

But we must not forget that true distinction is to be gained by a wide and varied range of such studies as conduce to the profitable enjoyment of life, in which, however, we must observe due proportion in the attention and time we devote to them.

First amongst such studies I place History: a subject which must not on any account be neglected by one who aspires to true cultivation. For it is our duty to understand the origins of our own history and its development; and the achievements of Peoples and of Kings.

For the careful study of the past enlarges our foresight in contemporary affairs and affords to citizens and to monarchs lessons of incitement or warning in the ordering of public policy. From History, also, we draw our store of examples of moral precepts. . . .

The great Orators of antiquity must by all means be included. Nowhere do we find the virtues more warmly extolled, the vices so fiercely decried. From them we may learn, also, how to express consolation, encouragement, dissuasion or advice. . . .

I come now to Poetry and the Poets—a subject with which every educated lady must shew herself thoroughly familiar. For we cannot point to any great mind of the past for whom the Poets had not a powerful attraction. . . . Hence my view that familiarity with the great poets of antiquity is essential to any claim to true education. For in their writings we find deep speculations upon Nature, and upon the Causes and Origins of things, which must carry weight with us both from their antiquity and from their authorship. Besides these, many important truths upon matters of daily life are suggested or illustrated. All this is expressed with such grace and dignity as demands our admiration.

But I am ready to admit that there are two types of poet: the aristocracy, so to call them, of their craft, and the vulgar, and that the latter may be put aside in ordering a woman's reading. A comic dramatist may season his wit too highly: a satirist describe too bluntly the moral corruption which he scourges: let her pass them by. . . .

But my last word must be this. . . . All sources of profitable learning will in due proportion claim your study. None have more urgent claim than the subjects and authors which treat of Religion and of our duties in the world; and it is because they assist and illustrate these supreme studies that I press upon your attention the works of the most approved poets, historians and orators of the past.

Sources 6 and 7 from Baldassare Castiglione, The Book of the Courtier, *trans. Charles S. Singleton, ed. Edgar Mayhew (Garden City, New York: Doubleday, 1959), pp. 32, 34, 70–71; pp. 206–208, 211–212. Copyright © 1959 by Charles S. Singleton and Edgar de N. Mayhew. Used by permission of Doubleday, a division of Random House, Inc.*

6. From Baldassare Castiglione, *The Courtier,* 1508–1516

"I hold that the principal and true profession of the Courtier must be that of arms which I wish him to exercise with vigor; and let him be known among the others as bold, energetic, and faithful to whomever he serves. And the repute of these good qualities will be earned by exercising them in every time and place, inasmuch as one may not ever fail therein without great blame.

And, just as among women the name of purity, once stained, is never restored, so the reputation of a gentleman whose profession is arms, if ever in the least way he sullies himself through cowardice or other disgrace, always remains defiled before the world and covered with ignominy. Therefore, the more our Courtier excels in this art, the more will he merit praise." . . .

Then signor Gasparo replied: "As for me, I have known few men excellent in anything whatsoever who did not praise themselves; and it seems to me that this can well be permitted them, because he who feels himself to be of some worth, and sees that his works are ignored, is indignant that his own worth should lie buried; and he must make it known to someone, in order not to be cheated of the honor that is the true reward of all virtuous toil. Thus, among the ancients, seldom does anyone of any worth refrain from praising himself. To be sure, those persons who are of no merit, and yet praise themselves, are insufferable; but we do not assume that our Courtier will be of that sort."

Then the Count said: "If you took notice, I blamed impudent and indiscriminate praise of one's self: and truly, as you say, one must not conceive a bad opinion of a worthy man who praises himself modestly; nay, one must take that as surer evidence than if it came from another's mouth. I do say that whoever does not fall into error in praising himself and does not cause annoyance or envy in the person who listens to him is indeed a discreet man and, besides the praises he gives himself, deserves praises from others; for that is a very difficult thing." . . .

"I would have him more than passably learned in letters, at least in those studies which we call the humanities. Let him be conversant not only with the Latin language, but with Greek as well, because of the abundance and variety of things that are so divinely written therein. Let him be versed in the poets, as well as in the orators and historians, and let him be practiced also in writing verse and prose, especially in our own vernacular; for, beside the personal satisfaction he will take in this, in this way he will never want for pleasant entertainment with the ladies, who are usually fond of such things. And if, because of other occupations or lack of study, he does not attain to such a perfection that his writings should merit great praise, let him take care to keep them under cover so that others will not laugh at him, and let him show them only to a friend who can be trusted; because at least they will be of profit to him in that, through such exercise, he will be capable of judging the writing of others. For it very rarely happens that a man who is unpracticed in writing, however learned he may be, can ever wholly understand the toils and industry of writers, or taste the sweetness and excellence of styles, and those intrinsic niceties that are often found in the ancients.

"These studies, moreover, will make him fluent, and (as Aristippus said to the tyrant) bold and self-confident in speaking with everyone. However, I would have our Courtier keep one precept firmly in mind, namely, in this as in everything else, to be cautious and reserved rather than forward, and take care not to get the mistaken notion that he knows something he does not know."

7. From Baldassare Castiglione, *The Courtier,* 1508–1516

I think that in her ways, manners, words, gestures, and bearing, a woman ought to be very unlike a man; for just as he must show a certain solid and sturdy manliness, so it is seemly for a woman to have a soft and delicate tenderness, with an air of womanly sweetness in her every movement. . . .

[Again] . . . many virtues of the mind are as necessary to a woman as to a man; also, gentle birth; to avoid affectation, to be naturally graceful in all her actions, to be mannerly, clever, prudent, not arrogant, not envious, not slanderous, not vain, not contentious, not inept, to know how to gain and hold the favor of her mistress [queen or presiding lady at court] and of all others, to perform well and gracefully the exercises that are suitable for women. And I do think that beauty is more necessary to her than to the Courtier, for truly that woman lacks much who lacks beauty. . . . I say that, in my opinion, in a Lady who lives at court a certain pleasing affability is becoming above all else, whereby she will be able to entertain graciously every kind of man with agreeable and comely conversation suited to the time and place and to the station of the person with whom she speaks, joining to serene and modest manners, and to that comeliness that ought to inform all her actions, a quick vivacity of spirit whereby she will show herself a stranger to all boorishness; but with such a kind manner as to cause her to be thought no less chaste, prudent, and gentle than she is agreeable, witty, and discreet: thus, she must observe a certain mean (difficult to achieve and, as it were, composed of contraries) and must strictly observe certain limits and not exceed them.

Now, in her wish to be thought good and pure, this Lady must not be so coy, or appear so to abhor gay company or any talk that is a little loose, as to withdraw as soon as she finds herself involved, for it might easily be thought that she was pretending to be so austere in order to hide something about herself which she feared others might discover; for manners so unbending are always odious. Yet, on the other hand, for the sake of appearing free and amiable she must not utter unseemly words or enter into any immodest and unbridled familiarity or into ways such as might cause others to believe about her what is perhaps not true; but when she finds herself present at such talk, she ought to listen with a light blush of shame. . . .

And to repeat briefly a part of what has already been said. I wish this Lady to have knowledge of letters, of music, of painting, and know how to dance and how to be festive, adding a discreet modesty and the giving of a good impression of herself to those other things that have been required of the

Courtier. And so, in her talk, her laughter, her play, her jesting, in short in everything, she will be most graceful and will converse appropriately with every person in whose company she may happen to be, using witticisms and pleasantries that are becoming to her.

Source 8 from Niccolo Machiavelli, The Prince and the Discourses, *translated by Luigi Ricci, revised by E. R. P. Vincent (New York: Random House, 1950), pp. 4, 53, 55, 56, 61–62. Reprinted by permission of Oxford University Press.*

8. From Niccolo Machiavelli, *The Prince*, 1513

I desire no honour for my work but such as the novelty and gravity of its subject may justly deserve. Nor will it, I trust, be deemed presumptuous on the part of a man of humble and obscure condition to attempt to discuss and direct the government of princes; for in the same way that landscape painters station themselves in the valleys in order to draw mountains or high ground, and ascend an eminence in order to get a good view of the plains, so it is necessary to be a prince to know thoroughly the nature of the people, and one of the populace to know the nature of princes. . . .

A prince should therefore have no other aim or thought, nor take up any other thing for his study, but war and its organisation and discipline, for that is the only art that is necessary to one who commands, and it is of such virtue that it not only maintains those who are born princes, but often enables men of private fortune to attain to that rank. And one sees, on the other hand, that when princes think more of luxury than of arms, they lose their state. The chief cause of the loss of states, is the contempt of this art, and the way to acquire them is to be well versed in the same. . . .

But as to exercise for the mind, the prince ought to read history and study the actions of eminent men, see how they acted in warfare, examine the causes of their victories and defeats in order to imitate the former and avoid the latter, and above all, do as some men have done in the past, who have imitated some one, who has been much praised and glorified, and have always kept his deeds and actions before them. . . .

It now remains to be seen what are the methods and rules for a prince as regards his subjects and friends. . . .

From this arises the question whether it is better to be loved more than feared, or feared more than loved. The reply is, that one ought to be both feared and loved, but as it is difficult for the two to go together, it is much safer to be feared than loved, if one of the two has to be wanting. For it may be said of men in general that they are ungrateful, voluble, dissemblers, anxious to avoid danger, and covetous of gain; as long as you benefit them, they are entirely yours; they offer you their blood, their goods, their life, and their children, as I have before said, when the necessity is remote; but when it approaches, they revolt. And the prince who has relied solely on their words, without making other preparations, is ruined; for the friendship which is gained by purchase and not through grandeur and nobility of spirit is bought but not secured, and at a pinch is not to be expended in your service. And men have less scruple in offending one who makes himself loved than one who makes himself feared; for love is held by a chain of obligation which, men being selfish, is broken whenever it serves their purpose; but fear is maintained by a dread of punishment which never fails.

Still, a prince should make himself feared in such a way that if he does not gain love, he at any rate avoids hatred; for fear and the absence of hatred may well go together, and will be always attained by one who abstains from interfering with the property of his citizens and subjects or with their women. And when he is obliged to take the life of any one, let him do so when there is a proper justification and manifest reason for it; but above all he must abstain from taking the property of others, for men forget more easily the death of their father than the loss of their patrimony. Then also pretexts for seizing property are never wanting, and one who begins to live by rapine will always find some reason for taking the goods of others, whereas causes for taking life are rarer and more fleeting.

But when the prince is with his army and has a large number of soldiers under his control, then it is extremely necessary that he should not mind being thought cruel; for without this reputation he could not keep an army united or disposed to any duty.

Source 9 from James Bruce Ross and Mary Martin McLaughlin, editors, The Portable Renaissance Reader *(New York: Viking, 1953), pp. 480–485, 490–492. Selection translated by James Bruce Ross. Copyright 1953, renewed 1981 by Viking Penguin Inc. Used by permission of Viking Penguin, a division of Penguin Putnam, Inc.*

9. From Leon Battista Alberti, *Autobiography*, after 1460(?)

In everything suitable to one born free and educated liberally, he was so trained from boyhood that among the leading young men of his age he was considered by no means the last. For, assiduous in the science and skill of dealing with arms and horses and musical instruments, as well as in the pursuit of letters[1] and the fine arts, he was devoted to the knowledge of the most strange and difficult things. And finally he embraced with zeal and forethought everything which pertained to fame. To omit the rest, he strove so hard to attain a name in modelling and painting that he wished to neglect

---

1. **letters:** Alberti means the humanist program of study, primarily the study of languages and literature.

nothing by which he might gain the approbation of good men. His genius was so versatile that you might almost judge all the fine arts to be his. Neither ease nor sloth held him back, nor was he ever seized by satiety in carrying out what was to be done.

He often said that not even in letters had he noticed what is called the satiety of all things among mortals; for to him letters, in which he delighted so greatly, seemed sometimes like flowering and richly fragrant buds, so that hunger or sleep could scarcely distract him from his books. At other times, however, those very letters swarmed together like scorpions before his eyes, so that he could see nothing at all but books. Therefore, when letters began to be displeasing to him, he turned to music and painting and exercise.

He played ball, hurled the javelin, ran, leaped, wrestled, and above all delighted in the steep ascent of mountains; he applied himself to all these things for the sake of health rather than sport or pleasure. . . .

At length, on the orders of his doctors, he desisted from those studies which were most fatiguing to the memory, just when they were about to flourish. But in truth, because he could not live without letters, at the age of twenty-four he turned to physics and the mathematical arts. He did not despair of being able to cultivate them sufficiently, because he perceived that in them talent rather than memory must be employed. At this time he wrote for his brother *On the Advantages and Disadvantages of Letters,* in which booklet, taught by experience, he discussed whatever could be thought about letters. And he wrote at this time for the sake of his soul several little works: *Ephebia, On Religion, Deiphira,* and more of this sort in prose; then in verse, *Elegies* and *Eclogues,* and *Discourses,* and works on love of such a kind as to inculcate good habits in those who studied them and to foster the quiet of the soul. . . .

Although he was affable, gentle, and harmful to no one, nevertheless he felt the animosity of many evil men, and hidden enmities, both annoying and very burdensome; in particular the harsh injuries and intolerable insults from his own relatives. He lived among the envious and malevolent with such modesty and equanimity that none of his detractors or rivals, although very hostile towards him, dared to utter a word about him in the presence of good and worthy men unless it was full of praise and admiration. Even by these envious ones he was received with honour face to face. But, in truth, when he was absent, those who had pretended to love him most slandered him with every sort of calumny, wherever the ears of the fickle and their like lay open. For they took it ill to be exceeded in ability and fame by him who, far inferior to them in fortune, had striven with such zeal and industry. There were even some among his kinsmen (not to mention others) who, having experienced his humanity, beneficence, and liberality, conspired against him most ungratefully and cruelly in an evil domestic plot, and those barbarians aroused the boldness of servants to strike him with a knife, blameless as he was.

He bore injuries of this kind from his kinsmen with equanimity, more in silence than by indignantly resorting to vengeance or permitting the shame and ignominy of his relatives to be made public. . . .

He could endure pain and cold and heat. When, not yet fifteen, he received a serious wound in the foot, and the physician, according to his custom and skill, drew together the broken parts of the foot and sewed them through the skin with a needle, he scarcely uttered a sound of pain. With his own hands, though in such great pain, he even aided the ministering doctor and treated his own wound though he was burning with fever. And when on account of a pain in his side he was continually in an icy sweat, he called in musicians, and for about two hours he strove by singing to overcome the force of the malady and the agony of the pain. His head was by nature unable to endure either cold or wind; but by persistence he learned to bear them, gradually getting used to riding bareheaded in summer, then in winter, and even in raging wind. By some defect in his nature he loathed garlic and also honey, and the mere sight of them, if by chance they were offered to him, brought on vomiting. But he conquered himself by force of looking at and handling the disagreeable objects, so that they came to offend him less, thus showing by example that men can do anything with themselves if they will. . . .

When his favourite dog died he wrote a funeral oration for him.

Source 10 from Denys Hay, editor and translator, The Anglia Historia of Polydore Vergil, *AD 1485–1537, book 74 (London: Camden Society, 1950), p. 147.*

10. From Polydore Vergil, *Anglia Historia,* ca 1540

Henry reigned twenty-three years and seven months. He lived for fifty-two years. By his wife Elizabeth he was the father of eight children, four boys and as many girls. He left three surviving children, an only son Henry prince of Wales, and two daughters, Margaret married to James king of Scotland, and Mary betrothed to Charles prince of Castile. His body was slender but well built and strong; his height above the average. His appearance was remarkably attractive and his face was cheerful, especially when speaking; his eyes were small and blue, his teeth few, poor and blackish; his hair was thin and white; his complexion sallow. His spirit was distinguished, wise and prudent; his mind was brave and resolute and never, even at moments of the greatest danger, deserted him. He had a most pertinacious memory. Withal he was not devoid of scholarship. In government he was shrewd and prudent, so that no one dared to get the better of him through deceit or guile. He was gracious and kind and was as attentive to his visitors as he was easy of access. His hospitality was splendidly generous; he was fond of having foreigners at his court and he freely conferred favours on them. But those of his subjects who were indebted to him and who did not pay him due honour or who were generous only with promises, he treated with harsh severity. He well knew how to maintain his royal majesty and all which appertains to kingship at every time and in every place. He was most fortunate in war, although he was constitutionally more inclined to peace than to war. He cherished justice above all things; as a result he vigorously punished violence, manslaughter and every other kind of wickedness whatsoever. Consequently he was greatly regretted[2] on that account by all his subjects, who had been able to conduct their lives peaceably, far removed from the assaults and evil doing of scoundrels. He was the most ardent supporter of our faith, and daily participated with great piety in religious services. To those whom he considered to be worthy priests, he often secretly gave alms so that they should pray for his salvation. He was particularly fond of those Franciscan friars whom they call Observants, for whom he founded many convents, so that with his help their rule should continually flourish in his kingdom. But all these virtues were obscured latterly only by avarice, from which (as we showed above) he suffered. This avarice is surely a bad enough vice in a private individual, whom it forever torments; in a monarch indeed it may be considered the worst vice, since it is harmful to everyone, and distorts those qualities of trustfulness, justice and integrity by which the state must be governed.

2. **regretted:** missed after he died.

QUESTIONS TO CONSIDER

The first step in exploring the history of ideas is to focus on and define the ideas themselves. Once you have done that by reading the selections and thinking about the questions proposed in Sources and Method, you need to take the next step, which is to compare the ideas of various thinkers. In this way you can trace the development of ideas, how they originate and mature and change in the mind of one thinker after another. First, ask specific questions, such as: What would Bruni think of Castiglione's court lady? How would Leon Battista Alberti be judged by Castiglione's standards? Did Polydore Vergil and Machiavelli have the same ideas about the personal qualities of a ruler? Would a man educated according to the ideas of Vergerius have fitted into Castiglione's ideal court? Would a ruler have wanted him? Would Bruni's learned lady have made a good member of Castiglione's court? Would Botticelli's Simonetta? Does Machiavelli's prince display the qualities Vergerius envisioned in a liberally educated man? How do the main qualities of Machiavelli's prince compare with those of Castiglione's courtier? Why might they be quite different? From the portrait, how might Dürer have been judged by each of the writers? Could we think of Verrocchio's sculpture of Colleoni as a portrait of a Machiavellian ruler? How did the artists' ideals for men, women, and rulers differ from the writers'?

Once you have made these specific comparisons, you can move on to broader comparisons of the basic assumptions of the authors and artists: What was the underlying view of human nature for these writers? Was this the same for men and women? You have probably noticed that all the writers and artists presented here are male. Given what you have now learned about ideals for men and women, would you have expected most Renaissance writers to be male?

Many intellectual historians are interested not only in the history of ideas themselves but also in their social and political origins. These historians want to know what people thought and why they thought the way they did. This type of intellectual history is called the *sociology of knowledge* because it explores the societal context of ideas in the same way that sociology examines past and present social groups. The sociology of knowledge is a more speculative field than the history of ideas alone because it attempts to discover the underlying reasons that cause people to develop different ways of thinking in different historical periods—a process that can be quite difficult to discern. Nevertheless, from the information your text provides about the social and political changes occurring during the Renaissance, you can also consider some sociology of knowledge questions: Why did humanism first arise in northern Italy and not elsewhere in Italy? Why was religion regarded as especially important for women? How did Castiglione's career affect his view of politics? How did

Machiavelli's? What transformation of the status of artists during the Renaissance allowed both Alberti and Dürer to depict themselves in the ways they did? Given that the documents range from 1392 to 1540, what political changes might have accounted for the varying ideals proposed for the individual? How did the ideals proposed for rulers reflect the actual growth of centralized political power? How might the growth of that power have shaped the ideals set forth by Machiavelli and Polydore Vergil? Questions such as these take us somewhat beyond the scope of our original enquiry, but they are important to ask in looking at any ideological change, particularly a sensibility as far-reaching as the Renaissance. Humanism did not spring up in a vacuum but at a very specific time and place.

We must also be careful, however, not to overemphasize social and political background in tracing the development of ideas. Intellectual historians prefer to speak of "necessary conditions" or "background factors" rather than "causes." A movement as diffuse and long lasting as humanism necessarily stemmed from a wide variety of factors, so do not feel concerned if you find yourself qualifying your answers to the questions in the last paragraph with such words as "might," "perhaps," and "possibly."

EPILOGUE

Scholars and writers throughout Western history have attempted to revive the classical past, but none of these efforts before or after were to produce the long-lasting effects of the Italian Renaissance. In many ways Petrarch was right: It was the dawn of a new age. As the ideas and ideals of humanism spread, writers all over Europe felt that they had definitely broken with the centuries-long tradition that directly preceded them. It was at this point that historians began the three-part division of Western history that we still use today: antiquity, the Middle Ages or medieval period, and the modern period. (If you pause to reflect on what "middle" implies, you will see that no one living in the tenth century would have described him- or herself as living in the "Middle Ages.")

The effects of the Renaissance were eventually felt far beyond the realms of literature and art. Humanist schools and academies opened throughout Europe, and eventually the older universities changed their curricula to add courses in Latin, Greek, and Hebrew language and literature. In northern Europe, humanists became interested in reforming the Church, bringing it back to the standards of piety and morality they believed had been present in the early Church, in the same way that Petrarch had tried to return the Latin language to its ancient standards. This movement, termed *Christian humanism*, would be one of the background factors behind the Protestant Reformation, as learned people began to realize from their studies that the Church was now far removed from the ideas and standards of the early Christians. The intense Renaissance interest in the physical world, combined with monetary greed and missionary impulses, led to the exploration and eventual colonization of much of the non-European world. This secular spirit was also important in setting the stage for the Scientific Revolution of the seventeenth century.

Humanist ideas about the perfect man, woman, and ruler were originally directed at the upper classes but would eventually find a much larger audience. Castiglione's *The Courtier* was translated into every European language, and the personal characteristics he outlined for the ideal courtier became those expected of the middle-class gentleman. Echoes of the Renaissance ideal for women are still with us; a glance at women's magazines or at contemporary advice manuals for girls will show you that physical beauty, morality, femininity, and religion are often still seen to be the most important personal qualities a woman can possess. Machiavelli's *The Prince* has more dramatic echoes, as many modern dictators clearly would agree that it is more important to be feared than loved.

We should not overemphasize the effects of the intellectual changes of the Renaissance on people living during that period, however. Only a very small share of the population, primarily wealthy, urban, and, as we have seen, male, participated at all in cultural life, whether as consumers

[269]

or as producers. Most people's lives were shaped much more during this period by economic changes and by religious practices than by the cultural changes we looked at in this chapter. In fact, in their efforts to stress the elitism of Renaissance culture, some historians have questioned whether the term "Renaissance" itself is a valid one, and prefer simply to use the more neutral phrase "late medieval and early modern period."

Even among the elites, many aspects of the Middle Ages continued during the Renaissance. Despite the emergence of individualism, family background remained the most important determinant of a person's social and economic standing. Despite an emphasis on the material, secular world, religion remained central to the lives of the elite as well as the common people. Though some artists were recognized as geniuses, they were still expected to be dependable, tax-paying members of society—that is, members of the community like everybody else. The fact that so many humanists felt it necessary to set standards and describe ideal behavior gives us a clue that not everyone understood or accepted that they were living in a new age: People have no need to be convinced of what they already believe is true.

CHAPTER TWELVE

PAGANS, MUSLIMS, AND CHRISTIANS IN THE

MENTAL WORLD OF COLUMBUS

THE PROBLEM

Along with inspiring a number of television specials, parades, scholarly conferences, and exhibitions, the 500th anniversary of the first voyage of Columbus in 1992 sparked a great debate about the man himself and the impact of his actions. Was he an intrepid explorer, one of the few Europeans not afraid to sail out of sight of land? Was he a religious zealot and mystic, convinced that God had called him to fight the power of Islam and convert people to Christianity by force if necessary? Was he an ethnocentric racist, unable to appreciate the cultures of the people with whom he came into contact? Did his voyages usher in a period of global interchange, bringing new crops across the Atlantic in both directions? Or did they instead bring demographic devastation to the New World, with European diseases killing the vast majority of the population of Central America? How did they set the stage for the African slave trade, which

became the largest forced movement of people in human history?

The debate surrounding these questions has perhaps become more polemical than it should, but one of its positive results has been a greater interest in seeing Columbus within his historical context. Earlier celebrations of Columbus, such as that in 1892, tended to present him as a lonely hero, a man who stuck to his dreams despite the ridicule and scorn of most of his contemporaries, and prevailed, proving that the earth was round when most people thought that it was flat. Columbus was often described as the first "modern man," in the sense that he was interested in venturing into the unknown simply to find what was there. This heroic view can still be found in the popular press, with Columbus portrayed as the direct ancestor to modern astronauts and praised as one of the few people who was able to throw off the shackles of medieval ideas.

By contrast, during the last several decades, many historians of the European explorations have downplayed

Chapter 12

Pagans,

Muslims, and

Christians in the

Mental World

of Columbus

the personal role of Columbus and other early explorers, and focused instead on technological, economic, political, and religious factors, arguing that without these, Columbus's voyages would not have happened. This is part of a more general rejection of what is often termed the "Great Man" school of history, with scholars examining factors other than individual personalities that contributed to major historical changes. In the case of the explorations, historians point to technological changes in the fifteenth and sixteenth centuries, such as improvements in shipbuilding, navigational instruments, and weaponry, that allowed Europeans to carry out the voyages they wished. In Portugal and Spain, the monarchies were gradually building up their authority, taking power away from the feudal nobility. They were developing new tax bases, which brought in steady revenue, and looking for ways to further expand both their wealth and their political power. The Portuguese hoped to reach gold mines in the African interior and find an alternative route for Eastern spices and luxury products, ending the monopoly of Italian merchants, who made enormous profits when they transported Eastern goods across the Mediterranean. In the late fifteenth century, Spain was in the final stages of the *reconquista,* the reconquering of Spain from the Muslims, which had begun centuries earlier. In 1492, under the leadership of King Ferdinand of Aragon and Queen Isabella of Castile, Aragonese and Castilian armies conquered Granada, a small territory in southern Spain that was

the last Muslim holding, and Christian soldiers no longer had a mission on the Spanish mainland.

Historians have concluded that all of these developments set the stage for Portugal and Spain, and religion provided additional motivation. Making contact with the East for spices would not only break the monopoly of Italian merchants, but also allow western Europeans to challenge the Muslims who controlled the spice trade before it reached the Mediterranean. Asia and Africa offered the prospect of millions of people who could be converted to Christianity, and then enlisted to oppose the Muslims. The Ottoman Turks were slowly advancing into Europe, taking Constantinople in 1453 and besieging Vienna half a century later, so that finding allies against Muslim power was becoming even more important in European eyes.

Looking at these factors in hindsight, it does appear that the voyages of Columbus were almost inevitable, and some scholarship pays very little attention to Columbus himself. Other scholars, however, have turned their attention back to Columbus as an individual, arguing that seeing him in context does not mean losing him in that context. These investigations have explored not only the economic, religious, and political setting of Columbus's voyages, but also his own intellectual background. As they have delved deeper into his motivations and ideas, they have discovered that he was influenced not only by his Christian faith and a desire for riches, but also by the works of earlier geographers and travelers, including classical-era pagans and medieval Muslims and Christians. Columbus spent his youth and young manhood in the port cities of Italy and the Iberian peninsula, where he read works of theoretical and practical geography and travel, and talked with sailors, scholars, and ship captains from a wide variety of backgrounds, all of whom had notions of what was to be found beyond the western horizon. Thus, when Columbus left Spain in 1492, he may have sailed off on waters that were unknown to European sailors, but he carried with him a clear idea of what he expected to find, as did other early explorers and the rulers who sent them. His preconceptions, and those of other early explorers, shaped his reactions to the Americas, Africa, and Asia, and the initial reactions of these early explorers in many ways set the patterns for racial and ethnic relations for centuries to come. Therefore, to understand why European exploration and colonization proceeded the way it did, we need to understand not only technological and political factors, but also the mental world of the earliest explorers.

Columbus provides an especially good entry into this, not only because he was regarded as the New World's "discoverer" for so long, but also because he left records of what he was reading and to whom he was talking. Your task in this chapter will be to read Columbus's own writings along with some of the works Columbus read or heard about to answer the following question: How did earlier works of geography and travel shape the mental world of Columbus, and thus influence the "Age of Discovery"?

SOURCES AND METHOD

This chapter focuses on the intellectual history of one individual, a topic that has been prominent in the writing of history for centuries. If you wander through the history, philosophy, and biography sections of any library or bookstore, you will find countless books devoted to "So-and-so's Thought About This" or "The Ideas of So-and-so" or "The Influence of So-and-so on This" (or "on Them"). The authors of these books have generally used the same method you will use in this chapter: careful reading of the writings of their subject. If they are especially interested in exploring the roots of their subject's ideas, intellectual historians and biographers generally start with the person's writings to identify key ideas, then work backwards to try to determine the sources of these notions. They turn to works that the individual is known to have read or possessed, searching through them for ideas that come out later in the writings or actions of the individual. This is exactly what we will be doing in this chapter: starting with Columbus's own words, and then turning to works he identifies as the sources of his ideas or is known to have possessed. Our task will be made easier by the fact that in some cases the actual books that he owned, complete

Chapter 12

Pagans,

Muslims, and

Christians in the

Mental World

of Columbus

with his own marginal notes, still survive. As many intellectual historians do, we will return to his words again at the end, and test our conclusions about his intellectual inheritance.

Source 1 is a letter written by Columbus to the king and queen of Spain in 1492, which serves as the prologue to his journal from his first voyage. The journal was not published during Columbus's lifetime, and the original has disappeared, although we do have an early-sixteenth-century copy by Bartolomé de las Casas, whose father and uncle had sailed with Columbus. Las Casas was one of the first missionaries to the natives of the New World and opposed their treatment at the hands of the Spanish, so there is some question as to whether he might have changed parts of the journal. Source 2 is another letter from Columbus to Ferdinand and Isabella, apparently written in 1501, and also contained in a different document, this time the biography of Columbus written by his son Ferdinand. As with las Casas's copy of Columbus's journal, there is also controversy about this biography, for Ferdinand's original Spanish manuscript has been lost and the first printed version is an Italian translation published in 1571. Most scholars accept that it was actually written by Ferdinand sometime in the 1530s and was based on his father's papers; Ferdinand was a scholar and book collector, and it is his library—now located in Seville—that contained his father's own books. Ferdinand was devoted to his father and also involved in litigation with the Spanish

crown about grants of property promised to his father, so the work highlights Columbus's heroism, but many things that it relates are supported by other sources. Thus, although there are disagreements about certain aspects of the works from which Sources 1 and 2 are taken, most scholars see these letters as authentic.

Read these two sources carefully. In Source 1, what does Columbus say motivated him to sail west? What did he (and Ferdinand and Isabella) expect to find? Why did he go in 1492, as opposed to some other year? In Source 2, to whom does Columbus say he spoke about his interests? What sorts of things did he learn in preparation for his voyage?

Source 3 is a further selection from Ferdinand's biography that describes in greater detail what Columbus was reading and hearing. What were the main ideas Columbus gained from the ancient Greek geographers Ptolemy and Marinus and the medieval Muslim geographer al-Farghani? How are these ideas supported by the other authors he has read, such as Marco Polo and Pierre d'Ailly? What did he learn from talking with Portuguese pilots and other acquaintances? From reading these first three sources, you now have some ideas about what Columbus expected and where his expectations came from.

One of the first actions we as modern historians take in studying any development is weeding out obviously fictitious or mythical material. Though we recognize that views of "the facts" vary greatly from observer to observer, we still attempt to exclude information that is clearly fictitious or impossible, or that sounds suspiciously like a myth created after the events. Modern scholarly biographies of George Washington, for example, do not include the story about him chopping down the cherry tree unless they are discussing the myths that have grown up around Washington. The distinction between fact and fiction is not a particularly useful one as we investigate Columbus's mental world, however, for Columbus and other sixteenth-century explorers read what we now recognize as the reports of mythological travelers just as carefully as they read the reports of real ones. Earlier real travelers were also steeped in the same myths, so that their reports repeat stories that had been told for centuries, often blending these seamlessly with descriptions of events and people that they actually saw. In answering the central question for this chapter, then, we need to take into account all the works that Columbus read or heard about, whether we now regard them as fiction, fact, or a combination of the two. (The dividing line between fact and fiction is often still not clear today, particularly for events for which there is no additional corroboration.) Thus you will need to read the next nine sources carefully, as you flesh out Columbus's mental world.

As is clear from the selections you have read, scholars from classical antiquity were very important to Columbus. Source 4 is a portion of Ptolemy's *Geography,* which was written in Greek in the second century A.D.

Ptolemy's work was unknown in western Europe in the Middle Ages, but this changed in the early fifteenth century when it was translated from Greek into Latin, quickly recopied many times, and by 1465 printed, using the newly developed printing press with movable metal type. Given the respect that Renaissance scholars had for the ancient world, Ptolemy's work quickly acquired the status of a classic, and his text and maps continued to be reprinted even after the Portuguese and Spanish voyages had proved them wrong. On his first voyage, Columbus had a copy of the Rome 1478 edition of Ptolemy's *Geography* in his sea chest. Source 5 is a brief selection from the *Natural History* of the first-century Roman official Pliny, the most popular Roman writer on natural phenomena. His work was frequently recopied throughout the Middle Ages and was printed in the fifteenth century; Columbus owned an Italian translation that had been printed in Venice in 1489. Read these selections carefully. How much of the globe in terms of longitude does Ptolemy propose is contained in the "known world," that is, Eurasia? What is the estimation of Marinus? What assurances does Ptolemy give his readers that his work is accurate? Conversely, how does he explain observations that might not match his? The selections from Pliny describe various peoples he has heard about in Asia. What physical and behavioral traits does he report?

As we saw in Sources 1 and 3, Columbus also studied the work of Muslim scholars and geographers,

Chapter 12

Pagans,

Muslims, and

Christians in the

Mental World

of Columbus

either in Latin translations or by talking with people who read and spoke Arabic. He took individuals who spoke Arabic on both his first and fourth voyages, assuming that they would have more luck communicating with the residents of the Indies and the great khan than those who spoke only European languages. Sources 6 and 7 are selections from medieval Muslim scholars: Source 6 is from the *Geography* of Abu Abdallah Mohammed Idrisi (1100–1166), who worked for many years as a geographer and cartographer at the court of King Roger II of Sicily, and Source 7 is from the enormous work of the scholar Ibn Fadl Allah al'Umari (d. 1358), the *Masalik al-Absar*. In Source 6, Idrisi describes several islands in the Atlantic off the coasts of Portugal and north Africa, and reports what some sailors who had set out sailing west from Lisbon said they had found. In Source 7, al'Umari reports what he was told the fourteenth-century Berber sultan of Mali, Mansa Musa, reported when talking with Egyptian officials while on his way to Mecca. Read these accounts carefully. What does Idrisi relate about the inhabitants of various Atlantic islands? What do the Maghrourins in Source 6 and the ship captain in Source 7 report that they have found? How might these accounts have contributed to Columbus's desire to sail westward, as well as shaping his expectations?

During the thirteenth century, the Mongols under Genghis and then Kublai Khan controlled an enormous empire stretching from eastern Europe to the Pacific. They welcomed trade and established enough order so that travelers could generally proceed safely, and large numbers of merchants, missionaries, and ambassadors crossed the Mongol Empire regularly. The next three sources all stem from this period of *Pax Mongolica* (Mongol Peace). Source 8 is an extract from a letter from John of Monte Corvino (1247–1328), a western Christian friar sent by the pope to the Mongols. John stayed for a long time as a missionary and wrote three letters back to members of his religious order, the Franciscans, asking for their support. Source 9 is a short part of *The Travels of Marco Polo* (ca 1253–1324). Polo was a Venetian merchant who apparently spent twenty years in Asia and often acted as a representative for Kublai Khan. His work was written, with the help of a writer of romance stories, shortly after he returned to Europe, and was widely translated, copied, and then published. Source 10 is from a work entitled *The Travels of Sir John Mandeville*, purportedly written by an English knight who traveled from Europe to Asia in the mid-fourteenth century. Mandeville claimed to have served the sultan of Egypt and the Mongol khan, but it is now believed that the work was largely fictional, based on Polo's reports, stories that dated back to Alexander the Great's eastern conquests, and Pliny's *Natural History*. Though its veracity is now questioned, in the fourteenth century it was not, and it was translated from the French in which it was originally written into every European language. Of these three, Columbus would have known about

John of Monte Corvino indirectly, and about Polo and Mandeville by reading their works: Columbus's own copy of Polo's book survives, with extensive notes in the margins in his own hand. Read these selections, which describe societies in central and southeast Asia. How does John of Monte Corvino describe his efforts at converting the residents of China? What else does he report about the realm of the khan? What do Polo and Mandeville both think is most important to report? How does their reaction to the people they describe differ from their reaction to the natural products of these areas?

Columbus was not the only person in fifteenth-century Europe who was speculating about traveling west and reading widely in geography and travel literature. Pierre d'Ailly, the bishop of Cambrai and chancellor at the University of Paris, relied on the works of ancient authors as well as medieval Muslims and Christians when writing his *Imago Mundi* in 1410, an encyclopedic account of the inhabitants of the world, of which Source 11 is a brief extract. Columbus made over 900 annotations in his copy, which was a Latin version printed in 1485. Paolo dal Pozzo Toscanelli was a physician, astronomer, and humanist who in 1474 sent a letter and world map to a cleric friend in Lisbon, and in 1481 sent a copy of these to Columbus. The map has been lost, but the letter survives, and is reprinted here as Source 12. Read both of these sources carefully. What geographical information do they contain? What do they report about the inhabitants of the western (or eastern) islands?

About the natural products of these places? What authorities do the authors rely on for their information?

Columbus's mental world was shaped not only by words, but also by visual images, particularly those contained on maps; as you read in Source 1, one of his goals was to "make a new chart for navigation . . . and show everything by means of drawing." None of Columbus's actual maps survive, but we have a good idea of what they were, as maps were often included with the books he read, and other contemporary maps have survived. Sources 13 and 14 are two maps from the fifteenth century. Source 13 is a world map from the edition of Ptolemy's *Geography* that Columbus owned—with Ptolemy's calculation of 177 degrees of longitude in the "known earth"; Source 14 is a sailor's chart of the islands of the Atlantic drawn in 1455 in Genoa, Columbus's home town. On these maps you can see many of the islands referred to in the written sources—the Fortunate Isles (labeled on Source 14 as the "Insulle Fortunate Sanct Brandanus" after the sixth-century Irish monk St. Brendan, who according to legend first discovered them), the Canaries (on the bottom of Source 14), the Madeira group (in the middle of Source 14 with each island named, including Porto Santo), the Azores (labeled "Insulla de ventura" on Source 14), and Taprobane near India on Source 13. (The Portuguese had reached Madeira and the Canaries in the fourteenth century, and the Azores in the early fifteenth; these island groups appear on medieval Muslim maps as well.)

Chapter 12

Pagans,

Muslims, and

Christians in the

Mental World

of Columbus

Source 14 also shows the large (and nonexistent) island of Antillia past the Azores, for which a Portuguese expedition set out in 1487. How would these maps have reinforced the ideas that Columbus gained through reading and conversation?

For the final reading in this chapter, we return to Columbus himself. Source 15 is a letter describing Columbus's first voyage, written while he was stopping near the Azores on his return from this voyage, and sent from Lisbon so that it would arrive at the court of Ferdinand and Isabella right before he got there. It was published in Spanish, the language in which he wrote, in 1493, translated into Latin and published in many editions in that language, and then translated into other European languages, including a rhymed version in Italian. It thus became very widely known, and formed the basis of many people's first impressions of the "New World."[1]

How do his descriptions of the natural features of the landscape reflect the things he had read? What natural products does he describe, and what does he promise Ferdinand and Isabella in terms of natural resources? What does he seem to have expected in terms of people, and how do his actual encounters fit with these expectations?

---

1. Columbus himself did not use the phrase "New World" until his discovery of the coast of South America on his third voyage in 1498.

At that point, he noted that he had found a "very great continent . . . until today unknown," and wrote that God had made him "the messenger of the new world." He still thought this new continent was off the coast of Asia, however, and on his fourth voyage, along the coast of Central America, he assumed that he was in Indochina and close to India. The phrase "New World" began to show up on world maps around 1505. Shortly after that, the word "America" also appeared, based on the name of Amerigo Vespucci, an Italian explorer-navigator who the German mapmaker Martin Waldseemüller mistakenly thought had discovered America. Waldseemüller commented that it was especially appropriate that America be named after a man, as both Europe and Asia had been named after demigoddesses. By 1513 Waldseemüller knew that he had been wrong and wanted to omit "America" from future maps, but the name had already stuck.

Source 1 from John Boyd Thacher, Christopher Columbus: His Life, His Work, His Remains *(New York: Kraus Reprints, 1967), vol. I, pp. 513–515. Reprinted by permission.*

1. Prologue to the Journal of Christopher Columbus (1492)

PROLOGUE

Because, most Christian and very exalted and very excellent and very powerful Princes, King and Queen of the Spains and of the Islands of the Sea, our Lords, in this present year of 1492 after your Highnesses had made an end to the war of the Moors, who were reigning in Europe, and having finished the war in the very great city of Granada, where in this present year on the 2nd day of the month of January, I saw the Royal banners of your Highnesses placed by force of arms on the towers of the Alhambra, which is the fortress of the said City: and I saw the Moorish King come out to the gates of the City and kiss the Royal hands of your Highnesses, and the hands of the Prince, my Lord: and then in that present month, because of the information which I had given your Highnesses about the lands of India, and about a Prince who is called Great Khan, which means in our Romance language, King of Kings,—how he and his predecessors had many times sent to Rome to beg for men learned in our Holy Faith that they might be instructed therein, and that the Holy Father had never furnished them, and so, many peoples believing in idolatries and receiving among themselves sects of perdition, were lost:—your Highnesses, as Catholic Christians and Princes, loving the Holy Christian faith and the spreading of it, and enemies of the sect of Mahomet and of all idolatries and heresies, decided to send me, Christopher Columbus, to the said regions of India, to see the said Princes and the peoples and lands, and learn of their disposition, and of everything, and the measures which could be taken for their conversion of our Holy Faith: and you ordered that I should not go to the east by land, by which it is customary to go, but by way of the west, whence until to-day we do not know certainly that any one has gone. So that, after having banished all the Jews from all your Kingdoms and realms,[2] in the same month of January, your Highnesses ordered me to go with a sufficient fleet to the said regions of India: and for that purpose granted me great favours and ennobled me, that from then henceforward I might entitle myself *Don* and should be High Admiral of the Ocean-Sea [*Atlantic*—Ed.] and Viceroy and perpetual Governor of all the

---

2. In January 1492, Ferdinand and Isabella issued a royal edict expelling all practicing Jews from Spain in their attempts to achieve total religious orthodoxy.

Chapter 12

Pagans,

Muslims, and

Christians in the

Mental World

of Columbus

islands and continental land which I might discover and acquire, and which from now henceforward might be discovered and acquired in the Ocean-Sea, and that my eldest son should succeed in the same manner, and thus from generation to generation for ever after. . . . Also, Lords and Princes, besides describing each night what takes place during the day, and during the day, the sailings of the night, I propose to make a new chart for navigation, on which I will locate all the sea and the lands of the Ocean-Sea, in their proper places, under their winds; and further, to compose a book and show everything by means of drawing, by the latitude from the equator and by longitude from the west, and above all, it is fitting that I forget sleep, and study the navigation diligently, in order to thus fulfil these duties, which will be a great labour.

Sources 2 and 3 from The Life of the Admiral Christopher Columbus by His Son Ferdinand, *translated and annotated by Benjamin Keen (New Brunswick, N.J.: Rutgers University Press, 1958), p. 10; pp. 15–18, 23, 24. Copyright © 1959, 1992 by Rutgers, The State University. Reprinted by permission of Rutgers University Press.*

2. Letter from Christopher Columbus to Ferdinand and Isabella (1501)

Very High Kings:[3]

From a very young age I began to follow the sea and have continued to do so to this day. This art of navigation incites those who pursue it to inquire into the secrets of this world. I have passed more than forty years in this business and have traveled to every place where there is navigation up to the present time. I have had dealings and conversation with learned men, priests, and laymen, Latins and Greeks, Jews and Moors, and many others of other sects. I found Our Lord very favorable to this my desire, and to further it He granted me the gift of knowledge. He made me skilled in seamanship, equipped me abundantly with the sciences of astronomy, geometry, and arithmetic, and taught my mind and hand to draw this sphere and upon it the cities, rivers, mountains, islands, and ports, each in its proper place. During this time I have made it my business to read all that has been written on geography, history, philosophy, and other sciences. Thus Our Lord revealed to me that it was feasible to sail from here to the Indies, and placed in me a burning desire to carry out this plan. Filled with this fire, I came to Your Highnesses. All who knew of my enterprise rejected it with laughter and mockery. They would not heed the arguments I set forth or the authorities I cited. Only Your Highnesses had faith and confidence in me.

3. Both Isabella and Ferdinand were rulers in their own right, Isabella of Castile and Ferdinand of Aragon, so that Columbus refers to them both here as "kings."

3. From *The Life of the Admiral Christopher Columbus by His Son Ferdinand*

Turning to the reasons which persuaded the Admiral to undertake the discovery of the Indies, I say there were three, namely, natural reasons, the authority of writers, and the testimony of sailors. With respect to the first—the natural reasons—he believed that since all the water and land in the world form a sphere, it would be possible to go around it from east to west until men stood feet to feet, one against the other, at opposite ends of the earth. In the second place, he assumed and knew on the authority of approved writers that a large part of this sphere had already been navigated and that there remained to be discovered only the space which extended from the eastern end of India, known to Ptolemy and Marinus,[4] eastward to the Cape Verde and Azore Islands, the westernmost land discovered up to that time. Thirdly, he believed that this space between the eastern end, known to Marinus, and the said Cape Verde Islands could not be more than the third part of the great circle of the sphere, because Marinus had already described in the East fifteen of the twenty-four [astronomical] hours or parts into which the world is divided; therefore, to reach the Cape Verdes barely required eight more hours, since even Marinus did not begin his description very far to the West. . . .

The fifth argument, which gave the greatest support to the view that this space was small, was the opinion of Alfragan,[5] and his followers, who assign a much smaller size to the earth than all the other writers and geographers, calculating a degree to be only 56⅔ miles;[6] whence the Admiral inferred that since the whole sphere was small, of necessity that space of the third part which Marinus left as unknown had to be small and therefore could be navigated in less time. From this he also inferred that since the eastern end of India was not yet known, that end must be the one which is close to us in the West; therefore any lands that he should discover might be called the Indies. . . .

The second reason that inspired the Admiral to launch his enterprise and helped justify his giving the name "Indies" to the lands which he discovered was the authority of many learned men who said that one could sail westward from the western end of Africa and Spain to the eastern end of India,

4. For Ptolemy, see Source 4. Marinus of Tyre was a Greek geographer of the second century A.D.

5. Alfragan (al-Farghani) was a Muslim astronomer and geographer from the end of the eighth century.

6. Alfragan was reckoning in Arabic miles of 2,164 meters; this works out to 66 nautical miles per degree.

Chapter 12

Pagans,

Muslims, and

Christians in the

Mental World

of Columbus

and that no great sea lay between. . . . Pliny, in the second book of his *Natural History*, Chapter 3, also says that the ocean surrounds the whole earth and that its length from east to west is that from India to Cádiz. . . .

Marco Polo, a Venetian, and John Mandeville tell in their travel accounts that they journeyed far beyond the eastern lands described by Ptolemy and Marinus; they do not speak of the Western Sea, but from their description of the East it could be argued that India neighbors on Africa and Spain. Pierre d'Ailly, in Chapter 8 "Concerning the Size of the Habitable Earth," of his treatise *Concerning the Form of the World,* and Julius Capitolinus,[7] in *Concerning the Habitable Places* and many other treatises, say that India and Spain are near each other in the West.

The Admiral's third and last motive for seeking the Indies was his hope of finding before he arrived there some island or land of great importance whence he might the better pursue his main design. He found support for this hope in the authority of many learned men and philosophers who were certain that the land area of the globe was greater than that of the water. This being so, he argued that between the end of Spain and the known end of India there must be many other islands and lands, as experience has since shown to be true.

He believed this all the more because he was impressed by the many fables and stories which he heard from various persons and sailors who traded to the western islands and seas of the Azores and Madeira. Since these stories served his design, he was careful to file them away in his memory. I shall tell them here in order to satisfy those who take delight in such curiosities.

A pilot of the Portuguese King, Martín Vicente by name, told him that on one occasion, finding himself four hundred and fifty leagues[8] west of Cape St. Vincent,[9] he fished out of the sea a piece of wood ingeniously carved, but not with iron. For this reason and because for many days the winds had blown from the west, he concluded this wood came from some islands to the west.

Pedro Correa, who was married to a sister of the Admiral's wife, told him that on the island of Pôrto Santo[10] he had seen another piece of wood brought by the same wind, carved as well as the aforementioned one, and that canes had also drifted in, so thick that one joint held nine decanters of wine. He said that in conversation with the Portuguese King he had told him the same thing and had shown him the canes. Since such canes do not grow anywhere in our lands, he was sure that the wind had blown them from some neighboring

---

7. For Pliny, see Source 5; for Marco Polo, Source 9; for John Mandeville, Source 10; and for Pierre d'Ailly, Source 11. Julius Capitolinus was a Roman writer of about A.D. 300.

8. **league:** usually around 3 nautical miles, though its exact distance has varied.

9. Cape St. Vincent is the southwest corner of Portugal.

10. Pôrto Santo is one of the islands of Madeira.

islands or perhaps from India. Ptolemy in the first book of his *Geography*, Chapter 17, writes that such canes are found in the eastern parts of the Indies.

Source 4 from Geography of Claudius Ptolemy, *translated and edited by Edward Luther Stevenson (New York: New York Public Library, 1932), extracts from chapters 3, 5, 6, 12. Courtesy of The New York Public Library, Astor, Lenox and Tilden Foundations. Used by permission of The New York Public Library.*

4. From Ptolemy's *Geography*

Those geographers who lived before us sought to fix correct distance on the earth, not only that they might determine the length of the greatest circle, but also that they might determine the extent which a region occupied in one plane on one and the same meridian. After observing therefore, by means of the instruments of which I have spoken, the points which were directly over each terminus of the given distance, they calculated from the intercepted part of the circumference of the meridian, distances on the earth.

[*Ptolemy then describes various instruments for measuring shadows, and notes how one uses measurements of the shadows at different points on the earth's surface to calculate the circumference of the earth. This method was first devised by Eratosthenes (ca 275–195 B.C.), librarian of the Museum of Alexandria and the first in the West to write a book titled "Geography."*]

After these preliminary remarks we are able to make a beginning of our work. Since, however, all regions cannot be known fully on account of their great size, or because they are not always of the same shape or because not yet satisfactorily explored, and a greater length of time makes our knowledge of them more certain, we think we should say something to the readers of our geography on the subject of varying traditions at various times, viz., of some portions of our continents, on account of their great size, we have as yet no knowledge; with regard to other parts we do not know what is their real nature, because of the negligence of those who have explored them in failing to give us carefully prepared reports; other parts of the earth are different to-day from what they were, either on account of revolution or from transformation, in which processes they are known to have partially passed into ruin.

We consider it necessary therefore for us to pay more attention to the newer records of our own time, weighing, however, in our description these new records and those of former times and deciding what is credible and what is incredible.

Marinus the Tyrian, the latest of the geographers of our time, seems to us to have thrown himself with the utmost zeal into this matter.

He is known to have found out many things that were not known before. He has searched most diligently the works of almost all the historians who

[283]

Chapter 12

Pagans,

Muslims, and

Christians in the

Mental World

of Columbus

preceded him. He has not only corrected their errors, but the reader can clearly see that he has undertaken to correct those parts of the work which he himself had done badly in the earlier editions of his geographical maps. . . .

[However,] He considers that our earth[11] extends a greater distance in longitude eastward, and to a greater distance in latitude southward than is right and true.

[Marinus had proposed that the Eurasian land mass extended 225°, but Ptolemy arrives at a different figure.]

. . . Hence, the length of the known earth, that is, from the meridian drawn through or terminated by the Fortunate Islands[12] in the extreme west, to Sera[13] in the extreme east is 177°15'.

Source 5 from Pliny, Natural History, *translated by H. Rackham. Loeb Classical Library (Cambridge, Mass.: Harvard University Press, 1938), vol. 2, pp. 377, 521.*

5. From Pliny, *Natural History*

After leaving the Caspian Sea and the Scythian Ocean our course takes a bend towards the Eastern Sea as the coast turns to face eastward. The first part of the coast after the Scythian promontory is uninhabitable on account of snow, and the neighbouring region is uncultivated because of the savagery of the tribes that inhabit it. This is the country of the Cannibal Scythians who eat human bodies; consequently the adjacent districts are waste deserts thronging with wild beasts lying in wait for human beings as savage as themselves. . . . Megasthenes[14] states that on the mountain named Nulus there are people with their feet turned backwards and with eight toes on each foot, while on many of the mountains there is a tribe of human beings with dogs' heads, who wear a covering of wild beasts' skins, whose speech is a bark and who live on the produce of hunting and fowling, for which they use their nails as weapons; he says that they numbered more than 120,000 when he published his work. Ctesias[15] writes that also among a certain race of India the women bear children only once in their life-time, and the children begin to turn grey directly after birth; he also describes a tribe of men called the

11. By "our earth" Ptolemy means the land mass of the world known to him, that is, Eurasia and Africa.

12. **Fortunate Islands:** the name given to various Atlantic Island groups. Here, probably the Canaries.

13. **Sera:** probably Seram (Ceram), an island in Indonesia.

14. Megasthenes was sent as an envoy to an Indian ruler by the ruler of Syria in about 300 B.C. His report survived, in fragments, to Pliny's time.

15. Ctesias was a Greek physician and historian of Persia and India who lived about 400 B.C.

Monocoli who have only one leg, and who move in jumps with surprising speed; the same are called the Umbrella-foot tribe, because in the hotter weather they lie on their backs on the ground and protect themselves with the shadow of their feet; and that they are not far away from the Cave-dwellers; and again westward from these there are some people without necks, having their eyes in their shoulders.

Source 6 from Pierre-Amédée Jaubert, La Géographie d'Édrisi, *translated from Arabic (Amsterdam: Philo Press, 1975), 3rd climate, 1st section, pp. 200–201; 4th climate, 1st section, pp. 26–29. English translation by Julius Ruff.*

6. From Abu Abdallah Mohammed Idrisi, *Geography*

In the same sea there is the Island of Calhan, the inhabitants of which are human in form but bear animal heads. They plunge into the sea, draw out of its depths the animals that they were able to catch, and then feed on them. Another island of the same sea is named the Island of the Two Magician Brothers. . . . It lies opposite the port of Asafi[16] and at such a distance that, when the atmosphere is free of mist over the sea, it is said that from the continent one can catch sight of the smoke that rises from the island. . . . "Curious details relative to this island were gathered from the words of the Maghrourins,[17] travelers from the town of Achbouna (Lisbon) in Spain when the port of Asafi received this name because of them. The account of this adventure is rather long, and we will have the opportunity to return to it when Lisbon is our subject."

In this sea there also lies an island of vast extent covered with thick darkness. It is named the Island of Sheep because there are indeed many of them there. But the flesh of these animals is so bitter that it is impossible to eat it, if we give credit to the account of the Maghrourins. Near the island that we have just mentioned there is Raca, the island of the birds.[18] . . .

It was from Lisbon that the Maghrourins' expedition departed "having the objective to know what comprises the ocean and what its limits are." As we said above, there still exists a street bearing the name Maghrourin Street (or Road) in Lisbon near the hot baths.

Here is how the thing came about. Eight close relatives got together and built a transport ship into which they loaded water and provisions sufficient for a voyage of several months. They set forth on the sea at the first east breeze.

16. **Asafi:** the town of Safi, on the west coast of present-day Morocco.
17. **Maghrourins:** the word means "adventurers."
18. Perhaps one of the Canary Islands.

Chapter 12

Pagans,

Muslims, and

Christians in the

Mental World

of Columbus

After having sailed for about eleven days, they reached a poorly-illuminated sea in which heavy waves emitted a rank odor and concealed numerous reefs. Fearing destruction, they changed the direction of their sails and hastened south for twelve days and reached the Island of Sheep, thus named because numerous flocks of sheep graze there without shepherds or anyone to guard them.

Having landed on this island, they found there a spring of flowing water and wild fig-trees. They caught and killed some sheep, but the flesh of them was so bitter that it was impossible to feed on it. They only kept the skins, sailed again twelve days, and finally caught sight of an island that seemed inhabited and cultivated. They approached it in order to learn what it was but were soon surrounded by boats, made prisoners, and led to a town situated on the seashore. They entered a house where they saw men of great height, swarthy, and of reddish color, wearing long hair, and women who were of a rare beauty. They remained three days in this house. On the fourth day they saw a man arrive who spoke the Arab language and who asked them who they were, why they had come, and what was their country. They told him all of their adventures; the latter gave them good hope and told them he was an interpreter. Two days later they were presented to the king of the land who asked them the same questions, to which they replied, as they had already replied to the interpreter, that they had ventured forth on the sea in order to learn what was strange and curious in it and to ascertain its extreme limits.

When the king heard them thus speak, he began to laugh and said to the interpreter: Explain to these people that once upon a time my father ordered some of his slaves to embark on this sea and that they traversed its breadth for a month until, the sky's light having entirely failed them, they were forced to give up this vain undertaking. The king, moreover, ordered the interpreter to assure the Maghrourins of his goodwill so that they might hold a good opinion of him, which was done. They then returned to their prison and remained there until a west wind arose and their captors blindfolded them, made them board a boat, and had them row for some time on the sea. We sailed, they said, for nearly three days and three nights and we reached a shore where they landed us, with our hands bound behind our backs, and where we were abandoned. We remained there until sunrise in the most dejected state because of the bonds which strongly tied us and which much troubled us. Finally, having heard bursts of laughter and human voices, we began to utter cries. Then some inhabitants of the country came to us and, finding us in such a miserable situation, talked with us and posed various questions to which we replied with the tale of our adventure. They were Berbers. One of them said to us: Do you know how far you are from your own country? Upon our negative reply, he added: It is a two-month journey from the spot where you find yourselves to your native land. Those among these individuals who seemed the most eminent said unceasingly: Wasafi (Alas!). This is why the name of the place is today still Asafi. It is the port that we have already described as being at the end of the west.

Source 7 from Ibn Fadl Allah al'Umari, Masalik al-Absar, *manuscript in Cairo MS. English translation in Abbas Hamdani, "An Islamic Background to the Voyages of Discovery," in Salma Khadra Jayyusi,* The Legacy of Muslim Spain *(Leiden: E.J. Brill, 1992), p. 276. Reprinted by permission of Abbas Hamdani.*

7. From Ibn Fadl Allah al'Umari, *Masalik al-Absar*

The ruler who preceded me did not believe it was impossible to reach the extremity of the ocean that encircles the earth [here meaning the Atlantic]; he wanted to reach that [end], and was determined to pursue his plan. So he equipped two hundred boats full of men, and many others with water, gold and provisions, sufficient for several years. He ordered the captain not to return until he had reached the other end of the ocean, or until he had exhausted the provisions and water. So they set out on their journey. They were absent for a long period, and at last just one boat returned. When questioned, the captain replied: "O Prince, we navigated for a long period, until we saw in the midst of the ocean a great river which flowed massively. My boat was the last one; others were ahead of me, and they were drowned in the great whirlpool and never came out again. I sailed back to escape this current."[19] But the Sultan would not believe him. He ordered two thousand boats to be equipped for him and for his men, and one thousand more for water and provisions. Then he conferred the regency on me for the term of his absence and departed with his men, never to return or show any sign of life. In this manner I became the sole ruler of the empire.

Source 8 from Henry Yule, editor and translator, H. Cordier, reviser of 2d ed., Cathay and the Way Thither *(London: Hakluyt Society, 1913–1916), vol. III, pp. 45–51. Notes from A. Andrea and J. Overfield,* The Human Record *(Boston: Houghton Mifflin, 1990), pp. 350–352. Copyright © 1990 by Houghton Mifflin Company. Used by permission.*

8. Letter of John of Monte Corvino

I, Friar John of Monte Corvino, of the order of Minor Friars,[20] departed from Tauris, a city of the Persians,[21] in the year of the Lord 1291, and proceeded to

19. A number of historians have concluded that this river was the Amazon in Brazil, as ocean currents in this region can carry ships across the Atlantic.
20. **Minor Friars:** the "lesser brethren," the official name of the Franciscans.
21. Tauris (modern Tabriz, Iran) was the capital city of the il-khan of Persia.

Chapter 12

Pagans,

Muslims, and

Christians in the

Mental World

of Columbus

India. And I remained in the country of India, wherein stands the church of St. Thomas the Apostle, for thirteen months, and in that region baptized in different places about one hundred persons. The companion of my journey was Friar Nicholas of Pistoia, of the order of Preachers[22] who died there, and was buried in the church aforesaid.

I proceeded on my further journey and made my way to Cathay, the realm of the Emperor of the Tatars[23] who is called the Grand Cham.[24] To him I presented the letter of our Lord the Pope, and invited him to adopt the Catholic Faith of our Lord Jesus Christ, but he had grown too old in idolatry. However he bestows many kindnesses upon the Christians, and these two years past I am abiding with him. . . .

I have built a church in the city of Cambaliech,[25] in which the king has his chief residence. This I completed six years ago; and I have built a belltower to it, and put three bells in it. I have baptized there, as well as I can estimate, up to this time some 6,000 persons; and if those charges against me of which I have spoken had not been made, I should have baptized more than 30,000. And I am often still engaged in baptizing.

Also I have gradually bought one hundred and fifty boys, the children of pagan parents, and of ages varying from seven to eleven, who had never learned any religion. These boys I have baptized, and I have taught them Greek and Latin after our manner. Also I have written out Psalters for them, with thirty Hymnaries and two Breviaries.[26] By help of these, eleven of the boys already know our service, and form a choir and take their weekly turn of duty as they do in convents, whether I am there or not. Many of the boys are also employed in writing out Psalters and other things suitable. His Majesty the Emperor moreover delights much to hear them chanting. I have the bells rung at all the canonical hours, and with my congregation of babes and sucklings I perform divine service, and the chanting we do by ear because I have no service book with the notes.

A certain king of this part of the world, by name George, belonging to the sect of Nestorian Christians,[27] and of the illustrious family of that great king

---

22. Also known as the Dominicans.

23. **Emperor of the Tatars:** Timur (1294–1307). Although Western visitors used the names Tatar (or, incorrectly, Tartar) and Mongol interchangeably, the Tatars, who spoke a Turkic language, were not Mongols. There was, however, some intermarriage among these various steppe nomads. For example, the Turkish warlord Timur the Lame (1336–1405) had some Mongol ancestry.

24. More often spelled "khan."

25. **Cambaliech:** Khanbalik.

26. Various prayer books.

27. **Nestorian Christians:** followers of Nestorius, a fifth-century Christian leader who held ideas about the relationship between the divine and human natures of Jesus Christ that differed from those held by a majority of church leaders. Nestorius's ideas were declared to be heresy, but they were accepted by many Christians in Iraq, Iran, and India. Nestorian Christians today number around 100,000, many of whom are in the United States.

who was called Prester John[28] of India, in the first year of my arrival here attached himself to me, and being converted by me to the truth of the Catholic faith, took the lesser orders,[29] and when I celebrated mass he used to attend me wearing his royal robes. Certain others of the Nestorians on this account accused him of apostasy, but he brought over a great part of his people with him to the true Catholic faith, and built a church on a scale of royal magnificence in honor of our God, of the Holy Trinity, and of our lord the Pope, giving it the name of the *Roman Church.*

This King George six years ago departed to the Lord a true Christian, leaving as his heir a son scarcely out of the cradle, and who is now nine years old. And after King George's death his brothers, perfidious followers of the errors of Nestorius, perverted again all those whom he had brought over to the church, and carried them back to their original schismatical creed. And being all alone, and not able to leave his Majesty the Cham, I could not go to visit the church above-mentioned, which is twenty days' journey distant.

Yet, if I could but get some good fellow-workers to help me, I trust in God that all this might be retrieved, for I still possess the grant which was made in our favor by the late King George before mentioned. So I say again that if it had not been for the slanderous charges which I have spoken of, the harvest reaped by this time would have been great!

Indeed if I had had but two or three comrades to aid me 'tis possible that the Emperor Cham would have been baptized by this time! I ask then for such brethren to come, if any are willing to come, such I mean as will make it their great business to lead exemplary lives. . . .

I have myself grown old and grey, more with toil and trouble than with years; for I am not more than fifty-eight. I have got a competent knowledge of the language and character which is most generally used by the Tatars. And I have already translated into that language and character the New Testament and the Psalter, and have caused them to be written out in the fairest penmanship they have; and so by writing, reading, and preaching, I bear open and public testimony to the Law of Christ. And I had been in treaty with the late King George, if he had lived, to translate the whole Latin ritual, that it might be sung throughout the whole extent of his territory; and whilst he was alive I used to celebrate mass in his church, according to the Latin ritual, reading in the before-mentioned language and character the words of both the preface and the Canon.[30]

And the son of the king before-mentioned is called after my name, John; and I hope in God that he will walk in his father's steps.

---

28. **Prester John:** a mythic Christian king of the East, who supposedly sought reunion with the West. His kingdom was variously located in Ethiopia, India, and Central Asia, all of which had Christian communities long separated from the West.

29. He was admitted to the four lesser clerical offices below those of priest, deacon, and subdeacon.

30. **preface and canon:** two parts of the Mass.

Chapter 12

Pagans,

Muslims, and

Christians in the

Mental World

of Columbus

As far as I ever saw or heard tell, I do not believe that any king or prince in the world can be compared to his majesty the Cham in respect to the extent of his dominions, the vastness of their population, or the amount of his wealth. Here I stop.

Dated at the city of Cambalec in the kingdom of Cathay, in the year of the Lord 1305, and on the 8th day of January.

Source 9 from Manuel Komroff, The Travels of Marco Polo *(New York: The Modern Library, 1953), pp. 259–260, 263, 267, 274, 280, 281–282, 289–290, 303–304. Copyright 1926 by Boni & Liveright, Inc., renewed 1953 by Manuel Komroff. Copyright 1930 by Horace Liveright, Inc., renewed © 1958 by Manuel Komroff. Reprinted by permission of Liveright Publishing Corporation.*

9. From *The Travels of Marco Polo*

Zipangu [Japan] is an island in the eastern ocean, situated at the distance of about fifteen hundred miles from the main-land, or coast of Manji.

It is of considerable size; its inhabitants have fair complexions, are well made, and are civilized in their manners. Their religion is the worship of idols. They are independent of every foreign power, and governed only by their own kings. They have gold in the greatest abundance, its sources being inexhaustible, but as the king does not allow it being exported, few merchants visit the country. Nor is it frequented by much shipping from other parts.

The extraordinary richness of the sovereign's palace, according to what we are told by those who have access to the place, is a wonderful sight. The entire roof is covered with a plating of gold, in the same manner as we cover houses, or more properly churches, with lead. The ceilings of the halls are of the same precious metal; many of the apartments have small tables of pure gold, of considerable thickness; and the windows also have golden ornaments. So vast, indeed, are the riches of the palace, that it is impossible to convey an idea of them.

In this island there are pearls also, in large quantities, of a pink colour, round in shape, and of great size equal in value to, or even exceeding that of the white pearls. . . .

In this island of Zipangu and the others in its vicinity, their idols are fashioned in a variety of shapes, some of them having the heads of oxen, some of swine, of dogs, goats, and many other animals. . . .

The various ceremonies practiced before these idols are so wicked and diabolical that it would be nothing less than an abomination to give an account of them in this book. The reader should, however, be informed that the idolatrous inhabitants of these islands, when they seize the person of an enemy who has not the means of effecting his ransom for money, invite to their house all their relations and friends. Putting their prisoner to death they cook and eat the body, in a convivial manner, asserting that human flesh surpasses every other in the excellence of its flavour. . . .

Departing from Ziamba, and steering between south and south-east, fifteen hundred miles, you reach an island of very great size, named Java. According to the reports of some well-informed navigators, it is the greatest in the world, and has a compass above three thousand miles. It is under the dominion of one king only, nor do the inhabitants pay tribute to any other power. They are worshippers of idols.

The country abounds with rich commodities. Pepper, nutmegs, spikenard, galangal, cubebs, cloves and all the other valuable spices and drugs, are the produce of the island; which occasion it to be visited by many ships laden with merchandise, that yields to the owners considerable profit.

The quantity of gold collected there exceeds all calculation and belief. . . .

In this kingdom are found men with tails, a span[31] in length, like those of the dog, but not covered with hair. The greater number of them are formed in this manner, but they dwell in the mountains, and do not inhabit towns. . . .

Leaving the island of Zeilan,[32] and sailing in a westerly direction sixty miles, you reach the great province of Maabar, which is not an island, but a part of the continent of the greater India, as it is termed, being the noblest and richest country in the world.

The natives of this part of the country always go naked, excepting that they cover with a piece of cloth those parts of the body which modesty dictates.

The king is no more clothed than the rest, except that he has a piece of richer cloth, and is honourably distinguished by various kinds of ornaments, such as a collar set with jewels, sapphires, emeralds, and rubies, of immense value. . . .

Distant from Kesmacoran about five hundred miles toward the south, in the ocean, there are two islands within about thirty miles from each other. One of these is inhabited by men, without the company of women, and is called Island of Males; and the other by women, without men, which is called the Island of Females.

The inhabitants of both are of the same race, and are baptized Christians, but hold the law of the Old Testament. The men visit the Island of Females, and remain with them for three successive months, namely, March, April, and May, each man occupying a separate habitation along with his wife. They then return to the male island, where they live the rest of the year, without the society of any female.

The wives retain their sons with them until they are of the age of twelve years, when they are sent to join their fathers. The daughters they keep at

31. **span:** nine inches.
32. **Zeilan:** Ceylon.

Chapter 12

Pagans,

Muslims, and

Christians in the

Mental World

of Columbus

home until they become marriageable, and then they bestow them upon some of the men of the other island.

Source 10 from The Travels of Sir John Mandeville *(London: Macmillan, 1905), pp. 103–104, 125–130.*

10. **From** *The Travels of Sir John Mandeville*

Beside that isle that I have spoken of, there is another isle that is clept[33] Sumobor. That is a great isle, and the king thereof is right mighty. The folk of that isle make them always to be marked in the visage[34] with an hot iron, both men and women, for great noblesse, for to be known from other folk; for they hold themselves most noble and most worthy of all the world. And they have war always with the folk that go all naked.

And fast beside is another isle, that is clept Betemga, that is a good isle and a plenteous. And many other isles be thereabout, where there be many of diverse folk, of the which it were too long to speak of all.

But fast beside that isle, for to pass by sea, is a great isle and a great country that men clepe Java. And it is nigh two thousand mile in circuit. And the king of that country is a full great lord and a rich and a mighty, and hath under him seven other kings of seven other isles about him. This isle is full well inhabited and full well manned. There grow all manner of spicery, more plenteously than in any other country, as of ginger, cloves-gilofre, canell, seedwall, nutmegs and maces. . . .

Many other spices and many other goods grow in that isle. For of all things is there plenty, save only of wine. But there is gold and silver, great plenty.

And the king of that country hath a palace full noble and full marvellous, and more rich than any in the world. . . .

In that isle is a dead sea, that is a lake that hath no ground; and if anything fall into that lake it shall never come up again. In that lake grow reeds, that be canes, that they clepe Thaby, that be thirty fathoms[35] long. . . . Of those canes they make houses and ships and other things, as we have here, making houses and ships of oak or of any other trees. And deem no man that I say it but for a trifle, for I have seen of the canes with mine own eyes, full many times, lying upon the river of that lake, of the which twenty of our fellows ne might not lift up ne bear one to the earth. . . .

33. **clept:** called.
34. **visage:** face.
35. **fathom:** six feet.

Afterward men go by many isles by sea unto an isle that men clepe Milke. And there is a full cursed people for they delight in nothing more than for to fight and to slay men. And they drink gladliest man's blood, the which they clepe Dieu. And the more men that a man may slay, the more worship he hath amongst them. And if two persons be at debate and, peradventure, be accorded[36] by their friends or by some of their alliance, it behoveth[37] that every of them shall be accorded drink of other's blood: and else the accord ne the alliance is nought worth: ne it shall not be no reproof to him to break the alliance and the accord, but if every of them drink of others' blood. . . .

Beside the land of Chaldea is the land of Amazonia, that is the land of Feminye. And in that realm is all women and no man; not, as some men say, that men may not live there, but for because that the women will not suffer no men amongst them to be their sovereigns.

For sometime there was a king in that country. And men married, as in other countries. And so befell that the king had war with them of Scythia, the which king hight[38] Colopeus, that was slain in battle, and all the good blood of his realm. And when the queen and all the other noble ladies saw that they were all widows, and that all the royal blood was lost, they armed them and, as creatures out of wit, they slew all the men of the country that were left; for they would that all the women were widows as the queen and they were. And from that time hitherwards they never would suffer men to dwell amongst them longer than seven days and seven nights; ne that no child that were male should dwell amongst them longer than he were nourished; and then sent to his father. And when they will have any company of man then they draw them towards the lands marching next to them. And then they have loves that use them; and they dwell with them an eight days or ten, and then go home again. And if they have any knave child they keep it a certain time, and then send it to the father when he can go alone and eat by himself; or else they slay it. And if it be a female they do away that one pap with an hot iron. And if it be a woman of great lineage they do away the left pap that they may the better bear a shield. And if it be a woman on foot they do away the right pap, for to shoot with bow turkeys: for they shoot well with bows.

36. **accorded:** reconciled.
37. **behoveth:** is necessary.
38. **hight:** was called.

Chapter 12

Pagans,

Muslims, and

Christians in the

Mental World

of Columbus

Source 11 from Pierre d'Ailly, Imago Mundi, *translated by Edwin F. Keever (Wilmington, N.C.: privately published, 1948), extracts from chapters 41, 42, 49.*

11. From Pierre d'Ailly, *Imago Mundi*

We also discuss other islands of the ocean which Isidore has in mind. . . .

The Fortunate Isles signify by their name that all things are usually propitious: fortunate because of the abundance of fruitage. The forests yield precious fruit trees; the slopes of the hills are clothed with promising grape vines. Hence it is an error of the gentiles to regard the islands as Paradise because of the fecundity of the soil. The first of them is called Nembriona, the second Juniona, the third Theode, the fourth Capraria, another Minaria, which is in a dense and vaporous cloud. Then Caninaria, abounding in dogs of immense size. All of the isles have many birds, good pastures, a great number of palms, nut trees and pines; rich in honey, and plentiful in animals, forests and fish. These islands are situated in the ocean opposite the left side of the Mauretania, between the south and the west, closest to the west, and scattered about over intervals of the sea.

The Gorgodes Islands of the ocean are in the direction of a promontory called 'Esperacerus'. They are inhabited by the Gorgodes, women of destructiveness, with coarse and hairy bodies. The islands were named for them. They are distant from the continent by a two-day sail. . . .

On account of its marvels special notice must be taken of Taprobane the island of India which, according to Orosius[39] contains ten cities. It lies in the east where the Indian Ocean begins, extending 875,000 paces in length, and 225,000 stadia in breadth. It is totally cut off by an interflowing stream. It is full of pearls and precious stones. Part of it abounds in beasts and elephants, and part is inhabited by the people, who are powerful in body beyond all measurements; with red hair, blue eyes and harsh voices. They hold no intercourse by speech with any other tribe. They offer their commodities with other merchants on the river-bank, and exchange amenities reluctantly. With them life is prolonged beyond human infirmity, so that one who dies a centenarian comes to his end immaturely. They take no sleep during the day. Annual harvests are never interrupted. Houses are small and humble; of cities they know nothing. Fruits are plentiful. They enjoy husbandry and hunting; indeed they take pleasure in pursuing tigers and elephants. Quite oddly they cover the capacious houses of their families with the backs of turtles. . . .

After having discussed the heavens and the earth and their respective parts it seems fitting to say something about water. . . .

39. **Orosius:** Paulus Orosius (fl. 390–417), a cleric and author of a popular geographic and historical treatise, *Historia adversum paganos.*

. . . The water runs down from one pole toward the other into the body of the sea and spreads out between the confines of Spain and the beginning of India, of no great width, in such a way that the beginning of India can be beyond the middle of the equinoctial circle and approach beneath the earth quite close to the coast of Spain. Likewise Aristotle and his commentator in the 'Libro Coeli et Mundi' came to the same conclusion because there are so many elephants in those regions. Says Pliny: 'Around Mt. Atlas elephants abound.' So also in India and even in ulterior Spain there are great herds of elephants. But, reasons Aristotle, the elephants in both those places ought to show similar characteristics; if widely separated they would not have the same characteristics. Therefore he concludes those countries are close neighbors and that a small sea intervenes; and moreover that the sea covers three-quarters of the earth; that the beginnings of the east and the west are near by, since a small sea separates them.

Source 12 from The Life of the Admiral Christopher Columbus by His Son Ferdinand, *trans. and annotated by Benjamin Keen (New Brunswick, NJ: Rutgers University Press, 1958), pp. 19–22. Copyright © 1959, 1992 by Rutgers, The State University. Reprinted by permission of Rutgers University Press.*

12. Letter to Columbus from Paolo dal Pozzo Toscanelli

Paolo the physician, to Christopher Columbus, Greetings.
   I perceive your noble and grand desire to go to the places where the spices grow; and in reply to your letter I send you a copy of another letter which some time since I sent to a friend of mine, a gentleman of the household of the most serene King of Portugal, before the wars of Castile,[40] in reply to another which by command of His Highness he wrote me on this subject; and I send you another sea-chart like the one I sent him, that your demands may be satisfied. A copy of that letter of mine follows:

Paolo the physician, to Fernão Martins, canon of Lisbon, Greetings.
   I was glad to hear of your intimacy and friendship with your most serene and magnificent King. I have often before spoken of a sea route from here to the Indies, where the spices grow, a route shorter than the one which you are pursuing by way of Guinea. You tell me that His Highness desires from me some statement or demonstration that would make it easier to understand and take that route. I could do this by using a sphere shaped like the earth, but I decided that it would be easier and make the point clearer if I showed that

40. Wars between Portugal and Castile 1475–1479, which ended in Castilian victory.

Chapter 12

Pagans,

Muslims, and

Christians in the

Mental World

of Columbus

route by means of a sea-chart. I therefore send His Majesty a chart drawn by my own hand, upon which is laid out the western coast from Ireland on the north to the end of Guinea, and the islands which lie on that route, in front of which, directly to the west, is shown the beginning of the Indies, with the islands and places at which you are bound to arrive, and how far from the Arctic Pole or the Equator you ought to keep away, and how much space or how many leagues intervene before you reach those places most fertile in all sorts of spices, jewels, and precious stones. And do not marvel at my calling "west" the regions where the spices grow, although they are commonly called "east"; because whoever sails westward will always find those lands in the west, while one who goes overland to the east will always find the same lands in the east.

The straight lines drawn lengthwise on this map show the distance from east to west; the transverse lines indicate distance from north to south. I have also drawn on the map various places in India to which one could go in case of a storm or contrary winds, or some other mishap.

And that you may be as well informed about all those regions as you desire to be, you must know that none but merchants live and trade in all those islands. There is as great a number of ships and mariners with their merchandise here as in all the rest of the world, especially in a very noble port called Zaiton,[41] where every year they load and unload a hundred large ships laden with pepper, besides many other ships loaded with other spices. This country is very populous, with a multitude of provinces and kingdoms and cities without number, under the rule of a prince who is called the Great Khan, which name in our speech signifies King of Kings, who resides most of the time in the province of Cathay. His predecessors greatly desired to have friendship and dealings with the Christians, and about two hundred years ago they sent ambassadors to the Pope, asking for many learned men and teachers to instruct them in our faith; but these ambassadors, encountering obstacles on the way, turned back without reaching Rome. In the time of Pope Eugenius[42] there came to him an ambassador who told of their great feeling of friendship for the Christians, and I had a long talk with him about many things: about the great size of their royal palaces and the marvelous length and breadth of their rivers, and the multitude of cities in their lands, so that on one river alone there are two hundred cities, with marble bridges very long and wide, adorned with many columns. This country is as rich as any that has ever been found; not only could it yield great gain and many costly things,

41. **Zaiton:** modern Tsinkiang, on the inlet of Formosa Strait.

42. Pope Eugenius IV (1431–1447), who convened a church council in Florence, attempting to unite the various branches of the Christian church. Representatives of eastern Christian churches attended this council, and the envoy Toscanelli reports speaking with who probably was a Nestorian Christian sent by a Mongol ruler.

but from it may also be had gold and silver and precious stones and all sorts of spices in great quantity, which at present are not carried to our countries. And it is true that many learned men, philosophers and astronomers, and many other men skilled in all the arts, govern this great province and conduct its wars.

From the city of Lisbon due west there are twenty-six spaces marked on the map, each of which contains two hundred and fifty miles, as far as the very great and noble city of Quinsay.[43] This city is about one hundred miles in circumference, which is equal to thirty-five leagues, and has ten marble bridges. Marvelous things are told about its great buildings, its arts, and its revenues. That city lies in the province of Mangi, near the province of Cathay,[44] in which the king resides the greater part of the time. And from the island of Antillia,[45] which you call the Island of the Seven Cities, to the very noble island of Cipango,[46] there are ten spaces, which make 2,500 miles, that is two hundred and twenty-five leagues. This land is most rich in gold, pearls, and precious stones, and the temples and royal palaces are covered with solid gold. But because the way is not known, all these things are hidden and covered, though one can travel thither with all security.

Many other things could I say, but since I have already told them to you by word of mouth, and you are a man of good judgment, I know there remains nothing for me to explain. I have tried to satisfy your demands as well as the pressure of time and my work has permitted, and I remain ready to serve His Highness and answer his questions at greater length if he should order me to do so.

Done in the city of Florence, June 25, 1474.

---

43. **Quinsay:** modern Hangchow.

44. Drawing on Marco Polo, Toscanelli uses the term "Mangi" for southern China, and "Cathay" for northern China.

45. **Antillia:** a mythical island in the Atlantic. See Source 14.

46. **Cipango:** Japan.

Chapter 12

Pagans,

Muslims, and

Christians in the

Mental World

of Columbus

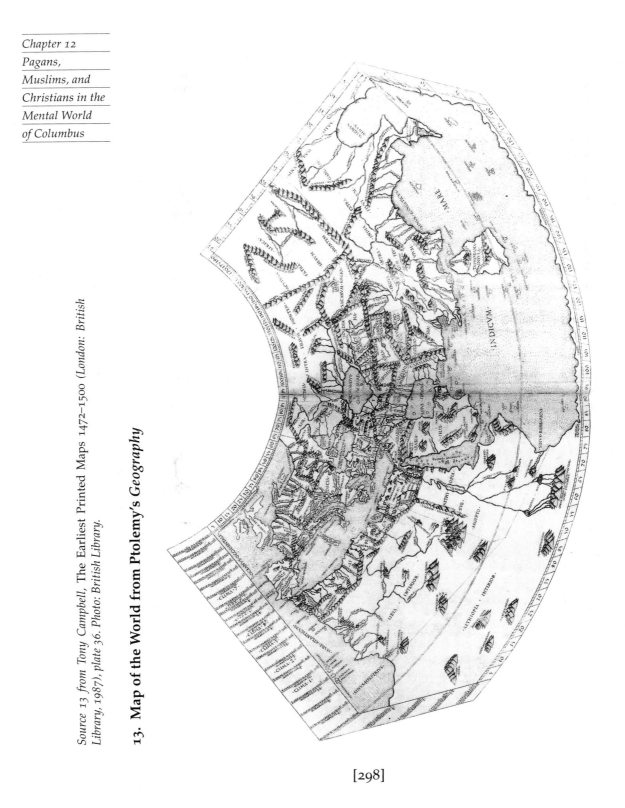

Source 13 from Tony Campbell, The Earliest Printed Maps 1472–1500 (London: British Library, 1987), plate 36. Photo: British Library.

13. Map of the World from Ptolemy's Geography

Source 14 from R. A. Skelton, Explorers' Maps: Chapters in the Cartographic Record of Geographical Discovery *(London: Routledge and Kegan Paul, 1958), fig. 29. Photo: Biblioteca Nazionale di Roma.*

14. Sailor's Chart (Detail) of the Atlantic Islands Drawn by Bartolomeo Pareto in Genoa (1455)

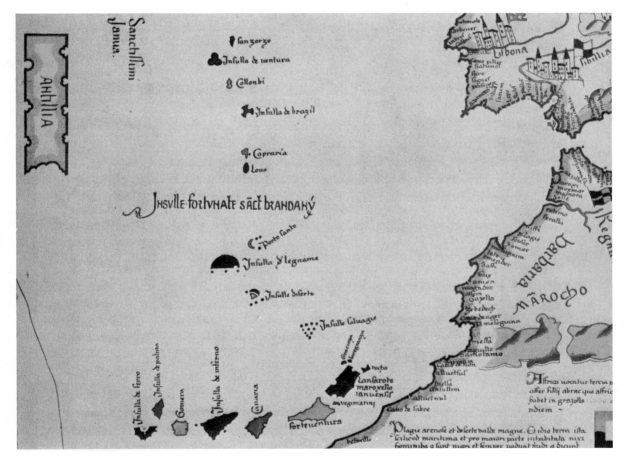

Chapter 12

Pagans,

Muslims, and

Christians in the

Mental World

of Columbus

Source 15 from R. H. Major, editor and translator, Select Letters of Christopher Columbus *(London: Hakluyt Society, 1847), pp. 1–15.*

15. Letter from Christopher Columbus (1493)

A letter addressed to the noble Lord Raphael Sanchez, Treasurer to their most invincible Majesties, Ferdinand and Isabella, King and Queen of Spain, by Christopher Columbus, to whom our age is greatly indebted, treating of the islands of India recently discovered beyond the Ganges, to explore which he had been sent eight months before under the auspices and at the expense of their said Majesties.

Knowing that it will afford you pleasure to learn that I have brought my undertaking to a successful termination, I have decided upon writing you this letter to acquaint you with all the events which have occurred in my voyage, and the discoveries which have resulted from it. Thirty-three days after my departure from Cadiz I reached the Indian sea, where I discovered many islands, thickly peopled, of which I took possession without resistance in the name of our most illustrious Monarch, by public proclamation and with unfurled banners. To the first of these islands, which is called by the Indians Guanahani, I gave the name of the blessed Saviour (San Salvador), relying upon whose protection I had reached this as well as the other islands. . . . In that island . . . which . . . we named Española,[47] there are mountains of very great size and beauty, vast plains, groves, and very fruitful fields, admirably adapted for tillage, pasture, and habitation. The convenience and excellence of the harbours in this island, and the abundance of the rivers, so indispensable to the health of man, surpass anything that would be believed by one who had not seen it. The trees, herbage, and fruits of Española are very different from those of Juana,[48] and moreover it abounds in various kinds of spices, gold, and other metals. The inhabitants of both sexes in this island, and in all the others which I have seen, or of which I have received information, go always naked as they were born, with the exception of some of the women, who use the covering of a leaf, or small bough, or an apron of cotton which they prepare for that purpose. None of them, as I have already said, are possessed of any iron, neither have they weapons, being unacquainted with, and indeed incompetent to use them, not from any deformity of body (for they are well-formed), but because they are timid and full of fear. . . . As soon . . . as they see that they are safe, and have laid aside all fear, they are very simple and honest, and exceedingly liberal with all they have; none of them refusing any thing he may possess when he is asked for it, but on the contrary inviting us

47. **Española:** Hispaniola, or San Domingo.
48. **Juana:** Cuba.

to ask them. . . . On my arrival at that sea, I had taken some Indians by force from the first island that I came to, in order that they might learn our language, and communicate to us what they knew respecting the country; which plan succeeded excellently, and was a great advantage to us, for in a short time, either by gestures and signs, or by words, we were enabled to understand each other. . . . In all these islands there is no difference of physiognomy, of manners, or of language, but they all clearly understand each other, a circumstance very propitious for the realization of what I conceive to be the principal wish of our most serene King, namely, the conversion of these people to the holy faith of Christ, to which indeed, as far as I can judge, they are very favourable and well-disposed. . . . As far as I have learned, every man throughout these islands is united to but one wife, with the exception of the kings and princes, who are allowed to have twenty: the women seem to work more than the men. I could not clearly understand whether the people possess any private property, for I observed that one man had the charge of distributing various things to the rest, but especially meat and provisions and the like. I did not find, as some of us had expected, any cannibals amongst them, but on the contrary men of great deference and kindness. Neither are they black, like the Ethiopians: their hair is smooth and straight: for they do not dwell where the rays of the sun strike most vividly,—and the sun has intense power there, the distance from the equinoctial line being, it appears, but six-and-twenty degrees. On the tops of the mountains the cold is very great, but the effect of this upon the Indians is lessened by their being accustomed to the climate, and by their frequently indulging in the use of very hot meats and drinks. Thus, as I have already said, I saw no cannibals, nor did I hear of any, except in a certain island called Charis,[49] which is the second from Española on the side towards India, where dwell a people who are considered by the neighbouring islanders as most ferocious: and these feed upon human flesh. The same people have many kinds of canoes, in which they cross to all the surrounding islands and rob and plunder wherever they can; they are not different from the other islanders, except that they wear their hair long, like women, and make use of the bows and javelins of cane, with sharpened spear-points fixed on the thickest end, which I have before described, and therefore they are looked upon as ferocious, and regarded by the other Indians with unbounded fear; but I think no more of them than of the rest. These are the men who form union with certain women, who dwell alone in the island Matenin,[50] which lies next to Española on the side towards India; these latter employ themselves in no labour suitable to their own sex, for they use bows and javelins as I have already described their paramours as doing, and for defensive armour have plates of brass, of which metal they possess great

49. **Charis:** Query Carib, the Indian name of Puerto Rico.
50. **Matenin:** one of the Virgin Islands—which is uncertain.

abundance. They assure me that there is another island larger than Española, whose inhabitants have no hair, and which abounds in gold more than any of the rest. I bring with me individuals of this island and of the others that I have seen, who are proofs of the facts which I state. Finally, to compress into few words the entire summary of my voyage and speedy return, and of the advantages derivable therefrom, I promise, that with a little assistance afforded me by our most invincible sovereigns, I will procure them as much gold as they need, as great a quantity of spices, of cotton, and of mastic[51] (which is only found in Chios), and as many men for the service of the navy as their Majesties may require.

51. **mastic:** a resin used as an astringent and in varnish.

QUESTIONS TO CONSIDER

Columbus was not simply a sponge soaking up ideas he had read or heard about, but selectively chose those that supported his goals. From what you have read, you can probably guess which estimate of the size of the known world he adopted, Marinus's view of 225 degrees of longitude or Ptolemy's smaller version of 177 degrees.[52] Can you see how the maps printed in Ptolemy's *Geography*, such as that in Source 13, might have actually reinforced this larger estimate? (A hint here: Do the maps show an east coast for Asia?) As his son notes in Source 3, Columbus's estimates were also based on his calculations of the size of a longitudinal degree, which he took from the Arabic geographer al-Farghani as about 45 miles, not realizing (or not choosing to realize) that al-Farghani had reckoned in Arabic miles, which

were longer than the Roman miles Columbus used.[53]

As you have seen, along with ideas about the size of the globe and the distance from Europe to Asia, Columbus also developed clear preconceptions about the natural world and human cultures to be found in "the Indies." You have now read reports about both the islands of the Atlantic (Source 6) and the Eastern regions of Asia (Sources 8 through 10). Do you see any common features in these? Do these features emerge in Columbus's own writings? How might these commonalities have affected Columbus's assessment of his location?

The letters of John of Monte Corvino (Source 8) and Paolo Toscanelli (Source 12) both discuss the conversion of people in China to Christianity, a goal that looms especially large in Columbus's discussion of his and his sovereigns' motivations in Source 1.

52. The actual size of the world known to Ptolemy and Marinus, which probably stretched from eastern Vietnam to the Canaries, is 127 degrees.

53. When the relative length of Arabic miles are taken into account, al-Farghani's estimates set the degree at 66 nautical miles, much closer to the actual distance of 60 nautical miles than Columbus's estimate of 45 miles.

What comments does he make about this in his actual description of the New World (Source 15)? How do these comments fit with the actual experiences of John of Monte Corvino and with Toscanelli's report of his discussion with the ambassador from Cathay?

When evaluating Columbus's preconceptions, we must realize that he not only discussed these with many people in Europe, but also shared them, as best he could, with the Native Americans he met. You can see from Columbus's letter that the people he met did not initially oppose him and (if we choose to believe him on this point) were interested in pleasing him. How might they have responded to his questions about cannibals, tailed humans, and Amazon women? To his questions about the availability of gold and spices? What do they apparently tell him about people and natural products found on nearby islands? Would such interchanges have worked to lodge Columbus's ideas more firmly or less firmly in his mind?

This chapter has asked you to focus on the mental world of Columbus, but you have probably noticed that most of the authors cite the same authorities that he does, that Aristotle, Ptolemy, Pliny, al-Farghani, and Marco Polo crop up everywhere. This reverence for standard authorities is often described as a hallmark of medieval European culture, with Columbus described as one of the first "modern men" who broke with this pattern. Based on your reading in this chapter, would you agree with this assessment? Does it surprise you that Columbus named the group of West Indian islands he discovered the Antilles (Antillia)? Would you say that Columbus regarded his voyages as extending earlier works of geography and travel, or as breaking with them?

EPILOGUE

Examining the ways in which Columbus's cultural assumptions shaped both his own and other Europeans' responses to the New World, the Mexican historian and philosopher Edmundo O'Gorman coined the phrase the "invention of America." The America that took shape in Europeans' minds—and in turn influenced their subsequent relations with indigenous peoples—was a blend of expectations and actual encounters. As we have seen in this chapter, those expectations were based on centuries of trade, warfare, missionary activity, and other encounters across much of the "Old World." In those encounters, people confronted others of different ethnicity, race, language, and religion, and they had to develop ways of understanding these differences. Some scholars describe this process as "creating the Other," or "constructing the Other," and note that as they created "the Other," groups also came to define themselves.

The encounter between Europeans and indigenous peoples in the New World was thus a continuation of a

Chapter 12

Pagans,

Muslims, and

Christians in the

Mental World

of Columbus

long-established process, but also something radically new and shocking, for these were people and lands that did not fit into a world-view based on Christian teachings and classical models. If the Flood described in the Old Testament truly covered the whole world, then the Indians must be descendants of Noah. But when and how did they get there? How could the ancient Greeks and Romans so revered by Renaissance humanists not have known about them? How were the differences between peoples to be explained? What was the true difference between civilized peoples and barbarians? Columbus's voyages intensified discussions about cultural difference, about self and Other.

A few Europeans argued that all peoples were equally rational and on the same road to civilization, but in most Europeans' minds the relative ease with which the Spanish conquered the Caribbean, Central America, and the Andes region intensified a sense of superiority. Columbus saw himself as called by God to spread Christianity, frequently signing his first name as *Christo-fero*—"Christ-carrier" in Latin—using the Greek letters for Christ as the first part of his name. Though later explorers rarely had as powerful a sense of personal destiny as Columbus, they shared his view of European cultural and spiritual preeminence.

The indigenous peoples of the New World were Others that were clearly inferior.

Criticism of this intellectual legacy and of the actual events of European conquest and colonization grew during the late twentieth century. Columbus Day (October 12) was made a U.S. federal holiday in 1937, but, beginning in the 1990s, some communities have renamed the day "Indigenous People's Day." In the early twentieth century, several countries in Latin America began celebrating October 12 as *Día de la Raza* (Day of the Race), commemorating the blending of European and indigenous cultures in the formation of their cultures. In 2002 Venezuela officially renamed Día de la Raza *Día de la Resistencia Indígena* (Day of Indigenous Resistance), with ceremonies highlighting domination and struggle. These revised holidays use Columbus as a symbol of European arrogance, and there is much in his writings and actions that supports this. As we have seen in this chapter, however, he can also provide a model of willingness to absorb ideas from many cultures. As he notes, "Latins and Greeks, Jews and Moors, and many others of other sects" all helped him "inquire in the secrets of this world," a world that all sides in the controversy over his legacy agree was radically changed because of his voyages.

CHAPTER THIRTEEN

THE SPREAD

OF THE REFORMATION

In 1517, an Augustinian monk in the German province of Saxony named Martin Luther (1483–1546) began preaching and writing against papal *indulgences*, those letters from the pope that substituted for earthly penance or time in Purgatory for Christians who earned or purchased them. Luther called for an end to the sale of indulgences because this practice encouraged people to believe that sins did not have to be taken seriously but could be atoned for simply by buying a piece of paper. In taking this position, he was repeating the ideas expressed more than one hundred years earlier by John Hus (1369?–1415), a Czech theologian and preacher. Many of Luther's other ideas had also been previously expressed by Hus, and even earlier by John Wyclif (1328–1384), an English philosopher and theologian. All three objected to the wealth of the Church and to the pope's claims to earthly power; called for an end to pilgrimages and the veneration of saints;

said that priests were no better than other people, and that in fact all believers were priests; and believed that the Bible should be available for all people to read for themselves in their own language.

Though Luther's beliefs were quite similar to those of Wyclif and Hus, their impact was not. Wyclif had gained a large following and died peacefully in his bed; less than twenty years after his death, however, English rulers ordered anyone espousing his beliefs to be burned at the stake as a heretic, and so the movement he started was more or less wiped out. Hus himself was burned at the stake in 1415 at the Council of Constance, which ordered the bones of Wyclif to be dug up and burned as well. Hus's followers were not as easily steered back to the fold or stamped out as Wyclif's had been, but his ideas never spread beyond Bohemia (modern-day Czech Republic). Martin Luther's actions, on the other hand, led to a permanent split in Western Christianity, dividing an institution that had existed as a unified body for almost 1,500 years. Within only a few years, Luther gained a huge number of followers in Germany and other countries, inspiring other religious reformers to break with the Catholic church in developing their own ideas. This movement has come to be known collectively as the "Protestant Reformation," though perhaps *Revolution* might be a more accurate term.

To understand why Luther's impact was so much greater than that of his predecessors, we need to examine a number of factors besides his basic set of beliefs. As with any revolution, social and economic grievances also played a role. Many different groups in early-sixteenth-century German society were disturbed by the changes they saw around them. Peasants wanted the right to hunt and fish as they had in earlier times and objected to new taxes that their landlords imposed on them. Bitter at the wealth of the Church, they believed that the clergy were more interested in collecting money from them than in providing spiritual leadership. Landlords, watching the price of manufactured goods rise even faster than they could raise taxes or rents, blamed urban merchants and bankers, calling them greedy and avaricious. Those with only small landholdings were especially caught in an inflationary squeeze and often had to sell off their lands. This was particularly the case for the free imperial knights, a group of about 3,000 individuals in Germany who owed allegiance directly to the emperor but whose landholdings were often less than one square mile. The knights were also losing their reason for existence because military campaigns increasingly relied on infantry and artillery forces rather than mounted cavalry. All these groups were becoming nationalistic and objected to their church taxes and tithes going to the pope, whom they regarded as primarily an Italian prince rather than an international religious leader.

Political factors were also important in the Protestant Revolution. Germany was not a centralized monarchy like France, Spain, and England, but a collection of hundreds of semi-independent territories loosely combined into a political unit called the Holy Roman Empire, under the leadership of an elected emperor. Some of these territories were ruled by nobles such as princes, dukes, or counts; some were independent cities; some were ecclesiastical principalities ruled by archbishops or bishops; and some were ruled by free imperial knights. Each territory was jealous of the power of its neighbors and was equally unwilling to allow the emperor any strong centralized authority. This effect usually worked to the benefit of the individual territories, but it could also work to their detriment. For example, the emperor's weakness prevented him from enforcing such laws against alleged heretics as the one the English king had used against Wyclif's followers, with the result that each territory was relatively independent in matters of religion. On the other hand, he was unable to place limits on papal legal authority or tax collection in the way the stronger kings of western Europe could, with the result that Germany supported many more indulgence peddlers than England or Spain.

The decentralization of the Holy Roman Empire also left each territory more vulnerable than before to external military threats, the most significant of which in the early sixteenth century was the Ottoman Turks. Originating in central Asia, the Turks had adopted the Muslim religion and begun a campaign of conquest westward. In 1453 they took Constantinople, and by 1500 they were nearing Vienna, arousing fear in many German rulers. The Turkish threat combined with social and economic grievances among many sectors of society to make western Europeans feel that the end of the world was near or look for a charismatic leader who would solve their problems.

Technological factors also played a role in the Protestant Revolution. The printing press was developed in Germany around 1450, and by Luther's time there were printers in most of the major cities in Europe. The spread of printing was accompanied by a rise in literacy, so that many more people were able to read than in the time of Wyclif or Hus. They were also more able to buy books and pamphlets, for the rag paper used by printers was much cheaper than the parchment or vellum used by copyists in earlier centuries. Owning a Bible or part of a Bible to read in one's own language was now a realistic possibility.

In many ways, then, the early sixteenth century was a favorable time for a major religious change in western Europe. Your task in this chapter will be to assess how that change occurred. How were the ideas of Luther disseminated so widely and so quickly? How were they made attractive to various groups within German society?

SOURCES AND METHOD

Before you look at the evidence in this chapter, think about how ideas are spread in modern American society. What would be the best ways to reach the greatest number of people if you wanted to discuss a new issue or present a new concept? You might want to use health issues as an example, for these often involve totally new ideas and information on one hand and are regarded as vitally important on the other. Think, for example, about the means by which the dangers of cigarette smoking or information about the spread of AIDS is communicated. To answer the first question, we will need to examine the sixteenth-century equivalents of these forms of communication. Health is an appropriate parallel because the most important such issue for many people in the sixteenth century was the health of their souls, a problem directly addressed by Luther and the other reformers.

The spread of the Reformation was perhaps the first example of a successful multimedia campaign; in consequence, as you might imagine, we will be using a wide variety of sources. As you read the written sources and look at the visual evidence, keep in mind that people were seeing, hearing, and reading all these materials at once. As in any successful advertising or propaganda campaign, certain ideas were reinforced over and over again to make sure the message was thoroughly communicated. You will need to pay particular attention, then, to those points that come up in more than one type of source.

Though they were seeing, hearing, or reading the same message, different groups within German society interpreted Protestant ideas differently. They latched on to certain concepts that had relevance for their own situations and often attached Protestant ideas to existing social, political, or economic grievances. Artists and authors spreading the Protestant message often conveyed their ideas in ways they knew would be attractive to various social groups. In answering the second question, it is important to note the portrayal of various social groups and pay attention to the frequency with which these portrayals appear. Thus, as you look at the visual sources and read the written ones, jot down one list of the ideas expressed and another of the ways in which various types of people are depicted. In this way, you will begin to see which ideas are central and perceived as popular, and which might be interpreted differently by different people.

Source 1 is a sermon delivered in 1521 by Martin Luther in Erfurt on his way to the Diet of Worms, a meeting of the leaders of the territories in the Holy Roman Empire. It is not based on Luther's own notes but was written down by a person in the audience, who then gave the transcript to a local printer. This sermon is thus a record of both how the Reformation message was spread orally—so many people wanted to hear him that the church where Luther preached could not hold them all—and how it was spread in written form, for seven editions of the sermon appeared in 1521 alone. What teachings of the Catholic church did Luther criticize, and what ideas of his own did he emphasize? In assessing how ideas are spread, we have to pay attention not only to the content of the message but also to the form. In what sorts of words and images did Luther convey his ideas to his large audience?

The next sources—three hymns—also serve as both oral and written evidence. Martin Luther believed that congregational hymn singing was an important part of a church service and an effective way to teach people about theology. In this tactic he anticipated modern advertisers, who recognize the power of a song or jingle in influencing people's choices. The first two hymns were written by Luther and the third by Paul Speratus, an early follower. As you read them, pay attention to both their content and their images. What ideas from Luther's sermon are reinforced in the hymns? What sorts of mental pictures do the words produce? (Keep in mind that you are reading these simply as poetry, whereas sixteenth-century people sang them. You may know the tune of "A Mighty Fortress," which is still sung in many Protestant congregations today; if so, you can use your knowledge of its musical setting to help you assess the impact of the hymn and its message.)

The Lutheran message would certainly not have spread as widely as it did if church services were its only forum. The remaining sources are those that people might have encountered anywhere. The woodcuts all come from Protestant pamphlets—small, inexpensive paperbound booklets written in German that were readily available in any city with a printer—or *broadsheets*—single-sheet posters that were often sold alone or as a series. These documents are extremely complex visually and need to be examined with great care. Most of the images used would have been familiar to any sixteenth-century person, but they may not be to you. Here, then, are some clues to help guide your analysis.

In Source 5, the person on the right wearing the triple crown with money on the table in front of him is the pope. The devils in front of the table are wearing the flat hats worn by cardinals; the pieces of paper with seals attached that they are handing out are indulgences. At the bottom are the flames of hell; at the top, heaven with a preacher and people participating in the two Church sacraments that the Protestants retained, baptism and communion.

Source 6, another heaven and hell image, shows Christ at the top deciding who will stay in heaven and two linked devils at the bottom dragging various people to hell. The right-hand devil wears the triple-crowned papal tiara, the left-hand one, the rolled turban worn by Turks. Included in the hell-bound group on the right are men wearing the flat cardinal's hat, the pointed hat of bishops, and the distinctive haircut of monks.

Source 7 comes from a series of woodcut contrasts. The left pictures show biblical scenes and the right the contemporary Church. The top left picture shows Christ with his disciples; the top right, the pope. From their hats and haircuts you can recognize some of the people gathered in front of the pope; those kneeling are wearing crowns, which in the sixteenth century were worn only by rulers. The bottom left picture shows Christ and the moneychangers at the temple at Jerusalem; the bottom right, the pope and indulgences.

Source 8 is the cover of a pamphlet called "The Wolf's Song." By now you recognize the hats and haircuts of the wolves at the top and sides; some of the geese wear crowns, and many carry jeweled necklaces. The choice of animals is intentional. Wolves were still a threat to livestock in sixteenth-century Europe, and geese were regarded as foolish, silly creatures willing to follow their leader blindly into dangerous situations.

Source 9 is a woodcut by the well-known German artist Lucas Cranach, whom Luther commissioned to illustrate his pamphlet "Against the Papacy at Rome, Founded by the Devil" (1545). It shows two men defecating into the papal triple crown.

Taking all of the images into account, what message do the woodcuts convey about the pope and other Catholic clergy? About the Protestant clergy? Which images and ideas are frequently repeated? How do these fit in with what was preached or sung in church?

The last source is a pamphlet by an unknown author printed in 1523. It is written in the form of a dialogue, a very common form for these Reformation printed materials. Read it, as you did the sermon and the hymns, for both content and tone. Why do you think the author chose these two characters to convey his message? What do they criticize about Catholic practices? How do the ideas expressed here compare with those in Luther's sermon? Which of the woodcuts might have served as an illustration for this pamphlet?

<hr>

THE EVIDENCE

Source 1 from John W. Doberstein, editor, Luther's Works, *vol. 51 (Philadelphia: Fortress, 1959), pp. 61–66. Reprinted by permission.*

1. Sermon Preached by Martin Luther in Erfurt (Germany), 1521

Dear friends, I shall pass over the story of St. Thomas this time and leave it for another occasion, and instead consider the brief words uttered by Christ: "Peace be with you" [John 20:19] and "Behold my hands and my side" [John 20:27], and "as the Father has sent me, even so I send you" [John 20:21]. Now, it is clear and manifest that every person likes to think that he will be saved and attain to eternal salvation. This is what I propose to discuss now.

You also know that all philosophers, doctors and writers have studiously endeavored to teach and write what attitude man should take to piety. They have gone to great trouble, but, as is evident, to little avail. Now genuine and true piety consists of two kinds of works: those done for others, which are the right kind, and those done for ourselves, which are unimportant. In order to find a foundation, one man builds churches; another goes on a pilgrimage to St. James'[1] or St. Peter's[2]; a third fasts or prays, wears a cowl, goes barefoot, or does something else of the kind. Such works are nothing whatever and must be completely destroyed. Mark these words: none of our works have any power whatsoever. For God has chosen a man, the Lord Christ Jesus, to crush death, destroy sin, and shatter hell, since there was no one before he came who did not inevitably belong to the devil. The devil therefore thought he would get a hold upon the Lord when he hung between the two thieves

---

1. St. James of Compostella, a cathedral in northern Spain.
2. A cathedral in Rome.

and was suffering the most contemptible and disgraceful of deaths, which was cursed both by God and by men [cf. Deut. 21:23; Gal. 3:13]. But the Godhead was so strong that death, sin, and even hell were destroyed.

Therefore you should note well the words which Paul writes to the Romans [Rom. 5:12–21]. Our sins have their source in Adam, and because Adam ate the apple, we have inherited sin from him. But Christ has shattered death for our sake, in order that we might be saved by his works, which are alien to us, and not by our works.

But the papal dominion treats us altogether differently. It makes rules about fasting, praying, and butter-eating, so that whoever keeps the commandments of the pope will be saved and whoever does not keep them belongs to the devil. It thus seduces the people with the delusion that goodness and salvation lies in their own works. But I say that none of the saints, no matter how holy they were, attained salvation by their works. Even the holy mother of God did not become good, was not saved, by her virginity or her motherhood, but rather by the will of faith and the works of God, and not by her purity, or her own works. Therefore, mark me well: this is the reason why salvation does not lie in our own works, no matter what they are; it cannot and will not be effected without faith.

Now, someone may say: Look, my friend, you are saying a lot about faith, and claiming that our salvation depends solely upon it; now, I ask you, how does one come to faith? I will tell you. Our Lord Christ said, "Peace be with you. Behold my hands, etc." [John 20:26–27]. [In other words, he is saying:] Look, man, I am the only one who has taken away your sins and redeemed you, etc.; now be at peace. Just as you inherited sin from Adam—not that you committed it, for I did not eat the apple, any more than you did, and yet this is how we came to be in sin—so we have not suffered [as Christ did], and therefore we were made free from death and sin by God's work, not by our works. Therefore God says: Behold, man, I am your redemption [cf. Isa. 43:3], just as Paul said to the Corinthians: Christ is our justification and redemption, etc. [I Cor 1:30]. Christ is our justification and redemption, as Paul says in this passage. And here our [Roman] masters say: Yes, *Redemptor*, Redeemer; this is true, but it is not enough.

Therefore, I say again: Alien works, these make us good! Our Lord Christ says: I am your justification. I have destroyed the sins you have upon you. Therefore only believe in me; believe that I am he who has done this; then you will be justified. For it is written, *Justicia est fides*, righteousness is identical with faith and comes through faith. Therefore, if we want to have faith, we should believe the gospel, Paul, etc, and not the papal breves,[3] or the decretals,[4] but rather guard ourselves against them as against fire. For everything that comes from the pope cries out: Give, give; and if you refuse, you are of

3. **breve:** letter of authority.
4. **decretal:** decree on matters of doctrine.

the devil. It would be a small matter if they were only exploiting the people. But, unfortunately, it is the greatest evil in the world to lead the people to believe that outward works can save or make a man good.

At this time the world is so full of wickedness that it is overflowing, and is therefore now under a terrible judgment and punishment, which God has inflicted, so that the people are perverting and deceiving themselves in their own minds. For to build churches, and to fast and pray and so on has the appearance of good works, but in our heads we are deluding ourselves. We should not give way to greed, desire for temporal honor, and other vices and rather be helpful to our poor neighbor. Then God will arise in us and we in him, and this means a new birth. What does it matter if we commit a fresh sin? If we do not immediately despair, but rather say within ourselves, "O God, thou livest still! Christ my Lord is the destroyer of sin," then at once the sin is gone. And also the wise man says: *Septies in die cadit iustus et resurgit.*" "A righteous man falls seven times, and rises again" [Prov. 24:16].

The reason why the world is so utterly perverted and in error is that for a long time there have been no genuine preachers. There are perhaps three thousand priests, among whom one cannot find four good ones— God have mercy on us in this crying shame! And when you do get a good preacher, he runs through the gospel superficially and then follows it up with a fable . . . or he mixes in something of the pagan teachers, Aristotle, Plato, Socrates, and others, who are all quite contrary to the gospel, and also contrary to God, for they did not have the knowledge of the light which we possess. Aye, if you come to me and say: The Philosopher says: Do many good works, then you will acquire the habit, and finally you will become godly; then I say to you: Do not perform good works in order to become godly; but if you are already godly, then do good works, though without affectation and with faith. There you see how contrary these two points of view are.

In former times the devil made great attacks upon the people and from these attacks they took refuge in faith and clung to the Head, which is Christ; and so he was unable to accomplish anything. So now he has invented another device; he whispers into the ears of our Junkers[5] that they should make exactions from people and give them laws. This way it looks well on the outside; but inside it is full of poison. So the young children grow up in a delusion; they go to church thinking that salvation consists in praying, fasting, and attending mass. Thus it is the preacher's fault. But still there would be no need, if only we had right preachers.

The Lord said three times to St. Peter: "*Petre, amas me? etc.; pasce oves meas*" [John 21:15–17]. "Peter, feed, feed, feed my sheep." What is the meaning of *pascere*? It means to feed. How should one feed the sheep? Only by preaching the Word of God, only by preaching faith. Then our Junkers come along

---

5. **junker:** member of the landowning nobility.

and say: *Pascere* means *leges dare*, to enact laws, but with deception. Yes, they are well fed! They feed the sheep as the butchers do on Easter eve. Whereas one should speak the Word of God plainly to guide the poor and weak in faith, they mix in their beloved Aristotle, who is contrary to God, despite the fact that Paul says in Col. [2:8]: Beware of laws and philosophy. What does "philosophy" mean? If we knew Greek, Latin, and German, we would see clearly what the Apostle is saying.

Is not this the truth? I know very well that you don't like to hear this and that I am annoying many of you; nevertheless, I shall say it. I will also advise you, no matter who you are: If you have preaching in mind or are able to help it along, then do not become a priest or a monk, for there is a passage in the thirty-third and thirty-fourth chapters of the prophet Ezekiel, unfortunately a terrifying passage, which reads: If you forsake your neighbor, see him going astray, and do not help him, do not preach to him, I will call you to account for his soul [Ezek. 33:8; 34:10]. This is a passage which is not often read. But I say, you become a priest or a monk in order to pray your seven canonical hours and say mass, and you think you want to be godly. Alas, you're a fine fellow! It [i.e., being a priest or monk] will fail you. You say the Psalter, you pray the rosary, you pray all kinds of other prayers, and say a lot of words; you say mass, you kneel before the altar, you read confession, you go on mumbling and maundering; and all the while you think you are free from sin. And yet in your heart you have such great envy that, if you could choke your neighbor and get away with it creditably, you would do it; and that's the way you say mass. It would be no wonder if a thunderbolt struck you to the ground. But if you have eaten three grains of sugar or some other seasoning, no one could drag you to the altar with red-hot tongs.[6] You have scruples! And that means to go to heaven with the devil. I know very well that you don't like to hear this. Nevertheless, I will tell the truth, I must tell the truth, even though it cost me my neck twenty times over, that the verdict may not be pronounced against me [i.e., at the last judgment].

Yes, you say, there were learned people a hundred or fifty years ago too. That is true; but I am not concerned with the length of time or the number of persons. For even though they knew something of it then, the devil has always been a mixer, who preferred the pagan writers to the holy gospel. I will tell the truth and must tell the truth; that's why I'm standing here, and not taking any money for it either. Therefore, we should not build upon human law or works, but rather have true faith in the One who is the destroyer of sin; then we shall find ourselves growing in Him. Then everything that was bitter before is sweet. Then our hearts will recognize God. And when that happens we shall be despised, and we shall pay no regard to human law, and then the pope will come and excommunicate us. But then we shall be so

---

6. Because of the rule that the priest must say mass fasting.

united with God that we shall pay no heed whatsoever to any hardship, ban, or law.

Then someone may go on and ask: Should we not keep the man-made laws at all? Or, can we not continue to pray, fast, and so on, as long as the right way is present? My answer is that if there is present a right Christian love and faith, then everything a man does is meritorious; and each may do what he wills [cf. Rom. 14:22], so long as he has no regard for works, since they cannot save him.

In conclusion, then, every single person should reflect and remember that we cannot help ourselves, but only God, and also that our works are utterly worthless. So shall we have the peace of God. And every person should so perform his work that it benefits not only himself alone, but also another, his neighbor. If he is rich, his wealth should benefit the poor. If he is poor, his service should benefit the rich. When persons are servants or maidservants, their work should benefit their master. Thus no one's work should benefit him alone; for when you note that you are serving only your own advantage, then your service is false. I am not troubled; I know very well what man-made laws are. Let the pope issue as many laws as he likes, I will keep them all so far as I please.

Therefore, dear friends, remember that God has risen up for our sakes. Therefore let us also arise to be helpful to the weak in faith, and so direct our work that God may be pleased with it. So shall we receive the peace he has given to us today. May God grant us this every day. Amen.

Source 2 from Ulrich Leupold, editor, Luther's Works, *vol. 53 (Philadelphia: Fortress, 1965), p. 305. Copyright © 1965 Fortress Press. Used by permission of Augsburg Fortress.*

2. Luther, *Lord, Keep Us Steadfast in Thy Word*, hymn, 1541–1542

1.   Lord, keep us steadfast in thy Word,
And curb the pope's and Turk's vile sword,
Who seek to topple from the throne
Jesus Christ, thine only Son.

2.   Proof of thy might, Lord Christ, afford,
For thou of all the lords art Lord;
Thine own poor Christendom defend,
That it may praise thee without end.

3.   God Holy Ghost, who comfort art,
Give to thy folk on earth one heart;
Stand by us breathing our last breath,
Lead us to life straight out of death.

3. Luther, *A Mighty Fortress Is Our God*, hymn, 1527–1528

1. A mighty fortress is our God,
A sword and shield victorious;
He breaks the cruel oppressor's rod
And wins salvation glorious.
The old satanic foe
Has sworn to work us woe!
With craft and dreadful might
He arms himself to fight.
On earth he has no equal.

2. No strength of ours can match his might!
We would be lost, rejected.
But now a champion comes to fight,
Whom God himself elected.
You ask who this may be?
The Lord of hosts is he!
Christ Jesus, mighty Lord,
God's only Son, adored.
He holds the field victorious.

3. Though hordes of devils fill the land
All threat'ning to devour us,
We tremble not, unmoved we stand;
They cannot overpow'r us,
Let this world's tyrant rage;
In battle we'll engage!
His might is doomed to fail;
God's judgment must prevail!
One little word subdues him.

4. God's Word forever shall abide,
No thanks to foes, who fear it;
For God himself fights by our side
With weapons of the Spirit.
Were they to take our house,
Goods, honor, child, or spouse,
Though life be wrenched away,

They cannot win the day.
The Kingdom's ours forever!

4. Paul Speratus, *Salvation unto Us Has Come*, hymn, 1524

1.   Salvation unto us has come
By God's free grace and favor;
Good works cannot avert our doom,
They help and save us never.
Faith looks to Jesus Christ alone,
Who did for all the world atone;
He is our mediator.

2.   Theirs was a false, misleading dream
Who thought God's law was given
That sinners might themselves redeem
And by their works gain heaven.
The Law is but a mirror bright
To bring the inbred sin to light
That lurks within our nature.

3.   And yet the Law fulfilled must be,
Or we were lost forever;
Therefore God sent his Son that he
Might us from death deliver.
He all the Law for us fulfilled,
And thus his Father's anger stilled
Which over us impended.

4.   Faith clings to Jesus' cross alone
And rests in him unceasing;
And by its fruits true faith is known,
With love and hope unceasing.
For faith alone can justify;
Works serve our neighbor and supply
The proof that faith is living.

5.   All blessing, honor, thanks, and praise
To Father, Son, and Spirit,
The God who saved us by his grace;
All glory to his merit
O triune God in heav'n above,
You have revealed your saving love;
Your blessed name we hallow.

5. Matthias Gerung, Broadsheet, Lauingen (Germany), 1546

Source 6 from the Mitchell Collection, London.

6. Matthias Gerung, Broadsheet, Lauingen, 1546

Source 7 from The Pierpont Morgan Library, New York/Art Resource NY.

7. Lucas Cranach, Pamphlet, Wittenberg (Germany), 1521

9. Lucas Cranach, Pamphlet, Wittenberg, 1545[7]

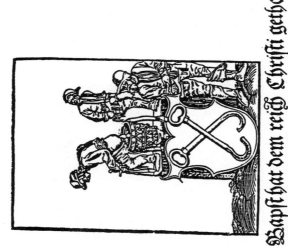

8. Unknown Artist, Pamphlet, Augsburg (Germany), 1522

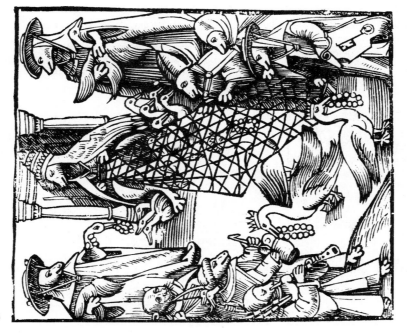

7. The lines below the woodcut read, "The pope has done to the kingdom of Christ/What is here being done to his own crown."

Source 10 from Oskar Schade, Satiren und Pasquille aus der Reformationszeit, *vol. 2, no. 15 (Hannover: 1863). Selection translated by Merry E. Wiesner.*

10. Anonymous German Pamphlet, 1523

A dialogue between two good friends named Hans Tholl and Claus Lamp, talking about the Antichrist[8] and his followers.

They are in a good mood while drinking wine and sit and discuss some ideas from the letters of Paul.

PREFACE

Dear Christians and brothers, if we want to recognize and know the Antichrist, we have to go to the brothers who can read, so that they will read us the second chapter of the second letter of Paul to the Thessalonians. There we will clearly find him, with his gestures and manners, how he acted and still acts, how he is now revealed so that we do not have to wait any longer but can know him despite his masks. How the devil sends his followers to knock us down, and how the old women and bath maids see him. We have long been blind to the lies and deceits of Satan, the devil. Because we have not paid attention to the divine warnings from Daniel, Paul, Christ, Peter, and the apocalypse of John, God has tormented us with ghosts and apparitions who will take us all with them to hell. Why should this cause God to suffer when He has offered you His holy word? If you don't want it, then go to the devil, for he is here now. He sees, finds, and possesses.

It happened that Hans Tholl and Claus Lamp were looking for each other and finally found each other in the evening.

CLAUS: My friend Hans, where have you been all day? I've been looking for you. The innkeeper has a good wine for two cents, and I wanted to drink a glass of wine with you.
HANS: Dear friend, I've been in a place that I wouldn't take six glasses of wine for.
CLAUS: So tell me where you have been.
HANS: I've got exciting news.
CLAUS: Well, what is it then? Tell me!
HANS: I was in a place where a friend read to four of us from the Bible. He read in the second chapter of the second letter of Paul to the Thessalonians about the Antichrist and how one is to recognize him.

---

8. **Antichrist:** the devil.

CLAUS: Oh I would have given a penny to have been there.

HANS: I want you to believe that I haven't heard anything like this in my whole life; I wouldn't have given three pennies to miss it.

CLAUS: Can't you remember anything, Hans? Can you tell me something about it?

HANS: I think I can tell you about almost the whole chapter, and only leave a little out.

CLAUS: So tell me! But let's get some wine first. I'll pay for yours.

HANS: Here's to your money!

CLAUS: Innkeeper, bring some wine.

HANS: What does he get for it?

CLAUS: He gets two cents. Now, tell me! I really want to hear what you will say about the Antichrist.

HANS: I'll tell you, but it will seem strange to you.

CLAUS: Why?

HANS: It seemed strange and odd to me, too, that people or states are the Antichrist.

CLAUS: Go ahead, then, you're boring me.

HANS: Stop that. All right, here's what the chapter says: "Dear brothers," Paul writes to the Thessalonians, "We ask you in the name of the coming of Christ and our coming together for the same, that you not be moved in your senses (or from your senses), or frightened by the spirit or the word or by letters supposedly coming from us, saying that the day of the Lord has come or will be coming soon. Let no one deceive you in any way, it will come only when there is disagreement and disunity (even though they all say they are preaching and believing nothing but the Gospel and Christianity) and the man of lawlessness will be disclosed, the son of damnation, who is against the gospel. Then he will be raised up (here Claus Lamp began to understand) above everything that is called a god (or is worshipped as a god) until he sits in the temple of God and lets himself be prayed to as if he were God." Claus, what are you thinking about? Do you know this man of lawlessness?

CLAUS: Now all the devils will come for you! He is no other beast than the Pope and his realm. I would never in my whole life have realized that if you hadn't been there [to hear it]. I'll buy you a second glass of wine!

HANS: Be quiet! I want to tell you more.

CLAUS: My dear friend, still more?

HANS: Of course. First I'll tell you the reason why I was talked to for so long.

CLAUS: My friend, for God's sake keep talking!

HANS: So listen! Here is the text: Paul says: "Don't you remember the things that I told you when I was with you? And now you know what is holding him (or what you should pay attention to), and that he will be revealed in his time. I tell you, that now he is doing so many evil and underhanded things, that only those who stop it now will stop it when his time comes fully. And then he will be revealed, the lawless one"—listen here, Claus—" who the lord Jesus Christ will slay with the breath of His mouth and will totally destroy with the light of His coming. But the coming of the Antichrist is through the activity of Satan, the devil, with great power and supposed signs and wonders, and with misguided celebration of the evil of those who will be destroyed. Because they would not accept the love of truth" (this clearly refers to the Gospel)" and be saved, God sends them the results of their errors, a great delusion, so that they believe the lies and are all condemned who did not believe the truth but agreed to the evil (and took it on themselves)." See that, Claus! Now you have heard why God has allowed error. Even though we have long wanted not to do wrong, we still hard-headedly keep doing it.

CLAUS: That says a lot. I would set my life on it, if it were only half as important. Now I hear and see that God allows very little understanding.

HANS: Yes, and why? People don't want to know very much and don't go to the Bible. God has hardened them and we are so godless. God will make us suffer because we don't ask about the truth. If we only had half as much concern about the health of our souls as we have about material goods, we wouldn't have come so far from the right path. As you have just heard, it isn't God who sent the so-called preachers [to lead us astray]. Here, I'll say it to you straight: Paul goes on to say: "Dear brothers, we should give thanks to God at all times because he chose you from the beginning, and he called you through the Gospel" (and not through other fairy-stories, as people are now saying).

CLAUS: Unfortunately you are right. Right now I hear strange things about the beast of the Antichrist from priests and monks. God help us!

HANS: Yes, we need to pray earnestly to God to send us good preachers, that preach the pure Gospel and leave the fairy stories at home.

CLAUS: My friend, I am still thinking about the Antichrist, that he has begun so many devilish things and made the whole world to be his fool.

HANS: That astonishers me, too. But you have now heard from Paul, when he says: "God has allowed them to be deluded because they have not accepted the truth." We haven't noticed this, and the priests have hidden it from us.

CLAUS: I believe that the devil has possessed them all so that they haven't preached to us about these things.

HANS: They are afraid that people would recognize that their God, the Pope, is the Antichrist. People are supposed to honor and pray to him, just like Paul says about the Antichrist. So they are afraid.

CLAUS: That's really true. They've thought: If we tell the lay people this, they will notice and think about how they have to kiss the Pope's foot and call him "most holy." And some know-it-alls even say: The Pope can't do any wrong; he can't sin.

HANS: It's amazing that God has allowed this to happen for so long, that it hasn't been made clear that we have been so blind. What really matters is that we have deserted the truth, my dear Claus. Let's ask God for the true faith!

[323]

I see clearly that everything will soon be over, that the Last judgment stands right before the door!

CLAUS: My dear brother Hans, I've thought that for a long time. Shall we go home?

HANS: Yes, let's drink up and go.

CLAUS: I don't want to drink any more, because I have been so seized by pity and compassion. I see that things will end soon. My dear Hans, I want to take this thing to its end with you, so I have to ask: what do you think about the fact that there is such a commotion now about Luther and his writings?

HANS: I think it's because he has discovered the Antichrist. He can't stand it, and I believe he will make many martyrs. I've heard that it has already started in some places; in Antwerp three people have been burnt because of his teachings. And I've heard that in some places they are imprisoning people and hunting them down.

CLAUS: If that's true, that's what's supposed to happen. I have always heard that the Antichrist will make martyrs and will pay money so that people will kill those who do not believe in him but instead preach the word of God.

HANS: I've heard that, too. Now to the next thing: when I want to hear more things read, I'll tell you.

CLAUS: My dear friend, I'll let everything be open to you, because I see clearly what will come out of it. I see clearly, if I want to be saved, I have to come back to the true faith, from which without a doubt the Antichrist and his horde have led us. God give you a good night!

HANS: Same to you! See that you don't forget what I've said.

CLAUS: I won't for the rest of my life. God be praised.

QUESTIONS TO CONSIDER

In exploring how the Reformation movement grew and took root throughout Europe, many scholars point to the printing press as the key factor in explaining why Luther's reforms had a much greater impact than those of Wyclif and Hus. After examining the sources, would you agree? What difference did it make that Luther's sermons were not only delivered but also printed? That hymns were taught not simply to choirs of monks or clergymen but to congregations of laypeople, out of hymnals that were printed and might be purchased by any fairly well-to-do member? That small pamphlets such as the one reproduced here were written in German and appeared in paperback?

Several historians have also pointed to the opposite effect, that the Protestant emphasis on individual reading of the Bible dramatically increased the demand for books. Judging by the language, what sort of person might have bought Luther's sermon or the pamphlet? What effects would you expect the Protestant Reformation to have had on literacy? The religious conflict itself was also a spur to book production and book buying, and religious works were the best sellers of the sixteenth century. What techniques did the pamphlet writer use to make his work more appealing to a buyer? How might including some of the woodcuts have affected sales?

Of course, the great majority of people in the sixteenth century could not read, so it may be wrong to overemphasize written sources of communication. As you noticed in the dialogue, however, people who could not read often turned to their neighbors who could, and so printed pamphlets were often heard by many who could not read them themselves. This dialogue itself was probably read out loud and may even have been acted out, which we know was the case with more elaborate dialogues containing stage directions and a whole cast of characters. Do you think this dialogue would have been effective read aloud rather than silently? The printing press also increased the circulation of visual images; woodcuts such as those reproduced here often became best sellers. Why did so many people purchase these woodcuts? If a person's only contact with Protestant thinking were images such as these, how would his or her beliefs have differed from those of a person who could read Luther's words as well?

To answer the second question— how the Protestant message was made attractive to people—look at your list of frequently repeated ideas and images. Which seem directed to all Christians? For example, what do the sources say about the role of good works in helping a person achieve salvation? The role of faith? Why might these ideas have been appealing? What was wrong with the Catholic clergy? In contrast, what did "good preachers" do and emphasize? Why might the contrast have made Luther's ideas attractive?

Though ideas and images were often repeated, not everyone understood them in the same way or was attracted to them for the same reasons. Different groups within German society responded to different parts of the Protestant message and must be examined separately. Begin with the peasants. How are they depicted in the various sources? Why did the pamphlet writer and the artist of Source 9 choose to make their characters peasants? In the heaven and hell woodcuts, where are peasants and poor people? Why would peasants have been particularly attracted to the criticism of indulgences? Why would Luther's ideas about the value of good works have appealed to them? Source 5 shows nobles in fancy feathered hats near hell, and Source 8 depicts rulers as geese; how would peasants have responded to these images? In the dialogue, Claus and Hans both agree that the Last Judgment is near. Why might sixteenth-century peasants have accepted this idea of the imminence of the end of the world?

Now consider the nobles and rulers. We have already noted that several of the woodcuts portray them negatively. How did Luther portray them in his sermon? Though hostility to nobles and rulers is evident in the Protestant message, many of the movement's ideas and images appealed to this class. Look, for example, at the upper-right picture in Source 7. How does this scene reflect the hostility of rulers to the papacy? The noble class was primarily responsible for military actions in sixteenth-century Germany. How would they have responded to the language of the hymns? What effect might linking the Turks and the pope in the hymn in Source 2 and the woodcut of Source 6 have had? Sources 1, 3, 6, and 10 all include devils attacking people or dragging them to hell at the Last Judgment. Why might nobles have been attracted to such imagery? What message would they have gotten from imagery linking such devils with the pope? In what ways did the reasons why Luther's ideas appealed to nobles contradict the reasons they appealed to peasants?

Other groups in German society appear only rarely in the sources given here, so you will not be able to discover as much about the ways in which the Protestant message attracted them as you can in the case of peasants and nobles. You may, however, want to review the sources for evidence relating to the middle class, which you can find most easily in the woodcuts. Which of your answers about the reasons certain ideas were appealing to peasants or nobles would also apply to middle-class people?

You are now ready to answer both questions posed in this chapter. How were the basic concepts of the Reformation communicated to a wide range of the population? How were these concepts made attractive to different groups?

EPILOGUE

Though Luther's initial message was one of religious reform, people quickly saw its social, economic, and political implications. The free imperial knights used Luther's attack on the wealth of the Church and his ideas about the spiritual equality of all Christians to justify their rebellion in 1521. Quickly suppressed, this uprising was followed by a more serious rebellion by peasants in 1525. Peasants in south Germany added religious demands, such as a call for taxes, to their long-standing economic grievances and took up arms. The Peasants' War spread eastward and northward but was never unified militarily, and it was brutally put down by imperial and noble armies later in the same year.

Given some of Luther's remarks about rulers and human laws (as you read in the sermon), the peasants expected him to support them. He did not, but urged them instead to obey their rulers, for in his opinion religion was not a valid justification for political revolution or social upheaval. When the peasants did not listen and continued their rebellion, Luther turned against them, calling them "murdering and thieving-hordes." He supported the rulers in their slaughter of peasant armies, and his later writings became much more conservative than the sermon you read here.

The nobles and rulers who accepted Luther's message continued to receive his support, however. Many of the German states abolished the Catholic Church and established their own Protestant churches under their individual ruler's control. This expulsion led to a series of religious wars between Protestants and Catholics that were finally ended by the Peace of Augsburg in 1555. The terms of the peace treaty allowed rulers to choose between Catholicism and Lutheran Protestantism; they were further given the right to enforce religious uniformity within their territories. By the middle of the sixteenth century, then, the only people who could respond as they chose to the Protestant message were rulers.

Achieving religious uniformity was not as simple a task as it had been earlier, however. Though rulers attempted to ban materials they did not agree with and prevent their subjects from reading or printing forbidden materials, religious literature was regularly smuggled from city to city. Because printing presses could produce thousands of copies of anything fairly quickly, ideas of all types spread much more quickly than they had earlier. Once people can read, it is much more difficult to control the information they take in; though rulers could control their subjects' outward religious activities, they could not control their thoughts.

Rulers were not the only ones who could not control thinking and the exchange of ideas during the sixteenth century. As Luther discovered to his dismay, once ideas are printed and widely disseminated, they take on a life of their own; no matter how much one might wish, they cannot be called back or be made to conform to their original meaning. Not only did German knights and peasants interpret Luther's message in their own way, but other religious reformers, building on what he had written, de-veloped their own interpretations of the Christian message. They used the same variety of methods that had been so successful in spreading Luther's ideas to communicate their own, and the Protestant Reformation became a multifaceted movement with many different leaders and numerous plans for action.

The Catholic church, learning from Protestant successes, began to publish its own illustrated pamphlets with negative images of Luther and other Protestant leaders along with explanations of its theology in easy-to-understand language. In this chapter we have looked exclusively at Lutheran propaganda, but the oral, written, and visual techniques of communication presented here were employed by all sides in the sixteenth-century religious conflict. Later they would be adapted for other political and intellectual debates.

CHAPTER FOURTEEN
STAGING ABSOLUTISM

THE PROBLEM

The "Age of Absolutism" is the label historians often apply to the history of Europe in the seventeenth and eighteenth centuries. In many ways it is an appropriate description because, with the exception of the Dutch Republic and England (where the Civil War of 1642–1648 and the Glorious Revolution of 1688 severely limited royal power), most major European states in this era had monarchs who aspired to absolute authority in their realms.

The royal absolutism that evolved in seventeenth-century Europe represents an important step in governmental development. In constructing absolutist states, monarchs and their ministers both created new organs of administration and built on existing institutions of government to supplant the regional authorities of the medieval state with more centralized state power. In principle, this centralized authority was subject to the absolute authority of the monarch; in practice, royal authority was nowhere as encompassing as that of a modern dictator. Poor communication

systems, the persistence of traditional privileges that exempted whole regions or social groups from full royal authority, and other factors all set limits on royal power. Nevertheless, monarchs of the era strove for the ideal of absolute royal power, and France was the model in their work of state building.

French monarchs of the seventeenth and early eighteenth centuries more fully developed the system of absolute monarchy. In these rulers' efforts to overcome impediments to royal authority, we can learn much about the creation of absolutism in Europe. Rulers in Prussia, Austria, Russia, and many smaller states sought not only the real power of the French kings, but also the elaborate court ceremony and dazzling palaces that symbolized that power.

Absolutism in France was the work of Henry IV (r. 1589–1610), Louis XIII (r. 1610–1643) and his minister Cardinal Richelieu, and Louis XIV (r. 1643–1715). These rulers established a system of centralized royal political authority that destroyed many remnants of the feudal monarchy. The reward for their endeavors was great: With Europe's largest population and immense wealth, France was potentially the mightiest country on the Continent in 1600 and its natural leader, if only these national strengths could be unified and directed by a strong government. Just as importantly, these monarchs endeavored to create strong central governments as proof against internal disorders, like rebellion and civil warfare, that plagued the medieval state. But French rulers confronted formidable problems, common to many early modern states, in achieving their goals. Nobles everywhere still held considerable power, in part a legacy of the system of feudal monarchy. In France they possessed military power, which they used in the religious civil wars of the sixteenth century and in their Fronde revolt against growing royal power in the mid-seventeenth century. Nobles also exercised considerable political power through such representative bodies as the Estates General and provincial assemblies, which gave form to their claims for a voice in government. Moreover, nobles served as the judges of the great law courts, the *parlements,* which had to register all royal edicts before they could take effect.

A second obstacle to national unity and royal authority in many states, in an age that equated national unity with religious uniformity, was the presence of a large and influential religious minority. In France the Protestant minority was known as the Huguenots. Not only did they forswear the Catholic religion of the king and the majority of his subjects, but they possessed military power through their rights, under the Edict of Nantes,[1] to fortify their cities.

A third and major impediment to unifying a country under absolute royal authority was regional differences. The medieval monarchy of France had been built province by province over several centuries, and the kingdom was not well integrated. Some provinces, like Brittany in the north, retained local estates or assemblies with which the monarch actually had to bargain for taxes. Many provinces had their own cultural heritage that separated them from the king's government centered in Paris. These differences might be as simple as matters of local custom, but they might also be as complex as unique systems of civil law. A particular problem was the persistence of local dialects, which made the French of royal officials a foreign and incomprehensible tongue in large portions of the kingdom.

The only unifying principle that could overcome all these centrifugal forces was royal authority. The task in the seventeenth century was to build a theoretical basis for a truly powerful monarch, to endow the king with tangible power that gave substance to theory, and to place the sovereign in a setting that would never permit the country to forget his new power.

To establish an abstract basis for absolutism, royal authority had to be strengthened and reinforced by a

1. **Edict of Nantes:** In this 1598 decree, King Henry IV sought to end the civil warfare between French Catholics and Huguenots. He granted the Protestants basic protection, in the event of renewed fighting, by allowing them to fortify some 200 of their cities. The edict also accorded the Protestants freedom of belief with some restrictions, and civil rights equal to those of Catholic Frenchmen.

veritable cult of kingship. Seventeenth-century French statesmen built on medieval foundations in this task. Medieval kings had possessed limited tangible authority but substantial religious prestige; their vassals had rendered them religious oaths of loyalty. French monarchs since Pepin the Short had been anointed in a biblically inspired coronation ceremony in which they received not only the communion bread that the Catholic Church administered to all believers, but also the wine, which was normally reserved for clerics; once crowned, they claimed to possess mystical religious powers to heal with the royal touch. All these trappings served to endow the monarch with almost divine powers, separating him from and raising him above his subjects. Many seventeenth-century thinkers emphasized this traditional divine dimension of royal power. Others, as you will see, found more practical grounds for great royal power.

To achieve greater royal power, Henry IV reestablished peace after the religious civil warfare of the late sixteenth century, and Cardinal Richelieu curbed the military power of the nobility. With the creation of loyal provincial administrators, the *intendants,* and a system of political patronage that he directed, the cardinal also established firmer central control in the name of Louis XIII. Richelieu, moreover, ended Huguenot political power by crushing their revolt in 1628, and he intervened in the Thirty Years' War to establish France as a chief European power.

The reign of Louis XIV completed the process of consolidating royal authority in France. Louis XIV created much of the administrative apparatus necessary to centralize the state. The king brought the nobility under even greater control, building in Europe's largest army a force that could defeat any aristocratic revolt and creating in Versailles a court life that drew nobles away from provincial plotting and near to the king, where their actions could be observed. The king also sought to extend royal authority by expanding France's borders through a series of wars and to eliminate the Huguenot minority completely by revoking the religious freedoms embodied in the Edict of Nantes.

The king supplemented his military and political work of state building with other projects to integrate France more completely as one nation. With royal patronage, authors and scholars flourished and, by the example of their often excellent works, extended the French dialect in the country at the expense of provincial tongues. In the king's name, his finance minister, Jean-Baptiste Colbert (1619–1683), sought to realize a vision of a unified French economy. He designed mercantilist policies to favor French trade and build French industry, and he improved transportation to bind the country together as one unit. The result of Louis's policies, therefore, was not only a stronger king and a more powerful France but a more unified country as well.

Far more than previous French monarchs, Louis XIV addressed the third task in establishing absolutism. In modern terms, it consisted of effective public relations, which required visible evidence of the new royal authority. The stage setting for the royal display of the symbols of absolute authority was Versailles, the site of a new royal palace. Built between 1661 and 1682, the palace itself was massive, with a façade one-quarter mile long pierced by 2,143 windows. It was set in a park of 37,000 acres, of which 6,000 acres were embellished with formal gardens. These gardens contained 1,400 fountains that required massive hydraulic works to supply them with water, an artificial lake one mile long for royal boating parties, and 200 statues. The palace grounds contained various smaller palaces as well, including Marly, where the king could entertain small, select groups away from the main palace, which was the center of a court life embracing almost 20,000 persons (9,000 soldiers billeted in the town; and 5,000 royal servants, 1,000 nobles and their 4,000 servants, plus the royal family, all housed in the main palace). Because the royal ministers and their secretaries also were in residence, Versailles was much more than a palace: It was the capital of France.

Royal architects deliberately designed the palace to impart a message to all who entered. As a guidebook of 1681 by Laurent Morellet noted regarding the palace's art:

The subjects of painting which complete the decorations of the ceilings are of heroes and illustrious men, taken from history and fable, who have deserved the titles of Magnanimous, of Great, of Fathers of the People, of Liberal, of Just, of August and Victorious, and who have possessed all the Virtues which we have seen appear in the Person of our Great Monarch during the fortunate course of his reign; so that everything remarkable which one sees in the Château and in the garden always has some relationship with the great actions of His Majesty.[2]

The court ritual and etiquette enacted in this setting departed markedly from the simpler court life of Louis XIII and were designed to complement the physical presence of the palace itself in teaching the lesson of a new royal power.

In this chapter we will analyze royal absolutism in France. What was the theoretical basis for absolute royal authority? What was traditional and what was new in the justification of royal power as expressed in late-sixteenth- and seventeenth-century France? How did such early modern kings as Louis XIV communicate their absolute power in the various ceremonies and symbols of royal authority presented in the evidence that follows?

SOURCES AND METHOD

This chapter assembles several kinds of sources, each demanding a different kind of historical analysis. Two works of political theory that were influential

2. Laurent Morellet, *Explication historique de ce qu'il y a de plus remarquable dans la maison royale de Versailles et en celle de Monsieur à Saint-Cloud* (Paris, 1681), quoted in Robert W. Hartle, "Louis XIV and the Mirror of Antiquity" in Steven G. Reinhardt and Vaughn L. Glasgow, eds., *The Sun King: Louis XIV and the New World* (New Orleans: Louisiana State Museum Foundation, 1984), p. 111.

in the formation of absolutism open the evidence. To analyze these works effectively, you will need some brief background information on their authors and on the problems these thinkers discussed.

Jean Bodin (1530–1596) was a law professor, an attorney, and a legal official. His interests transcended his legal education, however. He brought a wide reading in Hebrew, Greek, Italian, and German to the central problem addressed in his major work, *The Six Books of the Republic* (1576), that of establishing the well-ordered state. Writing during the religious wars of the sixteenth century, when government in France all but broke down, Bodin offered answers to this crisis. Especially novel for the sixteenth century was his call for religious toleration. Although he was at least formally a Catholic[3] and recognized unity in religion as a strong unifying factor for a country, Bodin was unwilling to advocate the use of force in eliminating Protestantism from France. He believed that acceptance was by far the better policy.

Bodin's political thought was also significant, and his *Republic* immediately was recognized as an important work. Published in several editions and translated into Latin, Italian, Spanish, and German, the *Republic* influenced

a circle of men, the *Politiques*, who advised Henry IV. Through the process of seeking to explain how to establish the well-ordered state, Bodin contributed much to Western political theory. Perhaps his most important idea was that there was nothing divine about governing power. Men created governments solely to ensure their physical and material security; to meet those needs, the ruling power had to exercise a sovereignty on which Bodin placed few limits.[4] Indeed, Bodin's concept of the ruler's power is his most important contribution to political thought. What is the essence of royal sovereignty for Bodin? What other governing power did the monarch possess? How did Bodin's vision point to the end of the feudal state that still partially existed in his time?

The second work of political theory was written by Jacques Bénigne Bossuet (1627–1704), Bishop of Meaux. A great orator who preached at the court of Louis XIV, Bossuet was entrusted with the education of the king's son and heir, the Dauphin. He wrote three works for that prince's instruction, including the one excerpted in this chapter, *Politics Drawn from the Very Words of the Holy Scripture* (1678).

As tutor to the Dauphin and royal preacher, Bossuet expressed what has been called the *divine right* theory of kingship: that is, the king was God's deputy on earth, and to oppose him was to oppose divine law. Here, of course, the bishop was drawing on

3. Bodin's religious thought evolved in the course of his life. Although he was brought up a Catholic and was briefly a Carmelite friar, his knowledge of Hebrew and early regard for the Old Testament led some to suspect that he was a Jew. The writings of his middle years indicate some Calvinist leanings. Later in life, his thought seems to have moved beyond traditional Catholic and Protestant Christianity. He was nevertheless deeply religious.

4. Bodin saw the sovereign power as limited by natural law and the need to respect property (which meant that the ruler could not tax without his subjects' consent) and the family.

those medieval beliefs and practices imputing certain divine powers to the king. Because Bossuet was an influential member of the court of Louis XIV, his ideas on royal authority carried considerable weight. Trained as a theologian, he buttressed his political theories with scriptural authority. In this selection, determine the extent of the royal link to God. Why might such a theory be particularly useful to Louis XIV?

Source 3 is a selection from the *Memoirs* of Louis de Rouvroy, duke of Saint-Simon (1675–1755). Saint-Simon's memoirs of court life are extensive, comprising forty-one volumes in the main French edition. They constitute both a remarkable record of life at Versailles and, because of their style, an important example of French literature. As useful and important as the *Memoirs* are, however, they must be read with care. All of us, consciously or unconsciously, have biases and opinions, and memoirists are no exception. In fact, memoir literature illustrates problems of which students of history should be aware in everything they read. The way in which authors present events, even what they choose to include or omit from their accounts, reflects their opinions. Because memoir writers often recount events in which they participated, they may have especially strong views about what they relate. Thus, to use Saint-Simon's work profitably, it is essential to understand his point of view. We must also ask if the memoir writer was in a position to know firsthand what he or she is relating or is simply recounting less reliable rumors.

Saint-Simon came from an old noble family that had recently risen to prominence when his father became a royal favorite. Ironically, no one was more deeply opposed to the policies of Louis XIV, which aimed to destroy the traditional feudal power of the nobility in the name of royal authority, than this man whose position rested on that very authority. Saint-Simon was, quite simply, a defender of the older style of kingship, in which sovereignty was limited by the monarch's need to consult with his vassals. His memoirs reflect this view and are often critical of the king. But even with his critical view of the king and his court, Saint-Simon was an important figure there, an individual privy to state business and court gossip, who gives us a remarkable picture of life at Versailles. Analyze the court etiquette and ritual that Saint-Simon describes as a nonverbal message from the king to his most powerful subjects. For example, what message did the royal waking and dressing ceremony convey to the most powerful and privileged persons in France, who crowded the royal bedroom and vied for the privilege of helping the king dress? What message did their very presence convey in turn to Louis XIV? Recall Bossuet's ideas of kingship. Why might public religious rituals such as that attending the royal rising be part of the agenda of a king who was not particularly noted for his piety during the first half of his life?

Studied closely, the three different kinds of written evidence presented—the work of a sixteenth-century political theorist, the writings of a contemporary supporter, and the memoirs of one of the king's opponents—reveal much about the growing power of the French monarchy. What common themes do you find in these works? What were the sources of the king's political authority?

From these written sources, we move on to pictorial evidence of the symbols of royal authority. Symbols are concrete objects possessing a meaning beyond what is immediately apparent. We are all aware of the power of symbols, particularly in our age of electronic media, and we all, perhaps unconsciously, analyze them to some extent. Take a simple example drawn from modern advertising: The lion appears frequently as an image in advertisements for banks and other financial institutions. The lion's presence is intended to convey to us the strength of the financial institution, to inspire our faith in the latter's ability to protect our funds. Using this kind of analysis, you can determine the total meaning of the symbols associated with Louis XIV.

Consider the painting presented as the fourth piece of evidence, *Louis XIV Taking Up Personal Government* in 1661. Louis XIV had been king in name since the age of five after his father's death in 1643, but only in 1661, as an adult, did he assume full power. Remember that such art was generally commissioned by the king and often had an instructional purpose. What do the following elements symbolize: the portrayal of Louis XIV as a Roman emperor; the positioning of a figure representing France on his right; the crowning of the king with a wreath of flowers; the figure of Time (note the hourglass

and scythe) holding a tapestry over the royal head; and the presence of herald angels hovering above?

Now go on to the other pictures and perform the same kind of analysis, always trying to identify the symbolic message that the painter or architect wished to convey. For Source 5, study the royal pose and such seemingly superficial elements in the picture as the king's dress and the background details. Ask yourself what ideas these were intended to convey. Source 6 presents the insignia Louis XIV chose as his personal symbol, which decorated much of Versailles. Reflect on Louis's reasons for this choice in reading his explanation:

The symbol that I have adopted and that you see all around you represents the duties of a Prince and inspires me always to fulfill them. I chose for an emblem the Sun which, according to the rules of this art [heraldry], is the noblest of all, and which, by the brightness that surrounds it, by the light it lends to the other stars that constitute, after a fashion, its court, by the universal good it does, endlessly promoting life, joy, and growth, by its perpetual and regular movement, by its constant and invariable course, is assuredly the most dazzling and most beautiful image of the monarch.[5]

Finally, Source 7 portrays Louis XIV costumed for one of the many pageants enjoyed by the king in his younger years. He wears the garb of a Roman emperor, an official who ruled much of the ancient world. What does the king's choice

5. Quoted in Reinhardt and Glasgow, *The Sun King,* p. 181.

of costume suggest about his vision of his own role in the world?

With Sources 8 through 13, we turn to analysis of architecture, which of course also served to symbolize royal power. You must ask yourself how great that concept of royal power was as you look at the pictures of Versailles. The palace, after all, was not only the royal residence but also the setting for the conduct of government, including the king's reception of foreign ambassadors. At the most basic level, notice the scale of the palace. What impression might its size have been intended to convey? At a second level, examine decorative details of the palace. Why might the balustrade at the palace entry have been decorated with statuary symbolizing Magnificence, Justice, Wisdom, Prudence, Diligence, Peace, Europe, Asia, Renown, Abundance, Force, Generosity, Wealth, Authority, Fame, America, Africa, and Victory?

Observe the views of the palace's interior, considering the functions of the rooms and their details. Source 10 offers a view of the royal chapel at Versailles. Richly decorated in marble and complemented with ceiling paintings such as that depicting the Trinity, the chapel was the site of daily masses as well as of royal marriages and celebrations of victories. Note that the king attended mass in the royal gallery, joining the rest of the court on the main floor only when the mass celebrant was a bishop. Why might such a magnificent setting be part of the palace? More important, what significance do you place on the position the king chose for himself in this grand setting?

Sources 11 and 12 present the sites of the royal rising ceremony described by Saint-Simon. The royal bedroom, Source 11, was richly decorated in gilt, red, and white, and was complemented by paintings of biblical scenes. Notice the rich decoration of the Bull's Eye Window Antechamber (Source 12), just outside the bedroom, where the courtiers daily awaited the king's arising. Why were the rooms decorated in such a fashion?

Source 13 offers an artist's view of Marly. Again, notice the scale of this palace, reflecting that it was, according to Saint-Simon, a weekend getaway spot for Louis XIV and selected favorites. How might the king have used invitations to this château, with the closeness to the royal person they entailed? Examine details of the palace. The central château had twelve apartments, four of which were reserved for the royal family, the others for its guests. The twelve pavilions around the lake in the center of the château's grounds each housed two guest apartments and represented the twelve signs of the zodiac. What symbolic importance might you attach to this?

Finally, return to Source 7, which recreates the pageant known as the Carousel of 1662, one of many such entertainments at court. The scale of such festivals could be huge. In 1662, 12,197 costumed people took part in a celebration that included a parade through the streets of Paris and games. Costumed as ancient Romans, Persians, and others, the participants must have made quite an impression on their audience. What kind of impression do you think it was?

What common message runs through the art and architecture you have analyzed? As you unravel the message woven into this visual evidence, combine it with the evidence you derived from Saint-Simon's portrayal of court life and the political theory of absolutism. Remember, too, the unstated message: that the monarchy of Louis XIV possessed in Europe's largest army the ultimate means for persuading its subjects to accept the divine powers of the king. You should be able to determine from all this material what was new in this conception of royal authority and the ways in which the new authority was expressed.

THE EVIDENCE

Source 1 from Francis William Coker, editor, Readings in Political Philosophy *(New York: Macmillan, 1926), pp. 235–236.*

1. From Jean Bodin, *The Six Books of the Republic,* Book I, 1576

The first and principal function of sovereignty is to give laws to the citizens generally and individually, and, it must be added, not necessarily with the consent of superiors, equals, or inferiors. If the consent of superiors is required, then the prince is clearly a subject; if he must have the consent of equals, then others share his authority; if the consent of inferiors—the people or the senate—is necessary, then he lacks supreme authority. . . .

It may be objected that custom does not get its power from the judgment or command of the prince, and yet has almost the force of law, so that it would seem that the prince is master of law, the people of custom. Custom, insensibly, yet with the full compliance of all, passes gradually into the character of men, and acquires force with the lapse of time. Law, on the other hand, comes forth in one moment at the order of him who has the power to command, and often in opposition to the desire and approval of those whom it governs. Wherefore, Chrysostom[6] likens law to a tyrant and custom to a king. Moreover, the power of law is far greater than that of custom, for customs may be superseded by laws, but laws are not supplanted by customs; it is within the power and function of magistrates to restore the operation of laws which by custom are obsolescent. Custom proposes neither rewards nor penalties; laws carry one or the other, unless it be a permissive law which nullifies the penalty of some other law. In short, a custom has compelling force only as long as the prince, by adding his endorsement and sanction to the custom, makes it a law.

6. **Chrysostom:** Saint John Chrysostom (ca 347–407), an early Father of the Greek church and a brilliant preacher whose religion led him to condemn the vices of the court of the Eastern Roman emperor.

It is thus clear that laws and customs depend for their force upon the will of those who hold supreme power in the state. This first and chief mark of sovereignty is, therefore, of such sort that it cannot be transferred to subjects, though the prince or people sometimes confer upon one of the citizens the power to frame laws (*legum condendarum*), which then have the same force as if they had been framed by the prince himself. The Lacedæmonians bestowed such power upon Lycurgus, the Athenians upon Solon;[7] each stood as deputy for his state, and the fulfillment of his function depended upon the pleasure not of himself but of the people; his legislation had no force save as the people confirmed it by their assent. The former composed and wrote the laws, the people enacted and commanded them.

Under this supreme power of ordaining and abrogating laws, it is clear that all other functions of sovereignty are included; that it may be truly said that supreme authority in the state is comprised in this one thing—namely, to give laws to all and each of the citizens, and to receive none from them. For to declare war or make peace, though seeming to involve what is alien to the term law, is yet accomplished by law, that is by decree of the supreme power. It is also the prerogative of sovereignty to receive appeals from the highest magistrates, to confer authority upon the greater magistrates and to withdraw it from them, to allow exemption from taxes, to bestow other immunities, to grant dispensations from the laws, to exercise power of life and death, to fix the value, name and form of money, to compel all citizens to observe their oaths: all of these attributes are derived from the supreme power of commanding and forbidding—that is, from the authority to give law to the citizens collectively and individually, and to receive law from no one save immortal God. A duke, therefore, who gives laws to all his subjects, but receives law from the emperor, Pope, or king, or has a co-partner in authority, lacks sovereignty.

Source 2 from Richard H. Powers, editor and translator, Readings in European Civilization Since 1500 *(Boston: Houghton Mifflin, 1961), pp. 129–130. Reprinted by permission of the Estate of Richard H. Powers.*

2. From Jacques Bénigne Bossuet, *Politics Drawn from the Very Words of the Holy Scripture,* 1678

TO MONSEIGNEUR LE DAUPHIN

God is the King of kings. It is for Him to instruct and direct kings as His ministers. Heed then, Monseigneur, the lessons which He gives them in His Scriptures, and learn . . . the rules and examples on which they ought to base their conduct. . . .

7. **Lacedæmonians:** the Spartans of ancient Greece. **Lycurgus:** traditional author of the Spartan constitution. **Solon:** sixth-century B.C. Athenian lawgiver.

BOOK II: OR AUTHORITY . . .

CONCLUSION: Accordingly we have established by means of Scriptures that monarchical government comes from God. . . . That when government was established among men He chose hereditary monarchy as the most natural and most durable form. That excluding the sex born to obey[8] from the sovereign power was only natural. . . .

BOOK III: THE NATURE OF ROYAL AUTHORITY . . .

FIRST ARTICLE: Its essential characteristics. . . . First, royal authority is sacred; Second, it is paternal; Third, it is absolute; Fourth, it is subject to reason. . . .

SECOND ARTICLE: Royal authority is sacred.

FIRST PROPOSITION: God establishes kings as his ministers and reigns over people through them.—We have already seen that all power comes from God. . . .

Therefore princes act as ministers of God and as His lieutenants on earth. It is through them that he exercises His empire. . . .

Thus we have seen that the royal throne is not the throne of a man, but the throne of God himself. So in Scriptures we find "God has chosen my son Solomon to sit upon the throne of the kingdom of Jehovah over Israel." And further, "Solomon sat on the throne of Jehovah as king."

And in order that we should not think that to have kings established by God is peculiar to the Israelites, here is what Ecclesiastes says: "God gives each people its governor; and Israel is manifestly reserved to Him.". . .

SECOND PROPOSITION: The person of the king is sacred.—It follows from all the above that the person of kings is sacred. . . . God has had them anointed by His prophets with a sacred ointment, as He has had His pontiffs and His altars anointed.

But even before actually being anointed, they are sacred by virtue of their charge, as representatives of His divine majesty, delegated by His providence to execute His design. . . .

The title of *christ* is given to kings, one sees them called *christs* or the Lord's *anointed* everywhere.

Bearing this venerable name, even the prophets revered them, and looked upon them as associated with the sovereign empire of God, whose authority they exercise on earth. . . .

THIRD PROPOSITION: Religion and conscience demand that we obey the prince.—After having said that the prince is the minister of God Saint Paul concluded: "Accordingly it is necessary that you subject yourself to him out of fear of his anger, but also because of the obligation of your conscience. . . ."

And furthermore: "Servants, obey your temporal masters in all things. . . ." Saint Peter said: "Therefore submit yourselves to the order established among

---

8. **sex born to obey:** women. The Salic Law, mistakenly attributed to the medieval Salian Franks, precluded women from inheriting the crown of France.

men for the love of God; be subjected to the king as to God . . . be subjected to those to whom He gives His authority and who are sent by Him to reward good deeds and to punish evil ones."

Even if kings fail in this duty, their charge and their ministry must be respected. For Scriptures tell us: "Obey your masters, not only those who are mild and good, but also those who are peevish and unjust."

Thus there is something religious in the respect which one renders the prince. Service to God and respect for kings are one thing. . . .

Thus it is in the spirit of Christianity for kings to be paid a kind of religious respect. . . .

BOOK IV: CONTINUATION OF THE CHARACTERISTICS OF ROYALTY

FIRST ARTICLE: Royal authority is absolute.

FIRST PROPOSITION: The prince need render account to no one for what he orders. . . .

SECOND PROPOSITION: When the prince has judged there is no other judgment. . . . Princes are gods.

Source 3 from Bayle St. John, translator, The Memoirs of the Duke of Saint-Simon on the Reign of Louis XIV and the Regency, *eighth edition (London: George Allen, 1913), vol. 2, pp. 363–365, vol. 3, pp. 221–227.*

3. The Duke of Saint-Simon on the Reign of Louis XIV

[*On the creation of Versailles and the nature of its court life*]

He [Louis XIV] early showed a disinclination for Paris. The troubles that had taken place there during the minority made him regard the place as dangerous;[9] he wished, too, to render himself venerable by hiding himself from the eyes of the multitude; all these considerations fixed him at St. Germains [sic][10] soon after the death of the Queen, his mother. It was to that place he began to attract the world by fêtes and gallantries, and by making it felt that he wished to be often seen.

---

9. During the Fronde revolt of 1648–1653, the royal government lost control of Paris to the crowds and the royal family was forced to flee the city. Because Louis XIV was a minor (only ten years of age) when the revolt erupted, the government was administered by his mother, Anne of Austria, and her chief minister, Cardinal Mazarin.

10. **St. Germains:** St. Germain-en-Layer, site of a royal château overlooking the Seine and dating from the twelfth century, where Louis XIV was born. The court fled there in 1649 during the Fronde.

His love for Madame de la Vallière,[11] which was at first kept secret, occasioned frequent excursions to Versailles, then a little card castle, which had been built by Louis XIII—annoyed, and his suite still more so, at being frequently obliged to sleep in a wretched inn there, after he had been out hunting in the forest of Saint Leger. That monarch rarely slept at Versailles more than one night, and then from necessity; the King, his son, slept there, so that he might be more in private with his mistress; pleasures unknown to the hero and just man, worthy son of Saint Louis, who built the little château.[12]

These excursions of Louis XIV by degrees gave birth to those immense buildings he erected at Versailles; and their convenience for a numerous court, so different from the apartments at St. Germains, led him to take up his abode there entirely shortly after the death of the Queen.[13] He built an infinite number of apartments, which were asked for by those who wished to pay their court to him; whereas at St. Germains nearly everybody was obliged to lodge in the town, and the few who found accommodation at the château were strangely inconvenienced.

The frequent fêtes, the private promenades at Versailles, the journeys, were means on which the King seized in order to distinguish or mortify the courtiers, and thus render them more assiduous in pleasing him. He felt that of real favours he had not enough to bestow; in order to keep up the spirit of devotion, he therefore unceasingly invented all sorts of ideal ones, little preferences and petty distinctions, which answered his purpose as well.

He was exceedingly jealous of the attention paid him. Not only did he notice the presence of the most distinguished courtiers, but those of inferior degree also. He looked to the right and to the left, not only upon rising but upon going to bed, at his meals, in passing through his apartments, or his gardens of Versailles, where alone the courtiers were allowed to follow him; he saw and noticed everybody; not one escaped him, not even those who hoped to remain unnoticed. He marked well all absentees from the court, found out the reason of their absence, and never lost an opportunity of acting towards them as the occasion might seem to justify. With some of the courtiers (the most distinguished), it was a demerit not to make the court their ordinary abode; with others 'twas a fault to come but rarely; for those who never or scarcely ever came it was certain disgrace. When their names were in any way mentioned, "I do not know them," the King would reply haughtily. Those who presented themselves but seldom were thus characterized: "They are people I never see;" these decrees were irrevocable. . . .

11. **Madame de la Vallière:** Louise de la Baume le Blanc, Duchesse de la Vallière (1644–1710), the king's first mistress.

12. Saint-Simon greatly admired Louis XIII, who he had never met, and for over half a century attended annual memorial services for the king at the royal tombs in the basilica of St. Denis.

13. Anne of Austria (1601–1666), the mother of Louis XIV.

Louis XIV took great pains to be well informed of all that passed everywhere; in the public places, in the private houses, in society and familiar intercourse. His spies and tell-tales were infinite. He had them of all species; many who were ignorant that their information reached him; others who knew it; others who wrote to him direct, sending their letters through channels he indicated; and all these letters were seen by him alone, and always before everything else; others who sometimes spoke to him secretly in his cabinet, entering by the back stairs. These unknown means ruined an infinite number of people of all classes, who never could discover the cause; often ruined them very unjustly; for the King, once prejudiced, never altered his opinion or so rarely, that nothing was more rare.

[On the royal day and court etiquette]

[The royal day begins.]

At eight o'clock the chief valet de chambre on duty, who alone had slept in the royal chamber, and who had dressed himself, awoke the King. The chief physician, the chief surgeon, and the nurse (as long as she lived), entered at the same time. The latter kissed the King; the others rubbed and often changed his shirt, because he was in the habit of sweating a great deal. At the quarter, the grand chamberlain was called (or, in his absence, the first gentleman of the chamber), and those who had, what was called the *grandes entrées*. The chamberlain (or chief gentleman) drew back the curtains which had been closed again, and presented the holy water from the vase, at the head of the bed. These gentlemen stayed but a moment, and that was the time to speak to the King, if any one had anything to ask of him; in which case the rest stood aside. When, contrary to custom, nobody had aught to say, they were there but for a few moments. He who had opened the curtains and presented the holy water, presented also a prayer-book. Then all passed into the cabinet of the council. A very short religious service being over, the King called, they re-entered. The same officer gave him his dressing-gown; immediately after, other privileged courtiers entered, and then everybody, in time to find the King putting on his shoes and stockings, for he did almost everything himself and with address and grace. Every other day we saw him shave himself; and he had a little short wig in which he always appeared, even in bed, and on medicine days. He often spoke of the chase, and sometimes said a word to somebody. No toilette table was near him; he had simply a mirror held before him.

As soon as he was dressed, he prayed to God, at the side of his bed, where all the clergy present knelt, the cardinals without cushions, all the laity remaining standing; and the captain of the guards came to the balustrade during the prayer, after which the King passed into his cabinet.

He found there, or was followed by all who had the entrée, a very numerous company, for it included everybody in any office. He gave orders to each for the day; thus within a half a quarter of an hour it was known what he meant to do; and then all this crowd left directly. The bastards, a few favourites, and the valets alone were left. It was then a good opportunity for talking with the King; for example, about plans of gardens and buildings; and conversation lasted more or less according to the person engaged in it.

All the Court meantime waited for the King in the gallery, the captain of the guard being alone in the chamber seated at the door of the cabinet.

[The business of government]

On Sunday, and often on Monday, there was a council of state; on Tuesday a finance council; on Wednesday council of state; on Saturday finance council. Rarely were two held in one day or any on Thursday or Friday. Once or twice a month there was a council of despatches[14] on Monday morning; but the order that the Secretaries of State took every morning between the King's rising and his mass, much abridged this kind of business. All the ministers were seated according to rank, except at the council of despatches, where all stood except the sons of France, the Chancellor, and the Duc de Beauvilliers.[15]

[The royal luncheon]

The dinner was always *au petit couvert*,[16] that is, the King ate by himself in his chamber upon a square table in front of the middle window. It was more or less abundant, for he ordered in the morning whether it was to be "a little," or "very little" service. But even at this last, there were always many dishes, and three courses without counting the fruit. The dinner being ready, the principal courtiers entered; then all who were known; and the first gentlemen of the chamber on duty, informed the King.

I have seen, but very rarely, Monseigneur[17] and his sons standing at their dinners, the King not offering them a seat. I have continually seen there the Princes of the blood and the cardinals. I have often seen there also Monsieur,[18] either on arriving from St. Cloud to see the King, or arriving from the council of despatches (the only one he entered), give the King his napkin and remain

14. **council of despatches:** the royal council in which ministers discussed the letters from the provincial administrators of France, the *intendants*.

15. **sons of France:** The royal family was distinguished from the rest of the nobility as "children of France." The "sons of France" in the last decade of the seventeenth century thus were the king's son, his grandsons, and his brother. **Duc de Beauvilliers:** Paul de Beauvilliers, Duc de St. Aignan (1648–1714), was a friend of Saint-Simon and tutor of Louis XIV's grandsons, the dukes of Burgundy, Anjou, and Berry.

16. *au petit couvert:* a simple table setting with a light meal.

17. **Monseigneur:** Louis, Dauphin de France (1661–1711), son of Louis XIV and heir to the throne.

18. **Monsieur:** Philippe, Duc d'Orléans (1640–1701), Louis XIV's only sibling. His permanent residence was at the Château of St. Cloud near Paris.

standing. A little while afterwards, the King, seeing that he did not go away, asked him if he would not sit down; he bowed, and the King ordered a seat to be brought for him. A stool was put behind him. Some moments after the King said, "Nay then, sit down, my brother." Monsieur bowed and seated himself until the end of the dinner, when he presented the napkin.

[The day ends.]

At ten o'clock his supper was served. The captain of the guard announced this to him. A quarter of an hour after the King came to supper, and from the antechamber of Madame de Maintenon[19] to the table again, any one spoke to him who wished. This supper was always on a grand scale, the royal household (that is, the sons and daughters of France) at table, and a large number of courtiers and ladies present, sitting or standing, and on the evening before the journey to Marly all those ladies who wished to take part in it. That was called presenting yourself for Marly. Men asked in the morning, simply saying to the King, "Sire, Marly." In later years the King grew tired of this, and a valet wrote up in the gallery the names of those who asked. The ladies continued to present themselves.

After supper the King stood some moments, his back to the balustrade of the foot of his bed, encircled by all his Court; then, with bows to the ladies, passed into his cabinet, where on arriving, he gave his orders. He passed a little less than an hour there, seated in an arm-chair, with his legitimate children and bastards, his grandchildren, legitimate and otherwise, and their husbands or wives. Monsieur in another arm-chair; the princesses upon stools, Monseigneur and all the other princes standing.

The King, wishing to retire, went and fed his dogs; then said good night, passed into his chamber to the *ruelle*[20] of his bed, where he said his prayers, as in the morning, then undressed. He said good night with an inclination of the head, and whilst everybody was leaving the room stood at the corner of the mantelpiece, where he gave the order to the colonel of the guards alone. Then commenced what was called the *petit coucher,* at which only the specially privileged remained. That was short. They did not leave until he got into bed. It was a moment to speak to him. Then all left if they saw any one buckle to the King. For ten or twelve years before he died the *petit coucher* ceased, in consequence of a long attack of gout he had had; so that the Court was finished at the rising from supper.

19. **Madame de Maintenon:** Françoise d'Aubigné, Marquise de Maintenon (1635–1719), married Louis XIV after the death of his first wife, Marie Thérèse of Spain.
20. *ruelle:* the area in the bedchamber in which the bed was located and in which the king received persons of high rank.

Source 4 from Château de Versailles/Cliché des Musées Nationaux–Paris. Art Resource, New York.

4. Charles Le Brun, *Louis XIV Taking Up Personal Government*, ca 1680, from the Ceiling of the Hall of Mirrors at Versailles

Source 5 from Réunion des Musées Nationaux/Art Resource, New York.

5. Hyacinthe-François-Honoré-Pierre-André Rigaud, *Louis XIV,*
King of France and Navarre, **1701**

7. Rousselet, Louis XIV as "Roman Emperor" in an Engraving from the Carousel of 1662

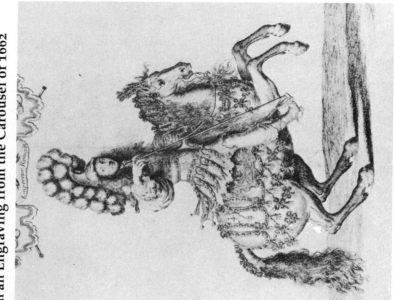

6. Mask of Apollo, God of Light, seventeenth century

[346]

Sources 8 and 9 from French Government Tourist Office.

8. Garden Façade of Versailles

Source 9 © Charles Rotbin/CORBIS.

9. Aerial View of Versailles

Sources 10 through 13 from Château de Versailles/Cliché des Musées Nationaux–Paris. Réunion des Musées Nationaux–Paris, Art Resource, New York.

10. The Royal Chapel at Versailles

11. Reconstruction of the King's Chamber at Versailles, after 1701

12. Antechamber of the Bull's Eye Window at Versailles

13. Pierre Denis Martin, *Château of Marly, 1724*

QUESTIONS TO CONSIDER

Louis XIV is reputed to have said, "I am the state." Whether the king actually uttered those words is immaterial for our purpose; they neatly summarize the unifying theme in all this chapter's evidence, which demonstrates how royal power was defined as absolute and how that authority was expressed in deeds, art, and architecture.

Consider first the theories of royal authority, comparing the political ideas of Bodin and Bossuet. What are the origins of sovereignty for Bodin and Bossuet? How do they differ? Why can Bodin be said to have justified absolutism on the basis of expediency, that is, that absolute royal power was the only way to ensure order? Do the two thinkers ultimately arrive at the same conclusions? What is the difference between Bodin's conclusion that the royal power permitted the king to hand down laws to his subjects and receive them from no one and Bossuet's definition of the king as virtually a god on earth?

Royal ceremony and etiquette enforced this view of the king. Consider Saint-Simon's *Memoirs* again. The selection describes only limited aspects of court etiquette, but it conveys to us a vivid image of court life. Who was the center of this court made up of the country's most prominent nobles? Analyze individual elements of court ceremony. How does each contribute to a consistent message? Consider the royal dining ritual. To reinforce the lesson of royal power,

who was kept standing during the king's luncheon? Who had the task, for most commoners performed by an ordinary waiter, of handing the king his napkin? A message of royal power is being expressed here in a way that is almost theatrical.

Indeed, the image of theater can be useful in further structuring your analysis. The stage setting for this royal display, the palace of Versailles, shows the work of a skilled director in creating a remarkably uniform message in landscape and architecture alike. Who do you suppose that director was? Examine his statement at Versailles. Look first at the exterior views of both Versailles (Sources 8 and 9) and Marly (Source 13). How do the grounds add to the expression of royal power? What view of nature might they suggest to a visitor? How did the stage set enhance the play described by Saint-Simon? How did it encourage the French to accept the authority of Louis XIV?

Look next at the interior of the palace. It was, of course, a royal residence. But do you find much evidence of its function as a place to live in? Examine the royal bedroom and its outer room (Sources 11 and 12). Modern bedrooms are generally intimate in size and decoration; how does the king's differ? Why? Notice, too, the art and use of symbols in the palace. Why might the king's artists and architects have decorated the palace so richly with biblical and classical heroes and themes (Sources 8 through 12)?

Finally, consider the principal actor, Louis XIV. Notice how his self-presentation is consistent with the trappings of the stage set. We find him consciously acting a role in Source 7, portraying an emperor in the Carousel of 1662. That engraving embodies a great deal of indirect information. What details reinforce the aura of royal power? Why should the king be mounted and in Roman costume? What strikes you about the king's attitude atop the prancing horse? Compare this picture with the Le Brun (Source 4) and Rigaud (Source 5) paintings. What elements do you find these pictures to have in common? How does the royal emblem of the sun (Source 6) contribute to the common message?

With these considerations in mind, return now to the central questions of this chapter. What was the theoretical basis for absolute royal authority? What was traditional and what was new in the justification of royal power expressed in late-sixteenth- and seventeenth-century France? How did such early modern kings as Louis XIV communicate their absolute power in the various ceremonies, displays, and symbols of royal authority presented in the evidence?

EPILOGUE

We all know that any successful act produces imitators. In the seventeenth century, the monarchy of Louis XIV looked for a long time like the most successful regime in Europe. Royal absolutism had seemingly unified France. Out of that unity came a military power that threatened to overwhelm Europe; an economic strength, based on mercantilism, that increased French wealth; and an intellectual life that gave the culture of seventeenth- and eighteenth-century Europe a distinctly French accent. Imitators of Louis XIV's work were therefore numerous. At the very least, kings sought physically to express the unifying and centralizing monarchical principle of government in palaces recreating Versailles.[21]

But the work of such monarchs as Louis XIV involved far more than the construction of elaborate palaces in which to stage the theater of their court lives. The act of focusing the state on the figure of the monarch began the transition to the centralized modern style of government and marked the beginning of the end of the decentralized medieval state that bound subjects in an almost contractual relationship to their ruler. The king now emerged as theoretically all-powerful and also as a symbol of national unity.

The monarchs of the age did their work of state building so effectively that the unity and centralization they created often survived the monarchy itself. The French monarchy, for example, succumbed to a revolution in

21. Palaces consciously modeled on Versailles multiplied in the late seventeenth and early eighteenth centuries. They included the Schönbrunn Palace in Vienna (1694); the Royal Palace in Berlin (begun in 1698); Ludwigsburg Palace in Württemberg, Germany (1704–1733); the Würzburg Residenz in Franconia, Germany (1719–1744); and the Stupinigi Palace (1729–1733) near Turin, Italy.

1789 that in large part stemmed from the bankruptcy of the royal government after too many years of overspending on wars and court life in the name of royal glory. But the unified state endured, strong enough to retain its sense of unity despite challenges in war and changes of government that introduced a new politics of mass participation.

The methods employed by Louis XIV and other monarchs also transcended their age. Modern governments understand the importance of ritual, symbolism, and display in creating the sense of national unity that was part of the absolute monarch's goal. Ritual may now be centered on important national observances. The parades on such days as July 4 in the United States, July 14 in France (commemorating one of the earliest victories of the Revolution of 1789), and the anniversary of the October 1917 Revolution as it was celebrated until 1990 in the former Soviet Union all differ in form from the rituals of Louis XIV. They are designed for a new political age, one of mass participation in politics, in which the loyalty of the whole people, not just that of an elite group, must be won. But their purpose remains the same: to win loyalty to the existing political order.

Modern states also use symbolism to build political loyalty. Artwork on public buildings in Washington, D.C., and the capital cities of other republics, for example, often employs classical themes. The purpose of such artwork is to suggest to citizens that their government perpetuates the republican rectitude of Athens and Rome. Display also is part of the political agenda of modern governments, even governments of new arrivals in the community of nations. This is why newly independent, developing nations of the twentieth and twenty-first centuries expend large portions of their meager resources on such things as grand new capital cities, the most sophisticated military weaponry, and the latest aircraft for the national airline. These are symbols of their governments' successes and thus the basis for these regimes' claims on their peoples' loyalty. These modern rituals, symbols, and displays perform the same function for modern rulers as Versailles did for the Sun King.